P9-DFG-038

War, Conflict and Human Rights

War, Conflict and Human Rights is an innovative interdisciplinary textbook combining aspects of law, politics, and conflict analysis to examine the relationship between human rights and armed conflict.

This second edition has been revised and updated, making use of both theoretical and practical approaches. Over the course of the book, the authors:

- examine the tensions and complementarities between protection of human rights and resolution of conflict, including the competing political demands and the challenges posed by internal armed conflict;
- analyse the different obligations and legal regimes applicable to state and non-state actors, including non-state armed groups, corporations and private military and security companies;
- explore the scope and effects of human rights violations in contemporary armed conflicts, such as those in Sierra Leone, Sudan, the Democratic Republic of Congo, and the former Yugoslavia, and implications for the "Arab Spring";
- assess the legal and institutional accountability mechanisms developed in the wake of armed conflict to punish violations of human rights law, and international humanitarian law such as the ad hoc tribunals for the former Yugoslavia and Rwanda, and the International Criminal Court;
- discuss continuing and emergent global trends and challenges in the fields of human rights and conflict analysis.

This volume will be essential reading for students of war and conflict studies, human rights, and international humanitarian law, and is highly recommended for students of conflict resolution, peacebuilding, international security and international relations generally.

Chandra Lekha Sriram is Professor of International Law and International Relations, the University of East London, UK.

Olga Martin-Ortega is Reader in Public International Law, the University of Greenwich, UK.

Johanna Herman is a Research Fellow, Centre on Human Rights in Conflict, the University of East London, UK.

"What makes this book such a superb teaching tool? The text begins by providing separate background chapters on human rights and conflict studies. This makes the case studies and topical chapters completely accessible for a wide range of students. Clearly written and completely up to date, *War, Conflict and Human Rights* will undoubtedly find itself on the mandatory reading list of many syllabi."

Julie Mertus, American University, USA

"[The authors] have tackled the most perplexing issues of humanitarian protection and conflict resolution, clarified the hard choices and explored their implications in probing case studies. They demonstrate that the tools now available to promote human rights, though far from adequate, can make a positive difference when they are mobilized vigorously and authentically, respecting both shared rights and legitimate differences."

Michael Doyle, Columbia University, USA

"This indispensable volume, useful for both teaching and research, navigates a path around the pitfalls inherent in the age-old conceptual struggle between peace and justice. In doing so it details a sophisticated agenda for conflict resolution and peacebuilding, through international humanitarian and human rights law, for the ultimate goal of conflict prevention."

Oliver Richmond, University of Manchester, UK

War, Conflict and Human Rights

Theory and practice

Second edition

**Chandra Lekha Sriram,
Olga Martin-Ortega and
Johanna Herman**

LONDON AND NEW YORK

First published 2009
by Routledge

Second edition published 2014
by Routledge
2 Park Square, Milton Park, Abingdon, Oxon, OX14 4RN

and by Routledge
711 Third Avenue, New York, NY 10017

Routledge is an imprint of the Taylor & Francis Group, an informa business

© 2014 Chandra Lekha Sriram, Olga Martin-Ortega and Johanna Herman

The right of Chandra Lekha Sriram, Olga Martin-Ortega and Johanna
Herman to be identified as authors of this work has been asserted by them in
accordance with sections 77 and 78 of the Copyright, Designs and Patents
Act 1988.

All rights reserved. No part of this book may be reprinted or reproduced or
utilised in any form or by any electronic, mechanical, or other means, now
known or hereafter invented, including photocopying and recording, or in
any information storage or retrieval system, without permission in writing
from the publishers.

Trademark notice: Product or corporate names may be trademarks or
registered trademarks, and are used only for identification and explanation
without intent to infringe.

British Library Cataloguing in Publication Data
A catalogue record for this book is available from the British Library

Library of Congress Cataloging-in-Publication Data
Sriram, Chandra Lekha, 1971–
War, conflict and human rights : theory and practice / Chandra Lekha
Sriram, Olga Martin-Ortega and Johanna Herman. – Second edition.
    pages cm
  Includes bibliographical references and index.
  1. War. 2. Human rights. 3. Peace-building. 4. War – Case studies.
  5. Human rights – Case studies. 6. Peace-building – Case studies.
  I. Martin-Ortega, Olga. II. Herman, Johanna. III. Title.
  JZ6385.S75 2014
  355.02–dc23   2013027217

ISBN13: 978-0-415-83225-0 (hbk)
ISBN13: 978-0-415-83226-7 (pbk)
ISBN13: 978-0-203-76422-0 (ebk)

Typeset in Times New Roman
by HWA Text and Data Management, London

MIX
Paper from
responsible sources
FSC   FSC® C013056
www.fsc.org

Printed and bound in Great Britain by
TJ International Ltd, Padstow, Cornwall

Contents

List of illustrations   vii
About the authors   x
How to use this book   xi
Acknowledgments   xiii

PART I
War and human rights: critical issues   1

1 The interplay between war and human rights   3

2 Conflict   14

3 Human rights   32

4 Humanitarian and human rights law in armed conflict   51

5 Nonstate actors and international humanitarian and international
   human rights law   65

PART II
Contemporary conflict: critical cases   81

6 The Former Yugoslavia   83

7 Sierra Leone   99

8 The Democratic Republic of Congo   116

9 Sudan   136

PART III
Building peace and seeking accountability: recent mechanisms and institutions **159**

10 Ad hoc tribunals   161

11 Enforcing human rights transnationally   183

12 Hybrid tribunals   199

13 The International Criminal Court   219

14 Enduring and emergent challenges and opportunities   238

    Glossary   243
    Selected further reading   247
    Index   250

Illustrations

Maps

6.1	Former Yugoslavia,1991	84
7.1	Sierra Leone	100
8.1	Democratic Republic of Congo	117
9.1	Sudan and South Sudan	137

Boxes

1.1	Conflict and human rights in practice: Northern Ireland, Kosovo, and Sierra Leone	5
1.2	UN mediation and amnesties	8
1.3	The relationship between conflict and human rights	9
1.4	Advocating human rights and conflict resolution: potential tension	9
1.5	Key international legal documents	10
1.6	Accountability institutions and responses	11
2.1	The so-called "Arab Spring"	16
2.2	The 2007 Kenyan post-election violence	19
2.3	UN bodies and agencies involved in conflict prevention	21
2.4	Do no harm	22
2.5	Current UN peacekeeping operations directed by DPKO	27
2.6	Peacebuilding Commission purposes	29
3.1	The difference between natural law and the liberal conception of rights	35
3.2	A world without human rights?	36
3.3	Human rights as politics and idolatry	37
3.4	The development of human rights	39
3.5	The rights of the homeless	40
3.6	Emerging solidarist rights	43
3.7	The Draft UN Declaration on the Right to Peace	44
3.8	Selected principles from the Bangkok Declaration	45
3.9	Conceptions of cultural relativism	46
4.1	Core human rights treaties and treaty monitoring bodies	53
4.2	Rights, duties, enforcement, and accountability under human rights and humanitarian law	54
4.3	The International Covenant on Civil and Political Rights (ICCPR)	56

4.4	The International Covenant on Economic, Social, and Cultural Rights (ICESCR)	56
4.5	The Torture Convention, Article 1	56
4.6	The Genocide Convention, Article 2	57
4.7	The Rome Statute, Article 7	58
4.8	The Geneva Conventions	59
4.9	Common Article 3 of the Geneva Conventions	60
4.10	Grave breaches of the Geneva Conventions	60
4.11	IHL and permissible weaponry: nuclear weapons and drones	61
5.1	Armed group commitments to IHL	67
5.2	*Kadić v. Karadžić*	69
5.3	Article 4 of the Third Geneva Convention	70
5.4	Additional Protocol II to the Geneva Conventions, Article 1	70
5.5	Extraordinary rendition	71
5.6	Offensive combat: PMSCs in Sierra Leone	73
5.7	Businesses under IHL	78
6.1	Key facts: Former Yugoslavia in 1991	85
6.2	The Dayton Accords	87
6.3	UN Security Council Resolution 1244	89
6.4	Key players in the Former Yugoslavia	90
6.5	ICJ judgment	92
6.6	Legacies of conflict and demands for reconciliation	94
6.7	Yugoslavia timeline	95
7.1	Key facts: Sierra Leone	101
7.2	Key players in Sierra Leone	104
7.3	The Lomé Agreement, Article 9	106
7.4	Abuja Agreement I, selected articles	107
7.5	Sierra Leone timeline	112
8.1	Key facts: Democratic Republic of Congo	118
8.2	Key players in the Second Congo War	120
8.3	Sexual and gender-based violence in the DRC	128
8.4	The DRC's case against Uganda, ICJ Hearing of April 27, 2005	130
8.5	The cases against the FPR in Spain	131
8.6	DRC timeline	132
9.1	Key facts: Sudan	138
9.2	Key facts: South Sudan	139
9.3	Key players in Sudan	144
9.4	*Presbyterian Church of Sudan v. Talisman Energy*	149
9.5	Genocide in Darfur? Conclusions of the International Commission of Inquiry	150
9.6	*The Prosecutor v. Omar Hassan Ahmad al-Bashir.* Second Warrant of Arrest, 12 July 2010	151
9.7	Sudan timeline	153
10.1	Key articles from the statute of the ICTY	163
10.2	The UN Charter, Article 41	166
10.3	Rule 11*bis* of the ICTY	172
10.4	Key articles from the Statute of the ICTR	172
10.5	Rule 11*bis* of the ICTR	177

11.1   The Spanish law that established universal jurisdiction   187
11.2   Civil actions in Spain   188
11.3   Universal jurisdiction and immunity   191
11.4   A new wave of universal jurisdiction venues?   193
11.5   Landmark ATCA cases: extension and limitation   196
11.6   Domestic accountability abroad   197
12.1   Hybrid tribunals to date   201
12.2   UNMIK Regulation no. 2000/64   202
12.3   UNTAET Regulation no. 2000/15   205
12.4   The Law on the Establishment of the Extraordinary Chambers   209
12.5   The civil party system   211
12.6   The Statute of the Special Court for Sierra Leone   213
13.1   The Rome Statute, Article 25   226
13.2   UN Security Council Resolution 1593 (March 31, 2005)   230

About the authors

Chandra Lekha Sriram is Professor of International Law and International Relations, the University of East London, School of Law and Social Sciences, and co-director of the Centre on Human Rights in Conflict. She received her PhD in Politics in 2000 from Princeton. Her research interests include human rights, international criminal justice, conflict prevention, and peacebuilding. Her most recent monograph is *Peace as Governance: Power-Sharing, Armed Groups, and Contemporary Peace Negotiations* (Palgrave 2008).

Olga Martin-Ortega is Reader in Public International Law at the University of Greenwich, United Kingdom. She received her PhD in law at the University of Jaen, Spain. Her research interests include business and human rights, postconflict reconstruction, and transitional justice. She is the author of *Empresas Multinacionales y Derechos Humanos en Derecho Internacional* (Bosch 2008) and co-author of *International Law* (Sweet and Maxwell, 7th edn, 2013).

Johanna Herman is Research Fellow at the Centre on Human Rights in Conflict, School of Law and Social Sciences, the University of East London. She received her MA in international affairs from Columbia University, with a concentration in human rights. She has worked for a number of United Nations agencies and international nongovernmental organizations. Her research interests include peacebuilding, transitional justice, and human rights.

Together, all three have co-edited *Transitional Justice and Peacebuilding on the Ground: Victims and Ex-combatants* (Routledge 2012, with Jemima Garcia-Godos), *Peacebuilding and Rule of Law in Africa: Just Peace?* (Routledge 2010), and *Surviving Field Research: Working in Violent and Difficult Situations* (Routledge 2009, with Julie A. Mertus and John C. King).

How to use this book

War and other forms of armed conflict often give rise to massive human rights violations, and violent conflict is indeed often provoked by grievances that may include serious violations of human rights and international humanitarian law. Demands for accountability for human rights violations are common in countries emerging from conflict, and postconflict countries have deployed a variety of mechanisms to address these demands. Indeed, demands for accountability can pose obstacles to peace negotiations. However, these crucial connections between war and human rights lie at the intersection of international human rights law and international humanitarian law, and conflict analysis and resolution. The issues at stake are not merely theoretical ones; they are central to the work of practitioners in international politics and international law. The knowledge needed to address these issues is therefore interdisciplinary, being both legal and political. There is thus a need to develop expertise that is both analytic as well as theoretical, and substantive knowledge of both politics and law.

The study of war, conflict, and human rights is a complex, interdisciplinary undertaking. Many students may have expertise in international human rights law, but not in conflict analysis, or may be familiar with particular conflicts, but not with the legal and institutional responses to those conflicts and abuses committed during their waging. This book attempts to bridge those gaps by presenting a comprehensive approach to the interaction between conflict resolution and human rights. This book is designed to support students in upper-division undergraduate and master's-level courses in conflict resolution and in human rights, as well as in hybrid studies of both.

Structure of the book

Part I addresses the theoretical issues underlying conflict and human rights, examining critical debates, politics, and law. Chapter 1 lays out the relationship between war and human rights, establishing the interaction that underpins the rest of the analysis in this book. Chapter 2 surveys the literature on critical conflict analysis, conflict resolution, and postconflict peacebuilding. It addresses the broad debates over the root causes of conflict; different methods of conflict prevention, mitigation, and resolution; and the challenges of postconflict peacebuilding. Chapter 3 examines the history of human rights and key debates in the human rights literature. These debates include those between universalist and particularist approaches, between individual and group rights, and between political and economic rights. Chapter 4 presents the relevant law, specifically international human rights law and international humanitarian law, and examines the specific challenge of addressing violations of these obligations in internal, as opposed to international, armed conflicts.

Chapter 5 examines the special problem of nonstate actors, especially armed groups, including terrorist groups and private companies, including multinational corporations and private military and security companies.

Part II moves from the theoretical to the concrete, examining serious internal conflict and attendant human rights violations in the context of five case studies. The first four case studies involve specific countries that have recently reached agreements ending armed conflict, while the fifth involves the global community. The country case studies examine the respective peace negotiations, and the choices made within those negotiations. Students will be able to explore the opportunities that were available for accountability, and to think about the various possibilities, without being constrained by what ultimately happened. Chapter 6 examines the wars in the former Yugoslavia during the 1990s, and the resolution reached through the Dayton Accords. Chapter 7 examines the peace process in Sierra Leone, which experienced violent conflict over resources and poor governance, and serious violations of human rights, including forcible conscription of child soldiers, mutilation, torture, and massacres. Chapter 8 considers the conflict and peace process in the Democratic Republic of Congo, which also experienced violent conflict over resources and governance, and gross human rights violations perpetrated by internal forces as well as militaries and militias sent or supported by multiple neighboring countries. Chapter 9 addresses the process in Sudan, where a protracted conflict over resources, religion, territory, and human rights violations raged in the south until recently, with the conflict and demands changing character over time. The conflict in the region of Darfur has seen violations which some have alleged constitute genocide.

Part III examines a range of accountability mechanisms that have been developed since the early to middle 1990s. Each chapter examines a different model of response to abuses linked to armed conflict: transnational, hybrid, and international. Chapter 10 discusses the ad hoc international criminal tribunals established for the former Yugoslavia and Rwanda in 1993 and 1994, respectively. Chapter 11 examines transnational methods of accountability, specifically the exercise of universal jurisdiction and transnational civil accountability. Chapter 12 addresses a relatively recent development in accountability—the hybrid or mixed tribunal—and discusses the operations of hybrid tribunals in Sierra Leone, East Timor, and Kosovo, and prospects for such a tribunal in Cambodia. Chapter 13 turns to the emerging practice of the International Criminal Court and its investigations and cases under way, as well as major policy and scholarly debates regarding the Court in the past ten years. Finally, Chapter 14 considers lessons learned from these cases, and prospects and challenges for the future.

Guidance for students and instructors

While the three parts of this volume differ in content and approach, guidance for students and instructors is provided throughout. A general glossary is provided, presenting key terms used in the human rights, international law, and conflict resolution literature. Whenever a key term is used for the first time in a chapter, it is highlighted so the reader will know that a definition is available in the glossary. To help guide class discussion and assist students in initiating future research, each chapter begins with an outline of key points, highlighting the main debates and concepts addressed in that chapter, and concludes with a set of discussion questions and group exercises, as well as a list of further readings and official documents and sources. The country-specific chapters in Part II of the volume also include maps, key facts about the country or territory under discussion, and a list of key players to help guide students through the complex web of groups and institutions involved in a given conflict.

Acknowledgments

As with all large projects, this book owes its completion to many individuals and institutions. We are especially grateful to the University of East London, School of Law, for its ongoing support to the Centre on Human Rights in Conflict, at which all three authors were based during the initial drafting of this book. We are also particularly grateful to Fiona Fairweather, Dean of the School of Law, for her active support in facilitating our work on a daily basis. Olga Martin-Ortega would also like to thank Professor Sarah Greer, Dean of the School of Law, Humanities and Social Sciences, University of Greenwich.

We are also indebted to Jordi Palou Loverdos for his kind assistance in accessing information on the international crimes committed in Rwanda and the Democratic Republic of Congo, as presented in court before the Spanish Audiencia Nacional resulting in the indictment order of February 6, 2008.

Finally, we thank our editor at Routledge, Andrew Humphrys, for initiating discussions on this project, and offering encouragement and feedback throughout.

Chandra Lekha Sriram, Olga Martin-Ortega, and Johanna Herman

Part I
War and human rights

Critical issues

1 The interplay between war and human rights

Key points

- The study of war and human rights is an interdisciplinary subject, involving knowledge of law, politics, and conflict analysis and resolution.
- Promotion of human rights and resolution of violent conflict are often viewed as being in tension by scholars and practitioners of each.
- The relationship between war and human rights is complex: human rights violations can underpin conflict, can emerge from conflict, and can transform conflicts already under way, and human rights accountability may be a critical demand within, but also an obstacle to, peace processes.
- Peace processes must not only address demands for accountability for past abuses, but also disarm combatants and reshape political processes and institutions of law and governance.
- A wide range of law exists that may be relevant in addressing human rights violations that arise during conflict, falling broadly under the rubrics of **international human rights law** and **international humanitarian law**.
- A wide range of responses to past abuses may be developed, through use of domestic courts or through international institutions and processes, including the **International Criminal Court**.
- Nonstate armed groups and private military and security companies play a critical role in contemporary armed conflicts, and pose challenges to peace processes, but also complicate the application of international humanitarian law.

Overview

This book examines key issues and debates regarding the connections between armed conflict and human rights, both theoretical and practical. It also examines the key legal sources and obligations in both international human rights law and international humanitarian law. And it does so from a grounded, real-world perspective, through in-depth case studies of particular countries involved in and emerging from armed conflict, paying attention to the specific human rights and conflict resolution challenges presented in each, and the compromises ultimately reached. The chapters in Part I examine in detail a wide range of human rights and accountability mechanisms that have been developed, each of which maps to one or more of the country case studies in Part II. This book thus examines an important set of issues that are directly located at the intersection of courses on human rights and international humanitarian law, and courses on conflict analysis and conflict resolution. The approach is explicitly hybrid, mixing disciplinary approaches, policy analyses, case studies, and legal analyses.

War, armed conflict, and human rights

The relationship between war and other violent conflict is complex and dynamic. As discussed later, violations of human rights can be both causes and consequences of violent conflict. Further, gross violations of human rights and violations of international humanitarian law can alter the course of conflicts, adding grievances and changing the interests of various actors, in turn making conflicts more intractable. Where this is the case, conflict resolution can become much more difficult, not least because many issues beyond the original "root causes" of conflict will be at stake, and because trust between the warring parties will be extremely low. Finally, demands for accountability will be made, whether by victims and relatives of victims, by local and international nongovernmental organizations, or by various international actors such as donor countries. The pursuit of legal accountability is often controversial, and is often resisted by one or more of the fighting parties; insisting upon legal accountability may impede negotiations or peace implementation. Nonetheless, there have been numerous attempts to pursue legal accountability while also making peace, and this book will examine many such cases.

These complex problems are both legal and political. Developing useful policy responses requires an understanding not only of international human rights and humanitarian law, but also of conflict dynamics and conflict resolution. We turn next, briefly, to the specific fields and disciplines of conflict analysis and resolution, human rights, and international humanitarian law, which will be developed in greater detail in subsequent chapters. We then address in greater detail the specific ways in which war and human rights violations may be intertwined, and the particular and competing demands and goals of conflict resolvers and human rights promoters.

Conflict analysis and causes of conflict

Conflict analysis, in theory and in practice, seeks to identify the "underlying" causes of conflict as well as to understand the dynamics of conflict once it is under way. In any given conflict there is always more than one cause, although some will be more salient in particular conflicts, as discussed in Chapter 2. Causes of conflict can include mistrust or grievances based upon ethnic discrimination or preferential treatment; competition over resources, whether political or economic; demands for political autonomy or independence; allegations of corruption; and myriad claims regarding current or past human rights abuses. Attempts to resolve conflicts will need to address many or all of these underlying causes, which means that in conflict resolution processes, human rights abuses are but one concern among many. Those seeking to resolve conflict will be concerned with bringing all relevant parties to the negotiating table, including the possibility of defection by some, particularly "spoilers"; building confidence among parties; and addressing the many grievances that parties may have against one another. They may also be concerned with allocating future economic and political resources; guaranteeing security for all parties, particularly those that fear for their survival; rebuilding institutions of law and order; and addressing specific demands for justice to rectify past abuses. They may also be concerned with setting the stage for

peacebuilding processes, often with a significant international presence, or with longer-term reconciliation and conflict transformation. Clearly, in many instances, human rights are not the first topic of concern for conflict resolution experts or practitioners. However, as we will see, human rights violations and human rights protections are intimately linked to the patterns of contemporary conflict in a number of ways, meaning that contemporary efforts to end wars have been compelled to deal with human rights and humanitarian law obligations. Encounters between human rights advocates and conflict resolution experts have thus been necessarily uneasy, with each "side" viewing the priorities of the other as suspect.

Human rights violations as causes of conflict

Human rights violations can be both causes and consequences of conflict. We begin with the ways in which human rights violations can generate conflict, with some examples for illustration in Box 1.1. In the most general sense, grievances over the real or perceived denial of rights can generate social conflict. This may be the case where there is systematic discrimination, differential access to education or health care, limited freedom of expression or religion, or denial of political participation, whether based upon race, ethnicity, caste, religion, language, gender, or some other characteristic. These violations may seem relatively minor, particularly in comparison to some of the grave crimes examined later in this book, including **war crimes** and **genocide**, but they can still generate real grievances and social unrest. In functional polities, such grievances may be handled through relatively peaceful, constitutional means, whether through litigation in the courts or through legislative reform or administrative policy change. However, in weak, corrupt, abusive, or collapsed and collapsing states, such conflict is more likely to become violent. That violence may be merely sporadic, if serious, or it may give rise to more systematic opposition.

Violent conflict may also emerge where there are more violent human rights abuses—illegal detention, extrajudicial execution, disappearances, **torture**, widespread killing, or even attempts at genocide. Where civilians have already been targeted by such violence, whether committed by the state or by **nonstate actors**, it is unlikely that peaceful resistance will have much effect, so it is yet more likely that affected individuals and groups will take up arms to defend themselves. In such situations, then, human rights violations are an important, underlying cause of conflict, although seldom the only one. Once war has erupted,

---

Box 1.1 Conflict and human rights in practice: Northern Ireland, Kosovo, and Sierra Leone

In Northern Ireland, the Catholic community claimed that they were the victims of systematic abuse and discrimination, and sought first to gain reforms through a nonviolent civil rights movement. When that failed, they resorted to the use of violence, and the Irish Republican Army emerged. The sustained denial of fundamental rights, even in the absence of serious bodily harm, can thus promote violent conflict.

In Kosovo, the Kosovo Liberation Army claimed that it took up arms in response to real and anticipated ethnic-cleansing efforts by the Serbs.

In Sierra Leone, the Civil Defense Forces emerged to protect local communities from the predations of both the government and Revolutionary United Front rebel forces.

any serious attempt at conflict resolution will also have to address the underlying sources of the original conflict, including abuses of human rights. Otherwise, violence, particularly retaliation for past abuses, is likely to re-emerge once third-party mediators, observers, or peacekeepers have departed.

Human rights violations as consequences of conflict

Alternatively, human rights abuses can emerge primarily as a result of violent conflict. A conflict may have been undertaken by the parties primarily out of concern to promote a political or ideological agenda, or to promote the welfare of one or more identity groups, or over access to resources. Examples abound: the leftist rebels in El Salvador ostensibly fought to redress the massive wealth imbalance in the country and the grinding poverty suffered by the majority, seeking land redistribution and a more egalitarian economic system. However, the conflict with the government that ensued generated vast human rights abuses, such as disappearances, torture, illegal detention, and execution, mostly committed by the government. In Argentina, the alleged threat of communist subversion was used by the military junta to maintain its own power and engage in systematic disappearances and repression. Conflicts over access to resources, such as diamonds in Sierra Leone, timber in Liberia, coltan in the Democratic Republic of Congo, and oil in Sudan, have taken a great toll beyond the cost to human life on the battlefield, resulting also in wide-scale killing and displacement of civilians, and gross human rights abuses. The vast majority of harm in recent conflicts has been inflicted on civilians, either incidentally or, more frequently, deliberately in the pursuit of resources. Violations may include human rights abuses such as torture and disappearances, but also frequently include war crimes, **crimes against humanity**, and even genocide.

Human rights violations as both causes and consequences of conflict

Of course, human rights violations are usually both causes and consequences of conflict, intertwined among other factors. For example, in Sudan, causes of conflict have included concerns about religious repression, access to resources, and control of land, as well as the human rights violations themselves, incurred over the course of the multi-decade conflict. It would be incorrect to suggest that the north–south conflict was generated by attempts of the government in the north to impose *sharia law* on the population of the south, who were largely Christian or animist. It would similarly be incorrect to argue that the conflict in Sudan was over access to oil alone. Rather, religious repression, discrimination and marginalization based on perceived racial distinctions and geography, and access to resources were at stake in that conflict, which reached a negotiated conclusion in 2005.

Human rights violations as transformers of conflict dynamics

Human rights violations are not only causes and consequences of violent conflict, however, they are also potentially transformative of conflicts and may make their resolution a greater challenge. Thus, conflicts that may begin over resources, religion, or ethnic or territorial claims, may, as they progress, create new grievances through the real and perceived violation of human rights by one or more parties. Further, such violations may reify divides in society, making it easier for leaders to mobilize people—civilian and armed—to violent action. In such mobilization, it becomes easy to demonize the "other," whether rebel group or state actor, which in turn facilitates not merely killing on the battlefield, but also the commission of further human rights violations. The conflict may be transformed, although not always, into one that is primarily about grievances, identity, and recrimination, even though other causes may have precipitated the original fighting. Further, and this is key from the perspective of conflict resolution, heightened mistrust and resentments make initial negotiations difficult, and may create impediments to long-term peacebuilding and reconciliation. Moreover, it is difficult to convince people and groups who have abused one another to sit face-to-face and negotiate; even if leaders take that step, ordinary individuals might be reluctant to set aside grievances. This fundamentally changes the terrain of peacebuilding; victims, civil society, and other actors may demand redress of past abuses, even though such redress is likely to be resisted by some or all of the warring parties.

Human rights and accountability as demands during peace negotiations and postconflict peacebuilding

Human rights protections and accountability for past violations are usually among the demands that parties consider when negotiating the end to an armed conflict. However, these are not the only demands, as discussed in Chapter 2. Human rights may emerge as a central concern in negotiations in a number of ways. First, the demand for accountability will likely be central for one or more parties at the negotiating table, with civil society, nongovernmental organizations, or the international community also pressing for some form of accountability beyond the negotiation table. The latter might take the form of prosecutions, lustration or vetting (removal or barring of abusers from certain public offices), **truth commissions**, or reparation. Any of these groups, and indeed some armed groups as well, might demand the restructuring and retraining security forces, so that they will respect human rights in the future. Yet simultaneously, individuals who have also been perpetrators of serious human rights violations, whether they are part of armed groups or the government, may fear imprisonment or, at the very least, loss of privileges through lustration, or public shaming through the release of a truth commission report. They may press for blanket amnesties or at least for their own protection. Thus demands for accountability can be serious obstacles during negotiations. Many have argued that the possibility of prosecution hampered negotiations with the Lord's Resistance Army (LRA) of northern Uganda: although the government provided reassurances regarding domestic prosecution during the Juba Peace Talks of 2006–2008, the International Criminal Court had already issued arrest warrants for LRA leader Joseph Kony and four others. A variety of provisions may be built into a peace agreement, or the issue may be held in abeyance to be dealt with subsequently. Demands for accountability and the various mechanisms to address past abuses after conflict are examined in greater detail in Parts II and III of this volume.

Alternatively, human rights protections may also be central to a negotiating process, important in laying the groundwork for democratic development, and may be useful in confidence building. Thus, for example, in El Salvador's multiple rounds of negotiations, one of the first operational agreements, the San José Agreement, approved the creation of a **United Nations** (UN) human rights observer mission. The functioning of the mission not only meant that human rights were prioritized during the negotiating process, but also introduced a third party on the ground in the country. Many scholars argue that the presence of a third party—as monitor, guarantor, and stabilizer—is essential if **peace negotiations** are to succeed.

Human rights protections and accountability for past abuses are also often claimed to be essential to **peacemaking** and peacebuilding. Analysts and advocates have argued that addressing human rights violations is essential for restoring the peace and building **rule**

***Box 1.2* UN mediation and amnesties**

A common demand of parties to conflicts are amnesties or other bars to accountability for serious crimes. These parties make such demands both out of fear of prosecution resulting in imprisonment, but also out of concern to maintain their own political legitimacy and viability in a post-agreement state. Thus, amnesties have historically been significant tools in the "toolbox" of mediators. However, such amnesties have faced increasing political criticism and growing arguments that some or all amnesties are illegal. While there remains legal debate about the constraints upon amnesty, there is consensus amongst some, though certainly not all, scholars, that blanket amnesties for serious international crimes such as genocide, war crimes, torture and crimes against humanity are not permissible. United Nations mediators receive explicit instruction that the UN cannot endorse any peace agreement with such provisions. With amnesty excluded or limited in many instances, other measures to reassure parties to negotiations, such as power-sharing arrangements, are often utilized, and may de facto limit accountability options.

Source: United Nations, *Guidance for Effective Mediation* at http://peacemaker.un.org/mediationapp#MediationOverview

of law, and in particular for demonstrating that a society is now on a different, nonviolent path. They have similarly argued that the absence of accountability may hamper long-term peacebuilding, because some former victims may seek vengeance, or the population more broadly may place little faith in postconflict institutions that have not addressed human rights abuses.

Conversely, the pursuit of accountability may hamper not only peace negotiations, but also peace implementation, where those who face accountability return to violence or threaten to return to violence. Thus in El Salvador, for example, the impending release of the truth commission report, which would find the armed forces responsible for the vast majority of human rights abuses committed during that country's conflict, caused unrest in the military. In Argentina, a country emerging from a severe internal repression that never became an official armed conflict, the attempt to prosecute the former military leadership resulted in with five coup attempts.

Other issues covered by peace processes might not seem directly related to human rights, but could have an important impact on demands for accountability and reconciliation processes. For example, peace negotiations and peace processes deal with the disarmament, demobilization, and reintegration of ex-combatants to guarantee that they do not return fighting. This may require a host of guarantees to parties that may be at cross-purposes with human rights protections, including **amnesty** but also other concessions to individuals or groups who may be responsible for grave violations of human rights or international humanitarian law. Thus the 1999 Lomé Agreement in Sierra Leone granted a blanket amnesty, and guaranteed notorious rebel leader Foday Sankoh a position in government. Negotiations will address an array of contentious issues, such as land tenure or access to resources, and restructuring of and access to governance and political representation. Particularly where governance has been poor, corrupt, or undemocratic, some domestic and international actors will be interested in rebuilding, or building for the first time, key elements needed to establish the rule of law—transparent legislation, a functional judiciary and correctional system, and

---

Box 1.3 **The relationship between conflict and human rights**

- Human rights violations as causes of conflict
- Human rights violations as consequences of conflict
- Human rights violations as both causes and consequences of conflict
- Human rights violations as transformative of conflict dynamics
- Human rights and accountability as demands during peace negotiations and postconflict peacebuilding

---

the like. Protection of human rights may also be an important component of postconflict rule of law promotion strategies.

Human rights concerns thus play a complex range of roles and have a complicated relationship to both peace negotiations and peacebuilding processes. The relationship is made more complex by the fact that specialists in the protection of human rights and specialists in conflict resolution form different communities, with different expertise.

Advocating human rights and conflict resolution: different communities, different agendas

Rhetorically, the goals of those who seek to protect human rights and those who seek to promote conflict resolution are complementary: both seek to reduce human suffering, in particular to prevent physical harm and violence to individuals, largely civilians, by governments or nonstate armed groups. However, the two groups may prioritize goals or assess success differently, with conflict resolution advocates typically prepared to place less importance on human rights concerns, at least temporarily, while details of peace agreements are being resolved, as explained in Box 1.4. Human rights advocates, conversely, will generally focus upon the underlying grievances as causes of the conflict, or on the abuses that occurred during the conflict, and insist that conflict might re-emerge if "justice" is not done. They may be less sensitive to the possibility that a demand for justice during peace negotiations might actually block conflict resolution.

Not surprisingly, conflict resolution advocates will prioritize different goals than human rights advocates. The latter will be suspicious of amnesties, and promote legal accountability, the creation of human rights institutions, the needs of victims, and public discussion of past abuses. Conflict resolution advocates, as noted above, will be interested primarily in reaching a negotiated settlement, and may be willing to sacrifice some human rights concerns to that

---

Box 1.4 **Advocating human rights and conflict resolution: potential tension**

- Human rights advocates prioritize accountability, public reckoning, national human rights institutions, and the needs of victims, and will be wary of any outcome that involves negotiation with or amnesty for human rights abusers.
- Conflict resolution advocates prioritize reaching a settlement that can bring an end to violent conflict, and will be prepared to negotiate with and even in some instances consider amnesty for human rights abusers.

end. However, they are also concerned with creating a sustainable, long-term peace and reducing the risk of return to conflict, and thus have an interest in the rule of law, democratic governance, and ultimately many human rights protections. Thus, while the primary goals of the two communities may appear to be at odds, given the intertwined nature of human rights violations and war, there may be a convergence to be identified, and each group of practitioners needs to be sensitized to the concerns of the other.

Relevant law

This book does not cover all obligations under international human rights law and international humanitarian law, as these are too vast to be addressed sufficiently here. The relevant legal obligations, developed in greater detail in Chapter 4, are primarily those that are closely tied to violent conflict as either causes or consequences. Further, the bulk of this book addresses situations in which violations of legal obligations are actually crimes, for which international, individualized criminal accountability is possible. These comprise a narrow set of violations, and are those for which postconflict regimes, or the international community, have prosecuted perpetrators.

The legal rights and obligations of greatest relevance here are the core international human rights documents, often referred to as the **International Bill of Rights**: the Universal Declaration of Human Rights (UDHR), the International Covenant on Civil and Political Rights (ICCPR), and International Covenant on Economic, Social and Cultural Rights (ICESCR). As we shall see in Chapter 4, these documents, where they do create obligations for states, do not create international crimes. The same is true of the Convention on the Elimination of Racial Discrimination in All Its Forms (CERD), the Convention on the Rights of the Child (CRC), and the Convention on the Elimination of Discrimination Against Women (CEDAW). Nonetheless, all of these documents articulate rights or obligations, the violation of which may serve to promote conflict, or result from conflict. Other human rights documents create more explicit obligations for states, and violations by individuals may be prosecutable crimes, as with the Convention on the Prevention and Punishment of the Crime of Genocide (the **Genocide Convention**) and the Convention Against Torture and Other Cruel, Inhuman, or Degrading Treatment or Punishment (the **Torture Convention**). Similarly, obligations

---

Box 1.5 **Key international legal documents**

- International Bill of Rights:
  - Universal Declaration of Human Rights
  - International Covenant on Civil and Political Rights
  - International Covenant on Economic, Social and Cultural Rights
- Convention on the Prevention and Punishment of the Crime of Genocide
- Convention Against Torture and Other Cruel, Inhuman, or Degrading Treatment or Punishment
- Four Geneva Conventions of 1949 and their two additional protocols of 1977
- Rome Statute of the International Criminal Court
- Convention on the Elimination of Racial Discrimination in All Its Forms
- Convention on the Rights of the Child
- Convention on the Elimination of Discrimination Against Women

under international humanitarian law, whether customary or based on treaty, may include **grave breaches**, known in common parlance as war crimes, for which individuals may be prosecuted. The key conventions of study here are the four **Geneva Conventions** of 1949 and their two additional protocols of 1977. Finally, the Rome Statute of the ICC defines three crimes for prosecution—war crimes, crimes against humanity, and genocide—and has defined a fourth over which it does not yet have active jurisdiction, the crime of aggression.

Responses to human rights abuses

Given the complex relationship between conflict and human rights, and the competing demands articulated above, a number of responses to significant human rights abuse have been developed—the domestic, transnational, hybrid, and ad hoc and permanent international, as noted in Box 1.6 and discussed in Part III of this volume. Domestic responses to end armed conflict and simultaneously grapple with human rights abuses may include all of the measures already noted, ranging from amnesty to prosecution, alongside lustration, reparation, retraining of security forces, and development of national human rights mechanisms. Transnational responses, whereby abuses are addressed in a different country than that in which they occurred, are most commonly the case in the pursuit of criminal accountability, with the exercise of **universal jurisdiction**, but accountability may also be pursued through civil suits. Most criminal cases have been brought in a few European countries, such as Belgium and Spain, while most civil cases have been brought in the United States, through the **Alien Tort Claims Act** (ACTA), or in the United Kingdom. Hybrid institutions for accountability have also been developed in recent years. These are tribunals created to function in the country where an armed conflict has occurred; they utilize not only domestic law and judges, but also a combination of domestic and international judges, prosecutors, and lawyers, and may rely on international human rights and humanitarian law or a combination of international and domestic law. There have been several such experiments to date—in Kosovo, East Timor, Sierra Leone, Cambodia, and Bosnia. Finally, there are international responses, through international criminal tribunals. Historically, after World War II, prosecutions were undertaken in the Nuremburg and Tokyo Tribunals, but new international bodies began to emerge in the 1990s with the creation of two ad hoc tribunals for the prosecution of crimes committed during the war in the former Yugoslavia and during the genocide in Rwanda. More recently, the ICC has undertaken formal investigations of crimes committed in numerous countries in Africa, to date Libya, Kenya, Uganda, the Democratic Republic of Congo, Sudan, the Central African Republic, Côte d'Ivoire and Mali. Each of these judicial bodies is somewhat different; although many refer to the same core legal obligations, their mandates and competence vary significantly.

Box 1.6 Accountability institutions and responses

- Domestic transitional justice
- Regional courts
- Ad hoc international tribunals
- Permanent international tribunals
- Hybrid or mixed tribunals
- Universal jurisdiction
- Civil accountability

Internal armed conflicts

Many of the conflicts examined in this book share a unique feature—they are internal armed conflicts, although many of them may involve a cross-border dimension. The internal nature of many contemporary conflicts generates particular legal and practical difficulties. While international human rights law functions in times of war and peace, and applies consistently whether the conflict is internal or international, the same cannot be said of international humanitarian law. The latter operates only where an armed conflict occurs. In some instances of civil strife, there may be genuine debate about whether an armed conflict is in fact occurring. Contemporary conflicts are seldom declared, and many low-intensity conflicts, while costly in lives and human rights violations, might not be treated as "wars." More important, however, international humanitarian law is traditionally dualistic, distinguishing between international and noninternational armed conflict, as is discussed in Chapter 4. This, as we shall see in Chapter 5, poses particular difficulty in pursuing accountability for armed groups and private military and security companies engaged in internal armed conflict.

Discussion questions

- What is the general relationship between war and human rights?
- How might human rights violations engender conflict? How does conflict engender human rights violations?
- Are amnesties permissible in peace agreements?
- How does the evolution of conflict, and human rights violations, change conflict?
- How might the interplay of conflict and human rights violations and protections affect conflict negotiation, resolution, and peacebuilding?

Further reading

Bell, Christine, *Peace Agreements and Human Rights* (Oxford: Oxford University Press, 2003), Chapters 1, 2, 10, and appendix, "A Decade of Peace Agreements."

Crimes of War Project, http://www.crimesofwar.org

Human Rights Watch, *Human Rights and Armed Conflict* (2004), http://hrw.org especially "Africa on Its Own," and "Right Side Up."

Lutz, Ellen, Eileen F. Babbitt, and Hurst Hannum, "Human Rights and Conflict Resolution from the Practitioners' Perspectives," *Fletcher Forum of World Affairs* vol. 27, no. 1 (Winter–Spring 2003) 173–193.

Manikkalingam, Ram, "Promoting Peace and Protecting Rights: How are Human Rights Good and Bad for Resolving Conflict?" *Essex Human Rights Review* vol. 5, no. 1 (July 2008): 1–11 http://projects.essex.ac.uk/ehrr/V5N1/Manikkalingam.pdf

Mertus, Julie A., and Jeffrey W. Helsing (eds), *Human Rights and Conflict: Exploring the Links Between Rights, Law, and Peacebuilding* (Washington, DC: US Institute of Peace Press, 2006).

Parlevliet, Michelle, "Rethinking Conflict Transformation from a Human Rights Perspective," (Berghof Research Centre, September 2009), Berlin: Berghof Research Centre. http://www.berghof-handbook.net/documents/publications/parlevliet_handbook.pdf

Vandeginste, Stef, and Chandra Lekha Sriram, "Power-sharing and Transitional Justice: A Clash of Paradigms?" *Global Governance* vol. 17, no. 4 (2011): 487–505.

Official documents and sources

United Nations, *Guidance for Effective Mediation,* http://peacemaker.un.org/mediationapp#Mediation Overview.

United Nations, *Report of the Independent Expert to Update the Set of Principles to Combat Impunity, Diane Orentlicher: Updated Set of Principles for the Protection and Promotion of Human Rights Through Action to Combat Impunity* (February 8, 2005), UN Doc. E/CN.4/2005/102/Add.1.

United Nations, *The Rule of Law and Transitional Justice in Conflict and Post-Conflict Societies: Report of the Secretary-General* (August 23, 2004), UN Doc. S/2004/616.

United Nations, *The Rule of Law and Transitional Justice in Conflict and Post-Conflict Societies: Report of the Secretary-General* (October 12, 2011), UN Doc. S/2011/634.

2 Conflict

Fundamentals and debates

Key points

- Current conflicts vary significantly in nature and in the actors involved compared to the traditional interstate conflicts prevalent when the **United Nations** (UN) architecture for the prevention and resolution was designed.
- Understanding the root causes of conflicts is essential in order to design adequate **conflict prevention** and resolution policies.
- Security and development actors share the same ultimate goal of avoiding conflicts, but do not necessarily share the same priorities in specific conflicts; their priorities may sometimes even appear contradictory.
- The UN institutional framework provides the main apparatus for international **peacekeeping** and **peacebuilding**.

Overview

After the end of the Cold War, internal conflicts proliferated significantly. Since then, collective efforts to prevent and resolve these conflicts have been a central focus for the international community. This chapter analyzes the characteristics and causes of contemporary armed conflicts, and how the international system copes with preventing and resolving them, as well as how it attempts to build durable peace afterward. This chapter examines the distinction between **peacemaking**, peacekeeping, and peacebuilding, and the historical evolution of these processes, as well as the main actors involved in conflict prevention, conflict resolution, and postconflict reconstruction, with special emphasis on the UN legal and institutional framework.

Today's conflicts

The international institutional architecture designed after World War II foresaw a system to prevent and resolve international disputes, focused on conflict between two or more states, which had been the most common form until then. The end of the Cold War marked a significant change in the nature and development of armed conflicts, and therefore also in the strategies to prevent, resolve, and mitigate their effects. The 1990s saw a spectacular proliferation of internal armed conflicts. Since then, interstate wars have decreased to a mere few, among them: the Gulf War in 1991, the wars between Ethiopia and Eritrea in

1998, the US-led invasions of Afghanistan and Iraq in 2001 and 2004, respectively, the war in the Democratic Republic of Congo, which involved some of its neighboring states (see Chapter 7), and the confrontation between Russia and Georgia in the summer of 2008.

Internal armed conflicts—intrastate—are different from interstate conflicts in many ways. Whereas an interstate war involves two standing armies fighting each other, a civil conflict involves a government army or militia fighting one or more rebel organizations. These rebel organizations are referred to, in much of the conflict and legal literature, as nonstate armed groups. In civil wars, these groups seek a range of objectives, including secession from or control over the state or parts of its territory, increased rights and freedom for the population or part of it, as well as resource exploitation, as discussed in the country case studies in Part II of this book. It is rare that armed groups target only each other. It is also rare that the parties in a conflict are completely isolated and not influenced by or do not receive support from external actors. When external military forces intervene and fight in support of at least one of the warring parties, the literature refers to them as internationalized intrastate conflicts. The violence generated in internal armed conflicts is commonly—and devastatingly—directed at civilians, who often flee both internally and to other countries in search of security. Thus the repercussions of a civil war commonly extend beyond the borders of the territory in which it takes place, affecting security and economic development at the regional level and provoking destabilization, displacement, and human rights abuse.

Today, because of their capacity for destabilization and threat to human rights, civil wars are addressed within the international peace and security framework. Even so, the proliferation of civil conflicts has tested the competence of the **UN Charter** to prevent and resolve them, as discussed in Part III.

Characteristics and causes of conflict

Civil conflict can be categorized in a variety of ways according to cause. Generally, there is a confluence of several causes for a given conflict, even if one cause can be identified as more prominent. Frequently cited causes of conflicts include ideological issues, such as moral and religious differences; political issues; identity issues, such as ethnicity; distributional issues, such as control of and access to natural resources; and unmet human needs and human rights violations. These causes can be classified in different ways: in terms of proximity of the cause to the actual violence, and mobilization; in terms of insecurity, inequality, private incentives, and perceptions; and in terms of "greed" versus "grievance."

Structural, proximate, and mobilizing causes

Structural causes are deeply rooted problems that have the potential to provoke violent conflict. Many structural causes emerge from the nature of political regimes, including the relationship between the state and its citizens, the legitimacy of the government and the involvement of civil society in its election, and the state's willingness or capacity to provide basic services. Both overly weak and overly strong governments may create conflict-prone situations. Structural causes can include inequality, discrimination, absence or breakdown of the **rule of law**, unequal access to recourses and services such as education and health care, and poverty.

However, the presence of structural causes does not mean that a conflict will ignite. Conflict generally requires a proximate cause as well—a significant change in the situation, such as the emergence of individuals or groups who seek to change the status quo. Proximate

---

Box 2.1 The so-called "Arab Spring"

In December 2010 a young man, Mohamed Bouazizi, set himself on fire and died in Tunisia in protest against his treatment by the police, which had confiscated his fruit and vegetable market stall. His death sparked a series of demonstrations to protest against the economic situation of the country and demanded increased civil liberties. After weeks of protests, then-President Zine al-Abadine Ali fled the country and an interim government was created in January 2011. Transitional Tunisia inherited the legacy of years of lack of freedom and democracy, abuse and corruption of the ruling class, compounded by the recent global economic crisis. The result was a situation of social instability, but it was the death of Bouazizi which acted as a mobilizing force. The protests in Tunisia spread quickly to the whole region and demonstrations for increased democracy, end of corruption and better economic conditions followed in Algeria, Bahrain, Iran, Iraq, Jordan, Lebanon, Libya, Morocco, Syria and Yemen, in what has been called the "Arab Spring," or "Arab uprisings." In some countries, such as Tunisia and Egypt, the demonstrations led to democratic elections, whilst the consequence in others such as Libya and Syria was armed conflict.

---

causes, then, may differ from structural causes only by degree. Examples of proximate causes include loss of citizenship for certain groups; restriction of the rights of certain groups (e.g., the introduction of quotas for entrance to universities); restriction of access to certain places; restriction of religious expression; manipulation of government powers, including abuse of security forces; heightened corruption; and widespread human rights violations.

Still, even in these situations, conflict may not necessarily occur. There generally needs to be a mobilizing cause too. These are causes that directly prompt the eruption of violence, such as the violent removal of a leader from office, electoral fraud, destruction of identity or religious symbols, and incitement of hatred or violence against a particular group of people.

Insecurity, inequality, private incentives, and perceptions

Insecurity

When the interests or agendas of two or more groups are at odds, such as over access to resources, political opinion, or religious beliefs, or when two or more groups perceive themselves as opponents because of ethnic or racial origins, there may arise what is sometimes called a security dilemma. In this scenario, actions taken by one group to increase its own security are seen by another group as threatening, provoking a competition for security that makes all groups less secure. The increased insecurity can have a range of consequences, from public disorder, to violence, to the collapse of the state, although the latter is rare as an end result. Conversely, the insecurity generated by the collapse of a state may also provoke a competition for security, which in turn may lead to violent conflict.

Inequality

Poverty is often cited as a cause of conflict. However, many of the countries in which violent conflicts have developed during the past decades, though they may have high levels of poverty, are also often home to a wealthy elite, and are often rich in natural resources. Thus, while poverty itself may be one of the underlying conditions that enable conflict, a structural cause, such as inequality, particularly horizontal inequality, is often what mobilizes the conflict. Horizontal inequality can be defined as differential access to specific goods across specific groups in a society, whether ethnic, linguistic, cultural, religious, or some other category of people. This access is not limited to economic resources, but may also include political resources, educational resources, and social status.

Private incentives

In some cases, leaders and would-be leaders mobilize specific sectors of the population, sparking confrontation and conflict. Some such leaders and their followers have legitimate security concerns, or are mobilized by specific grievances, but others have purely predatory intentions. In the latter scenario, the pursuit of private incentives, such as pursuit of political power (whether to obtain or maintain it) and economic gain (control over natural resources including minerals and illicit crops), may promote conflict.

Perceptions

Perceptions can also mobilize conflict, if certain societal groups feel threatened by others. This is frequently the case where there has been a history of ethnic animosity. The perception of unequal treatment by the government, or of discrimination over access to power or resources, may mobilize groups and exacerbate the security dilemma, as actions taken by one group to increase its own security in such circumstances are likely to be viewed by other groups as threatening. In many cases, leaders and aspiring leaders manipulate perceptions for their own benefit.

* * *

As illustrated in the country case studies in Part II, these causes are interrelated—they normally coexist and intersect—and in any given conflict it is difficult to identify one that has primacy over others. Conditions of inequality may exist, and in tandem with a history of ethnic violence, yet conflict might not ignite until leaders seek to manipulate perceptions and foment violence for their own ends. Equally, attempts to provoke violence may not work in the absence of a specific history of ethnic hostility, or where perceptions are more difficult to manipulate. The conflicts in the former Soviet bloc and in parts of Africa are examples of the interaction of such causes. Conflicts often emerge as weak states become repressive in an effort to retain power, or where there is competition among multiple groups for power or security in the absence of functional states. Inequality has been a common feature, but certainly the perceptions of such discrimination have been the proximate causes in conflicts such as those of the former Yugoslavia and Rwanda. Private incentives have played an important role in many contemporary conflicts especially in relation to access to natural resources, in Africa.

Greed v. grievance

An important debate in conflict analysis concerns the relative priority of "greed" and "grievance" as causes. Is it greed, such as the pursuit of control over economic or natural resources, or grievance, such as ethnic hatred or resentment over inequality or past abuses, that really underpins most conflicts? Some of the conflicts that arose after the end of the Cold War were depicted, particularly in the media, as motivated by "ancient ethnic hatreds." According to this analysis, conflicts both in former Soviet-bloc countries and in parts of Africa emerged because the end of the bipolar international order which kept internal conflicts in check allowed the unleashing of historical ethnic resentment. This argument is rather simplistic, and does not take into account the broader range and interrelation of conflict causes discussed previously. While it is certainly the case that conflicts in the former Yugoslavia and Rwanda involved violence between ethnic groups, intermarriage among ethnic groups was common in Yugoslavia, particularly Bosnia-Herzegovina, and to a lesser degree in Rwanda, undermining claims that ethnic hatreds make peaceful coexistence impossible.

Conflict prevention

The term *conflict prevention* encompasses the range of activities taken to mitigate the risk of an imminent conflict, as well as those activities that seek to address deep-rooted causes that can lead to conflict in the future. Traditionally, in conflicts involving one or more states, the means for preventing a resort to violence involves diplomatic negotiations between the parties, sometimes with the involvement of a third, neutral party. The proliferation of internal conflicts has demanded new prevention activities outside this traditional framework of **diplomacy**. These preventive activities can be categorized as structural (long-term) and operational (short-term). Recently the **UN Secretary-General** introduced a third category: systemic prevention.

Structural v. operational prevention

The theory and practice of conflict prevention have been guided by the distinction between structural and operational prevention. Structural prevention refers to the activities undertaken to address the root causes of conflict, while operational prevention, also called direct prevention, comprises activities undertaken to reduce or eliminate more immediate sources of violence.

   Structural prevention activities include poverty alleviation, reduction of corruption and inequality, reform of governance and institution-building programs, and reform of the security sector. Structural prevention, therefore, seeks to alleviate possible underlying causes of conflict, where no conflict appears imminent.

   Operational prevention seeks to address proximate and mobilizing causes of conflict, attempting to maintain stability and prevent grievances. These activities include provision of "good offices" by external actors; addressing sources of tension and friction before they lead to violence; meeting humanitarian needs, including access to basic resources such as food and water, and addressing immediate health needs; and even the use of targeted sanctions and military pressure. Targeted sanctions have been used in countries such as Angola, Sierra Leone, and Côte d'Ivoire.

   Traditionally, structural prevention and operational prevention were undertaken by somewhat different sets of actors. Structural prevention was conducted by development and humanitarian actors, while operational prevention was conducted by security actors. UN prevention practice in the 1990s could be characterized in this way. However, research into the practice of conflict prevention shows that the distinction between structural and operational measures is often too rigid. Structural and operational activities and actors have complementary roles to play in addressing conflict prevention. Recent UN practice often involves actors from "security" and "development" agencies working together on similar types of prevention efforts.

Systemic prevention

In 2001 the UN Secretary-General, Kofi Annan, developed a strategy to transform the United Nations from a culture of conflict reaction to a culture of conflict prevention, the latter comprising two categories: structural prevention and operational prevention. Later, Annan evolved the strategy further by adding a third category: systemic prevention. This third category refers to global measures to address the risk of conflict—measures that transcend particular states, including reduction of the illicit trade in small arms and light weapons, as well as the spread of nuclear, chemical, and biological weapons; reduction of environmental degradation; treatment of pandemic diseases such as HIV/AIDS; regulation of industries that are known to fuel conflict; and advancement of global development. Thus, while structural and operational preventive measures are conflict-specific, systemic measures have global scope. According to the Secretary-General, systemic initiatives, combined with ongoing, country-specific structural and operational preventive measures, increase the possibility of peace and reduce vulnerability to armed conflicts.

The recent Kenyan conflict illustrates a case in which prevention allowed violence to end before the conflict became intractable (see Box 2.2).

Box 2.2 The 2007 Kenyan post-election violence

In December 2007, fighting broke out in Kenya after a disputed general election. Both President Mwai Kibaki, who had been in office since 2002, and Raila Odinga, leader of the opposition, claimed to have won the election. A reported 1,500 people died in the fighting and 600,000 were displaced. The conflict was rooted in historical tensions and inequality between the several ethnic groups, as well as systemic corruption, but the immediate trigger was the disputed election, exacerbated by violence between the Kalenjin and Kukuyu ethnic groups. Immediately after the elections and the start of the conflict, the European Union and the United States pressured Kibaki and Obinga to end the fighting. Mediation was attempted by US envoy Jendayi Frazer and Ghanaian president John Kufuor, on behalf of the African Union, and assisted by four former African heads of state and the ambassadors from the United States, Britain, and France. In January 2008, former UN Secretary-General Kofi Annan took over the mediation. His intervention as mediator led to a power-sharing deal between the opposing parties, who formed a coalition government, in April 2008, in which Kibaki became president and Odinga the prime minister. The International Criminal Court opened an investigation into the situation (see Chapter 13). The next presidential elections in 2013 were accompanied by instability, but did not result in widespread violence. However, two politicians charged with crimes against humanity before the ICC, Uhuru Kenyatta and William Ruto, became president and deputy president, respectively.

Key actors in conflict prevention

There are a multiplicity of security and development actors who participate in conflict prevention, making coordination of their efforts difficult, especially when prevention actors are driven by competing political agendas.

Security actors are those that can exercise a certain degree of coercion. These include the United Nations, in particular the **UN Security Council**, and many **regional organizations** such as the European Union (EU), the **North Atlantic Treaty Organization** (NATO), the Organization for Security and Cooperation in Europe (OSCE), the Organization of American States (OAS), the **African Union** (AU), the **Economic Community of West African States** (ECOWAS), and the Association of Southeast Asian Nations (ASEAN). While some have played only a minimal role in conflict prevention to date, all have engaged in dialogue or collaboration with the UN.

Development actors include international financial institutions such as the World Bank and the International Monetary Fund (IMF), international agencies such as the UN Development Programme (UNDP), national development agencies such as the United Kingdom's Department for International Development (DFID) and the US Agency for International Development (USAID), and specialized nongovernmental organizations such as the International Committee of the Red Cross (ICRC). Other entities may also be involved in the prevention of specific conflicts, including the private sector and the media.

Among the international actors, however, perhaps the most important for conflict prevention is the United Nations, as conflict prevention is now understood to be one of its central missions. The main UN organ for coordinating conflict prevention efforts is the **Department of Political Affairs** (DPA). It provides political analysis and advice, and direct support for preventive diplomacy and "good offices." It plays a central role in monitoring and assessing global political developments; warning of potential crises before they break out; advising the UN Secretary-General on actions that could advance the cause of peace; providing support and guidance to UN peace envoys and political missions in the field; engaging member states directly through electoral assistance; and supporting interdepartmental relations and partnerships with other UN entities, regional organizations, and civil society. Box 2.3 lists the wide range of the UN bodies and agencies involved in these tasks.

Conflict resolution

Conflict resolution seeks to terminate a conflict which has already erupted and to achieve peace. The international conflict resolution system established after World War II, mainly within the UN framework, was primarily designed to address interstate wars, and thus inevitably it has experienced some difficulty adapting to intrastate conflicts. The UN Charter establishes a fundamental obligation for all member states to resolve their international disputes "by peaceful means in such a manner that international peace and security, and justice, are not endangered" (Article 2.3).

During the Cold War, many internal conflicts proliferated; however, the competition between East and West resulted in a stalemate, and the UN system was limited in its capacity to address internal as well as international conflicts. The end of the Cold War created new opportunities for the international community to promote resolution to civil wars. In the 1990s, peacemaking tools were further developed and new mechanisms created, and the number of actors involved in conflict resolution increased.

Box 2.3 **UN bodies and agencies involved in conflict prevention**

- Security Council
- General Assembly
- The office of the Secretary-General and its special representatives and envoys
- Department of Political Affairs (DPA)
- Department of Peacekeeping Operations (DPKO)
- UN Development Programme (UNDP)
- Office for the Coordination of Humanitarian Affairs (OCHA)
- Department of Economic and Social Affairs (DESA)
- UN High Commissioner for Human Rights (UNHCHR)
- World Food Programme (WFP)
- Food and Agriculture Organisation (FAO)
- World Health Organization (WHO)
- UN Children's Fund (UNICEF)
- Department of Disarmament Affairs (DDA)
- UN Development Fund for Woman (UNIFEM)
- UN Educational, Scientific and Cultural Organization (UNESCO)

Actors

Traditionally, the primary actors involved in conflict resolution were the official actors, largely international governmental organizations and state representatives. However, more and more **nonstate actors** now participate in conflict resolution in different capacities and perform a range of functions, including strictly diplomatic efforts to bring parties together, providing humanitarian assistance, and mitigating the effects of conflict and preventing escalation.

Official actors

A central official actor is the United Nations. The UN's competence to participate in conflict resolution is confirmed in Chapters VI and VII of the UN Charter. These chapters outline the role of UN organs in the peaceful resolution of disputes that could endanger the maintenance of international peace and security. Chapter VI deals with peaceful settlement of disputes, while Chapter VII deals with responses to threats to peace, breaches of peace, and acts of aggression.

The main responsibilities in the UN Charter are those of the Security Council to call upon the parties to settle their disputes by peaceful means (Article 33.2), investigate any dispute or situation that might lead to international conflict (Article 34), and recommend appropriate responses (Articles 36.1 and 38). In the event of a threat to the peace, a breach of the peace, or an act of aggression, the Security Council decides the measures that shall be taken to maintain or restore international peace and security (Article 39). Though use of force may be authorized if deemed necessary, softer measures such as economic sanctions and interruption of diplomatic relations are often the first course of action (Article 41).

In principle, UN peacemaking efforts are not intended to address civil conflicts through use of force, as such conflicts theoretically pose no threat to international peace and security.

However, many civil conflicts have involved significant harm to civilians, and there have been demands for the use of force to protect them. While such humanitarian intervention remains hotly disputed by international lawyers, intervention has been justified on the basis of the threats to international peace and security that internal conflicts may pose. The UN has engaged in peacekeeping operations not originally envisaged by the UN Charter, for which there has been no clear, strictly legal basis. This is why the first operations of this kind were known as "Chapter VI½" operations, as they did not fall strictly under Chapter VI (peacemaking) or Chapter VII (peace enforcement) of the UN Charter. Beyond peacekeeping, peacemaking may involve noncoercive actions by the UN Secretary-General, through provision of "good offices" to help parties resolve a conflict peacefully.

Recently, other intergovernmental organizations, in particular **regional organizations**, have participated in conflict resolution, through both peacemaking and peacekeeping. Organizations such as NATO, the EU, the OSCE, the AU, and ECOWAS have participated in the resolution of conflicts in such places as the former Yugoslavia and Sierra Leone.

Unofficial actors

It is not just state representatives or intergovernmental organizations who are involved in conflict resolution. Other nongovernmental actors (also called informal intermediaries) include religious institutions, academics, former government officials, nongovernmental and humanitarian organizations, think tanks, and even businesses. These actors differ in their agendas, aims, and methods, but they generally attempt to provide an adequate environment for conflict resolution in which participants feel free to share their perceptions and needs and explore options for resolution, outside the more constraining governmental framework.

The participation of unofficial actors in conflict resolution and conflict prevention raises questions related to their accountability and the need to monitor their activities. In certain circumstances, well-intentioned individuals and organizations can do more harm than good

---

Box 2.4 **Do no harm**

Mary B. Anderson, a development economist and director of the Collaborative for Development Action, launched a project titled "Local Capacities on Peace" in 1995, to assist peace workers and organizations, which later became known as the "Do No Harm" project. In 1999 she published the book *Do No Harm: How Aid Can Support Peace or War,* in which she illustrated how aid that was intended to do good could end up doing harm. Anderson argued that aid actions directed at building peace in one area could reinforce divisions and conflict in another. She provided a framework for analyzing the impact of aid on conflict, which was implemented and tested in the field from 1997 to 2000 by different organizations. In 2000, Anderson's booklet *Options for Aid in Conflict: Lessons from Field Experience* was published, and at the request of donors and organizations involved in the implementation phase of "Do No Harm," the project began a "mainstreaming" strategy to disseminate the findings of the project widely throughout the aid community and to assist organizations in adapting the framework to their procedures. This project and the framework for analyzing the impact of aid on conflict have importantly influenced the way international donors now conduct their conflict prevention strategies.

when intervening in conflict zones. Among these organizations, there is a growing concern about how to avoid unintended negative consequences when participating in conflict mitigation, and this concern is increasingly taken into account in program and funding design.

Mechanisms

Diplomacy

Peace negotiation, mediation, conciliation, and arbitration are traditional conflict resolution methods. Official diplomacy is developed by official actors—international governmental organizations and states. It is referred to as "track-one" diplomacy, while the interaction of nonstate actors and individuals is termed "track-two" diplomacy.

Official actors are those that act in representation of a state, or with statelike authority. They engage with other states or statelike authorities to bring conflict to an end through diplomatic efforts. Therefore, track-one diplomacy may take place bilaterally between two states, multilaterally among several states, and even regionally or globally through intergovernmental organizations. Bilateral diplomatic efforts between Russia and Estonia sought to solve the conflict of Russian-speaking minorities, while the OSCE High Commissioner on National Minorities held consultations not only with Estonia and Russia, but also with other Baltic states.

The United Nations generally engages in track-one diplomacy when developing its peacemaking activities, and its work has been described as "global" track-one diplomacy. Such activities are considered to be an extension of the parties' own efforts. The Secretary-General is the lead UN actor in conducting conflict resolution diplomacy, acting personally or through special envoys and special representatives.

Track-two diplomacy is also known as citizen diplomacy, multi-track diplomacy, back-channel diplomacy, and supplemental diplomacy. Track-two diplomacy can be undertaken by private citizens or groups of individuals, as well as by representatives from conflicting parties. Activities can include the organization of interactive problem-solving workshops, such as the Inter-Tajik Dialogues organized to address the Tajik civil conflict. The Tajik discussions, which began in March 1993 in Moscow, involved a roundtable meeting of seven individuals from various factions to provide support to the official peace process.

Unofficial actors also engage in what is called "track-three" diplomacy, or interventions at the grassroots level. These actions seek to build or rebuild relationships among ordinary citizens and change attitudes and perceptions of hostility. Examples include radio stations that broadcast programs dedicated to fostering peace and national reconciliation dialogue among groups, such as Radio Ijambo in Burundi, founded in 1995 by Search for Common Ground, a US-based nongovernmental organization; and activities that promote the inclusion of youth, such as the International Camp for Conflict Resolution, organized by the nongovernmental organization Seeds of Peace in the Middle East.

Diplomatic interventions include mediation and good offices, facilitation, fact-finding, and arbitration.

MEDIATION AND GOOD OFFICES

"Good offices" are a traditional means of conflict resolution in which parties to a conflict consent to the participation of a third party during peace negotiations. The third party must abstain from expressing any opinion on the merits of the controversy and from pushing the parties toward a single solution. Mediation, however, involves seeking the consent of the parties to evaluate the merits of their dispute and persuade them to adopt a specific solution. The line between these two methods can sometimes become blurred. Both require the consent of the parties involved in the conflict, are not imposed, and consist only of the provision of advice.

Traditionally, good offices and mediation were developed by a third party, normally a state, in interstate conflicts, although the UN Secretary-General is authorized by Article 99 of the UN Charter to offer good offices. With the proliferation of internal conflicts and the end of the Cold War, the UN Secretary-General increasingly offered good offices. The UN Secretary-General or his envoys and special representatives have provided their good offices on a case-by-case basis, and their role has evolved within peace processes. Parties must consent to the participation of the Secretary-General in the resolution of a particular conflict, and the Secretary-General's mandate might change during the process according to the needs of the parties, their level of trust, the effectiveness of other mediating actors, or the level of international support received.

FACILITATION

External actors engaged in facilitation can engage in a range of activities, from providing neutral facilities or transportation, to chairing negotiation sessions or meeting the parties separately to help them move discussions forward. The role of UN officials as facilitators changes according to the situation and the needs of the parties.

FACT-FINDING

Fact-finding enables external actors involved in conflict resolution to verify, authenticate, or investigate an incident that has given rise or might give rise to a dispute. The participation of an impartial actor is meant to legitimate the findings. Within the UN, such people are designated by the Secretary-General or the Security Council on the basis of reputation or expertise. The Office of the High Commissioner for Human Rights (OHCHR) can also engage in fact finding. In Kenya (see Box 2.2), the OHCHR deployed a 21-day mission to investigate the violence and allegations of grave human rights violations that followed the December 2007 election. The mission found that the state appeared to have failed to take appropriate measures to prevent or stop the violence and the human rights violations.

ARBITRATION

Arbitration is a traditional method of conflict resolution in which an impartial third party, an arbitrator, is designated by relevant parties to issue a decision to resolve the conflict. The parties agree to be bound by the decision of the arbitrator. This mechanism of conflict resolution has been most common in interstate disputes. For example, arbitration was used to determine the borders of the disputed region of Abyei between Sudan and the now-independent state of South Sudan. The Sudan Comprehensive Peace Agreement established the Abyei Borders Commission, which produced its report in 2005. However, the report was disputed and the parties submitted it to the Permanent Court of Arbitration, which produced a final binding decision in 2009.

Peace negotiations

Contemporary conflicts seldom conclude with the military victory of one of the parties, but rather through negotiated settlements between the state and one or more nonstate armed groups. The motive for participating in peace negotiation for each group varies, but their inclusion is essential in order to achieve complete, implementable, peace agreements. Peace agreements often include provisions relating to the security of the groups involved; their disarmament, demobilization, and reintegration into society; their representation in new governmental structures, including their transformation into political parties; their insertion into new transitional governments and the security forces; territorial and resource distribution; and increasingly, mechanisms of accountability for the human rights violations committed during the conflict. Agreements are frequently reached with the support of external parties, including their guarantees during the negotiation to support and monitor implementation. The cases presented in this book illustrate examples of conflicts terminated with peace agreements. The UN has been a key actor in monitoring and supporting the implementation of peace agreements since the end of the Cold War, through peacekeeping and peacebuilding missions.

Often the situation before and after implementation of peace agreements is so fragile that the international community opts to deploy foreign forces to monitor truces while diplomatic negotiations are taking place and monitor the protection of human rights. An example of a United Nations observer mission is the UN Observer Mission in Georgia (UNOMIG), established by Security Council Resolution 858 in August 1993 with a mandate to monitor and verify the cease-fire agreement between the Georgian and Abkhaz sides of the conflict, and to oversee the safe and orderly return of refugees and displaced persons. In April 2012 the UN established an observer mission in Syria (UN Supervision Mission in Syria, UNSMIS), however the mission closed in August that year following the deterioration of the situation and the escalation of violence.

Peacekeeping

Peacekeeping is primarily conducted by the United Nations, although regional organizations have engaged in peacekeeping as well, as when a European Union police mission took over from the UN Mission in Bosnia-Herzegovina (UNMIBH) on January 1, 2003. In 2004, the African Union deployed its AU Mission in Sudan (AMIS) to aid peacekeeping efforts in Darfur; AMIS was subsequently incorporated into the UN-AU Hybrid Mission in Darfur (UNAMID). In 2012, the UN Security Council renewed the mandate of the AU Mission in Somalia (AUMISOM).

To understand contemporary peacekeeping, it is important to understand its evolution since the adoption of the UN Charter, and particularly since the end of the Cold War. Since the 1990s, peacekeeping has evolved from an emphasis on interstate conflicts to encompass a wide range of operations. UN peacekeeping operations continue to increase, not only in number but also in complexity. In 2013 there were 15 active peacekeeping operations involving over 90,000 uniformed personnel (including military troops, police and military observers) and over 17,000 civilians. At the time of writing, the current annual budget for UN peacekeeping is US$7.33 billion. UN peacekeeping mission operate with personnel transferred by individual countries. In 2013, 114 countries provided uniformed personnel to UN peacekeeping missions, with the leading contributors being Bangladesh, India, Pakistan, Ethiopia and Nigeria.

The United Nations has been involved in peacekeeping since its creation, but peacekeeping operations have evolved significantly since the end of the Cold War. The peacekeeping operations that developed between the end of World War II and the end of the 1980s are known as first-generation, classic, or traditional peacekeeping operations. They were designed to respond to interstate crises, the primary concern of the international community in the postwar period. These operations required the consent of the parties to the conflict, who allowed or invited the deployment of UN troops to monitor a truce, withdraw armed forces, or create a buffer zone during political negotiations. The UN forces were unarmed or lightly armed and adopted a neutral role; they could use force only in self-defense. Their primary objective was to serve as deterrents to renewed conflict. Examples of these first peacekeeping operations include the UN Emergency Force (UNEF) in the Sinai, which was sent to separate Israel and Egypt following the Franco–British–Israeli intervention in Suez in 1956; as well as the UN Peacekeeping Force in Cyprus in 1964 and the UN Transitional Assistance Group (UNTAG) in Namibia in 1989, the latter of which marked the transition to the second generation of peacekeeping operations. In some cases, as in Cyprus, conflict was only delayed rather than resolved.

During the 1990s, the so-called second generation of peacekeeping operations developed to address the proliferation of internal conflicts that began to emerge following the end of the Cold War. As with earlier operations, second-generation peacekeeping operations rely on the consent of the parties to a conflict, but they do not limit their engagement to traditional military functions; they also engage in policing and civilian tasks. Their main goal is not only to monitor peace arrangements, but also to achieve long-term settlements by confronting conflicts at their roots. These operations are also known as multidimensional operations, as they involve the implementation of complex peace agreements that seek to build the foundations of self-sustaining, durable peace and establish legitimate governments. This is done through developing the social, political, and economic infrastructure necessary to prevent future violence, which may include economic reconstruction, rebuilding of civil society, and reform of the security forces, judicial system, and electoral system. The civilian components of second-generation peacekeeping operations include policing functions, electoral monitoring and democratization activities, humanitarian relief, economic reconstruction and longer-term development work, civil engineering projects, the promotion, monitoring, and protection of human rights, and de-mining. Since the 1990s, the operations under this second-generation model of peacekeeping have been particularly successful (as in Namibia [UNTAG] from 1989 to 1990, El Salvador [ONUSAL] from 1991 to 1995, Cambodia [UNTAC] from 1991 to 1992, Mozambique [ONUMOZ] from 1992 to 1994, and Croatia [UNCRO] from 1995 to 1996), and the growth of their civilian components has led to the emergence of peacebuilding operations.

Peace enforcement

At the end of the Cold War, the international community sought to extend its capacity to intervene in civil conflicts through enforcement action. These operations are also known as third-generation peacekeeping operations. Unlike prior generations, these operations do not necessarily have the consent of the parties to a conflict, and may proceed in the absence of a comprehensive peace agreement. Their mandate is based on Chapter VII of the UN Charter, which authorizes the Security Council to take necessary action to maintain or restore international peace and security (Article 42). Activities include low-level military operations to protect the delivery of humanitarian assistance, the enforcement of cease-fires,

Box 2.5 Current UN peacekeeping operations directed by DPKO

Operation	Start date
UN Truce Supervision Organization in Middle East (UNTSO)	May 1948
UN Military Observer Group in India and Pakistan (UNMOGIP)	January 1949
UN Peacekeeping Force in Cyprus (UNFICYP)	March 1964
UN Disengagement Observer Force in Syria (UNDOF)	June 1974
UN Interim Force in Lebanon (UNIFIL)	March 1978
UN Mission for the Referendum in Western Sahara (MINURSO)	April 1991
UN Interim Administration Mission in Kosovo (UNMIK)	June 1999
UN Mission in Liberia (UNMIL)	September 2003
UN Operation in Côte d'Ivoire (UNOCI)	April 2004
UN Stabilization Mission in Haiti (MINUSTAH)	June 2004
AU-UN Hybrid Mission in Darfur (UNAMID)	July 2007
UN Stabilisation Mission in the Democratic Republic of Congo (MONUSCO)	July 2010
UN Interim Security Force for Abyei (UNISFA)	June 2011
UN Mission in the Republic of South Sudan (UNMISS)	July 2011

For updates on peacekeeping missions, see http://www.un.org/en/peacekeeping

using force to persuade parties to settle the conflict by negotiation, forceful implementation of the terms of comprehensive peace agreements, and assistance in the rebuilding of so-called failed states. The use of force involved in these activities has led some commentators to refer to them to be effectively "war-making." Landmark operations of this type include those in 1992 in Somalia (UNOSOM) and Croatia, Bosnia-Herzegovina (UNPROFOR), which also exposed the practical limitations of this approach.

UN peacekeeping operations are coordinated by the **Department of Peacekeeping Operations** (DPKO), whose mission is to assist the member states and the Secretary-General in their efforts to maintain international peace and security. Its functions are to plan, prepare, manage, and provide political and executive direction of peacekeeping operations. The DPKO is responsible for the implementation of UN Security Council mandates, which involves maintaining contact with the Security Council, the troops and financial contributors, and parties to the conflict, and engaging with other governmental and nongovernmental entities involved in peacekeeping efforts.

Postconflict reconstruction: peacebuilding

Since the end of the Cold War, peace operations have increasingly developed postconflict *peacebuilding* elements. Peacebuilding refers to the efforts of the international community to maintain a lasting peace in war-torn societies once initial peace has been achieved. Peacebuilding generally follows peacemaking and peacekeeping, but multidimensional peacekeeping operations contain significant peacebuilding elements. Even after conflicts are formally terminated, there remain risks that violence will resume during peacebuilding.

Peacebuilding ideally seeks to contribute to a so-called positive or participatory peace. A positive peace, contrary to a negative or sovereign peace, in which one of the factions is eliminated (a so-called peace of the grave), seeks to promote wider participation and participatory governance or democratic rule. Postwar states often suffer from weak or contested national identity, sometimes opposing ethnic identities, corrupted or destroyed state institutions, poverty and the absence of a substantial working class, and a civilian economy that has been looted or destroyed. Peacebuilding operations seek to address underlying economic, social, cultural, and humanitarian challenges in order to prepare for a more inclusive and competitive political system, with the aim of enabling a shared national identity, functioning state institutions, a significant middle class, and a growing economy. Peacebuilding operations also seek to develop stable constitutional and judicial means for dispute resolution, in order to avoid resort to force in the event of future disputes. The main aim of peacebuilding is thus to achieve a "sustainable" peace.

Peacebuilding includes a wide range of activities: monitoring cease-fires; demobilizing and reintegrating former combatants; helping organize and monitor elections of a new government; supporting democratic reform and improved governance, with particular focus on justice and security sector reform as well as restoration of the rule of law; assisting the return of refugees and displaced persons; enhancing human rights protection; and fostering reconciliation after past atrocities.

Peacekeeping and peacebuilding are inextricably linked. In 2001, in his report *No Exit Without Strategy*, the UN Secretary-General called for peacekeeping operations to include peacebuilding elements in their mandates, in order to help dismantle the structures of violence and create the conditions conducive to durable peace and sustainable development. Most contemporary peacekeeping operations include these elements. The United Nations is the primary international actor involved in peacebuilding, but regional bodies have recently become increasingly involved in peacebuilding as well, just as they have in conflict prevention and peacekeeping. The complexity of contemporary missions has led to a so-called division of labor between the UN and other international actors. Thus, military tasks can be delegated, as in Afghanistan to NATO; the activities of specialized UN departments, funds, and agencies, such as the UNDP, can be shared with regional organizations, such as the OAS, the EU, and the OSCE; and financial institutions, such as the IMF, World Bank, and regional development banks, can address aspects of economic reconstruction. In this book, we focus mainly on the UN system when addressing peacebuilding actors. Though most UN agencies are involved, in one way or the other, in the implementation of peacebuilding programs, the primary responsibility for the coordination and direction of activities in the field lies with the DPA and DPKO.

Until recently, peacekeeping and peacebuilding operations lacked an overall strategic approach and coherence, even within the UN organs and bodies themselves. For example, some missions were under the supervision of DPA, such as the UN Assistance Mission in Iraq (UNAMI) and the UN Support Mission in Libya (UNSMIL) and its peacebuilding support offices in Guinea-Bissau, the Central African Republic, Sierra Leone, and Somalia. These are relatively small operations compared with the peacekeeping missions administered by the DPKO (see Box 2.5), which also have a substantial peacebuilding component.

To address this lack of coherence, the UN Peacebuilding Commission was created by agreement of the UN member states at the 2005 world summit. The Peacebuilding Commission is an intergovernmental advisory body, designed to coordinate the actors

---

Box 2.6 **Peacebuilding Commission purposes**

Extract of UN General Assembly Resolution A/RES/60/180 (2005):

a. To bring together all relevant actors to marshal resources and to advise on and propose integrated strategies for post-conflict peacebuilding and recovery;

b. To focus attention on the reconstruction and institution building efforts necessary for recovery from conflict and to support the development of integrated strategies in order to lay the foundation for sustainable development;

c. To provide recommendations and information to improve the coordination of all relevant actors within and outside the United Nations, to develop best practices, to help to ensure predictable financing for early recovery activities and to extend the periods of attention given by the international community to post-conflict reconstruction.

---

and resources involved in postconflict reconstruction. The commission is supported by the Peacebuilding Support Office, within the UN Secretariat. This office also assists the Secretary-General in coordinating UN agencies in their peacebuilding efforts.

The countries on the agenda of the Peacebuilding Commission in its first six years of work were all from the African continent. In 2013 they were: Burundi, Sierra Leone, Guinea, Guinea-Bissau, Liberia and Central African Republic, where the Peacebuilding Commission engages in developing comprehensive "integrated" strategies for coordinating peacebuilding activities. The main aim of these strategies is to guide government's engagement with all stakeholders in the country, and with the international community, during postconflict processes. In 2006, the UN Peacebuilding Fund was established to provide funding when other mechanisms are not available. It works closely with the Peacebuilding Commission to address the most immediate challenges in the early stages of peacebuilding. The fund is administered by the Peacebuilding Support Office. The three institutions together are collectedly referred to as the UN's new peacebuilding architecture.

Peacebuilding and accountability for past atrocities

As discussed in more detail in Chapter 1, addressing the demands of victims of human rights violations and the reconciliation of societies who have been subjected to suffering during conflicts could also be considered part of the process of building sustainable peace. The range of processes and mechanisms through which such societies and the international community attempt to come to terms with a legacy of large-scale past abuse is known as postconflict accountability, often referred to as **transitional justice**. Transitional justice mechanisms are designed to provide accountability for the perpetrators, reparations for the victims, and reconciliation among the wider society. Transitional justice mechanisms include judicial mechanisms for individual prosecution, both national and international (addressed in Part III of this book): ad hoc tribunals, transnational prosecutions, mixed or **hybrid tribunals**, and the **International Criminal Court**. Transitional justice mechanisms also include nonjudicial mechanisms, such as traditional or customary conflict resolution methods, including traditional cleansing and reconciliatory ceremonies; truth commissions and national reparation processes, including symbolic processes such as changing street names and erecting monuments; and institutional reform, accompanied by vetting processes and dismissals of individuals who participated in repressive regimes or abuses of human rights.

Accountability and reconciliation are essential to peacebuilding. However, as discussed in Chapter 1, even if the goals of accountability and conflict resolution may overlap significantly, there are also significant tensions, particularly with respect to the use of specific tools, including those described in this book. As discussed in both Part II and Part III, the demands and processes of accountability can not only jeopardize the chances to achieve a peace agreement, but also destabilize the process of reconstruction and the chances for sustainable peace.

Discussion questions

- How can addressing potential structural causes of conflict help prevent conflict?
- What is the role of the UN Secretary-General in conflict mediation, both currently and historically, and what political constraints are involved?
- How important is it to have a coordination body for peacebuilding activities within the UN?

Group exercise

Study the facts of the following two conflicts and compare them in terms of warring parties, structural and mobilizing causes, and conflict resolution options:

- The conflict between Russia and Georgia during the summer of 2008
- The ongoing (though now waning) conflict in Colombia between the government and the Revolutionary Armed Forces of Colombia (Fuerzas Armadas Revolucionarias de Colombia [FARC])

Further reading

Anderson, Mary B., *Do No Harm: How Aid Can Support Peace or War* (Boulder, CO: Lynne Rienner, 1999).

Call, Charles T., with Vanessa Wyeth, *Building States to Build Peace* (Boulder, CO: Lynne Rienner, 2008).

Doyle, Michael W., and Nicholas Sambanis, *Making War and Building Peace* (Princeton, NJ: Princeton University Press, 2006).

Jenkins, Rob, *Peacebuilding. From Concept to Commission* (London: Routledge, 2013).

Kaldor, Mary, *New and Old Wars: Organized Violence in a Global Era* (Stanford, CA: Stanford University Press, 3rd edition, 2012).

Paris, Roland, *At War's End: Building Peace after Civil Conflict* (Cambridge: Cambridge University Press, 2004).

Sriram, Chandra L., and Karin Wermester, *From Promise to Practice: Strengthening UN Capacities for the Prevention of Violent Conflict* (Boulder, CO: Lynne Rienner, 2003).

Official documents

United Nations, *An Agenda for Peace: Preventive Diplomacy, Peacemaking, and Peacekeeping* (June 17, 1992), UN Doc. A/47/277–S/24111.

United Nations, *Report of the Panel on United Nations Peace Operations* (August 21, 2000), UN Doc. A/55/305–S/2000/809.

United Nations, *No Exit Without Strategy: Security Council Decision-Making and the Closure or Transition of United Nations Peacekeeping Operations—Report of the Secretary-General* (April 20, 2001), UN Doc. S/2001/394.

United Nations, *Prevention of Armed Conflict – Report of the Secretary General* (June 7, 2001), UN Doc. A/55/985–S/2001/574.

United Nations, *In Larger Freedom: Towards Development, Security, and Human Rights for All— Report of the Secretary-General* (March 21, 2005), UN Doc. A/59/2005

United Nations, *The Rule of Law and Transitional Justice in Conflict and Post-Conflict Societies: Report of the Secretary-General* (August 23, 2004), UN Doc. S/2004/616 and (October 12, 2011), UN Doc. S/2011/634.

Online sources

European Union, "Conflict Prevention, Peace Building and Mediation," http://eeas.europa.eu/cfsp/conflict_prevention/

Human Security Report Project, http://www.hsrgroup.org/

Organisation for Security and Economic Cooperation (OSCE), Conflict Prevention Centre, http://www.osce.org/cpc

United Nations Department of Peacekeeping Operations, http://www.un.org/en/peacekeeping/

United Nations Peacebuilding Commission, http://www.un.org/peace/peacebuilding.

Uppsala Conflict Data Program, http://www.pcr.uu.se/research/UCDP/

3 Human rights

History and debates

Key points

- Although the Universal Declaration on Human Rights declares that human rights are universal, there is no universally accepted definition of the content of human rights.
- There are many areas of contention within the field of human rights, including "group rights," feminist critique, and civil and political rights versus social, economic, and cultural rights.
- There is criticism concerning the implications of a "Western" interpretation of human rights.
- Human rights and conflict are inextricably linked. There are a range of ways in which denial of rights can lead to conflict, and numerous human rights violations occur as a consequence of conflict.

Overview

Although the term "human rights" is used across the world in a way that suggests universal acceptance and understanding, the actual source of these rights and the implications of holding such rights are highly contentious. An understanding beyond the daily usage of the term is needed, one that examines competing claims and critiques and provides the context for discussion of the interplay between conflict and human rights.

The conventional account of human rights points to their emergence during the Enlightenment and articulation in the declarations from the American and French Revolutions. The discourse from this period focused on the goals of liberty and specific political and civil rights of individual citizens, with the backdrop of revolution leading to such claims being made against one's own state. Although specific countries may have outlined the concept of citizen rights in their own constitutions, it was only following World War II that the concept of rights evolved into international human rights as enshrined in the Universal Declaration of Human Rights. This particular narrative proves problematic, due to the focus on the individual and his or her rights, which has led to criticism that they are a Western concept rooted in a particular historical account and are therefore not appropriate to non-Western cultures and traditions, as the latter may put less emphasis on the individual. Even among those who accept the concept of individual rights, the content of such cannot be assumed, and there is ongoing debate over the importance of civil and political rights compared with social, economic, and cultural rights, which have historically been given less prominence.

The Development of International Human Rights

The term "human rights" is so widely used today that it may seem to be common sense that these rights exist. Since first usage of the term in international law in the mid–twentieth century, the concept of human rights has become so powerful that individuals, groups, and even governments identify with and use such rights for their own purposes. However, although the words "human rights" are used to call for or defend certain actions, there is little questioning of what they mean. Although human rights nongovernmental organizations make demands on governments to uphold the rights of individuals, the actual concept is seldom challenged. How did this idea of international standards for protection of human rights by national authorities emerge and become so established? If we recognize the high value that states place on the notion of national sovereignty, their acceptance of constraints on their behavior through human rights laws and mechanisms would seem contradictory, and it is to be expected that reaching agreements imposing such constraints would be difficult.

The content and widespread acceptance of international human rights standards emerged largely in the post–World War II period, following the atrocities that transformed human rights from a domestic matter into an international concern. The victorious Allies, meeting in Dumbarton Oaks to discuss and negotiate the formation of the international body that would become the **United Nations** (UN), stated that ensuring respect for human rights and fundamental freedoms would be one of its purposes. This was subsequently reflected in the preamble of the **UN Charter** with the words

> We the Peoples of the United Nations … Determined to reaffirm faith in fundamental human rights, in the dignity and worth of the human person, in the equal rights of men and women and of nations large and small.

This was the first time the words "human rights" were used in an international treaty. As one of the fundamental principles of the new organization, the protection of human rights paved the way for a new era. The **Nuremberg Charter**, followed by the Nuremberg trials, elaborated on the concept of **crimes against humanity** and led to the **Genocide Convention** (Convention on the Prevention and Punishment of the Crime of Genocide). The Genocide Convention was the first international treaty specifically focused on human rights.

These postwar events created momentum within the international community and laid the foundations of an international framework for human rights. This framework was enshrined in the source of **international human rights law**, the **International Bill of Rights**, which comprises the Universal Declaration of Human Rights (UDHR), the International Covenant on Civil and Political Rights (ICCPR), and the International Covenant on Economic, Social and Cultural Rights (ICESCR). The drafting of the UDHR in 1948 signaled a change in the concept of human rights, from the purely domestic to the international. During the drafting, representatives from across the world were consulted about how they conceived of human rights. This wide-ranging process resulted in a declaration, rather than placing specific obligations on states to uphold individual rights. Although some human rights advocates were disappointed that the UDHR was not a binding international treaty, the acceptance of the importance of human rights was demonstrated by the fact that forty-eight countries voted in the **UN General Assembly** to adopt the declaration, with no countries voting against (eight countries abstained).

Beyond the UDHR, there are treaties and conventions that create rights for individuals and also create obligations for states that ratify them. In comparison to the UDHR, the ICCPR and ICESCR were beset by delays as governments debated standards for an internationally binding treaty, and the impact of the Cold War made reconciling different ideas concerning human rights difficult. However, international conventions supplement the rights of the ICCPR and ICESCR with specific rights concerning the rights of women, children and migrant workers, the prevention of torture, the elimination of racial discrimination, and discrimination against women. Within these international human rights treaties are a number of important distinctions. The content of each treaty addresses different types of rights and also provides different mechanisms through which to protect them. This means that not all human rights treaties can be enforced in the same way, which is explored further in Chapter 4.

The foundations for human rights claims

It is important to understand the underlying conceptualizations of human rights that form the foundations of the legal agreements discussed in Chapter 4. In particular, it is critical to understand the range of perspectives from different cultural and religious traditions in order to evaluate challenges and critiques. How we conceptualize human rights has wider implications in terms of which rights can or should be included or defended. How and why can the human rights treaties discussed above be justified?

The UN Human Rights Commission sought to develop a common basis for human rights through the drafting of the UDHR. This included commissioning the UN Educational, Scientific and Cultural Organization (UNESCO) to consult with leading thinkers and writers from around the world by questionnaire. This exercise was an attempt to achieve a representative idea of how human rights were conceived by countries with cultural, religious, and political differences. The aim was to find roots for human rights in all cultures, to demonstrate that human rights transcended national boundaries and refute the idea that human rights were particular to Western history. Respondents such as René Cassin pointed to the Old Testament conception of rights, while others noted that Hinduism and Buddhism also protected fundamental freedoms and contributed rules of morality. Other thinkers, such as the Chinese philosopher Chung Shu-Lo, explored the contributions of Confucius, while Indian poet and philosopher Hamayun Kabir commented on the influence of the Quran.

Although the UNESCO consultation does demonstrate that some concept of an objective moral standard can be found in all societies, human rights as conceived in the UDHR and subsequent human rights treaties originated in the Enlightenment period in Europe and America. Although we can point to similar ideas in other countries and at other periods, it is this particular development that led to the form that rights have taken today. The development of human rights is intrinsically tied to ideas of natural law and natural rights, which are specifically tied to Western philosophy and history.

The concept of natural law first appeared in ancient Greece and Rome, with the idea that a natural law exists beyond positive laws as decided by humans. This is a higher form of law (which can be conceived as coming from a creator or as something inherent in all humanity) and thus cannot be breached by human-made rules. This provided a form of moral code, insofar that men had a duty to follow natural law. The conceptualization of natural rights rather than just duties under natural law was articulated in the seventeenth and eighteenth centuries. With agitation for freedom of religion, particularly through the Protestant Reformation, the idea of natural law imposing duties on citizens, with no concomitant rights for them or obligations of the sovereign, began to be disputed. Natural law was recast as providing individuals with natural rights that were inherent within them, in the state of nature—before social rules were decided. Jean-Jacques Rousseau was a key proponent of

---

Box 3.1 **The difference between natural law and the liberal conception of rights**

	Account of human rights	*Sources of human rights*	*Nature of human rights*
Natural law	Rights exist and are bestowed by a deity or inhere in humans	From a deity or from human nature	Universal and natural
Liberal conception	Rights are individual, largely civil and political	Granted by a state internally and agreed by states internationally	Rights are universal

---

such claims, arguing that man moves from the state of nature to civil society, where he is governed by a sovereign, but only with his consent (the social contract). Sovereignty of political authority stems from the consent of the governed, and they do not lose their rights in accepting the rule of a sovereign. John Locke further developed this concept in his discussion of the social contract, which enables individuals to hold rights against their government, including protection of private property. The political, social, and economic changes during this period were instrumental in allowing the concepts of individual rights and freedoms to evolve, with groups such as the Levellers in England campaigning for wider suffrage and religious toleration.

These ideas were highly influential in the American and French Revolutions, with the concepts forming the basis of the new republics. The American Declaration of Independence (1776) stated: "We hold these truths to be self-evident, that all men are created equal, that they are endowed by their Creator with certain unalienable Rights, that among these are Life, Liberty and the Pursuit of Happiness." While in France, the Declaration on the Rights of Man and of the Citizen (1789) claimed that "men are born and remain free and equal in rights" and that "the aim of every political association is the preservation of the natural and imprescriptible rights of man." These declarations shaped the content of rights retained by the individual against the state, and the freedom of the individual became central to liberal thought in Western countries. The concept of human rights then developed through the nineteenth and twentieth centuries, central to social struggles for universal suffrage, rights of women, abolition of slavery, labor rights, education and economic welfare, until it achieved its centrality in the UDHR.

The problem of universality

Although the UDHR invokes the term "human rights," it does not define it. It is unlikely that the drafters could have envisaged that human rights would develop into an international movement and that a set of legal obligations would emerge through agreements such as the **Torture Convention** (Convention Against Torture and Other Cruel, Inhuman, or Degrading Treatment or Punishment) or the Genocide Convention, culminating in some ways in the creation of the **International Criminal Court**. Despite the rapid growth of and widespread adherence to human rights agreements, they are still contested in some quarters, particularly by those who argue that human rights are culturally specific, and Western.

As discussed above, the concept of rights as elaborated in the UDHR does stem from the Western experience. Cultural relativists object that the concept of human rights does not transcend culture and thus should not be imposed on other societies that do not share the same outlook or history (an example is the idea that "Asian" values are different than Western values, as discussed later in this chapter). However, even those who do not accept the arguments of cultural relativists may recognize that different conceptions of the content of human rights exist, and that societies could function according to justifiable principles that do not invoke individual human rights. Consider the work of two authors, Steven Lukes and Michael Ignatieff. Lukes considers how society could use other philosophies to achieve the greater good, and ultimately demonstrates the uniqueness of human rights (see Box 3.2). Ignatieff does not deny that we can make a claim for human rights, but he sees them as

---

Box 3.2 A world without human rights?

A synopsis of Steven Lukes, "Five Fables on Human Rights," in Stephen Shute and Susan Hurley, eds., *On Human Rights: The Oxford Amnesty Lectures, 1993* (New York: Basic Books, 1994).

To understand the impact of human rights, it is helpful to imagine alternative ways that society could be organized without such an idea. Steven Lukes's essay "Five Fables on Human Rights" considers how other ideologies put forward by critics of human rights could be taken to their logical conclusion. He challenges readers to go beyond the recognized content of human rights and think about the actual concept, by presenting alternate worlds in which the principles of human rights are not accepted.

Utilitaria

Utilitarians believe in the greatest good for the greatest number. Therefore the most important thing in Lukes's utilitaria is to measure what is good in order to calculate the costs of good, and sacrifice and measure them against each other. Problems may occur where there are fundamental disagreements in what is understood as good. Also, such an outlook would mean that each individual could be asked to sacrifice for the greater good. This implies that it would probably be beneficial for the majority but bad for minorities.

Communitaria

Communitarians prize the connections, understanding, and relationships between individuals. They live according to evolving traditions and customs, which they identify, and identify with. In this world, there are no universal principles; the community decides the rules. However, communitaria does not exist in a vacuum, and as new populations arrive, despite attempts by multiculturalism to recognize each new community's identity, problems still occur. The most difficult decision is how to determine which groups are included and how to deal with communities who have beliefs that are incompatible with each other. In addition, some beliefs and practices would not be challenged, as they are important to the group, although they may cause harm in practice to individuals.

Proletaria

In this world, there are no social classes and people identify with each other as human rather than as belonging to a particular community. There is no state, and society is purely egalitarian. Lukes points out that the problem is that there are no problems; it is a utopia that would be impossible to achieve in the real world. It is unlikely in any configuration that there would be no tensions over such issues as scarcity of resources or self-interest.

Why human rights?

Lukes explains what human rights offer that these alternate possible societies cannot:

- Unlike utilitaria, human rights act as a restraint upon society—the good of the majority cannot be claimed at the expense of minorities.
- Unlike communitaria, human rights allow individuals to conform or deviate from specific practices according to their individual desire.
- Unlike proletaria, human rights acknowledge that human beings will be cruel and act in self-interest and have to deal with scarcity of resources, and protect individuals accordingly.

Box 3.3 **Human rights as politics and idolatry**

A synopsis of Michael Ignatieff, *Human Rights as Politics and Idolatry* (Princeton, NJ: Princeton University Press, 2001).

Michael Ignatieff criticizes the foundations used for human rights, such as natural law or religion, or claims about human nature or society. He criticizes human rights as either inherently political or engaging in idolatry, and thus argues that, at most, only a thin conception of human rights can be defended.

Human rights as politics

Ignatieff argues that human rights are implemented and enforced according to the political interests of states in the international community. He highlights various key problems. First, human rights activists and nongovernmental organizations from the West will often have a "Western agenda" and hold values and principles specific to their countries. Moreover, Ignatieff points to a more fundamental problem—that in this situation, claims based on the idea of human rights as "trumps" can lead to conflict between competing rights and be used to challenge the claims of others. Human rights can be used to halt political disputes by elevating the debate above interest or preference. According to Ignatieff, the assertion of rights to supersede another claim is a type of politics.

The solution is to engage in dialogue rather than competition over rights and other claims. Thus, for example, granting self-determination could destabilize a larger state or even a region. To uphold the right to self-determination could actually have a more severe impact than the denial of that right. Ignatieff would argue that because rights are politics, we must consider the consequence of rights because they are not in fact all universal or "trumps" that can be applied to every situation. In addition, the international community makes a political decision in such a situation about whether to intervene or not. In sum, Ignatieff's argument of human rights as politics exposes flaws due to bias, the political nature of rights, and the practical implications of enforcing rights without thought to consequence.

Human rights as idolatry

Ignatieff believes that human rights have been separated from links to natural law and religion, and have become a "secular religion" built on the concept of human nature and dignity. Human rights advocates seek to depict human rights as universal because they are deemed innate in human beings. Ignatieff argues that this view of humanity as sacred is too disputed to be universal, as are religious claims, and that there is a need for a more widely accepted basis. His suggestion is to defend human rights on the grounds of what they do for human beings, which is defend human agency. This is a minimal theory of human rights, one that does not necessarily emphasize individual rights: if individuals find meaning in a community, then collective understandings of human rights may also be defensible.

political or a form of idolatry, and he thus supports a "thin" version of rights, which may not include all the rights that we would consider (see Box 3.3).

If human rights cannot be defended as universal, an alternative could be to seek a consensus on human rights—basic norms that all can agree upon. Even if the underlying reasoning for specific norms differs—for example, some may use religious arguments against torture, whereas others may refer to human dignity—the agreed norm would still be the same. Nonetheless, it would be difficult to build such consensus in practice (the attempt to balance between universalism and multiculturalism is explored later in this chapter). In practice, it is possible for countries to accept the overall framework of a human rights agreement but make exceptions based on what is viewed as appropriate for their cultural contexts. States can make reservations to certain treaties, and some rights are derogable in states of emergency (although some abuses, such as torture, can never be permitted). Reservations to treaties are controversial; for example, although 187 countries have ratified or acceded to the Convention on the Elimination of All Forms of Discrimination Against Women (CEDAW), some states have made reservations that could be seen as undermining the spirit of signing the treaty. Although reservations that contravene the object and purpose of CEDAW are prohibited under Article 28(2), countries from the Middle East and North Africa have made reservations to some provisions on the grounds that they are incompatible with *sharia* law or national legislation. These include reservations to Article 2 provisions condemning discrimination against women, Article 9 provisions on equal rights concerning nationality, and Article 16 provisions on marriage and family relations. This raises the question of whether it is better to have a widely ratified human rights instrument with many reservations, or a less widely ratified instrument but with fuller commitment from party states.

Box 3.4 The development of human rights

First generation

Individual civil and political rights.

Second generation

Economic, social, and cultural rights. May attach to individual or groups.

Third generation

Group or community rights, which may include solidarity rights.

Challenges and disputes in human rights

Understanding the foundations of rights helps us understand the distinction between so-called first-, second-, and third-generation rights (see Box 3.4). First-generation rights (civil and political) seek to protect individuals against the state, while second-generation rights (economic, social, and cultural) allow the individual to make baseline welfare claims against the state. Third-generation rights involve claims about the need of the community for individuals to flourish. The struggle for equality in civil and political rights is well documented and is probably what most people associate with "human rights." However, within the field of human rights is an ongoing debate concerning the centrality of first-generation rights and the emphasis upon "individual" human rights.

Second-generation rights

After World War II, there was a definite split between Western states, which promoted individual civil and political rights, and communist states, which argued that economic rights were crucial for achieving freedom. The United States sought to exclude economic rights from the UDHR, and was instrumental in separating the binding covenants, the ICCPR and ICESCR. The United States has not yet ratified the ICESCR. Although, according to the Vienna Declaration on Human Rights, civil and political rights, and economic, social, and cultural rights are indivisible and interrelated, they have been treated very differently and accorded different priorities.

Communist countries argued that they provided a better living environment for their citizens, which was essential for the securing of other rights, even though these states regularly engaged in abuse of civil and political rights. With the collapse of communism in the Soviet bloc, arguments for the primacy of economic, social, and cultural rights have fewer state supporters but this primacy still functions as a basis for a critique of liberal emphasis on individual civil and political rights. This separation can be understood as a distinction between positive rights, the duty to provide a baseline of welfare, versus negative rights, the duty to refrain from violating specific rights. Those who define human rights in terms of negative freedoms would argue that only civil and political rights can be upheld and that they provide the basis for freedom and protection of the individual. Proponents of economic, social, and cultural rights believe that the right to vote or freedom of expression have little meaning to people who live in poverty, are unemployed, or lack basic needs such as health and food.

This was famously elaborated by Amartya Sen in *Development as Freedom*, in which he argued that rights to subsistence are as crucial to freedom as civil and political rights. Other theorists have demonstrated that critics of economic, social, and cultural rights use an artificial distinction between positive and negative rights, and that in fact, economic, social, and cultural rights can be defined using this negative definition (see Box 3.5). Beyond these theoretical distinctions, the main obstacle for those who support economic, social, and cultural rights is how to implement them in practice. Such an argument, based on the premise of positive rights, means that governments are required to act to provide guarantees of subsistence or welfare. The difficulty with such requirements is that it is much harder to build a consensus to agree on the substance. The question of enforcement is even more difficult: there would be problems in defining and measuring a baseline as well as in determining penalties for failing to achieve the minimum standard. In terms of poverty or unemployment, these are structural problems, and interference in such political and social organization of a country would be vehemently resisted by a government, hence the refusal of the United States to sign the ICESCR.

As the human rights community debates the place of economic, social, and cultural rights within the broader framework of rights, treatment of these rights by the United Nations, human rights organizations, and nongovernmental organizations has evolved. The UN

Box 3.5　**The rights of the homeless**

A synopsis of Jeremy Waldron, "Homelessness and the Issue of Freedom" in Jeremy Waldron, *Liberal Rights: Collected Papers, 1981–1991* (Cambridge: Cambridge University Press, 1993).

> Without a home, a person's freedom is his freedom to act in public, in places governed by common property rules. That is the difference between our freedom and the freedom of the homeless.

In this essay, Jeremy Waldron addresses the question of homelessness and how it should be considered in relation to the concept of freedom. He argues that concerns about the homeless are usually classified under social and economic concerns, but are actually as important as other human rights such as freedom from torture and freedom of expression. In this way, freedom from homelessness is as much a human right as a civil right and a political right. He argues that although those who argue for the rights of the homeless or poor are often cast as arguing for a "positive" freedom, this can actually be considered a "negative" freedom.

Waldron begins by explaining that all societies have rules that divide property in the following way: property governed by private property rules, property governed by common property rules, and property governed by state property rules. The combination among each varies with the rules of each society. A homeless individual is someone who has no property governed by private property rules where he can reside safely, and Waldron argues that "the homeless person is utterly and completely at all times at the mercy of others."

Consequently, rules that formalize the distinction between public and private, banning private activities in public areas such as sleeping in subway tunnels and washing in public lavatories, affect the homeless, who must live their lives on common property. Waldron argues that the freedom to be somewhere and the freedom to do something are interconnected. An individual who is not free to be in any place is not free to do anything and therefore is not free. The homeless therefore depend on common property for the freedom to perform actions.

If we understand negative freedom as freedom from obstructions to an individual doing something, then a homeless person is not free to be in any place governed by a private property rule. Waldron argues that, therefore, demands for social and economic rights for the homeless are demands for negative, not positive, freedom. In this manner, private property rules restrict individual action just as legislation might restrict political freedoms such as those of speech or religion.

Waldron concludes by stating that a theory of human rights chooses actions that people should have the freedom to perform no matter what other restrictions there are on their conduct. The rights that should be secured for the homeless are not enshrined in a charter, but are preconditions to autonomy and as such should be valued.

Human Rights Commission has appointed special rapporteurs on education, food, and health, and an expert on the right to development. There has been a broader movement on the development of rights-based approaches to work undertaken by UN agencies and aid agencies such as Oxfam. However, human rights organizations such as **Amnesty International** and **Human Rights Watch** have seldom engaged with economic, social, and cultural rights, in part because of their approach to advocacy. Their typical strategy is to find a specific violation, name and shame those responsible, and make simple policy recommendations, and this approach is easier to apply to violations of civil and political rights than to the more structural economic, social, and cultural rights. Nevertheless, recently, several organizations that work only on economic, social, and cultural rights have emerged, as well as networks of activists, such as ESCR-Net. These developments demonstrate the evolution of debates about the importance of economic, social, and cultural rights.

More recently, the Optional Protocol to the ICESCR (OP-ICESCR) offers the possibility of greater enforcement of economic, social, and cultural rights. The OP-ICESCR creates a complaint mechanism to which individuals or groups of individuals can bring complaints if they have been unable to obtain remedies from their own governments. The ratifying countries recognize the competence of the Committee on Economic, Social and Cultural Rights to receive and examine these complaints. The decisions of the committee will provide clarification of economic, social, and cultural rights obligations and provide guidance to states and national courts on adequate remedies for victims. The committee will also seek to identify the root causes of grave and systematic violations. The OP-ICESCR was adopted by the UN on December 10, 2008, opened to signature and ratification on September 24, 2009 and came into force on May 5, 2013. Forty-two countries have signed the OP-ICESCR, and ten have ratified it so far (Ecuador, Mongolia, Spain, El Salvador, Argentina, Bolivia, Bosnia-Herzegovina, Slovakia, Portugal, and Uruguay). The NGO Coalition for an OP-ICESCR states the OP-ICESCR will reinforce state compliance with economic, social, and cultural rights obligations, support access to legal remedies in cases of violations, strengthen the activities of NGOs working in the field, and empower claimants to help develop the content of economic, social, and cultural rights obligations. Although the complaint mechanism offers one venue to address violations of economic, social, and cultural rights, in the absence of wider ratification and the completion of any successful claims, its effects remain to be seen.

Third-generation or group rights

Advocates of group rights argue that individuals suffer harm not only as individuals, but also due to their membership of a particular group. Further, individuals live and receive fulfillment in groups, and thus communities need protection through group rights. There are three types of claims that can be made under the rubric of group rights: collective, corporate, and solidarity.

Collective group rights

Individuals hold rights as individuals and also as members of groups. They come together to claim rights collectively. Their claims may be more powerful in certain situations than an aggregation of individual claims. There are also some rights that cannot be exercised individually, such as the right to culture, which cannot be practiced by an individual on his or her own.

Corporate group rights

Corporate group rights are asserted when a group claims rights not as collective rights on behalf of individuals, but on the grounds that the group itself has rights and that it itself has moral standing. A key example of this might be indigenous peoples claiming specific land rights as a group.

Solidarity rights

Solidarity rights may be invoked on behalf of, essentially, all humanity, rather than on behalf of particular communities, or ethnic groups, or other self-identified groups. Instead, rights such as rights to development, to environment, and to peace (see Box 3.6) are understood to be rights held collectively by all of humanity, such that their violation in any location undermines collective enjoyment of these rights.

These documents represent a range of obligations; some are asserted merely in declarations, while others are enshrined in treaties and conventions. In addition, the content between instruments differs; some assertions are of very general rights, while others indicate a more express requirement of states to actually secure those rights. Nonetheless, none of these rights are currently honored to any measurable extent. Beyond the question of enforceability, there are practical challenges. It is difficult to determine how to balance solidarist rights with other rights. For example, a situation could arise where solidarist rights come at the cost of rights for smaller groups, such as minorities or individuals. Would the right of everyone to peace be prioritized over a group's right to self-determination? This tension illustrates the difficulty of articulating rights in such a broad manner.

Further objections to group rights may be raised. First, groups are not humans, but rather are entities made up of humans—so it is unclear how specific rights can be attached to them. Second, it not necessarily the case that a group will better protect an individual, and it is unclear how a balance between individual and group rights could be determined. Furthermore, the corporate conception of group rights may threaten the individual by making it possible for the moral standing of the group to supersede the standing of individuals within the group. Beyond these objections, it may be asked whether separate group rights are necessary, since some first-generation and second-generation rights are already framed as collective rights, such as freedom of association.

Box 3.6 Emerging solidarist rights

Right	Instruments	Description
Right of peoples	ICCPR and ICESCR	Rights of peoples to self-determination and to freely dispose of natural wealth and resources
Right to development	UN Declaration on the Right to Development, 1986	Right to development, also linked to self-determination
	UN Millennium Declaration, 2000	Confirms UN commitment to the right to development
Right to environment	African Charter on Human and Peoples' Rights, 1981	Right to environment as a condition necessary for development
	Stockholm Declaration on the Human Environment, 1972	
	Right to quality of environment to permit a life of dignity	
	World Charter for Nature, 1982	Enshrines respect for nature
	Rio Declaration on Environment and Development, 1992	Access to information, participation and effective remedies
Right to peace	Preamble to UN Charter	Goal of the United Nations is "to save succeeding generations from the scourge of war"
	UN General Assembly Declaration on the Preparation of Societies for Life in Peace, 1978	Inherent right of every nation and person to peace
	African Charter of Peoples' Rights, 1981	Right to international peace and security

Relativism and the "Asian values" debate

The UDHR is founded on the concept of human dignity, and the ICCPR and ICESCR state that human rights derive from the inherent dignity of the human person. The presumption is that every person has inalienable rights by virtue of being human, which she or he can claim against the state. However, as discussed previously, non-Western countries have objected that such a concept of rights is not universal, and that elsewhere the concept of the individual and his or her relationship to community and society is quite different. This position is exemplified by the so-called "Asian values" objection and debate.

The objection was first presented strongly in the 1990s by a number of political leaders, such as Lee Kuan Yew, president of Singapore. This school of thought gained support from adherents in Asian countries as well as from critics of the Western liberal conception of human rights elsewhere. In what may be seen as a simplification, but nonetheless one that found many supporters, Lee argued that Asian societies are culturally distinct, and in particular do not prioritize the individual in the way that Western societies do, but rather prioritize social goods such as order and security. Thus, for example, Lee claimed that discipline in Asian countries, such as corporal punishment, may seem to be at odds with international human rights standards, but is important to ensure order and security in Singapore. While

---

Box 3.7 **The Draft UN Declaration on the Right to Peace**

Since 2009, the UN Human Rights Council has elaborated the concept of the right to peace through a number of workshops and resolutions. The Human Rights Council passed Resolution 20/15 in July 2012, establishing an open-ended intergovernmental working group to negotiate a draft United Nations declaration on the right to peace. Civil society groups around the world are contributing to the process. The discussions of the concept have involved some controversy: the first report of the intergovernmental working group in February 2013 reported that some delegations emphasized that there was no right to peace under international law and felt it was inappropriate to discuss themes treated by other UN mechanisms, such as refugees and disarmament. Further, while some delegations believed the right to peace derived from the UDHR, other delegations rejected the idea of peace as a prerequisite to human rights. There was also some debate as to whether the right to peace was an individual or collective right. It remains to be seen how these negotiations on the draft declaration will develop when there are such substantive disagreements, and demonstrates the difficulties in articulating solidarist rights.

Western society places great importance on the individual in structuring both economy and society, Lee and others argued that the importance of the individual is unique to the West. They claimed that Asian countries have a very different conception of economic and social organization, with the individual existing in the context of the family and wider community and society. Thus advocates of Asian values sought to justify prioritizing the welfare state and social and economic rights over civil and political rights.

These claims were formally articulated in the Bangkok Declaration, adopted by several Asian states in 1993 (see Box 3.8). The Bangkok Declaration emphasized the importance of economic, social, and cultural rights, stated that the creation of international human rights norms should go hand in hand with endeavors to work toward a just and fair world economic order and highlighted the importance of development and the environment. The declaration also stated that human rights should not be promoted through confrontation and the imposition of incompatible values, but rather that human rights must be considered in the context of a dynamic and evolving process of international norm-setting, bearing in mind the significance of national and regional particularities and various historical, cultural, and religious backgrounds.

These arguments have also been made outside Asia, with Islamic and African states raising similar objections. However, critics of these arguments would hold that objections raised by these states are really designed to justify repressive domestic measures, not as genuine criticisms of human rights. Although the Bangkok Declaration is a moderate document, it could provide some grounds for those who want to limit the effects of human rights in closed societies and repressive states. However, this objection does not mean that the relativist position (see Box 3.9) or Asian values should be ignored, as there are merits to concerns about the universality of human rights.

There are several possible ways to resolve the tension between universalism and multiculturalism. First, a middle ground could be sought. It may be feasible to recognize baseline rights, such as the right to life and the right to access justice, and also include the right to culture. This approach would recognize that the individual has some basic rights but also allow individuals to choose culturally specific practices important to them. However,

---

Box 3.8: **Selected principles from the Bangkok Declaration**

Report of the Regional Meeting for Asia of the World Conference on Human Rights (Bangkok, March 29–April 2, 1993).

3. *Stress* the urgent need to democratize the United Nations system, eliminate selectivity and improve procedures and mechanisms in order to strengthen international cooperation, based on principles of equality and mutual respect, and ensure a positive, balanced and non-confrontational approach in addressing and realizing all aspects of human rights.

8. *Recognize* that while human rights are universal in nature, they must be considered in the context of a dynamic and evolving process of international norm-setting, bearing in mind the significance of national and regional particularities and various historical, cultural and religious backgrounds.

9. *Recognize further* that States have the primary responsibility for the promotion and protection of human rights through appropriate infrastructure and mechanisms, and also recognize that remedies must be sought and provided primarily through such mechanisms and procedures.

10. *Reaffirm* the interdependence and indivisibility of economic, social, cultural, civil and political rights, and the need to give equal emphasis to all categories of human rights.

18. *Recognize* that the main obstacles to the realization of the right to development lie at the international macroeconomic level, as reflected in the widening gap between the North and the South, the rich and the poor.

19. *Affirm* that poverty is one of the major obstacles hindering the full enjoyment of human rights.

20. *Affirm also* the need to develop the right of humankind regarding a clean, safe and healthy environment.

26. *Reiterate* the need to explore the possibilities of establishing regional arrangements for the promotion and protection of human rights in Asia.

---

in practice, such a balance would be difficult to strike, particularly because it would be states that would seek to select which cultural rights should be promoted, and serious debates would arise about which cultural practices should be excluded as inconsistent with recognized basic rights. For example, if the right to life and the right to freedom from torture are among basic rights to be protected, culturally specific practices such as female genital cutting or amputation as punishment for stealing would be inconsistent with those rights, but societies with such practices would nonetheless seek to defend them as cultural rights.

Even engaging in dialogue about the subject is problematic. There is a risk of treating culture as static and unchanging. It would also be difficult to determine who has the right to represent any particular community. Vulnerable groups may be at risk where powerful groups seek to institutionalize inequality or abuse as culturally protected.

Critics will reject such claims of group rights and their relativistic underpinnings and advocate instead the rights of individuals above all. This is an ongoing debate that will prove controversial for the foreseeable future.

Box 3.9 **Conceptions of cultural relativism**

Elizabeth M. Zechenter, "In the Name of Culture: Cultural Relativism and the Abuse of the Individual," *Journal of Anthropological Research* vol. 53 (Autumn 1997): 319–347.

There is more than one type of cultural relativism, as explained by Elizabeth Zechenter:

Descriptive or weak relativism

Cultures vary.

Normative or strong relativism

There cannot be universal ethical or moral standards because these depend on culture.

Epistemological relativism

Humans are shaped by their culture and there are no cross-cultural characteristics.

Feminist and gender critiques

Equality between men and women is enshrined in the Universal Declaration of Human Rights. However, in the early days of the development of the human rights movement, gender equality was not given the same prominence as the focus on civil and political rights or even race equality. The Convention on the Elimination of All Forms of Discrimination Against Women (CEDAW) was only drafted in 1979, nearly fifteen years after Convention on the Elimination of All Forms of Racial Discrimination (CERD), the ICESCR and ICCPR, and other treaties. A feminist critique of human rights emerged in the 1980s, arguing that a gendered perspective was needed in order to identify and address specific abuses not adequately addressed by the traditional human rights approach.

Feminists argue that the language and mechanisms of human rights enable structural gendered inequalities to exist, and that the emphasis on civil liberties ignores the possibility that some rights, such as freedom of religion, could be used to oppress women. One way to understand the challenge of protecting women's rights is to consider the distinction between public and private in international law. This distinction provides for state responsibility and in some instances for individual criminal accountability for abuses in the public sphere, such as torture, but does not address abuses in the private sphere, such as domestic violence, sexual violence, or infanticide. Although there are women who do suffer torture, for example as political prisoners, the position of women within families in many societies means that many abuses that they may face take place within the private sphere and as such are ignored by international human rights treaties. As with the critiques already outlined, this critique also challenges the liberal emphasis on civil and political rights. The feminist perspective is further complicated by efforts to account for the fact that women do not have the same experiences globally; their concerns may vary because of their economic standing personally or their location in a country that has specific economic difficulties or social norms, or because of additional dimensions such as race, membership in a particular group, and sexuality.

Economic, social, and cultural rights can provide one means to address structural inequalities, where women are subject to abuses or suffer a particular burden because they are women. Women are more likely than men to be poor, suffer malnourishment, and have less access to health services—this is sometimes referred to as the feminization of poverty. However, the distinction between public and private remains relevant, because women's domestic work within the family is not recognized as equal to the work carried out by men in the public sphere. Thus invocation of Article 7 of the ICESCR to promote women's rights to just and favorable conditions of work, for example, would not be easy. Furthermore, as we have seen, claims to culture can in fact be detrimental to the position of women.

A gendered perspective on life and liberty has led to greater acknowledgment of women's rights. The Vienna Declaration and Programme of Action, an outcome of the World Conference on Human Rights in 1993, specifically called on governments and the United Nations to ensure the equal enjoyment by women of all human rights. It called for integration and cooperation within the UN system, including access to implementation procedures of the treaty-monitoring bodies and the use of gender-specific data. The declaration particularly stressed the importance of

> the elimination of violence against women in public and private life, the elimination of all forms of sexual harassment, exploitation and trafficking in women, the elimination of gender bias in the administration of justice and the eradication of any conflicts, which may arise between the rights of women and the harmful effects of certain traditional or customary practices, cultural prejudices and religious extremism.
>
> (Vienna Declaration and Programme of Action, para 38)

That conference was followed by the World Conference on Women in Beijing in 1995, which issued a declaration that affirmed women's rights are human rights and called for the prevention and elimination of violence against women and girls, the promotion and protection of all their human rights, and respect for international law to protect women and girls. The Beijing conference identified twelve areas of concern in its platform for action, including the "human rights of women." Three strategic objectives were put forth: (1) promote and protect the human rights of women, through the full implementation of all human rights instruments, especially the Convention on the Elimination of All Forms of Discrimination Against Women; (2) ensure equality and nondiscrimination under the law and in practice; and (3) achieve basic knowledge of the law amongst women. Progress on these objectives has been assessed during reviews after five, ten, and fifteen years. Member states reaffirmed the declaration and its platform for action. In addition, there have been evaluations of implementation of the commitments made at Beijing at the national, regional, and global level, as member states reported on national implementation and regional meetings were held by the UN regional commissions to synthesize regional progress and challenges.

A number of key milestones in the recognition of sexual and gender-based violence against women are particularly relevant to conflict situations. The UN General Assembly's Declaration on the Elimination of Violence Against Women, in December 1993, defined violence against women as including violence in the family, violence in the general community, and violence by the state. States were asked to condemn violence against women and not invoke any custom, tradition, or religious consideration to avoid their obligations with respect to its elimination. Efforts to address the targeting of women during conflict proved decisive in the work of the **International Criminal Tribunal for Rwanda** (ICTR) and the **International Criminal Tribunal for the Former Yugoslavia** (ICTY) in prosecuting wartime rape and gender-related crimes. The Rome Statute of the International Criminal Court now recognizes rape and sexual violence as crimes against humanity and crimes of war. Crimes against humanity are defined to include rape, sexual slavery, enforced prostitution, forced pregnancy, enforced sterilization, or any other form of sexual violence of comparable gravity. Imposing measures intended to prevent births within a particular group can be considered **genocide**. The definition of **war crimes** also adopts a gendered perspective, including rape, sexual slavery, enforced prostitution, forced pregnancy, and enforced sterilization among acts that may constitute crimes.

Human rights and conflict

As explored in Chapter 1, there are several intersections between human rights and conflict. Human rights can be both causes and consequences of conflict, and can also transform the nature of conflict. Debates over the universality or content of human rights can sometimes be manipulated in order to silence criticism when real violations happen. There are a range of ways in which denial of civil and political rights might provoke conflict. For example, if an election is not free and fair, political protests may escalate. If a group is systematically denied political access—to voting, to standing as candidates for elected office—it may protest in ways that might result in violence. Similarly, a group whose exercise of religion is infringed upon may protest, to the point of violence. Or, as occurred in February 2006 with the controversy over cartoons in Denmark that offended some Muslims, a group who feels that its religion has been slighted may protest, and that protest may become violent. Of course, such sporadic violence will not always escalate into broader civil conflict.

Although these grievances from denial of civil and political rights are well documented, denial of second- and third-generation rights can potentially provoke conflict, as discussed in Chapter 2. Protest may emerge over the denial of a wide range of economic, social, and cultural rights, such as over poor and insufficient provision for health, education, or housing. Or protest may arise where specific segments of the populace are particularly and systematically disadvantaged, whether intentionally or unintentionally, in their exercise of these rights. Such protest is mostly channeled peacefully through elections. But in dysfunctional states it might lead to more violent protest and conflict. If we consider revolutionary left-wing guerrilla movements in places such as Guatemala and El Salvador, for example, at least part of the reason they resorted to violence was that the state apparatus would not provide basic needs for the poor, and a wealthy elite had captured and controlled the state.

There are many violations that occur as consequences of conflict, with many internal conflicts targeting civilians as much as combatants. Abuses are not confined to the actual fighting; often children are abducted and forced to fight, or young girls are taken as "wives" to the combatants. Violence during conflict includes torture and killing of combatants as well as indiscriminate massacres and serious injury of civilians, with women and girls particularly targeted as victims of sexual violence. A much larger number will be internally displaced within the country in their escape from the fighting, or they may flee to neighboring countries. Often, the camps established for internally displaced persons and refugees are no more secure than their places of origin, and health, sanitation, and food provision are poor or nonexistent.

There have been a number of advances in promotion of rights related to conflict, particularly the recognition of gender-related violence, violence targeting children, and recruitment of child soldiers. The **UN Secretary-General** has appointed a Special Representative on Children and Armed Conflict, and the **UN Security Council** passed Resolution 1325 to acknowledge the impact of war on women and their role in conflict resolution and **peacebuilding**.

In any conflict, many basic human rights will be violated. The emphasis of this book is on the interplay between human rights and conflict, and deals largely with responses to gross violations of the right to bodily integrity; thus the following chapters will not detail violations of CEDAW or the Convention on the Rights of the Child (CRC), for example. The focus here is those abuses that result in criminal punishment, particularly of the types of crimes that can now be prosecuted before the International Criminal Court, but that were punishable before the creation of this institution.

Discussion questions

- Should advocacy organizations such as Amnesty International concentrate more on economic, social, and cultural rights than on civil and political rights?
- If there are solidarity rights emerging on an international level, what might they be?
  - Right to development?
  - Right to environment?
  - Right to peace?
- Upon whom are they binding?
  - States?
  - Individuals?
  - Public and private groups?
- What are the implications of a state making a reservation to an important article of a human rights treaty?
- Why was it so important for a feminist critique to use the phrase "women's rights are human rights"?
- Which human rights are most likely to be violated in a conflict situation?

Group exercise

Imagine that you are drafting a new international declaration on human rights:

- Write a list of five basic or core rights. Decide which economic, social, and cultural rights should be included, and which civil and political rights.
- Devise a strategy to decide which criteria a group must meet to be recognized, what rights they can be accorded, and how to determine when a group is restricting the rights of its members. Decide how you will mediate if conflicts emerge between groups.
- Discuss the potential impact of the declaration, although it is widely ratified, several countries have made reservations to key articles; discuss the potential impact if fewer countries have ratified it but with no reservations.

Further reading

Alston, Phillip, and Ryan Goodman, *International Human Rights* (Oxford: Oxford University Press, 2012).

Cook, Rebecca, *Human Rights of Women: National and International Perspectives* (Philadelphia, PA: University of Pennsylvania Press, 1994).

Donnelly, Jack, *Universal Human Rights in Theory and Practice* (New York: Cornell University Press, 2003).

Dunne, Tim, and Nicholas J. Wheeler, *Human Rights in Global Politics* (Cambridge: Cambridge University Press, 1999).

Ignatieff, Michael, *Human Rights as Politics and Idolatry* (Princeton, NJ: Princeton University Press, 2001).

Ishay, Micheline R., *The History of Human Rights: From Ancient Times to the Globalization Era* (Berkeley, CA: University of California Press, 2004).

Kymlicka, Will, *Multicultural Citizenship: A Liberal Theory of Minority Rights* (Oxford: Oxford University Press, 1996).

Lauren, Paul Gordon, *The Evolution of International Human Rights: Visions Seen* (Philadelphia, PA: Pennsylvania State University Press, 2011).

Lukes, Steven, "Five Fables on Human Rights," in Stephen Shute and Susan Hurley (eds), *On Human Rights: The Oxford Amnesty Lectures, 1993* (New York: Basic Books, 1994).

Sen, Amartya, *Development as Freedom* (Oxford: Oxford University Press, 2001).

Waldron, Jeremy, "Homelessness and the Issue of Freedom," in Jeremy Waldron, *Liberal Rights: Collected Papers, 1981–1991* (Cambridge: Cambridge University Press, 1993).

Zechenter, Elizabeth M., "In the Name of Culture: Cultural Relativism and the Abuse of the Individual," *Journal of Anthropological Research* vol. 53 (Autumn 1997): 319–347.

Official documents and sources

Bangkok Declaration on Human Rights (1993), http://www.unhchr.ch/Huridocda/Huridoca.nsf/TestFrame/9d23b88f115fb827802569030037ed44?Opendocument.

Charter of the United Nations (UN Charter) (1945), http://www.un.org/en/documents/charter/index.shtml

Convention Against Torture and Other Cruel, Inhuman or Degrading Treatment or Punishment (Torture Convention) (1984), http://www.hrweb.org/legal/cat.html

Convention on the Elimination of All Forms of Discrimination Against Women (1979), http://www.hrweb.org/legal/cdw.html

Convention on the Elimination of All Forms of Racial Discrimination (1965), http://www.ohchr.org/EN/ProfessionalInterest/Pages/CERD.aspx

Convention on the Prevention and Punishment of the Crime of Genocide (Genocide Convention) (1948), http://www.hrweb.org/legal/genocide.html

Declaration on the Right to Development (1986), http://www.ohchr.org/Documents/Issues/Development/DeclarationRightDevelopment_en.pdf

International Covenant on Civil and Political Rights (1966), http://www.hrweb.org/legal/cpr.html

International Covenant on Economic, Social and Cultural Rights (1966), http://www.hrweb.org/legal/escr.html

Report of the Open-ended Inter-Governmental Working Group on the Draft United Nations Declaration on the Right to Peace, 26 April 2013, UN Doc. A/HRC/WG.13/1/2.

Rio Declaration on Environment and Development (1992), http://www.unep.org/documents.multilingual/default.asp?documentid=78&articleid=1163

Universal Declaration of Human Rights (1948), http://www.un.org/en/documents/udhr/

United Nations Millennium Declaration (2000), http://www.un.org/millennium/declaration/ares552e.htm

Vienna Declaration and Programme of Action (1993), http://www.ohchr.org/EN/ProfessionalInterest/Pages/Vienna.aspx

Online sources

Status of Ratifications of Key Human Rights Instruments, www2.ohchr.org/english/bodies/treaty/docs/HRChart.xls

4 Humanitarian and human rights law in armed conflict

Key points

- There are many types of international human rights law and international humanitarian law.
- Some law creates no rights or obligations, while some law makes it possible to bring criminal charges against individuals.
- International humanitarian law imposes obligations primarily upon states, and distinguishes between international and non-international armed conflicts.
- Individual criminal accountability may be imposed in a range of institutions.

Overview

This chapter discusses the legal instruments that may be used to respond to serious human rights violations during war or political violence, specifically the key rights and obligations established by both **international human rights law** and **international humanitarian law**. While these two sets of rights and obligations share superficial similarities, their sources, purposes, applicability, and content differ. International human rights law recognizes rights for individuals and obligations for states, and applies whether an armed conflict exists or not. International humanitarian law establishes rights for individuals and obligations for both states and individuals, and applies where armed conflict exists, but differently depending upon whether the conflict is international or noninternational. Obligations under both international human rights law and international humanitarian law are contained in treaties and customary law. By signing an international human rights treaty, states assume the responsibility to respect, protect, and promote the human rights of individuals under their jurisdiction. In contrast, customary law binds all states, regardless of whether they have signed any international document agreeing to human rights obligations.

Rights and obligations under humanitarian and human rights law

International human rights law and international humanitarian law establish distinct types of rights and obligations, and not all breaches of obligations have the same legal consequences for states, or even for individuals. Simply stating that an individual or group of individuals have rights does not necessarily mean that such persons can act to enforce them, or have them enforced by a third party. There are various mechanisms to ensure that obligations are upheld, ranging from the monitoring of specialized bodies, including human rights courts, established by treaties, to legal accountability for individuals, including international prosecutions.

Declarations of individual rights

The Universal Declaration of Human Rights (UDHR) is a document that simply asserts rights. It describes the rights vested in all individuals, but is understood to be a declaration and as such is not legally binding, although it is now considered part of customary international law. While the UDHR declares a set of rights, it does not indicate who, if anyone, has specific obligations to protect those rights. The UDHR's section on duties applies only to persons and is extremely general. Finally, the UDHR creates no enforcement or monitoring mechanisms, in part because it creates no specific obligations.

Treaties and conventions may create rights for individuals as well as vest the obligation to protect these rights in states that are signatory to those agreements.

The International Covenant on Civil and Political Rights (ICCPR) and the International Covenant on Economic, Social and Cultural Rights (ICESCR) are such conventions. These two instruments, together with the UDHR, constitute what is known as the **International Bill of Rights**. Other rights are contained in other specialized conventions, such as the Convention on the Elimination of All Forms of Racial Discrimination (CERD), the Convention on the Rights of the Child (CRC), and the Convention on the Elimination of All Forms of Discrimination Against Women (CEDAW), discussed in Chapter 3. These conventions also support the establishment of monitoring bodies to which signatory states are required to report on the measures they have taken to protect the enumerated rights. However, violation of these rights and obligations by a state does not have significant further consequences beyond, perhaps, international condemnation. The state cannot be sued in any court by any victim, and while one state might sue another before the **International Court of Justice** (ICJ), such suits are unlikely, because few states would be affected by internal breaches by another state, and thus would have no grounds to bring a case.

Treaties and conventions may articulate rights for individuals, and impose obligations upon states.

Instruments such as the **European Convention on Human Rights**, the Inter-American Convention on Human Rights, and the African Charter for Human and Peoples' Rights create institutions that can not only monitor compliance, but also adjudicate violations. A few relevant cases identifying state abrogations of obligations of human rights in the context of conflict have been adjudicated by the inter-American and European courts and more recently in the African court, but this book focuses on mechanisms that more extensively and directly address abuses during conflict, largely by imposing international criminal accountability.

Treaties and conventions may obligate states not merely to protect rights, but also to prevent and punish violations.

Such obligations are enshrined in the **Torture Convention** (Convention Against Torture and Other Cruel, Inhuman, or Degrading Treatment or Punishment) and the **Genocide Convention** (Convention on the Prevention and Punishment of the Crime of Genocide).

Box 4.1 Core human rights treaties and treaty monitoring bodies

Human rights treaty	Monitoring body
Convention on the Elimination of All Forms of Racial Discrimination (CERD) (December 21, 1965)	CERD
International Covenant on Civil and Political Rights (ICCPR) (December 16, 1966)	CCPR
International Covenant on Economic, Social and Cultural Rights (ICESCR) (December 16, 1966)	CESCR
Convention on the Elimination of All Forms of Discrimination Against Women (CEDAW) (December 18, 1979)	CEDAW
Convention Against Torture and Other Cruel, Inhuman, or Degrading Treatment or Punishment (CAT) (December 10, 1984)	CAT
Convention on the Rights of the Child (CRC) (November 20, 1989)	CRC
International Convention on the Protection of the Rights of All Migrant Workers and Members of Their Families (ICRMW) (December 18, 1990)	CMW

Even between these two conventions, however, there are important distinctions. The Torture Convention imposes obligations upon states in their own territories, or in territories over which they have control. The Genocide Convention creates obligations that are more universal: states must prevent and punish the act of **genocide**, but nowhere in the convention is there a territorial requirement, essentially giving rise to **universal jurisdiction** (discussed in greater detail in Chapter 11). According to universal jurisdiction, states can exercise extraterritorial jurisdiction over certain acts in the absence of a territorial nexus. This is particularly important when considering human rights violated during conflict, since states may be unwilling or unable to carry out prosecutions on their own territory. Notwithstanding the differences between the language of the Torture and Genocide Conventions on territoriality, over time **torture** has come to be viewed as a crime over which all states can exercise jurisdiction. Similarly, violations of some provisions of the four 1949 **Geneva Conventions** may constitute what are referred to as **war crimes**. These are known as **grave breaches**, which may be committed only in the context of an international armed conflict (discussed below) and are also part of customary international law. Individuals found to have violated grave breaches provisions may be subject to criminal prosecution.

Instruments that obligate states not only to respect and protect human rights, but also to prevent and punish violations, may give rise to individual accountability through creating categories of international crime. Thus violations of these conventions may therefore result not merely in a breach by a state, but also in a crime by an individual, who can be tried in a domestic tribunal or an international court. It is important to understand that while the Torture and Genocide Conventions define identifiable crimes, which may therefore be punished, the bulk of human rights law articulates rights that states are bound not to infringe upon, or upon which they may only infringe in specific, narrow circumstances. Thus in many instances, a violation of a human rights agreement may not be a crime, unless it is defined as such in domestic law. However, a state might still be found to have violated a treaty and suffer sanction from the international community. It may be the subject of claims by other

Box 4.2 Rights, duties, enforcement, and accountability under human rights and humanitarian law

Instrument	Level of rights	Duties	Measures for enforcement	Criminal punishment or accountability
Universal Declaration of Human Rights	Specific rights for individuals	No clear duties imposed on states	None	None
ICCPR and ICESCR	Specific rights for individuals	States have duties to provide	None	None
Genocide Convention	No specific rights for individuals	States prevent and punish, with no territorial limitations	Between states at the International Court of Justice (ICJ)	Individual criminal accountability; state responsibility
Torture Convention	No specific rights for individuals	States prevent and punish domestically	Monitored by the Committee Against Torture; states can bring suits against each other at the International Court of Justice	Individual criminal accountability; state responsibility
European Convention on Human Rights; American Convention on Human Rights; African Court on Human and Peoples' Rights	Specific rights for individuals	States have duties to provide	Systems include courts to adjudicate disputes and violations by states of obligations	No individual criminal accountability; state responsibility
Geneva Conventions of 1949	No specific rights for individuals	States criminalize grave breaches in international armed conflict	By states against individuals for grave breaches; states may also bring suit against one another at the ICJ	Individual criminal accountability; state responsibility
Rome Statute of the International Criminal Court ICC)	No specific rights for individuals	States punish crimes or extradite to court	By states against individuals via the Court or through domestic prosecutions of ICC crimes	Individual criminal accountability

Note: criminal jurisdiction has been proposed for the African Court of Human and Peoples' Rights.

states or by their own citizens that they have violated obligations in the regional human rights courts for Africa, Europe and the Americas. A state might also be the subject of suit before the International Court of Justice that it has abrogated its international legal obligations in respect of specific states or conventions (discussed below). The result is not a finding of state commission of a crime, but instead of state responsibility for an internationally wrongful act.

International humanitarian law, by contrast, places more extensive obligations upon states, and articulates rules that states must apply to their officials and combatants. The relative rights, duties and obligations of international humanitarian law (IHL) and international human rights law (IHRL) instruments are shown in Box 4.2.

Substantive human rights obligations

Here we focus on the three documents that comprise the International Bill of Rights—the UDHR, the ICCPR, and the ICESCR—as well as the Genocide and Torture Conventions. Other treaties are excluded from extensive discussion in this book because they are less frequently invoked in postconflict jurisprudence considering human rights violations. However, this does not mean that the rights enshrined in these other treaties, such as those concerned with elimination of racial discrimination and protection of women and children, are not frequently affected by conflict, and do not deserve protection during conflict and redress afterward.

International treaties and customary international law obligations

The International Covenant on Civil and Political Rights

The ICCPR establishes largely individual rights, ranging from protection of bodily integrity to freedom from discrimination, as shown in Box 4.3.

The International Covenant on Economic, Social and Cultural Rights

The ICESCR also enshrines rights for individuals, but its emphasis is upon economic rights such as the right to work, and cultural rights such as the right to engage in one's culture, as shown in Box 4.4. The ICCPR and the ICESCR are necessarily interdependent, although not all countries that have ratified the former have also ratified the latter.

The Torture Convention

The definition of torture is articulated in Article 1 of the Torture Convention (see Box 4.5), and includes the infliction of both physical and mental suffering, for a variety of ends, committed by an official or a person acting in an official capacity. However, despite the relatively straightforward language of the convention, the precise meaning of torture has been the subject of dispute, particularly by the United States with regard to its use of "enhanced interrogation techniques" upon alleged terrorists.

Under the convention, states are not merely obliged to refrain from engaging in such activities. They are further obliged to prevent acts of torture on their territory; criminalize torture and punish such acts; not extradite or otherwise deport individuals to locations where they could be tortured; and extradite those accused of torture to other countries seeking to punish acts of torture, on appropriate request.

Box 4.3 The International Covenant on Civil and Political Rights (ICCPR)

- Physical integrity of the individual, including protection against torture, arbitrary arrest, and arbitrary deprivation of life.
- Procedural fairness when an individual has been deprived of liberty by a government: provisions on arrest, trial procedure, and conditions of imprisonment.
- Equal protection: protections against discrimination along racial, religious, gender, or other lines.
- Freedom of belief, speech, and association.
- Right to political participation.

Box 4.4 The International Covenant on Economic, Social and Cultural Rights (ICESCR)

- Right to work, and to enjoyment of just and favorable conditions of work, such as fair wages and equal pay, safe working environment, equal opportunity for promotion, and the right to form trade unions.
- Right to social security, including social insurance.
- Special measures of protection for the family and for children.
- Right to an adequate standard of living, including food, clothing, and housing.
- Right to enjoyment of the highest attainable standard of physical and mental health.
- Right to education, including provision of compulsory primary education free of charge for all.
- Right to take part in cultural life, to benefit from scientific progress, and to benefit from any moral or material interests emerging from productions of which one is the author.

Box 4.5 The Torture Convention, Article 1

For the purposes of this Convention, torture means any act by which severe pain or suffering, whether physical or mental, is intentionally inflicted on a person for such purposes as obtaining from him or a third person information or a confession, punishing him for an act he or a third person has committed or is suspected of having committed, or intimidating or coercing him or a third person, or for any reason based on discrimination of any kind, when such pain or suffering is inflicted by or at the instigation of or with the consent or acquiescence of a public official or other person acting in an official capacity. It does not include pain or suffering arising only from, inherent in or incidental to lawful sanctions.

Box 4.6 The Genocide Convention, Article 2

In the present Convention, genocide means any of the following acts committed with intent to destroy, in whole or in part, a national, ethnical, racial or religious group, as such:

a. Killing members of the group;
b. Causing serious bodily or mental harm to members of the group;
c. Deliberately inflicting on the group conditions of life calculated to bring about its physical destruction in whole or in part;
d. Imposing measures intended to prevent births within the group;
e. Forcibly transferring children of the group to another group.

The Genocide Convention

The definition of genocide is articulated in Article 2 of the Genocide Convention (see Box 4.6), and includes two broad components: the intent to destroy particular groups, and the commission of specific acts in support of that intent. As discussed in Chapter 8 in the context of the situation in the Darfur region of Sudan, acts that fall merely within the definition do not suffice where evidence of intent cannot be found.

States are not merely obliged to refrain from the commission of genocide; they are also required to punish and prevent it, and to that end the convention requires that states commit to a number of specific measures. First, states are obliged to punish persons responsible for genocide, and to enact the legislation necessary for such punishment. Such legislation can be applicable to the commission of genocide anywhere in the world, not only to acts that take place on the territory of states that have signed the convention. States are also obliged to extradite suspects when appropriate—for example, if they are unable to prosecute, or if another state offers a more appropriate forum.

Crimes against humanity

Crimes against humanity initially formed part of customary international law, but were later formally codified in the Rome Statute of the **International Criminal Court** (ICC) (see Box 4.7). Crimes against humanity are a unique category. They are distinct from international humanitarian law in that the presence of armed conflict is not necessary, and in that they emerged not through international agreement, but through custom, as *jus cogens* obligations carrying greater weight than many human rights obligations. They have now been firmly established in jurisprudence, ranging from rulings of the Nuremburg Tribunal to those of the ad hoc tribunals for the former Yugoslavia and Rwanda. Crimes against humanity involve specific acts undertaken in the context of a widespread or systematic attack on the civilian population. Such acts may include murder, extermination, enslavement, deportation, imprisonment, torture, rape, sexual slavery, persecution, disappearances, and apartheid. The threshold for crimes against humanity has been the subject of some dispute before the ICC, as one judge in the Kenya situation objected that there was no evidence of a sufficient organizational plan or policy, a requirement in the statute not traditionally included in pre-ICC Statute definitions of crimes against humanity.

Box 4.7 **The Rome Statute, Article 7**

1. For the purpose of this Statute, "crime against humanity" means any of the following acts when committed as part of a widespread or systematic attack directed against any civilian population, with knowledge of the attack:
    a. Murder;
    b. Extermination;
    c. Enslavement;
    d. Deportation or forcible transfer of population;
    e. Imprisonment or other severe deprivation of physical liberty in violation of fundamental rules of international law;
    f. Torture;
    g. Rape, sexual slavery, enforced prostitution, forced pregnancy, enforced sterilization, or any other form of sexual violence of comparable gravity;
    h. Persecution against any identifiable group or collectivity on political, racial, national, ethnic, cultural, religious, gender as defined in paragraph 3, or other grounds that are universally recognized as impermissible under international law, in connection with any act referred to in this paragraph or any crime within the jurisdiction of the Court;
    i. Enforced disappearance of persons;
    j. The crime of apartheid;
    k. Other inhumane acts of a similar character intentionally causing great suffering, or serious injury to body or to mental or physical health.

Substantive international humanitarian law obligations

It is important to distinguish international human rights law from international humanitarian law, as the two bodies of law have distinct purposes and histories, even though violations of international humanitarian law are often charged along with violations of human rights, in cases brought before domestic, international, or hybrid courts. While the purpose of international human rights law is to articulate the rights of humans, with an emphasis upon individual rights, the purpose of international humanitarian law is to regulate behavior in armed conflict. While this purpose is broadly humanitarian—to prevent abuses by armed forces of prisoners of war, civilians under occupation, and injured combatants—international humanitarian law aims to regulate conflict rather than protect rights. While laws regulating war have existed for centuries, the impetus for contemporary international humanitarian law was Henri Dunant, founder of the precursor to the International Committee for the Red Cross, who was supposedly so appalled by the excesses he witnessed at the Battle of Solferino in June 1859 that he began campaigning for stricter regulation.

We explore here the substantive obligations established by international humanitarian law. But we do not address much of the international humanitarian law predating the 1949 Geneva Conventions, because many key principles are subsumed in the 1949 agreements and their two additional protocols (see Box 4.8), or are customary law.

What is the content of international humanitarian law, and what are its legal sources? International humanitarian law emerges from a range of sources, beginning with custom, and including the 1899 Hague Conventions, the four 1949 Geneva Conventions, and the

---

Box 4.8 The Geneva Conventions

The Four Geneva Conventions of 1949

First Geneva Convention: treatment of sick and wounded in the armed forces.
Second Geneva Convention: treatment of sick and wounded at sea.
Third Geneva Convention: treatment of prisoners of war.
Fourth Geneva Convention: protection of civilians.

The Two Additional Protocols of 1977

Protocol I: protection of victims of international armed conflicts.
Protocol II: protection of victims of noninternational armed conflicts.

---

two 1977 additional protocols to the Geneva Conventions. International humanitarian law regulates the behavior of combatants in armed conflict, and variously sets forth rules for the treatment of prisoners of war, sick and wounded combatants, and civilian populations, particularly in circumstances of occupation.

For the purposes of this book, the Geneva Conventions, specifically the grave breaches that constitute war crimes and may call forth individual criminal accountability, are of most relevance. The drafters of the conventions specifically avoided creating a category of "war crimes": instead they identified a list of "grave breaches" for which individual responsibility may be imposed. A comprehensive list of grave breaches can be found among the website sources listed at the end of this chapter, and includes willful killing, torture, willfully causing great suffering or serious injury to body or health, extensive destruction or appropriation of property not justified by necessity, compelling a prisoner of war or civilian to serve in the armed forces of a hostile power, willfully depriving a prisoner of war or protected person the rights of a fair trial, unlawful deportation, transfer, or confinement of a protected person, and hostage-taking. There are a range of prohibitions in Article 3 of each of the four Geneva Conventions, known as **Common Article 3** (see Box 4.9), that prohibit similar acts in all conflicts, whether internal or international. However, the traditional regulations of international humanitarian law differ in international and noninternational armed conflicts: acts which could constitute grave breaches in international armed conflicts would, in noninternational armed conflicts, constitute violations of Common Article 3 but not be criminalized. Although the Rome Statute essentially eliminates this distinction for signatory states, for situations over which the court does not have jurisdiction, this important distinction continues to apply under the Geneva Conventions. The Geneva Conventions and international humanitarian law generally regulate the conduct of armed conflict, and therefore are not applicable in the absence of conflict.

Individuals who violate international humanitarian law under the grave breaches provisions (see Box 4.10) can be held to account in a domestic court of their state of nationality (see Chapter 10), in a domestic court of a third state (not party to the conflict) under universal jurisdiction (see Chapter 11), in a hybrid tribunal (see Chapter 12), and in the International Criminal Court (see Chapter 13).

While international human rights law begins with the rights of individuals, and may in a few circumstances be specifically enforceable, or in some cases create a category of crimes, such as torture or genocide, international humanitarian law sets forth limitations on the

***Box 4.9* Common Article 3 of the Geneva Conventions**

In the case of armed conflict not of an international character occurring in the territory of one of the High Contracting Parties, each Party to the conflict shall be bound to apply, as a minimum, the following provisions:

1. Persons taking no active part in the hostilities, including members of armed forces who have laid down their arms and those placed "hors de combat" by sickness, wounds, detention, or any other cause, shall in all circumstances be treated humanely, without any adverse distinction founded on race, colour, religion or faith, sex, birth or wealth, or any other similar criteria.

    To this end, the following acts are and shall remain prohibited at any time and in any place whatsoever with respect to the above-mentioned persons:
    a. violence to life and person, in particular murder of all kinds, mutilation, cruel treatment and torture;
    b. taking of hostages;
    c. outrages upon personal dignity, in particular humiliating and degrading treatment;
    d. the passing of sentences and the carrying out of executions without previous judgment pronounced by a regularly constituted court, affording all the judicial guarantees which are recognized as indispensable by civilized peoples.
2. The wounded and sick shall be collected and cared for.

    An impartial humanitarian body, such as the International Committee of the Red Cross, may offer its services to the Parties to the conflict.

    The Parties to the conflict should further endeavour to bring into force, by means of special agreements, all or part of the other provisions of the present Convention.

    The application of the preceding provisions shall not affect the legal status of the Parties to the conflict.

***Box 4.10* Grave breaches of the Geneva Conventions**

First Geneva Convention, Article 50

Grave breaches to which the preceding article relates shall be those involving any of the following acts, if committed against persons or property protected by the convention: wilful killing, torture, or inhuman treatment, including biological experiments, wilfully causing great suffering or serious injury to body or health, and extensive destruction and appropriation of property, not justified by military necessity and carried out unlawfully and wantonly.

Note: The grave breaches provisions of the Four Geneva Conventions, and of Additional Protocol I of 1977, are not identical. For comparisons, see the analysis provided by the International Committee of the Red Cross at http://www.icrc.org/eng/resources/documents/misc/5zmgf9.htm

---

Box 4.11 IHL and permissible weaponry: nuclear weapons and drones

IHL focuses extensively on impermissible acts in armed conflict, but to a far lesser degree on categories of weaponry. Yet clearly, some modern forms of weaponry with their destructive power and capacity to be used remotely might present greater concerns than traditional weapons. Advocates have sought to argue that some forms of weaponry necessarily violate international humanitarian law on a number of grounds: that they cannot distinguish sufficiently between combatants and civilians, thus violating the principle of distinction and that they cause harm disproportionate to any legitimate military goal, and that they cause unnecessary suffering. Similar arguments have been raised, nearly two decades apart, in relation to nuclear weapons and unmanned drones. In 1996, the ICJ issued an advisory opinion on the *Legality of the Threat or Use of Nuclear Weapons* which concluded that the threat or use of nuclear weapons did not necessarily violate principles of international humanitarian law, but that any use would be legal only if it did satisfy the principle of distinction and other core principles. Similar claims began to be raised in relation to the use by the United States of unmanned planes, or drones, to strike targets in Afghanistan and Pakistan. There have been no judicial determinations as yet, but the ICRC has argued that the use of drones is not illegal *per se* but must comply with IHL.

Human rights organizations have also sought for some time to limit the trade in other types of weapons that can be used during conflict. In 2013 a major legal milestone was achieved with the adoption of the Arms Trade Treaty, which regulates international trade in conventional certain weapons. It was adopted by the UN General Assembly with an overwhelming majority of 154 states in favor, three against and 23 abstentions.

---

conduct of armed conflict, and identifies specific obligations whose breach *may* constitute crimes. This distinction is complicated, and has been blurred somewhat with the codification of war crimes provided by the Rome Statute of the International Criminal Court: the ICC includes war crimes, crimes against humanity, and genocide among the crimes subject to its jurisdiction, thus combining violations of international humanitarian law and violations of international human rights law. However, commission of torture is not included as a separate crime in the statute, although it is a proscribed act within the definition of war crimes.

International criminal accountability

Key principles

International criminal accountability may be imposed in a range of national or international venues, as discussed later in this book, and with reference to one or more of the treaties outlined in Box 4.1. Regardless of venue or substantive law, however, a number of key principles have been established in practice.

First, for crimes of international concern such as genocide and crimes against humanity, the defense of superior orders is not accepted. The **Nuremberg Charter** (Charter of the International Military Tribunal) established the tribunal to try crimes committed by Germans during World War II. As the Nuremberg Charter explicitly states: "the fact that the defendant acted pursuant to an order of his government or of a superior shall not free him from responsibility, but may be considered in mitigation of punishment." The defense of duress may be acceptable in limited circumstances, and is allowed by the Rome Statute, Article 31(1)(d), in situations where the harm to others sought to be avoided by the person who committed the crime was far greater than the crime he or she actually committed.

The principle of command responsibility, according to which superiors are responsible for actions of their subordinates, also applies. The ad hoc ICTY required three elements in the *Čelebići* case: superior/subordinate relationship, mental element or intent, and failure to act to prevent or punish violations.

In order to commit the crimes in question, defendants must have *mens rea,* a mental state involving intent to commit the crime. Defendants may raise defenses of mistake of fact, or mistake of law, meaning that they had not intended to commit a crime, but the defense of mistake of law is limited to situations where an element of the crime involves a legal evaluation.

General principles of criminal law found in most domestic criminal systems apply in international criminal law. Thus the accused is presumed innocent until proven guilty. The principle of nonretroactivity also applies. Thus the principles of **nullem crimen sine lege** (no crime without law) and **nulla poena sine lege** (no punishment without law) apply.

As with domestic law, group criminal accountability is generally not recognized under international law, in part because of due process concerns. While the Nuremberg Tribunal recognized the concept of joint criminal enterprise, it was not to be used to convict an individual in the absence of evidence of individual responsibility. There was even discussion of providing for jurisdiction of the ICC over not just natural persons—human individuals—but also legal persons—groups, corporations, and the like. This provision, however, was not included in the final draft of the Rome Statute.

Finally, in recent decades, judicial decisions and international agreements such as the Rome Statute of the ICC have progressively limited claims of immunity from prosecution by reason of official status. Before the ICC, no claims of official immunities may be invoked to prevent the assertion of jurisdiction, and the same appears to be the case before any international court. Before domestic courts, sitting heads of state and high-level officials may invoke immunity while in office, but may not raise it as a defense once they have left office.

Specific institutions

Part III of this book examines specific institutions and processes that may impose sanctions upon individuals for the violations of law discussed here. It is important to understand that while it is the state that undertakes the obligations enumerated under international human rights and humanitarian law, the actual crimes addressed are crimes committed by individual persons that call for individual criminal accountability. Thus an individual may face accountability for grave breaches of the Geneva Conventions, or for the commission of crimes against humanity, or genocide, or torture. A state cannot be similarly prosecuted.

This does not mean that a state cannot be held to account—after all, it is the state that undertakes these obligations. A state may be sued for actions that violate its obligations under relevant conventions, or that violate customary international law. Such a suit would occur before the International Court of Justice (ICJ), the key judicial organ of the United Nations system, if the Court has jurisdiction, or by another supranational court. As discussed in Chapter 7, the Democratic Republic of Congo brought cases against

Rwanda and Uganda before the ICJ for violations of human rights and humanitarian law. In December 2005 the case against Uganda reached a substantive judgment, while in early February 2006 the ICJ dismissed the case against Rwanda for lack of jurisdiction. Similarly, Bosnia brought suit at the ICJ against Serbia and Montenegro for alleged commission of or complicity in genocide during the conflict in the former Yugoslavia (discussed in Chapter 6). In 2007, the ICJ did not find that there was state responsibility for these crimes, but did find that Serbia and Montenegro had failed in their obligation to *prevent* genocide. Further, states can face claims by their citizens or other states that they have violated regional and/or international legal obligations before the regional human rights courts established in Africa, Europe and the Americas. There have also been initiatives to expand the jurisdiction of the African Court of Human and Peoples' Rights to include criminal jurisdiction over individuals for international crimes. The African Union Commission first requested a study on the matter in 2009, amidst significant backlash amongst many African states over the ICC's exclusively African caseload (see Chapter 13), but the expansion of jurisdiction has not been agreed.

Discussion questions

* What are the key distinctions between international human rights law and international humanitarian law? How do they vary in terms of purpose and subjects, and applicability?
* What are the key human rights protections that may be of interest during armed conflict? How might these rights be affected by conflict?
* Discuss the conventions and custom that together compose international humanitarian law. What do they regulate, and how do they work?
* Consider the distinction between international and non-international armed conflicts in key documents, and its effect upon what acts may be criminalized. Is this distinction evolving?

Further reading

Abbas, Ademola, "The Proposed International Criminal Jurisdiction for the African Court: Some Problematical Aspects," *Netherlands International Law Review* vol. 60, no. 1 (2013): 27–50.

Aksar, Yusuf, *Implementing International Humanitarian Law: From the Ad Hoc Tribunals to a Permanent International Criminal Court* (London: Routledge, 2004).

Alston, Phillip, Ryan Goodman, and Henry J. Steiner, *International Human Rights in Context: Law, Politics, Morals* (Oxford: Oxford University Press, 2007).

Nino, Carlos S., "The Duty to Punish Past Human Rights Violations Put into Context: The Case of Argentina," *Yale Law Journal* vol. 100 (1991): 2619–2641.

Orentlicher, Diane, "Settling Accounts: The Duty to Prosecute Human Rights Violations of a Prior Regime," *Yale Law Journal* vol. 100 (1991): 2537–2618.

Paust, Jordan J., M. Cherif Bassiouni, Michael Scharf, Jimmy Gurul, Leila Sadat, Bruce Zagaris, and Sharon A. Williams, *International Criminal Law* (Durham, NC: Carolina Academic Press, 2000).

Ratner, Steven R., and Jason S. Abrams, *Accountability for Human Rights Atrocities in International Law and Practice* (Oxford: Oxford University Press, 2001).

Schabas, William A., *The Universal Declaration of Human Rights: The Travaux Préparatoires* (Cambridge: Cambridge University Press, 2013).

Wippman, David, and Matthew Evangelista (eds), *New Wars, New Laws? Applying the Laws of War in 21st Century Conflicts* (Ardsley, NY: Transnational, 2005).

Official documents and sources

Additional Protocols to the Geneva Conventions (1977):

Additional Protocol I, http://treaties.un.org/doc/Publication/UNTS/Volume%201125/volume-1125-I-17512-English.pdf

Additional Protocol II, http://treaties.un.org/doc/Publication/UNTS/Volume%201125/volume-1125-I-17513-English.pdf

Convention Against Torture and Other Cruel, Inhuman, or Degrading Treatment or Punishment (Torture Convention) (1984), http://www.hrweb.org/legal/cat.html

Convention on the Elimination of All Forms of Discrimination Against Women (1979), http://www.hrweb.org/legal/cdw.html

Convention on the Elimination of All Forms of Racial Discrimination (1965), http://www.ohchr.org/EN/ProfessionalInterest/Pages/CERD.aspx

Convention on the Prevention and Punishment of the Crime of Genocide (Genocide Convention) (1948), http://www.hrweb.org/legal/genocide.html

Convention on the Rights of the Child (1989), http://www.hrweb.org/legal/child.html

Geneva Conventions (1949): http://www.icrc.org/eng/war-and-law/treaties-customary-law/geneva-conventions/index.jsp

International Covenant on Civil and Political Rights (1966), http://www.hrweb.org/legal/cpr.html

International Court of Justice, Advisory Opinion, Legality of the Threat or Use of Nuclear Weapons (8 July 1996) at http://www.icj-cij.org/docket/files/95/7495.pdf

International Court of Justice, Application of the Convention on the Prevention and Punishment of the Crime of Genocide (Bosnia and Herzegovina v. Serbia and Montenegro) (27 February 2007) at http://www.icj-cij.org/docket/index.php?p1=3&p2=3&k=8d&case=91&code=bhy&p3=4.

International Covenant on Economic, Social, and Cultural Rights (1966), http://www.hrweb.org/legal/escr.html

Universal Declaration of Human Rights (1948), http://www.un.org/en/documents/udhr/

Online sources

African Court of Human and Peoples' Rights website, at http://www.african-court.org/en/

Status of ratifications of key human rights instruments, http://www1.umn.edu/humanrts/research/ratification-index.html

5 Nonstate actors and international humanitarian and international human rights law

Key points

- Nonstate actors present distinct questions for international humanitarian and international human rights law in terms of both the protection of their members during combat and their potential responsibility for violations.
- International humanitarian law distinguishes between state and nonstate combatants as well as international and noninternational armed conflicts.
- The presence of private military and security companies in most contemporary conflicts has brought important practical and legal challenges.

Overview

Since the end of the Cold War, and with the proliferation of noninternational armed conflicts, the challenge of regulating activities of nonstate actors (including multinational corporations, nonstate armed groups, groups designated as terrorist, and private military and security companies) has become more pronounced given the fact that international humanitarian law and international human rights law were created by states and designed in the first instance to regulate state behavior. Increased internal armed conflicts involve an increased number of nonstate actors, resulting in an increased number of actors who may be protected differently than state actors and present distinct challenges for the imposition of responsibility for crimes. The challenge is made all the more complex by the diversity of actors which might broadly be characterized as nonstate actors and of the patchwork of domestic and international law which may apply to them. For the purposes of this chapter, we treat actors as falling into several categories: **nonstate armed groups**, and the related category of terrorist groups; multinational corporations, and **private military and security companies**. While the groups are diverse, they also share some commonalities: there are often questions as to whether and how international humanitarian law obligations and protections may apply to them, the nature of their human rights obligations, and what types of international crimes for which either groups or individual members may be considered responsible. The shared questions arise from the distinction in international humanitarian law between international and non-international armed conflicts, which entails differential obligations and protections depending upon the type of conflict and the role of the combatant, and is grounded in the state-centric nature of international law and the desire which states have not to treat nonstate actors as equivalents. States, after all, are traditionally the primary subjects of international law, the bearers of rights and responsibilities.

However, states are not the only subjects of international law. International humanitarian law does purport to place binding obligations on nonstate armed groups, and international human rights law enshrines rights for individuals, even though neither set of actors can consent to international legal obligations.

The problem of nonstate armed groups

As the international community has become more concerned with addressing internal armed conflict, the difficulty of addressing nonstate armed groups has grown in salience and importance. Since the events of September 11, 2001, dealing with nonstate armed groups categorized as terrorists has become the top priority for the United States, the **United Nations** (UN), and many of the world's governments. Yet neither political nor legal strategies seem up to the challenge of addressing these groups, which, while not state actors, pursue largely political goals through armed force.

There is thus an apparent gap between law and practice regarding the human rights obligations and accountability of nonstate armed groups. International human rights and humanitarian legal conventions that impose duties upon states regarding the conduct of conflict largely apply to states that are party to those conventions; these legal standards, even where they have reached the status of customary international law, are traditionally understood to regulate state activities in armed conflict. At the same time, conduct of states has been limited regarding the use of repressive measures through a host of human rights instruments, such as the Torture Convention. It is important to note that this body of law does not just preclude states' engagement in such abuses, whether in time of war or not, but also enables or requires the establishment of procedures for punishing individuals responsible for such abuses. Thus it is not merely states, but also individuals, that are limited in their exercise of certain forms of violence. Individual responsibility has been further extended through the creation of ad hoc criminal tribunals, the establishment of the International Criminal Court (ICC), and the exercise of universal jurisdiction.

Regulation and control of nonstate armed groups, by comparison, remain relatively underdeveloped. These groups are diverse, including rebel groups seeking to overthrow the state in whole or in part, resistance movements challenging state activities, paramilitary and parastatal forces, and autonomous militias as well as groups designated as terrorist organizations. The constraints placed upon states that are party to a host of international human rights and humanitarian treaties have limited application to such groups, given that only states can accede to international legal obligations. However, international humanitarian law does seek to regulate behavior in armed conflict as well as provide protections to combatants who have ceased to engage in combat due to illness, injury, or because they are prisoners of war. International human rights law prohibits acts such as genocide regardless of who the perpetrator may be, and while the official definition of torture requires that the perpetrator be a state official or acting in another official capacity, many nonstate armed groups do act in such a capacity.

At the same time, individual criminal accountability does not apply to groups but only to their members, and it is perhaps neither feasible nor wise that criminal accountability should be extended to groups as groups. Responding to abuses by nonstate armed groups is increasingly important given the prevalence of internal armed conflict since the end of the Cold War. This is compounded by the spillover effects of the movements of armed rebel groups and militias, and the phenomenon of cross-border terrorism. The result is that key players in contemporary domestic and international security remain relatively unregulated

---

Box 5.1 **Armed group commitments to IHL**

While nonstate armed groups cannot formally sign and adhere to international treaties and conventions, some groups have sought to publicly declare their commitment to abide by international humanitarian law. They often do so through an international nongovernmental organization known as Geneva Call, which receives declarations of armed groups regarding their commitments to, for example, refrain from the use of child soldiers and landmines, or more generally to follow the rules in the Geneva Conventions and their Additional Protocols. The agreements purport to be "treaty-like" and are signed by the group and the cantonal government of Geneva. Thus, for example, six nonstate armed groups in Burma/Myanmar have signed instruments committing to refrain from the use of landmines. Similarly, the United Nations Special Representative of the Secretary-General for Children and Armed Conflict obtains commitments by nonstate armed groups to refrain from the recruitment of child soldiers. Such groups make these commitments for a variety of reasons, including to garner domestic and/or international legitimacy which may aid in their pursuit of a peace agreement, future political status, or to reinforce claims to act on behalf of the populace against an illegitimate government.

For more information, see the websites of Geneva Call: http://www.genevacall.org and the Office of the UN Special Representative of the Secretary-General for Children and Armed Conflict: http://childrenandarmedconflict.un.org.

---

and unaddressed by international human rights or humanitarian law. This is particularly the case, as we shall see, because of the distinctions made in traditional international humanitarian law between international and noninternational armed conflicts.

The Rome Statute of the ICC resolves some of these issues by essentially eliminating the distinction between international and noninternational armed conflicts, making the acts prohibited by Common Article 3 of the Geneva Conventions war crimes. However, the ICC's jurisdiction is only over natural persons, and it can only impose individual criminal responsibility. There is no possibility of punishing groups or legal persons, only the natural persons within them. However, there are mechanisms through which armed groups can and have committed to compliance with international humanitarian law standards (Box 5.1).

Nonstate armed groups, and indeed terrorist organizations and activities, are not a new phenomenon. However, the rapid increase in internal armed conflicts since the end of the Cold War, as well as the rise of global terrorism and counterterrorism activities exemplified by Al-Qaida and the US global "war on terror," have sparked debates about the efficacy of both human rights law and international humanitarian law in regulating and punishing activities by nonstate armed groups, whether criminal or not.

Human rights violations and nonstate actors

Because the provisions of Common Article 3 and Additional Protocol II refer to activities in situations defined as armed conflict, they can encompass and regulate armed groups as well as states. However, the same cannot be straightforwardly said for human rights obligations. In human rights treaties, generally, it is states that undertake to protect certain rights or refrain from violation of them. Treaties are driven by state consent, and speak to the relationship between the state and its citizens. Therefore, at least traditionally, armed groups do not have specific obligations under human rights agreements, such as the ICCPR, the CRC, CEDAW, and others. However, many practitioners and advocates have increasingly proposed applying human rights treaties to armed groups, supported, in part, by former UN Secretary-General Kofi Annan. However, while individual members of groups may be subject to punishment for violations of international humanitarian law and a limited set of international human rights violations, groups as groups are not subject to punishment or sanction of the type arising where there is state responsibility for internationally wrongful acts. The reason for this is relatively straightforward, deriving from the nature of the international legal order and the premium placed upon state sovereignty. States create international law, and traditionally were viewed as the only creators and subjects of international law. Nonetheless, states will generally reject any claim by bodies other than states, particularly armed groups that challenge the power or legitimacy of states, for standing under international law. To say that such groups have obligations, like states, under this body of law, would appear to accord them greater legitimacy.

The provisions of the Torture Convention illustrate well the challenges of applying the terms of some human rights law to **nonstate actors**, not only where groups themselves are not subject to the provisions of the law, but also where some element of state action is required in order for a crime to have been committed. Traditionally, this has been the understanding of the Torture Convention. Why is this the case? Consider the language in Article 1 of the convention, which defines torture as suffering "inflicted by or at the instigation of or with the consent or acquiescence of a public official or other person acting in an official capacity." This provision would appear to require state action, but has more recently been understood to include the acts of those who exercise effective control over a territory, as was the case with Bosnian Serb leader Radovan Karadžić during the conflict in the former Yugoslavia (see Chapters 6 and 10). In a civil suit against Karadžić, a US court rejected his defense that obligations under international law regarding genocide, crimes against humanity, war crimes, and torture did not apply to him because he was not a state official. Instead, the court found that he was subject to suit in the United States under the Alien Tort Claims Act (see Chapter 11), because he had exercised effective control over the territory of Srpska during the time of the alleged acts were committed, even though he was not a state official.

However, while human rights agreements generally only articulate state obligations, even if broader obligations may be interpreted, international humanitarian law does deal with the obligations and violations of nonstate actors in more detail.

Proscribed violations in internal conflict

As we have seen, the Geneva Conventions and their additional protocols define proscribed conduct in war, regarding the treatment of both civilians and combatants. Violation of any of the grave breaches provisions of the Geneva Conventions may constitute a war crime.

However, traditional international humanitarian law has had difficulty addressing acts that might otherwise be war crimes when they are committed in the context of noninternational, or internal, armed conflict. First, the grave breaches provisions of all four Geneva Conventions apply only in international armed conflicts. States that are party to the conventions undertake to criminalize and punish these grave breaches, but not in *noninternational* armed conflicts. The only provisions that would apply to internal conflicts, then, are those of Common Article 3, which articulates proscribed acts in conflict of a noninternational character, but does not explicitly require states to make them criminal, nor does it call such acts "grave breaches," the terminology used in the conventions elsewhere to enumerate acts that constitute war crimes.

Box 5.2 *Kadić v. Karadžić*

Opinion of 2nd Circuit re: Subject Matter Jurisdiction
United States Court of Appeals for the Second Circuit
Docket Nos. 94-9035, -9069, Decided: October 13, 1995

The plaintiffs-appellants are Croat and Muslim citizens of the internationally recognized nation of Bosnia-Herzegovina, formerly a republic of Yugoslavia. Their complaints, which we accept as true for purposes of this appeal, allege that they are victims, and representatives of victims, of various atrocities, including brutal acts of rape, forced prostitution, forced impregnation, torture, and summary execution, carried out by Bosnian-Serb military forces as part of a genocidal campaign conducted in the course of the Bosnian civil war. Karadžić, formerly a citizen of Yugoslavia and now a citizen of Bosnia-Herzegovina, is the President of a three-man presidency of the self-proclaimed Bosnian-Serb republic within Bosnia-Herzegovina, sometimes referred to as "Srpska," which claims to exercise lawful authority, and does in fact exercise actual control, over large parts of the territory of Bosnia-Herzegovina. In his capacity as President, Karadzic possesses ultimate command authority over the Bosnian-Serb military forces, and the injuries perpetrated upon plaintiffs were committed as part of a pattern of systematic human rights violations that was directed by Karadžić and carried out by the military forces under his command. The complaints allege that Karadžić acted in an official capacity either as the titular head of Srpska or in collaboration with the government of the recognized nation of the former Yugoslavia and its dominant constituent republic, Serbia.

Legitimate combatants in internal conflict: beneficiaries of protection

Addressing abuses in internal conflict is made more complex insofar as the Geneva Conventions recognize combatants in internal conflict as legitimate combatants, and thus subject to protections of prisoner of war status, *only* if they satisfy a number of criteria (see Box 5.3). These include being a member of the state's armed forces, without further qualification, whereas the standard is set significantly higher for irregular or internal opposition forces, be they rebel groups or militias.

Opposition groups often will not fulfill these criteria, which are not imposed upon state armed forces. The standards for armed groups to be considered prisoners of war, subject to protections of the convention, are higher. However, this standard is relaxed in Additional Protocol II of 1977 (see Box 5.4), relative to noninternational armed conflict. Similarly, this protocol recognizes the possibility of armed groups being directly bound by its terms.

Of most interest here is that the protections of Additional Protocol II, prohibiting the harms previously enumerated by Common Article 3, now apply in internal armed conflict, even if the armed group in question *does not* have a distinctive emblem or carry arms openly. Rather, the provisions apply to armed groups exercising control over territory and responsible command, and having the capacity to implement the protocol. This more relaxed standard might be of use in more fully ensuring the application of the content of international humanitarian law in internal armed conflicts. One area in which Additional Protocol II may set a higher standard than Common Article 3 is in its definition of conflict

---

Box 5.3 Article 4 of the Third Geneva Convention

A. Prisoners of war, in the sense of the present Convention, are persons belonging to one of the following categories, who have fallen into the power of the enemy:

…

    2.   Members of other militias and members of other volunteer corps, including those of organized resistance movements, belonging to a Party to the conflict and operating in or outside their own territory, even if this territory is occupied, provided that such militias or volunteer corps, including such organized resistance movements, fulfil the following conditions:

        a. That of being commanded by a person responsible for his subordinates;

        b. That of having a fixed distinctive sign recognizable at a distance;

        c. That of carrying arms openly;

        d. That of conducting their operations in accordance with the laws and customs of war.

Box 5.4 Additional Protocol II to the Geneva Conventions, Article 1

1.   This Protocol, which develops and supplements Article 3 common to the Geneva Conventions of 12 August 1949 without modifying its existing conditions of application, shall apply to all armed conflicts which are not covered by Article 1 of the Protocol Additional to the Geneva Conventions of 12 August 1949, and relating to the Protection of Victims of International Armed Conflicts (Protocol I) and which take place in the territory of a High Contracting Party between its armed forces and dissident armed forces or other organized armed groups which, under responsible command, exercise such control over a part of its territory as to enable them to carry out sustained and concerted military operations and to implement this Protocol.

2.   This Protocol shall not apply to situations of internal disturbances and tensions, such as riots, isolated and sporadic acts of violence and other acts of a similar nature, as not being armed conflicts.

---

itself: Common Article 3 requires the presence of armed conflict, while Additional Protocol II offers a stringent definition, excluding much violence as no more than internal disturbance. Similarly, Common Article 3 does not set any requirement of effective control over territory for armed groups in order for them to be subject to its terms, while Additional Protocol II does.

Alleged terrorists and "illegitimate" or "unlawful" combatants as a special problem

While not all nonstate armed groups can be classified as terrorists, many states, regional organizations, or international organizations have classified a significant number of nonstate armed groups as terrorist groups. While there are a large number of international treaties and conventions prohibiting terrorist acts, there is not yet an agreed international legal definition of what constitutes terrorism or a terrorist group. Nonetheless, terrorism has presented a special set of challenges which can be distinguished from those presented by "ordinary" armed groups, insofar as states, particularly the United States, have sought to treat individuals or groups designated as terrorists as illegitimate or unlawful combatants not eligible for protection in international humanitarian law. Thus, for example, the administration of George W. Bush, following the attacks in the United States on September 11, 2001, classified hundreds of foreigners and some Americans as "enemy combatants" as part of the so-called global war on terror, denying them access to counsel, holding them without charge or trial, notwithstanding the protections afforded under the Geneva Conventions to prisoners of war, or afforded to US citizens under the US constitution. The US took a step further with the creation of a detention facility at Guantanamo, and the designation of alleged Al-Qaida or Taliban members as "unlawful combatants", a term coined by the US and not widely recognized. As a result, these individuals were deprived of their rights as prisoners of war under the Third Geneva Convention or as civilians under the Fourth Geneva Convention. Taliban fighters, as combatants of the government of Afghanistan prior to its overthrow, would appear to have been eligible for prisoner of war status, while alleged Al-Qaida members would not perhaps have been legitimate combatants, failing to satisfy the criteria of having a fixed emblem, carrying arms openly, complying with the rules of war and having a responsible chain of command. Nonetheless, individuals captured would then be designated civilians who, even if they engaged in activities considered hostile would retain protections under the Fourth Geneva Convention, including the right to a fair trial. In *Rasul v. Bush* (June 29, 2004), the US Supreme Court ruled that foreign detainees at Guantanamo Bay had the right to petition for a writ of *habeas corpus*, challenging their detention. The Bush Administration subsequently created military tribunals to review the status of detainees. Nonetheless, many prisoners were subjected to extended detention without charge or trial, many for more than 10 years. While the majority of prisoners were released to their countries of origin or third countries, some 160 remain in detention as of mid-2013. Foreigners have also been subjected to interrogation and alleged torture at the hands of American and foreign interrogators overseas as part of the US program of "extraordinary rendition" (Box 5.5).

Box 5.5 Extraordinary rendition

Extraordinary rendition involves the extrajudicial apprehension and transfer of a person to a foreign country. The United States, with the assistance of allies including the United Kingdom and Poland, engaged in this activity extensively during the so-called Global War on Terror, removing persons from American or foreign soil and transferring them to secret detention facilities overseas, where they were denied access to courts, legal counsel, or supervision and protection of human rights and humanitarian law watchdogs such as the International Committee of the Red Cross. Individuals detained were often subjected to what the US termed "enhanced interrogation techniques" which have been characterized by others as torture. These renditions resulted in the violation of international human rights such as the right to life, protection against arbitrary deprivation of liberty, the right to a fair trial, the right to be free from torture, and to be free from cruel, inhuman and degrading treatment.

Terrorism as a distinct international crime?

While a precise definition of terrorism in international law remains elusive, some scholars and practitioners have argued for treating terrorism as a distinct international crime during peacetime. Arguably, in wartime terrorism does not require a distinct characterization, as any act which might be designated terrorist would also meet the definition of an act constituting a war crime. However, in peacetime the question may be more complex. Acts of terrorism might simply constitute domestic crimes. In the context of transnational networks and attacks, this might seem a limited approach. Some scholars have suggested that acts of terrorism fit comfortably within the definition of crimes against humanity. Should terrorism be a distinct international crime or does it fall within the definition of existing crimes? At the Rome Conference, during the negotiations for the Statute of the International Criminal Court, several states proposed that it be included as a distinct crime, others that it fall under the rubric of crimes against humanity. Terrorism was ultimately not included in the statute, although a resolution of the Rome Conference proposed that a review conference on the statute consider both drug crimes and terrorism for inclusion in the statute at a later date, but these issues were not taken up at the 2010 Review Conference in Kampala.

Private military and security companies

Definition

The participation of private companies in conflict and conflict related activities is a relatively new phenomenon. However, the participation of individuals in conflict or in support of fighting forces, for profit, who are not part of an army, militia or paramilitary group and with no personal connection to a conflict is not new. These individuals have been commonly referred to as mercenaries. The use of mercenaries declined and nearly disappeared in the first part of the twentieth century, but saw the resurgence in the 1960s during the decolonization of Africa and Asia. Private military and security companies (PMSCs) however, have only started to be used more systematically in the past 15 years, since the military interventions in Iraq and Afghanistan, although they were used earlier in conflicts in Africa, such as that in Sierra Leone, to a lesser degree.

PMSCs are corporations offering security, defense and military services to a range of actors. It is often thought that PMSCs contract mainly with states, but international organizations, nongovernmental organizations and private companies are now frequently their clients. UN agencies, including UNICEF, UNDP, UNHCR, have used private security services. Humanitarian organizations increasingly rely on them to protect their personnel and infrastructure when delivering humanitarian aid. These companies not only participate in conflict, but increasingly participate in postconflict reconstruction activities, such as security sector reform. Their services include provision of armed guards; protection of persons and objects, including buildings; protection of roads and trade routes, including protection of marine commerce against pirates; maintenance and operation of weapons systems; prisoner detention and interrogation; intelligence, risk assessment and military research and analysis; and advice to or training of local forces and security personnel. Whilst their participation in direct combat is not as common as in the early years of their involvement in conflicts, their services may involve direct confrontation with combatants and participation in the conflict.

Over the past decade the outsourcing of military and security services to these private contractors has challenged the traditional monopoly of the state over the legitimate use of

---

Box 5.6 Offensive combat: PMSCs in Sierra Leone

In early 1990s several PMSCs performed offensive combat operations in Africa, including the South African company Executive Outcomes and the British company Sandline International. These early operations involved fighting on behalf of governments immersed in civil wars which had limited military capacity, including Angola, Sierra Leone and Papua New Guinea. Their activities were controversial and sparked an intense debate about the legitimacy of the industry. In Sierra Leone, the government hired Executive Operations in March 1995 to help the national army fight the Revolutionary United Front (RUF), just as the rebel group approached to the capital of Freetown. In less than a year Executive Operations led a counter-offensive which induced the rebels into peace negotiations. In May 1997 the peace process collapsed after a coup staged by the RUF. Notwithstanding the presence of a peacekeeping mission by the Economic Community of West African States, President Kabbah turned to a PMSC again, this time Sandline, which supported the counter-coup with weapons and military training. Sandline's intervention in the Sierra Leone conflict violated the UN arms embargo and proved an embarrassment for the British government, which had been informed by the company of its activities in the African country. Both Executive Outcomes and Sandline have now ceased operations.

---

force, particularly as these entities increase in size and importance and take on roles that were previously part of governmental functions, such as the control over armed forces, defense of the territory and security of citizens. In certain situations private contractors are more numerous than state armed forces, develop more activities or have even replaced members of them. Their presence in virtually every conflict and postconflict situation has created significant practical and legal challenges. Perhaps the most severe challenges arise from their implication in human rights abuses and the difficulty in holding them legally accountable.

Human rights violations

From the their early operations in conflict countries, PMSCs have been the subject of allegations of human rights violations. Their alleged abusive practices, including extrajudicial killings, torture, sexual violence, arbitrary detention and disappearance and participation in weapons, drugs and human trafficking have drawn fire, as has the composition of their work force, and the lack of accountability for their activities. Weak vetting procedures and the incentives to hire cheap labor have meant that PMSCs have employed individuals previously involved in human rights violations or other forms of criminal or socially unacceptable behavior. For example, some PMSCs have made extensive use of former police officials from apartheid South Africa, and Pinochet-era Chilean military personnel.

The participation of PMSCs in Iraq has resulted in numerous incidents involving human rights abuses. In 2007 the personnel of the US company Blackwater fired indiscriminately into a crowd of civilians in Nisour Square in Baghdad, killing 17 civilians, among them women and children, and injuring 20 more. This incident created further tension between the US and the Iraqi governments, and led to the end of the activities of Blackwater in Iraq. Victims sought justice in US courts, and after years of proceedings six of the victims settled with the company for an undisclosed sum in January 2012. Two other US companies, CACI

International Inc. and Titan Corp., were involved in the abuses of Iraqi detainees in the Abu Ghraib prison, where they provided services of interrogation and translation. A group of 250 Iraqis sued both companies in the US under the Alien Tort Claims Act for torture and illegal acts. However, the claims in that case, *Saleh v. Titan,* were dismissed. The US Supreme Court refused to consider an appeal in 2011, effectively ending the case.

The lack of comprehensive regulation, the low level of supervision by both home and host or territorial governments and the difficulties victims face in accessing judicial remedies has meant that many of these violations have been committed with impunity. In some cases, territorial states' jurisdiction has been explicitly circumvented via immunity clauses. For example, Order 17 of the now-disbanded Coalition Provisional Authority – the transitional government established after the fall of Saddam Hussein – established that contractors would be immune from the Iraqi legal process with respect to acts performed by them under the terms and conditions of their contract. The corporate structure of these entities also enables their impunity. They can dissolve themselves, rename and rebrand easily, and individual employees can move from company to company leaving little trace. This makes it even more difficult for victims to pursue justice for these violations.

In certain situations, the working practices of PMSCs can mean that their employees have their rights violated. Their working conditions tend to be dangerous and unhealthy and in many occasions lack sufficient security measures, which has meant that in some conflicts there have been larger casualties amongst private contractors than official fighting forces. They have also in many instances subjected to violations of labor laws.

International regulation

PMSCs and their personnel operate in a multilayered regulatory system rather than a total legal vacuum. They are legally bound by their contracts with states or other entities to which they provide their services and therefore to the domestic legal systems in which their contracts are formalized. Contracts have tended to be vague, and have generally not included any provisions regarding human rights protection or accountability. But these activities are nonetheless in principle covered by IHL and IHRL. The novelty of the structure of PMSCs and their participation in conflict make it difficult to apply some of the traditional concepts of IHL or IHRL to them, resulting in impunity for many of their activities.

Antecedents: the regulation of mercenaries

The first IHL provision, which specifically addressed the issue of the use of mercenaries was Article 47.2 of Protocol I to the 1949 Geneva Conventions. This article establishes a very narrow definition of a mercenary as any person who: (a) is specially recruited locally or abroad in order to fight in an armed conflict; (b) takes a direct part in the hostilities; (c) is motivated by the desire for private gain and is promised material compensation substantially in excess of that promised or paid to combatants of similar ranks and functions in the armed forces of that party; (d) is neither a national of a party to the conflict nor a resident of territory controlled by that party; (e) is not a member of the armed forces of a party to the conflict; and (f) has not been sent by a state which is not a party to the conflict on official duty as a member of its armed forces. The six conditions must all be fulfilled for an individual to qualify as a mercenary, which means the coverage of this provision is limited.

During the 1970s and 1980s two treaties were concluded which specifically address the question of mercenaries: the 1977 Organisation of African Unity (OAU) Convention for the Elimination of Mercenarism in Africa, which entered into force in 1985, and the 1989 UN International Convention Against the Recruitment, Use, Financing and Training of Mercenaries which entered into force in 2001. The definition of mercenary in these conventions is equally narrow. The OAU Convention relies on its members to implement it through national legislation, but only South Africa, which is not party to it, has adopted an anti-mercenary law. Both the OAU and the UN Conventions have received few ratifications.

All of the conventions make the status of mercenary conditional upon a number of requirements which PMSCs can easily avoid, and which often appear inapplicable even to traditional mercenaries. This, together with the fact that the conventions have not been well-received by many states, mean that existing legal instruments fail to sufficiently address the challenge of private contractors participating in conflict.

The application of international humanitarian law

As discussed above IHL makes a distinction between legitimate combatants (*de jure* or *de facto*) and civilians, which has a direct effect on the protections afforded to persons during conflict. The status of PMSCs and their employees under IHL is problematic. In principle, PMSCs and their personnel should be bound by IHL when they directly participate in the hostilities and are involved in combat. If PMSCs do not participate directly in the hostilities or are not incorporated into the armed forces of the state party to the conflict, then they will be considered civilians under IHL. But the distinctions in practice are more difficult and the categories are blurred, as is the nature of the protection due to them and their responsibility in cases of violations.

If they participate directly in hostilities, the most significant challenge is defining the relationship between the party to the conflict and the private contractor. Some authors have argued that they could be considered as incorporated into the armed forces of a state party to the conflict, given that the state has entitled them to intervene in the conflict in their behalf. However, other authors argue that formal incorporation in the state armed forces is required in order to place the private contractors within the military chain of command and control. This would be consistent with the criteria established in Article 43 of Additional Protocol I for armed forces: that they act on behalf of a party to the conflict; that they are organized; that they are under the chain of command of that party, which would in turn be responsible for the conduct of subordinates.

If they are not considered as part of state armed forces, the question remains whether they could still be considered legitimate combatants. In principle they could fall within the definition of Article 4 of the Third Geneva Convention (see Box 5.3.). However, the International Criminal Tribunal for the Former Yugoslavia in its *Tadić* judgment in interpreting this provision added the need for control by the state over the group in order to establish the link between the state and the nonstate armed group. The amount of control that the contracting state exercises over the PMSC in order to comply with the *Tadić* requirement could be difficult to assess.

Most PMSCs are only occasionally directly involved in conflict. Thus, they might instead be considered to be civilians taking direct part in the hostilities. Civilians who directly participate in the hostilities lose their civilian protection. This concept has been a source of controversy in recent years. In 2008, the International Committee of the Red Cross (ICRC) published its Interpretative Guidance on the Notion of Direct Participation in Hostilities under IHL and made specific reference to PMSCs and their employees. The ICRC Guidance acknowledged that the great majority of private contractors and civilian employees currently active in armed conflicts have not been incorporated into state armed forces and assume functions that clearly do not involve their direct participation in hostilities on behalf of a party to the conflict. Therefore, the guidance concluded that under IHL, they generally fall within the definition of civilians. It expressly stated that private contractors and employees of a party to an armed conflict who are civilians are entitled to protection against direct attack, unless they take a direct part in hostilities. Their activities or location may, however, expose them to an increased risk of incidental death or injury even if they do not take a direct part in hostilities. The ICRC also acknowledged however that, in some cases, it may be extremely difficult to determine the civilian or military nature of contractor activity. For this reason, work has been undertaken at the United Nations to develop a convention to regulate such forces.

Proposed draft convention on the regulation, oversight and monitoring of private military and security companies

The UN Special Rapporteur on the use of mercenaries, appointed in 1987, was replaced in 2005 by the Working Group on the Use of Mercenaries as a Means of Violating Human Rights and Impeding the Exercise of the Right of Peoples to Self-determination. The group comprises five regional experts, and its mandate includes an expectation that it will

> elaborate and present concrete proposals on possible complementary and new standards aimed at filling existing gaps, as well as general guidelines or basic principles encouraging the further protection of human rights, in particular the right of peoples to self-determination, while facing current and emergent threats posed by mercenaries or mercenary-related activities.
>
> (UN Human Rights Council Resolution 7/21)

In 2010, the group presented a proposed draft convention, the International Convention on the Regulation, Oversight and Monitoring of Private Military and Security Companies.

The proposed draft convention establishes the responsibility of a state for the military and security activities of the PMSCs registered or operating in its jurisdiction, whether they are contracted by the state or not. The state is obliged to pass legislation to establish the procedures for contracting, licensing the export and import of military and security services. The proposed draft convention contains specific prohibitions on outsourcing or contracting inherent state functions, which include the use of force, thus effectively excluding PMSC participation directly in hostilities. Article 7 of the proposed draft convention establishes that state parties should establish measures to ensure respect for IHL and IHRL and that PMSCs and their personnel are held accountable for their violations. Part IV contains a series of provisions regarding criminal, civil and administrative responsibility for the companies and their employees, as well as provisions for asserting jurisdiction, for prosecution and extradition. Part V establishes the creation of a Committee on the Regulation, Oversight and Monitoring of PMSCs, which would be composed by independent experts. The committee would be responsible, among other things, of maintaining an international register of PMSCs.

The United Nations Human Rights Council has created an open-ended intergovernmental working group to consider the possibility of elaborating such an instrument, but so far states have not moved to formalize the proposed convention.

Voluntary regulation and self-regulation

States have not agreed on a binding document at international level; however some states have produced a document in which they outline best state practice. The Montreux Document on Pertinent International Legal Obligations and Good Practices for States related to Operations of Private Military and Security Companies during Armed Conflict was elaborated through a joint initiative of the Swiss government and the ICRC, with the participation of 17 governments, including home and host states of PMSCs and in consultation with representatives of the industry and civil society. It was launched in 2009. The Montreux Document is not legally binding, but rather seeks to outline current international legal obligations and good practices. It reaffirms the obligation of states to ensure that private military and security companies operating in armed conflicts comply with international humanitarian and human rights law. Among the most important recommendations are that states verify the track record of companies and examine the procedures they use to vet their staff and take measures to ensure that the personnel of private military and security companies can be prosecuted when serious breaches of the law occur.

The industry prefers and has lobbied strongly for self-regulation. There are several industry associations, of which the British Association of Private Security Companies (BAPSC) and the International Stability Operations Associations (ISOA) have their own codes of conduct for their members. However, a limitation of voluntary self-regulation is that codes are often not monitored, and when they are, there are no serious consequences for non-compliance.

Multinational corporations operating in conflict environments

Multinational corporations may also find themselves immersed in conflict situations. As discussed in Chapter 2, many contemporary conflicts involve the struggle to control natural resources, and in many instances such corporations are involved in exploitation, trade and production of raw materials and goods. Diamonds in Sierra Leone and Angola, coltan, cassiterite, and wolframite in the Democratic Republic of Congo, legal and illegal crops in Colombia, and oil in the Niger Delta are just some of the examples of natural resources, which have fuelled and continue to fuel conflict and human rights abuses worldwide. These resources may be exploited by repressive regimes and/or armed groups, which use the revenues to continue fighting and often in the process engage in human rights violations. These resources are later sold in the global market and enter the global supply chain. While multinational corporations are seldom directly engaged in the exploitation of most of these "conflict resources," by manufacturing and commercializing these products they contribute to processes, which entail ongoing human rights violations. On occasions some companies have been sufficiently engaged in a conflict situation that they have in some form aided and abetted abuses, as discussed in Chapter 11 with regard to companies operating in Burma, and in Chapter 9 with regard to Talisman Oil in Sudan.

Human rights initiatives for companies

For the past two decades, international human rights organizations have been trying to make companies, whether operating in conflict zones or not, accountable for their activities which have a direct impact on human rights. However, the main legal hurdle is that, as nonstate actors, corporations are not legally bound by international law and therefore by human rights norms. This means that most of the initiatives which address the behavior of corporations with regard to human rights must rely on the voluntary commitment of companies and states. Among the most widely accepted voluntary schemes is the UN Global Compact, which consists of ten voluntary principles to which companies can adhere and commit to insert in their operations and relations with their business partners. The principles include the respect of human rights, labor rights, the environment and the commitment to work against corruption. The Global Compact acts as a network where companies share best practices and get support on their social commitments. Over ten years of operation, the Global Compact has addressed the relationship between companies, peace, and stability.

In 2011, after six years of operation, the UN Special Representative on Business and Human Rights published his Guiding Principles on Business and Human Rights, which contained distinct sets of recommendations and guidance for states and companies. The Guiding Principles state that states have the duty to protect the population under their jurisdictions from the harmful activities of business whilst corporations have the responsibility to respect human rights. The Guiding Principles also establish the need for states and companies to develop remedies for victims and guarantee that they have access to meaningful procedures of redress. The Guiding Principles contain a series of recommendations for states in relation to conflict zones which include engaging with companies to help them identify, prevent and mitigate the human rights-related risks of their activities and business relationships; providing them with adequate assistance to assess and address the heightened risks of human rights abuses, paying special attention to gender-based and sexual violence; denying access to public support and services for companies which are involved in gross human rights abuses and which have refused to cooperate in addressing the situation; and ensuring that they have policies, legislation, regulations and enforcement measures which effectively address the risk of business involvement in gross human rights abuses. The Guiding Principles do not, however, contain an enforcement mechanism.

Human rights organizations have created partnerships with governments and companies to develop initiatives, which address specific problems related to corporate activities in conflict or weak governance zones. Among the first ones of these multi-stakeholder initiatives was the Kimberley Process for the Certification of Rough Diamonds, to control the trade of diamonds and avoid the export of so-called "blood diamonds." Other initiatives include the Voluntary Principles on Human Rights and Security and the Extractive Industries Transparency Initiative.

Companies and international humanitarian law

IHL may have implications for corporations, which operate in conflict situations. It is clear that a corporation's assets and personnel (provided they do not take part directly in armed hostilities) are protected by IHL. It is more difficult to assess, however, how these corporations, and their personnel, are limited in their activities by IHL.

Box 5.7 Businesses under IHL

In a 2006 study, the ICRC warned companies that their activities may be affected by IHL when operating in conflict environments, and urged them to use extreme caution and be aware that their actions may be considered to be linked to the conflict even though such activities do not occur during fighting or on the battlefield. The ICRC contended that it is not necessary for these companies or their managers to intend to support a party to the hostilities for their activities to be considered to be closely linked to the conflict.

The ICRC recommended that companies should be aware of IHL obligations with regard to:

- The security of their infrastructure and personnel, especially if they come under attack.
- The legality of acquisition of resources and property, since they may not have been obtained with the consent of the owner this could potentially amount to pillage.
- The labor conditions of those working for their business partners, since they might benefit from forced labor of prisoners of war or concentration camp detainees in violation of IHL.
- The displacement of local population who may have been forcibly evicted from their land to guarantee access to transport routes which may also amount to pillage or breach the rules regulating occupation.
- The impact on the environment of their operations, especially if they supply products—such as chemical or biological weapons, or exfoliants (commonly known as defoliants)—that can cause such damage during armed conflict, as forms of warfare that may be expected to cause widespread, long term and severe damage to the natural environment are forbidden by IHL.
- The production and trade of specific types of weapons, which are prohibited by international law, such as anti-personnel landmines, or biological and chemical weapons, including poisonous gases. The ICRC also asks companies to give consideration to how other products not traditionally used as weapons could be used to perpetrate war crimes.
- Source: "An Introduction to the Rights and Obligations of Business Enterprises under International Humanitarian Law" (ICRC, 2006), available http://www.icrc. org/eng/resources/documents/misc/business-ihl-150806.htm

To address the issue, in 2006 the ICRC published a document entitled "An Introduction to the Rights and Obligations of Business Enterprises under International Humanitarian Law" exploring the potential situations in which commercial companies could find themselves affected by IHL (Box 5.7).

Discussion questions

- Upon whom are international humanitarian law obligations imposed? States or individuals?
- Is the following statement correct? Why or why not? While international bodies have addressed accountability of individual leaders of armed opposition groups, they have so far largely ignored the accountability of the groups in favor of the accountability of individual members.
- Is international law adequately equipped to address the new challenge of international terrorism? What type of international law violation might terrorism constitute?
- Should humanitarian law apply to captured alleged terrorists, and if so, how?
- Does IHL apply to commercial companies operating in conflict zones? Why or why not?

Group exercise

In two groups argue for and against self-regulation for the private military and security industry.

Further reading

Andreopoulos, George J., "The International Legal Framework and Armed Groups," *Human Rights Review* vol. 11 (2010): 223–246.

Bakker, Christine and Mirko Sossai (eds), *Multilevel Regulation of Military and Security Contractors: The Interplay between International, European and Domestic Norms* (Oxford: Hart, 2012).

Cassese, Antonio, "The Multifaceted Criminal Notion of Terrorism in International Law," *Journal of International Criminal Justice* vol. 4 (2006): 933–958.

Chesterman, Simon and Chia Lehnardt (eds), *From Mercenaries to Market: The Rise and Regulation of Military Companies* (Oxford: Oxford University Press, 2007).

Clapham, Andrew, "Extending International Criminal Law beyond the Individual to Corporations and Armed Opposition Groups," *Journal of International Criminal Justice* vol. 6 (2008): 899–926.

Duffy, Helen, *The "War on Terror" and the Framework of International Law* (Cambridge: Cambridge University Press, 2005), especially pp. 332–78, 379–442.

Ehrenreich Brooks, Rosa, "War Everywhere: Rights, National Security Law, and the Law of Armed Conflict in the Age of Terror," *University of Pennsylvania Law Review* vol. 153, no. 2 (December 2004): 675–761.

Francioni, Francesco and Natalino Ronzitti (eds), *War by Contract: Human Rights, Humanitarian Law and Private Contractors* (Oxford: Oxford University Press, 2011).

Gomez del Prado, Jose, "A United Nations Instrument to Regulate and Monitor Private Military and Security Contractors," *Notre Dame Journal of International and Comparative Law*, vol. 1 (2011): 1–79.

Greenwood, Christopher, "A Critique of the Additional Protocols to the Geneva Conventions of 1949," in Helen Durham and Timothy L. H. McCormack (eds), *The Changing Face of Conflict and the Efficacy of International Humanitarian Law* (The Hague: Kluwer, 1999).

Martin-Ortega, Olga, "Business and Human Rights in Conflict," *Ethics & International Affairs* vol. 22, no. 3 (2008): 273–283.

Montreux Document on Pertinent International Legal Obligations and Good Practices for States related to Operations of Private Military and Security Companies during Armed Conflict, (2009), http://www.icrc.org/eng/resources/documents/publication/p0996.htm

Tonkin, Hannah, *State Control over Private Military and Security Companies in Armed Conflict* (Cambridge: Cambridge University Press, 2011).

Official documents

Report of the Working Group on the Use of Mercenaries as a Means of Violating Human Rights and Impeding the Exercise of the Right of Peoples to Self-Determination, UN Doc. A/HRC/15/25 (July 5, 2010).

Special Representative of the Secretary-General on the issue of human rights and transnational corporations and other business enterprises, *Guiding Principles on Business and Human Rights: Implementing the United Nations "Protect, Respect and Remedy" Framework*, UN Doc. A/HRC/17/31, (March 21, 2011).

Online sources

UN Global Compact, www.unglobalcompact.org

Voluntary Principles on Human Rights and Security, www.voluntaryprinciples.org

Part II
Contemporary conflict
Critical cases

6 The Former Yugoslavia

Key points

- The conflicts in the former Yugoslavia have been complex, involving multiple belligerent parties and dissolution of the state.
- The conflicts have involved mass atrocities attributable to both state and nonstate forces.
- The shift from internal to international conflict may affect the applicability of certain international humanitarian law.
- The conflicts have led to the creation of the first international war crimes tribunal since World War II.
- The legacies of the conflict continue to affect electoral politics in the post-Yugoslav republics and further efforts at accountability and reconciliation continue.

Overview

The conflicts in the former Yugoslavia have been complex and have occurred both within states and between states since the end of the Cold War, after which many nation-states within the former Soviet Union and across Eastern Europe began to fragment. As a result, several successor states emerged, partially along the lines of the former Yugoslavia's administrative division into a number of republics, and also along ethnic lines (see Box 6.1 for key facts on Yugoslavia). Conflicts between 1991 and 1995 largely in the territory of what are now Bosnia-Herzegovina, and Croatia, sparked international outrage, intervention by the **United Nations** (UN) and the **North Atlantic Treaty Organization** (NATO), and eventually the creation of the first international war crimes tribunal, the ad hoc **International Criminal Tribunal for the Former Yugoslavia** (ICTY), since the Nuremberg and Tokyo Tribunals. The 1999 conflict in Kosovo sparked a three-month bombing campaign by NATO in Serbia, and led to the creation of a UN interim administration in the province.

This chapter examines the historical background of the conflict in the former Yugoslavia, human rights violations as both causes and consequences of conflict, the **international humanitarian law** and **international human rights law** applicable to the abuses committed, and prospects for accountability. Chapter 10 discusses the ICTY in greater detail.

Map 6.1 Former Yugoslavia,1991
Source: Adapted from the PCL Map Collection, University of Texas Libraries, the University of Texas at Austin, http://www.lib.utexas.edu/maps/europe/former_yugoslavia.jpg

Background to the conflict

The former Yugoslavia was the result of the unification of the Kingdom of Serbs, Croats, and Slovenes in 1918. While each population resided across the territory, and intermarriage existed, Serbs comprised the majority in the areas now known as Serbia, Croats in the areas now known as Croatia, and Slovenians in the areas now known as Slovenia. The territory now known as Bosnia-Herzegovina was mixed, but with a majority Bosnian Muslim population. Albanians resided largely in the territory now known as Kosovo, with a Serb minority. In 1929 the unified country became known as Yugoslavia. During World War II, Germany sought to occupy the territory, and faced resistance from paramilitary groups, but also found allies in Croatia in the Ustache (a Croatian ultranationalist organization), which engaged in ethnic cleansing and expulsion of Serbs, gypsies, and Muslims. With the defeat of the Germans and Croatian collaborators, Josip Broz Tito took control of Yugoslavia, a federation of six republics: Serbia, Montenegro, Croatia, Bosnia-Herzegovina, and Slovenia. He established a communist regime, which endured after his death in 1980, independent of the Soviet Union and held together by authoritarian rule. In 1989, Slobodan Milošević

Box 6.1 **Key facts: Former Yugoslavia in 1991**

Geography

Location: Balkans, neighboring Albania, Austria, Bulgaria, Greece, Hungary, Italy, Romania
Disputes: Kosovo's status; the official name of Macedonia disputed by Greece
Area: Total area 255,800 km^2, land area: 255,400 km^2, water area: 400 km^2
Natural resources: coal, copper, bauxite, timber, iron ore, antimony, chromium, lead, zinc, asbestos, mercury, crude oil, natural gas, nickel, uranium

People

Population: 24 million, growth rate 0.6%
Nationality: Yugoslav
Ethnic groups: Serb 36.3%, Croat 19.7%, Muslim 8.9%, Slovene 7.8%, Albanian 7.7%, Macedonian 5.9%, Yugoslav 5.4%, Montenegrin 2.5%, Hungarian 1.9%, other 3.9% (1981 census)
Religions: Eastern Orthodox 50%, Roman Catholic 30%, Muslim 9%, Protestant 1%, other 10%
Languages: Serbo-Croatian, Slovene, Macedonian (all official); Albanian, Hungarian
Literacy: 90% (male 96%, female 84%) age 15 and older can read and write (1981 census)

Government

Country name: Socialist Federal Republic of Yugoslavia (SFRY)
Government type: Federal republic; four of six republics have noncommunist governments
Capital: Belgrade
Administrative territorial divisions: Six republics: Bosnia-Herzegovina, Croatia, Macedonia, Slovenia, and Serbia; two nominally autonomous provinces within Serbia: Kosovo and Vojvodina
Independence: December 1, 1918; independent monarchy established from the Kingdoms of Serbia and Montenegro, parts of the Turkish Empire, and the Austro-Hungarian Empire; SFRY proclaimed November 29, 1945

Economy

Gross national product: US$120.1 billion, per capita US$5,040; real growth rate 6.3% (1990)
Unemployment rate: 16% (1990)

Source: Central Intelligence Agency, *World Factbook*
http://www.theodora.com/wfb1991/yugoslavia/yugoslavia_people.html
http://www.theodora.com/wfb1991/yugoslavia/yugoslavia_economy.html
http://www.theodora.com/wfb1991/yugoslavia/yugoslavia_geography.html

became president of the Serbian Republic, within Yugoslavia, and began calling for Serbian domination of the country. This ultranationalism sparked separatism, and ultimately the violent breakup of the state along ethnic lines. The conflict in the former Yugoslavia was largely, although not purely, based upon ethnicity or religion, with political leaders using identity and historical grievances to stoke conflict. The three largest ethnic groups in the country, Serbs (composing about 33 percent of the population), Croatians (about 20 percent), and Muslims (largely Bosnian Muslims, about 9 percent), were far less integrated by the end of the conflict, and longer-term resentment and mistrust continue.

Conflict in Bosnia-Herzegovina and Croatia

In 1991, Croatia, Slovenia, and Macedonia declared independence from Yugoslavia, followed in 1992 by Bosnia-Herzegovina. The remaining republics of Serbia and Montenegro declared a new republic, the Federal Republic of Yugoslavia (FRY) in April 1992. While the FRY rejected Croatia's declaration of independence, Milošević initially reached a pact with Croatian leader Franjo Tuđjman to partition Bosnia-Herzegovina into Serb- and Croat-controlled regions. The independence of Macedonia and Slovenia came relatively peacefully (as did Montenegro's independence in 2006), at least by comparison to the wars that ensued in Croatia and Bosnia-Herzegovina. In the latter regions, Serbia under Milošević promoted violent military campaigns, through support to local nationalist groups, to create a "Greater Serbia."

Bosnia-Herzegovina followed its declaration of sovereignty in October 1991 with a declaration of independence from the former Yugoslavia on March 3, 1992, following a referendum boycotted by ethnic Serbs. The Bosnian Serbs—supported by neighboring Serbia and Montenegro, led by Milošević —responded with armed resistance aimed at partitioning the republic along ethnic lines and joining Serb-held areas of Bosnia-Herzegovina to form a "Greater Serbia." They were led by Radovan Karadžić and his army chief Ratko Mladić, who like Milošević would later be indicted by the International Criminal Tribunal for the Former Yugoslavia for alleged involvement in war crimes and atrocities, in particular the massacre in Srebrenica. In Croatia, Croatian Serbs resisted Croatian independence and engaged in fighting with the support of Serbia. Bosnian forces and Croatian forces fought not only the Serb forces in their territories, but occasionally also each other, creating a three-way, albeit asymmetrical, conflict. The atrocities, involving targeted killing and widespread abuse of civilians of different ethnic groups, were committed by the major parties to the conflict, but in significantly greater numbers by Serb forces against Croat and Bosniak civilians. While these acts might have been characterized as **genocide**, they were termed "ethnic cleansing" by the international community. In March 1994, Bosniaks and Croats signed an agreement creating the joint Bosniak/Croat Federation of Bosnia-Herzegovina, ending fighting between these two parties.

Conflict continued in these territories, with intense international pressure to reach a peaceful, negotiated settlement. The **UN Secretary-General** appointed a personal envoy, Cyrus Vance, in October 1991, to seek a resolution. On February 15, 1992, despite objections by many in Serbia, the Secretary-General recommended to the **UN Security Council** the establishment of the UN Protection Force (UNPROFOR). This plan was approved in a **UN Security Council resolution**, Resolution 743 of 1992. The expectation at the time was that this would be an interim measure, while a cease-fire was secured. However, the fighting endured, with atrocities, massacres, and targeting of civilians frequent and the UN force unable to halt them, given a relatively weak mandate. The UN force designated three original

Box 6.2 **The Dayton Accords**

General Framework Agreement for Peace in Bosnia-Herzegovina

The Republic of Bosnia-Herzegovina, the Republic of Croatia and the Federal Republic of Yugoslavia (the "Parties"),

Recognizing the need for a comprehensive settlement to bring an end to the tragic conflict in the region,
Desiring to contribute toward that end and to promote an enduring peace and stability,
Affirming their commitment to the Agreed Basic Principles issued on September 8, 1995, the Further Agreed Basic Principles issued on September 26, 1995, and the cease-fire agreements of September 14 and October 5, 1995,
Noting the agreement of August 29, 1995, which authorized the delegation of the Federal Republic of Yugoslavia to sign, on behalf of the Republika Srpska, the parts of the peace plan concerning it, with the obligation to implement the agreement that is reached strictly and consequently,

Have agreed as follows:

Article I
The Parties shall conduct their relations in accordance with the principles set forth in the United Nations Charter, as well as the Helsinki Final Act and other documents of the Organization for Security and Cooperation in Europe. In particular, the Parties shall fully respect the sovereign equality of one another, shall settle disputes by peaceful means, and shall refrain from any action, by threat or use of force or otherwise, against the territorial integrity or political independence of Bosnia-Herzegovina or any other State.

Annex 6: Agreement on Human Rights
Chapter One: Respect for Human Rights
Article I: Fundamental Rights and Freedoms
The Parties shall secure to all persons within their jurisdiction the highest level of internationally recognized human rights and fundamental freedoms, including the rights and freedoms provided in the European Convention for the Protection of Human Rights and Fundamental Freedoms and its Protocols and the other international agreements listed in the Appendix to this Annex.

protected areas: Eastern Slavonia, Western Slavonia, and Krajina, with others to follow. However, despite increases in the size and mandate of UNPROFOR by the Security Council, it was unable to halt much of the violence and targeting of civilians, with the most notable failures being its inability to prevent the massacre of Srebrenica and the siege of Sarajevo.

International efforts at mediation promoted numerous peace plans, but all were doomed to fail. However, international pressure increased, and finally, on November 21, 1995, in Dayton, Ohio, the warring parties signed a peace agreement. The Dayton Accords (see Box 6.2) retained Bosnia-Herzegovina's international boundaries and created a multiethnic, democratic government with a rotating presidency. The peace agreement also recognized two entities within that state: the Bosniak/Croat Federation of Bosnia-Herzegovina, and the Bosnian Serb–led Republika Srpska (RS).

Conflict in Kosovo

The conflict in Kosovo involved efforts by Serbia to consolidate control over Serbs in the territory of the former Yugoslavia where they were in the minority. Serbs had been present in what is now Kosovo since the seventh century, but the territory did not fall under Serbian rule until the thirteenth century. Following defeat by the Ottomans in the Battle of Kosovo in 1389, large numbers of Turks and Albanians moved to Kosovo, and Albanians became the dominant ethnic group in Kosovo; this battle served as a symbolic tool for Serb nationalists such as Milošević to invoke in stoking the fires of nationalism during the 1990s. Serbia regained control over Kosovo from the Ottoman Empire in 1912. Following the creation of the Yugoslav government under Tito, Kosovo was recognized as an autonomous province within Serbia, and was given progressively greater powers. Kosovo was granted near-republic status in the 1974 Yugoslav constitution. Nonetheless, Albanian nationalism, including riots and demands for independence, increased in the 1980s. Serbs in Kosovo complained that they were being mistreated, and such claims were exploited by Serb nationalist leaders such as Milošević. Serbia passed a new constitution in 1989 that limited Kosovo's autonomy. In 1991, Kosovo Albanian leaders held a referendum in which Kosovo declared itself independent. Serbia responded with repressive measures, and Ibrahim Rugova, a moderate ethnic Albanian leader, established a parallel unofficial government, seeking to resist this repression peacefully, but without success. In response, Kosovo Albanians created the Kosovo Liberation Army (KLA) in 1995 and began fighting to oust Serb control. Both the US and the Yugoslav governments viewed the KLA as a terrorist organization due to its attacks on Serb targets, including police and civilians. The KLA also established a political wing, headed by Hashim Thaçi, who would become the prime minister of Kosovo when it declared independence in 2008. Serbia responded with a counterinsurgency campaign that entailed massacres and massive expulsions of ethnic Albanians by Serbian military, police, and paramilitary forces.

Attempts at negotiation culminated in the Rambouillet Accords in 1999, which set forth principles of interim self-government for Kosovo, enshrined principles of nondiscrimination and self-determination, and promised the right of return, protection of humanitarian assistance, and a halt to the use of force. The Rambouillet agreement was ultimately rejected by Milošević. NATO initiated a three-month bombing campaign in Serbia, beginning in March 1999, and Serbia was forced to withdraw military and police forces in June 1999. UN Security Council Resolution 1244 (1999) (see Box 6.3) placed Kosovo under a transitional administration, the UN Interim Administration Mission in Kosovo (UNMIK), until Kosovo's final status could be resolved. The resolution recognized Serbia's territorial integrity, with UNMIK engaged in actual governance of Kosovo. In 2001, UNMIK set out a constitutional framework that established Kosovo's provisional institutions of self-government and began to devolve responsibilities to it. In late 2005 the UN initiated proceedings to determine Kosovo's future status. Negotiations held intermittently between 2006 and 2007 failed to reach a compromise between Serbia's insistence on its territorial integrity, with significant autonomy for Kosovo, and the Kosovo Albanians' demand for full independence. On February 17, 2008, Kosovo declared its independence from Serbia. To date, Kosovo has been recognized a sovereign state by over 100 countries, including many European nations, but not by Serbia.

Box 6.3 **UN Security Council Resolution 1244**

UN Doc. S/RES/1244 (June 10, 1999)

3. Demands in particular that the Federal Republic of Yugoslavia put an immediate and verifiable end to violence and repression in Kosovo, and begin and complete verifiable phased withdrawal from Kosovo of all military, police and paramilitary forces according to a rapid timetable, with which the deployment of the international security presence in Kosovo will be synchronized;

4. Confirms that after the withdrawal an agreed number of Yugoslav and Serb military and police personnel will be permitted to return to Kosovo to perform the functions in accordance with annex 2;

5. Decides on the deployment in Kosovo, under United Nations auspices, of international civil and security presences, with appropriate equipment and personnel as required, and welcomes the agreement of the Federal Republic of Yugoslavia to such presences;

...

7. Authorizes Member States and relevant international organizations to establish the international security presence in Kosovo as set out in point 4 of annex 2 with all necessary means to fulfil its responsibilities under paragraph 9 below; establish the international security presence in Kosovo as set out in point 4 of annex 2 with all necessary means to fulfil its responsibilities under paragraph 9 below;

...

10. Authorizes the Secretary-General, with the assistance of relevant international organizations, to establish an international civil presence in Kosovo in order to provide an interim administration for Kosovo under which the people of Kosovo can enjoy substantial autonomy within the Federal Republic of Yugoslavia, and which will provide transitional administration while establishing and overseeing the development of provisional democratic self-governing institutions to ensure conditions for a peaceful and normal life for all inhabitants of Kosovo.

The fall of Milošević

Milošević's grip on power was first loosened with disputed elections in 2000; he was forced to resign amid mass protests. In 2001 he was arrested by the FRY government on charges of corruption, embezzlement, and abuse of power. However, he had also been indicted by the ICTY (see Chapter 10) on charges of crimes relating to the wars in Bosnia-Herzegovina and in Kosovo. He died in tribunal custody in March 2006.

Human rights violations in the Former Yugoslavia

Human rights violations as underlying causes of conflict

Domestic grievances

Past abuses, even historically remote, were invoked by various sides to the conflict as justifications, among others, for fighting. Serb forces inside and outside Serbia justified fighting Croatian forces in part by invoking the memory of abuses by the Nazi-allied Croatian Ustache.

Box 6.4 **Key players in the Former Yugoslavia**

Individuals

Radovan Karadžić: founder of the Serbian Democratic Party in Bosnia-Herzegovina
    and first president of Republika Srpska. In ICTY custody.
Slobodan Milošević: President of the Serbian Republic within Yugoslavia, and then
    of the Federal Republic of Yugoslavia (Serbia and Montenegro). Died in 2006.
Ratko Mladić: Chief of staff of the Army of Republika Srpska during the Bosnian
    conflict of 1992–95. In ICTY custody.
Ibrahim Rugova: Moderate Kosovar political leader. Died in 2006.
Hashim Thaçi: Leader of the KLA's political and subsequently prime minister of
    Kosovo.
Franjo Tuđjman: Leader of the Croatian Democratic Union; declared Croatian
    independence 1991. Died in 1999.

National armies

Kosovo Liberation Army (KLA).

International and Regional Missions

UN Interim Administration Mission in Kosovo (UNMIK).
UN Protection Force (UNPROFOR).

Other actors

International Court of Justice (ICJ).
International Criminal Tribunal for the Former Yugoslavia (ICTY).
North Atlantic Treaty Organization (NATO).

Milošević also justified support to Serb forces in Bosnia-Herzegovina, and fighting in Kosovo, in the defense of Serb minorities, who, according to Milošević, were being discriminated against and attacked, or were at risk of such treatment. Milošević's rhetoric surrounding the need to fight in Kosovo, and indeed in Bosnia as well, repeatedly harkened back to the 1389 battle that established Ottoman control, and his nationalist rhetoric was seen as ushering in repression by Serbs of various minorities. Kosovar Albanians took up arms under the banner of the KLA on the grounds that they were being abused by the regime in Belgrade, and were in danger of suffering ethnic cleansing. However, their struggle against repression from Belgrade also involved attacks on the Serb minority in Kosovo. Bosniak and Croat forces fought separately and together to defend against Serb military attacks, and attacks targeted specifically against civilians, which were viewed as ethnic cleansing.

    These invocations of discrimination, abuses, and threats to survival were based on a mixture of truth and conveniently deployed mythmaking. In many instances, most evidently in assaults by Serb forces in Bosnia-Herzegovina and in Kosovo, abuses were currently taking place, perhaps offering the greatest justification for resort to force. Where historical grievances were invoked, however, the human rights justification for force appeared somewhat more remote.

Internal or international conflict?

Was the conflict in the former Yugoslavia an internal or an international (transborder) conflict? It was in fact both, and its character changed over time, although precisely when may be disputed. At the outset, the conflict was largely internal in character. However, with the declarations of independence by Croatia and Bosnia-Herzegovina, the war became internationalized. These declarations were rapidly recognized by a few states; EU recognition of Croatia came in January 1992, and Croatia, Slovenia, and Bosnia-Herzegovina were admitted into the United Nations as member states in May 1992. By this date, they were clearly independent states and the conflicts were potentially both internal (purely Bosnian Serb, Croat, and Muslim forces fighting in the territory of Bosnia-Herzegovina, and purely Croatian Serb and Croat forces fighting in the territory of Croatia) and international (conflicts between Bosniak and Croat fighters, and material support from the FRY to Croatian and Bosnian Serb forces fighting in Bosnia-Herzegovina and Croatia). Characterization of the conflict as internal or international may shape the applicable law.

Human rights violations emerging from and transforming the conflict

A wide range of atrocities took place during the conflicts, the majority of which were perpetrated by Serb forces in Croatia and Bosnia-Herzegovina, although Bosniak and Croat forces also engaged in abuses. Similarly in Kosovo, Serb forces appear to have been responsible for the majority of abuses, with the KLA far from innocent of abuses itself. In both conflicts, violence by state and **nonstate actors** targeted civilians, forcing them to flee as part of a strategy of ethnic cleansing. Methods included massacres of civilians, **torture**, disappearances, rape and forced impregnation, and bombardment of population centers having no evident military value. We focus here upon three specific sets of events: the siege of Sarajevo, the massacre at Srebrenica, and the 1998–99 violence in Kosovo, which led to the NATO bombing campaign.

The siege of Sarajevo

The siege of Sarajevo, the capital city of Bosnia-Herzegovina, by Serb and Bosnian Serb forces, is classed as the longest siege in modern conflict, lasting from April 1992 until February 1996 and outlasting the signature of the Dayton Accords. An estimated 12,000 were killed, 85 per cent of whom were civilians. The siege also forced many to flee, a depopulation that reduced the size of Sarajevo to just over 60 percent of its former size. The siege involved massive shelling upon the city, as well as a campaign of sniper attacks designed to terrorize civilians. The city was blockaded, preventing necessities such as food, medicine, water, and electricity from reaching it. The shelling targeted government buildings, hospitals, UN facilities, markets, and even civilians standing in line for water.

The massacre at Srebrenica

The town of Srebrenica was designated a "safe area" by UN Security Council Resolution 819 in 1993, in response to the systematic attacks on civilians by Serb paramilitary forces. Despite this designation, siege of the town and violence against its civilians continued, with Serb forces capturing Srebrenica in July 1995. The violence reached its pinnacle with the massacre, in July 1995, of an estimated 8,000 Bosniak men and boys by a unit under the command of Mladić. This was the largest massacre of civilians in Europe since the end of

World War II, and, with its specific targeting of men and boys of a single ethnic group, was viewed by many as genocide. The small Dutch contingent of UN peacekeepers was unable to halt either the fall of Srebrenica or the massacre. Beyond their removal and massacre of the men and boys, Serb forces engaged in widespread rape of women, although, under a UN-brokered agreement, some women were evacuated to government-held territory.

The 1998–99 violence in Kosovo

As part of their counterinsurgency campaign, Serbian forces engaged in widespread violence against civilians and civilian property in Kosovo. They committed mass rapes of women, engaged in forced disappearances, and undertook efforts at ethnic cleansing and forced migration of populations. A massacre by Serb forces in Račak sparked Western condemnation and intensified diplomatic efforts and threats. By March 1999, Serbian authorities had initiated an ethnic cleansing campaign of forced population movement on a massive scale. Ethnic Albanian refugees and internally displaced persons were driven from their homes by Serbian forces at gunpoint, with many loaded onto trains and other vehicles and expelled from Kosovo. Serbian forces drove out the majority of Kosovar Albanians from urban areas such as Đjakovica. Those who were kept behind were used as human shields, compelled to accompany Serbian forces as protection against NATO airstrikes; Serbian forces also disguised themselves as nongovernmental workers to avoid being targeted by NATO aircraft. In addition, Serbian forces coerced many refugees into signing statements saying that they were leaving the province of their own free will, seized identity and property documents, and destroyed civilian property. Police systematically looted, destroyed, and burned villages, and shot livestock, with the apparent goal of depopulating certain regions, especially the villages near the border with Albania. According to the **UN High Commissioner for Refugees** (UNHCR), approximately 850,000 people fled to neighboring countries and hundreds of thousands were internally displaced. KLA forces also engaged in attacks on ethnic Serbian civilians as well as in plunder, including the looting of an Orthodox Serb monastery.

NATO forces have also been accused of violating international law for the manner in which they conducted the bombing campaign. High-level flight paths increased the risks of misdirected bombs hitting civilian targets, and indeed there were a number of nonmilitary targets, including the Chinese embassy in Belgrade and a prison. NATO also targeted what it termed "dual-use" sites, such as a state-controlled television tower. These attacks have been condemned by some human rights advocates as failing to distinguish between military and civilian targets. So too has the use of cluster munitions, some of which remain on

---

Box 6.5 ICJ judgment

"The Court concludes that the acts committed at Srebrenica falling within Article II *(a)* and *(b)* of the Convention were committed with the specific intent to destroy in part the group of the Muslims of Bosnia-Herzegovina as such; and accordingly that these were acts of genocide, committed by members of the VRS in and around Srebrenica from about 13 July 1995."

Source: International Court of Justice, *Application of the Convention on the Prevention and Punishment of the Crime of Genocide (Bosnia-Herzegovina v. Serbia and Montenegro)* (February 26, 2007).

the ground unexploded and have led to civilian deaths long after the conflict ceased. Two cases were brought before the **European Court of Human Rights** regarding the effects of cluster munitions: *Behrami and Behrami v. France* and *Saramati v. France, Norway, and Germany*. However, the Court deemed the cases inadmissible because the acts in question were considered acts of the UN, not of individual states. Serbia also attempted to bring a case before the **International Court of Justice** (ICJ) against all NATO member states in 1999, claiming that they had violated obligations under the **UN Charter** limiting use of force. However, the Court found that it lacked jurisdiction and the case was unable to proceed.

Applicable law and possible subjects of legal accountability

State responsibility for genocide

Under international law, states are obligated to take measures to prevent genocide. While many of the atrocities that occurred in the former Yugoslavia were loosely termed "ethnic cleansing," some could constitute genocide or war crimes. Chapter 10 deals in greater detail with the jurisprudence of the International Criminal Tribunal for the Former Yugoslavia, established to consider individual criminal responsibility for particular acts committed during the conflicts there. However, states may also be responsible for breaches, such as failure to prevent genocide. Bosnia-Herzegovina brought a case against Serbia before the ICJ, alleging both Serbia's responsibility for genocide and its failure to prevent genocide in the context of attacks on a variety of civilian targets. In its application, filed in March 1993 as the conflict raged, Bosnia-Herzegovina alleged:

> Not since the end of the Second World War and the revelations of the horrors of Nazi Germany's "Final Solution" has Europe witnessed the utter destruction of a People, for no other reason than they belong to a particular national ethnical, racial, and religious group as such. The abominable crimes taking place in the Republic of Bosnia-Herzegovina at this time can be called by only one name: genocide.

The application referred to plans to create a "Greater Serbia" and the siege of Sarajevo as evidence of genocidal intent and action. The court's final judgment encompassed a range of atrocities that had not yet occurred at the time of the original application, including the Srebrenica massacre.

In February 2007 the ICJ held that the acts committed in Srebrenica constituted genocide (see Box 6.5).

However, while the ICJ found that Serbia was responsible for its failure to take measures within its power to prevent the genocide (e.g., controlling its proxy Bosnian Serb leaders), it did not find that Serbia was directly responsible for the commission of genocide. It did find, though, that Serbia was obligated to cooperate with the ICTY and transfer to the court all those who had been indicted by it but were still hiding in Serbia or Republika Srpska within Bosnia-Herzegovina.

International humanitarian law

Applicable law is a critical issue in considering possible responses and individual criminal accountability for the crimes committed in the former Yugoslavia. Determining what international humanitarian law applies is complex, because the conflicts and abuses that occurred in the context of the breakup of the state require determining whether, at any given time, the conflict was internal or international. As discussed in Chapter 4, under conventional and customary international law, particularly the **Geneva Conventions** of 1949 and their additional protocols of 1977, the characterization of a conflict as internal or international affects whether commission of **grave breaches** (or war crimes) can be considered. The statute of the ICTY, as established by the UN Security Council, included grave breaches of the Geneva Conventions and of customary international humanitarian law, suggesting that the council viewed the conflict as international. However, at the time of some of the violations in Bosnia-Herzegovina, the independence of breakaway states was being contested internationally; and in the case of Kosovo, it was not recognized at all. Thus grave breaches provisions might not apply where the conflicts are treated as internal. A final obstacle is that if some of the successor states were not internationally recognized during a portion of the conflict, they could thus not be considered parties to the conventions. However, given that the content of the Geneva Conventions is now considered customary law, key provisions would continue to apply. Should grave breaches provisions apply, potential violations could be found with respect to attacks upon civilians and civilian property.

International human rights law

The situation is clearer with respect to applicable human rights law. Clearly, *jus cogens* proscriptions of genocide and torture applied to all participants in the conflicts, even if Serbia and Montenegro were not parties to the relevant conventions at the time of the conflicts. The judgment of the ICJ discussed previously confirms this assessment. Finally, **crimes against humanity** could potentially be identified in these conflicts, as those in both Bosnia-Herzegovina and Kosovo involved widespread and/or systematic attacks upon the civilian population.

Box 6.6 Legacies of conflict and demands for reconciliation

Although the Dayton Agreement formally ended the conflict in Bosnia and Croatia in 1995, and the Kosovo conflict ended in 1999, the legacies of the conflicts endure. Although there have been significant juridical responses to abuses committed during the conflict, including the ICTY, hybrid trial processes in Kosovo and more recently war crimes chambers in Bosnia and Serbia, societies remain deeply divided in each entity. In Bosnia-Herzegovina, the 2010 presidential and parliamentary elections results ran along ethnic lines, following campaigns filled with ethnic rhetoric and with few parties seeking to bridge the divide. The entity continues to have a presidency that rotates amongst ethnic groups. In Serbia, there were fierce reactions amongst ethnic hardliners but also some ordinary citizens to the trial of Slobodan Milošević and the arrests of Radovan Karadžić and Ratko Mladić by the ICTY (see Chapter 10). These developments reflect the degree to which the divides which generated the conflict or developed as a result of it have not been fully addressed. In an attempt to address the legacy of the past beyond prosecutions, civil society groups in republics of the former Yugoslavia have developed an initiative known as RECOM, which would create a region-wide truth commission. While they developed a draft statute in 2011, this would require parliamentary adoption by the relevant states, which has not taken place.

Box 6.7 Yugoslavia timeline

1918	Kingdom of Serbs, Croats, and Slovenes created.
1929	Kingdom renamed Yugoslavia.
1945	Yugoslavia becomes a communist nation, under the tight control of Josip Broz Tito.
1980	Death of Tito.
1989	Slobodan Milošević becomes president of the Serbian Republic; initiates ultranationalist rhetoric and revision of Yugoslav constitution to reduce Kosovo's autonomy.
1991	Slovenia and Croatia declare independence.
1992	*January:* Macedonia declares independence; European Union recognizes Croatia.
	April: Bosnia-Herzegovina declare independence; Serbia and Montenegro form the Federal Republic of Yugoslavia with Milošević as leader.
	May: Croatia, Slovenia, and Bosnia-Herzegovina admitted to the United Nations as member states.
1992	UNPROFOR established.
1992–96	Siege of Sarajevo.
1993	International Criminal Tribunal for the Former Yugoslavia created.
1995	Srebrenica massacre.
1995	Dayton Accords signed.
1995	Kosovo Liberation Army formed.
1998–99	Intensified fighting between KLA and counterinsurgency Serb forces deployed by Milošević in Kosovo.
1999	NATO bombing campaign in response to Serb attacks in Kosovo.
2000	Milošević steps down.
2001	*April:* Milošević arrested and charged with corruption, embezzlement, abuse of power.
	June: Milošević handed over to the ICTY.
2003	New state, a federation of Serbia and Montenegro, replaces the former Yugoslavia.
2006	*March:* Milošević dies in ICTY custody.
	May: Montenegro holds a referendum in favor of independence.
	June: Montenegro becomes a UN member.
2008	Kosovo declares independence, and is now recognized by over 100 states but is not a member of the United Nations.
2008	Radovan Karadžić arrested and handed over to the ICTY.
2011	Ratko Mladić extradited to the ICTY.

However, a further complication was that, regardless of the status of states that had newly declared themselves independent, many of the accused perpetrators were not state officials. The **Torture Convention** criminalizes torture by state officials, creating the possibility that leaders of nonstate political groupings and paramilitary forces, such as Radovan Karadžić and Ratko Mladić, might evade responsibility. These were critical issues to be addressed by the ICTY, as discussed in Chapter 10.

Discussion questions

This complex conflict raises critical questions regarding applicable law and appropriate subjects of legal proceedings. The purpose of this discussion is to consider what types of institutions might have been established to address any of the possible crimes identified through the previous discussion, not to discuss the proceedings actually under way in the ICTY (discussed in Chapter 10), nor those conducted before transnational mechanisms elsewhere (discussed in Chapter 11) or before hybrid mechanisms (discussed in Chapter 12). The questions posed here are hypothetical, in the sense that they do not take into account where individuals have actually been charged, or the death of Milošević.

Determining accountability

There may be practical difficulties in identifying specific perpetrators, or when considering prosecution of senior state or nonstate actors; demonstrating their connection to and responsibility for specific events can be problematic. Further, the distinction in international humanitarian law between international and noninternational conflict could affect when war crimes can be said to have occurred, and which actors might be held responsible.

- What law should apply in considering abuses in the former Yugoslavia? Be specific about which human rights treaties and which elements of international humanitarian law apply.
- What specific crimes can be identified, given these bodies of law? Bear in mind whether the conflict was international or noninternational at the time.
- Who might be charged for any of these crimes? Clarify the connections to the potential actors.

Prospects for addressing violations

Selection of institutions

Selecting appropriate institutions for addressing violations can be made more difficult by the fact that the country in which the crimes occurred became several countries, and by the fact that, in the case of Serbia and to a lesser degree Bosnia and Croatia, nationalists still hold significant political power.

- What are the pros and cons of establishing an international tribunal for this situation?
- Could or should domestic prosecutions be pursued in any of the new states emerging from the breakup of Yugoslavia?
- Could the International Criminal Court have jurisdiction over any of the events discussed here?

Balancing human rights and security

Because nationalists continue to hold significant power in successor states to Yugoslavia, attempts to prosecute anyone, and particularly top political leaders, might have the potential to destabilize a fragile peace agreement.

• What potential for disruption was or is present in the prosecutorial pursuit of powerful political figures?
• What charges might be brought, if any, against officials responsible for NATO's bombing campaign?

Dealing with the regional dimension

The breakup of the former Yugoslavia may have regional dimensions in two senses: first, in that an internal armed conflict became an international, regional conflict; and second, in that it had the potential to destabilize the wider Balkans and Europe.

• When would you argue that the conflict became international?
• Are there crimes that cannot be prosecuted because the conflict had not yet become international when those crimes were committed?
• Have prosecutions been affected by the dissolution of the state into several states? How or why or why not?

Group exercise

Form two groups. The first group should argue for a strategy of domestic justice, addressing the following questions:

• What are the advantages of domestic justice?
• Which particular events would you address?
• Who would you hold accountable?
• How would you manage security threats?
• What are the obstacles to applying particular laws?
• How would the elements of prosecutions, **truth commissions**, and vetting work together? What could be the problems?
• How would a lack of regional accountability affect the situation?

The second group should argue for strategy of international justice, addressing the following questions:

• Who should international justice pursue?
• What are the advantages of international justice?
• What are the challenges of international justice?
• What are the similarities and differences between the conflict in the former Yugoslavia and other situations?

Further reading

D'Amato, Anthony, "Peace vs. Accountability in Bosnia," *American Journal of International Law* vol. 88 (1994): 500–6.

Glenny, Misha, *The Fall of Yugoslavia* (London: Penguin, 1996).

Meron, Theodor, "International Criminalization of Internal Atrocities," *American Journal of International Law* vol. 89 (1995): 554–7.

Nettelfield, Lara, *Courting Democracy in Bosnia and Herzegovina* (Cambridge: Cambridge University Press, 2010).

Ramet, Sabrina P., *Thinking About Yugoslavia: Scholarly Debates About the Yugoslav Breakup and the Wars in Bosnia and Kosovo* (Cambridge: Cambridge University Press, 2005).

Rich, Roland, "Recognition of States: The Collapse of Yugoslavia and the Soviet Union," *European Journal of International Law* vol. 14, no. 1 (1993): 36–65.

Silber, Laura, and Alan Little, *The Death of Yugoslavia* (London: Penguin, 1995).

Official documents and sources

International Court of Justice, *Application of the Convention on the Prevention and Punishment of the Crime of Genocide (Bosnia and Herzegovina v. Serbia and Montenegro),* Judgment of February 26, 2007, http://www.icj-cij.org/docket/files/91/13685.pdf

United Nations, *Report of the Secretary-General Pursuant to General Assembly Resolution 53/35: The Fall of Srebrenica* (November 15, 1999), UN Doc. A/54/49.

Updated Statute of the International Criminal Tribunal for the Former Yugoslavia, (February 2008), http://www.un.org/icty

Online sources

Human Rights Watch annual reports, http://www.hrw.org

International Crisis Group reports, http://www.crisisweb.org

United Nations Department of Peacekeeping Operations sites for UNPROFOR and other related missions, http://www.un.org/depts/dpko/missions

United States Department of State human rights country reports, http://www.state.gov

7 Sierra Leone

Key points

- The civil war in Sierra Leone lasted over a decade and also included a regional dimension through the intervention of Liberia and the involvement of mercenaries.
- Civilians were systematically targeted and atrocities included the recruitment and use of child soldiers and the abduction of "wives."
- Although the Revolutionary United Front (RUF) carried out the majority of abuses, all sides to the conflict were involved in human rights violations; even so, the public perceived the Civil Defense Forces (CDF) as heroes for defending the government against the RUF.
- The peace process comprised a number of failed agreements, including a controversial provision granting combatants amnesty.

Overview

The conflict in Sierra Leone resulted in the deaths of tens of thousands, and a significant number of the population fell victim to the worst forms of human rights abuses, with rebel forces using maiming and sexual violence as a central strategy for intimidation of civilians. Fighting commenced in March 1991 and was declared officially ended in 2002, with failed attempts at peace processes in 1991, 1996, and 1999. Not only did several international actors become involved, but there were also regional implications for the conflict, since Liberia played a key role in prolonging the fighting.

This chapter examines the historical underpinnings to the conflict, the sources of human rights violations, and the social and political cleavages that led to such widespread abuses. Chapter 12 presents the legal and institutional responses to the conflict, including the creation of the Special Court for Sierra Leone (SCSL) and the Truth and Reconciliation Commission (TRC).

Background to the conflict

Postcolonial turmoil

Sierra Leone gained independence from Britain in 1961 and subsequently entered a period of great political unrest, with attempts at democratic multiparty elections resulting in successive coups and one-party government rule. The Sierra Leone People's Party (SLPP) formed the

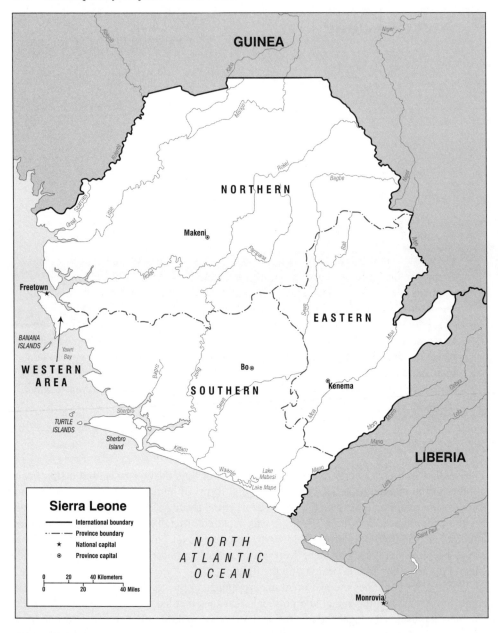

Map 7.1 Sierra Leone
Source: Adapted from the PCL Map Collection, University of Texas Libraries, the University of Texas at Austin, http://www.lib.utexas.edu/maps/africa/sierra_leone_pol_2005.jpg

Box 7.1 Key facts: Sierra Leone

Geography

Location: West Coast of Africa, sharing borders with Guinea and Liberia
Area: 71,740 km^2
Natural resources: Diamonds, titanium ore, bauxite, iron ore, gold, chromite

People

Population: 5.6 million
Ethnic groups: Temne 35%, Mende 31%, Limba 8%, Kono 5%, Kriole (Krio) 2%,
    Mandingo 2%, Loko 2%, other ethnic groups 15%
Religions: Islam 60%, Christian 10%, indigenous beliefs 30%
Languages: English (official), Temne (north), Mende (south), Krio (English-based
    Creole)
Literacy: 35.1% (male 46.9%, female: 24.4%) age 15 and older can read and write
    English, Mende, or Temne

Government

Country name: Republic of Sierra Leone
Government type: Constitutional democracy
Capital: Freetown
Administrative territorial divisions: Three provinces: Eastern, Northern, Southern;
    and the Western Area
Independence: April 27, 1961 (from the UK)

Economy

Gross domestic product: US$8.412 billion, GDP per capita US$1,400 (2012 est.)

Source: Central Intelligence Agency, *World Factbook,* Sierra Leone country profile, https://
www.cia.gov/library/publications/the-world-factbook/geos/sl.html (accessed June 2013).

first postcolonial government, from 1961 to 1967. The SLPP was supported primarily by the Mende, from the south of the country, while the opposition party, the All People's Congress (APC), was supported primarily by the Limba and Temne, from the north. Following the victory of the APC in the 1967 elections, the SLPP refused to concede its position. Siaka Stevens, the leader of the APC, was deposed by a military coup immediately following the elections, but was able to take his position as head of state in 1968 when another military coup was staged to support him. These events set a precedent for future undermining of democratic processes and paved the way for a pattern of military intervention and the weakening of state institutions.

Stevens neglected the apparatus of the state and relied instead on patronage networks to consolidate his power, culminating in the enactment of a new constitution that established Sierra Leone as a one-party state in 1978. During this period, Stevens ensured that the Limba and Temne were favored both in government and in the security forces, somewhat worsening ethnic relations. Under Stevens's leadership, accountability and transparency was progressively eroded, and the general public eventually became resigned to widespread corruption in government. Stevens's approach had far-reaching influence, filtering down to regional and local levels. After 19 years in power, in August 1985, Stevens stood down and handed power to General Joseph Momoh. Momoh's corrupt rule led to economic collapse, with a declaration in 1987 of a state of economic emergency. The combination of Momoh's and Steven's leadership undermined the country's economic development following independence, with Sierra Leone consistently ranking at the bottom of the Human Development Index since the **United Nations** (UN) introduced the index in 1990.

Emergence of the RUF

The Revolutionary United Front, led by Foday Sankoh, initiated a rebellion in March 1991 that led to a civil war lasting over a decade. The RUF claimed to be fighting to bring down the corrupt government, espousing a populist agenda that also aimed at igniting pan-African revolution. The RUF received critical support from Liberian fighters, due to Sankoh's connections with Liberian warlord Charles Taylor, who had initiated a civil war in Liberia in 1989 to overthrow Major Samuel Doe. Taylor sought to punish Sierra Leone for participating in the 1990 intervention by the Economic Community of West African States Monitoring Group (ECOMOG) against his rebellion. It was widely believed that supporting the RUF was his means of retaliation. This backing also ensured supplies of arms in addition to fighters. With this support, the initial RUF attack comprised two contingents, one entering eastern Sierra Leone and the other entering the southwest of the country. The RUF initially gained control of the eastern provincial district of Kailahun and the region of Kono, where many diamond mines were located. The fighting would continue for the next ten years, with the war intensifying in the south and east of the country and even reaching the capital, Freetown.

Meanwhile, the impact of mismanagement and corruption by both Stevens's and Momoh's regimes paved the way for removal of Momoh by the Sierra Leone Army (SLA), driven by its own grievances. Angered by a lack of pay or medical treatment, the junior officers of the SLA staged a military uprising in April 1992. Following the coup, Momoh fled to Guinea and Captain Valentine Strasser was elected head of the National Provisional Ruling Council (NPRC), the name taken by the military junta. Strasser had been part of the Sierra Leonean contingent of ECOMOG that fought against Taylor in Liberia, and had been subsequently dispatched in 1991 to fight the RUF. His initial promises included the defeat of the RUF, an end to corruption, and the return of the country to civilian rule.

The NPRC was unable to defeat the RUF, and also failed to successfully restructure and organize the army. The years of neglect under Stevens and Momoh had severely weakened the military, which suffered from depletion of numbers, with only about 3,000 troops, as well as low morale. Strasser increased recruitment, resulting in the army's expansion to an official number of 17,000 troops by 1996. However, it is not possible to confirm this estimate, since there was no accounting or census system in place. Strasser's attempt to expand the army was inadequate, however, with the SLA still ill-equipped to prevent RUF advances. Moreover, due to the rushed recruitment process, the caliber of soldiers was low, and the army increasingly colluded with the RUF at the expense of the civilian population.

During this period, the RUF developed its practice of targeting and terrorizing the civilian population, which was to become a cornerstone of its strategy. The NPRC was able to advance against the RUF only by hiring the South Africa–based private military company Executive Outcomes (EO) in April 1995. EO succeeded in pushing back the RUF to Sierra Leone's borders and, amid this conflict, presidential and legislative elections were set to be held at the Bintumani Conference Center in March of the following year. The Bintumani conference was a consultative forum for the active civil society groups that were pressing for the elections, with political representatives also participating. In January 1996, Brigadier-General Julius Maada Bio ousted Strasser as head of the NPRC following Strasser's insistence that he be nominated for the presidential election. Due to the success of Executive Outcomes, the RUF agreed to a cease-fire in January 1996 and the presidential election was held in February. The election was won by SLPP candidate and former UN official Ahmad Tejan Kabbah.

Peace talks between the RUF and the government began in April 1996 and culminated in the signing of a peace agreement in November in Abidjan, Côte d'Ivoire. Negotiations over the presence of EO and foreign troops were particularly difficult. The government finally conceded that EO would leave the country, at the RUF's request. The departure of EO proved to be instrumental in changing the balance of military power, and the RUF's retreat was short-lived. The Abidjan peace process broke down, with each side accusing the other of breaching the cease-fire. A key development at this point was the arrest of Sankoh by Nigerian authorities in Lagos for illegal possession of weapons. He was placed under house arrest until July 1998 while his field commanders in Sierra Leone ensured that RUF attacks continued.

President Kabbah mobilized traditional Mende hunters known as the Kamajors to defend their communities, and these local militia formed the basis of the Civil Defense Forces (CDF), which fought against the RUF. The CDF achieved some gains in its campaign against the RUF, but its limited victories were insufficient to secure Kabbah's personal position as president. There was still concern in the Sierra Leone Army over lack of provisions, as well as fear over the SLA's future under a civilian government. With the security situation in the country precarious due to the departure of Executive Outcomes, Kabbah was overthrown in a military coup on May 25, 1997, and went into exile. Paul Koroma was declared leader of the Armed Forces Revolutionary Council (AFRC) and claimed that the AFRC's goal was to restore peace and political stability following a lack of "commitment" from President Kabbah. Following the coup, a nine-month struggle for control in Freetown led to a large-scale evacuation of the international community and foreigners, and the exile of thousands of Sierra Leoneans.

Koroma invited the RUF to join a coalition government in June 1997, and **rule of law** completely collapsed under the AFRC/RUF junta, which was never recognized as legitimate by the population or the international community. Eventually, after a failed attempt at negotiation in which the AFRC/RUF junta reneged on a promise to restore Kabbah to power in October 1997, ECOMOG forces (Nigerian forces acting under a regional Economic Community of West African States [ECOWAS] mandate) were dispatched to Freetown. In the same month, sanctions were imposed under a **UN Security Council resolution**, Resolution 1132, aimed at preventing the supply of petrol and arms to the country and calling on the military junta to relinquish power to the democratically elected government. The pressure of sanctions encouraged the AFRC/RUF junta to sign the Conakry Accords, in which it agreed to a process of disarmament and demobilization by the end of the year and the eventual return of Kabbah. However, the RUF failed to comply with the disarmament process outlined within the accords, continuing to bring arms into Sierra Leone from Liberia and carrying out attacks on ECOMOG troops. In response, ECOMOG began a full offensive in February 1998 and finally ousted the AFRC and forced the RUF to retreat. On March 10, Kabbah returned to Freetown as president and the following week the UN embargo was lifted.

Box 7.2 **Key players in Sierra Leone**

Political parties

All People's Congress (APC)
Sierra Leone People's Party (SLPP)

Individuals

Ahmad Tejan Kabbah: SLPP candidate who won the February 1996 Presidential
    elections.
Paul Koroma: Leader of the AFRC, which deposed Kabbah in a military coup.
Milton Margai: Prime minister after the SLPP won the first elections since
    independence.
Joseph Momoh: Elected president in 1985 in a one-candidate election.
Sam Hinga Norman: Leader of the CDF. Died in 2007.
Foday Sankoh: Head of the RUF.
Siaka Stevens: Leader of the APC. Won the 1967 elections to become prime minister
    in 1968, and became president in 1971 after parliament declared Sierra Leone
    a republic.
Valentine Strasser: Head of the NPRC, the military junta that ruled following the coup
    against Momoh.
Charles Taylor: Liberian warlord who became president of Liberia in 1997. Supported
    the RUF since 1991.

Countries

Liberia: Provided support to the RUF through the actions of Charles Taylor.

Armed groups

Armed Forces Revolutionary Council (AFRC): A group of soldiers from the SLA who
    overthrew the government in 1999.
Civil Defense Forces (CDF): Assisted the government in fighting against the RUF.
Kamajors: Traditional Mende hunters who formed part of the CDF.
Revolutionary United Front (RUF): Started the civil war, and was invited to join the
    coalition government with the AFRC in 1997.

National armies

Sierra Leone Army (SLA).

International and regional missions

Economic Community of West African States Monitoring Group (ECOMOG):
    Majority of troops provided by Nigeria.
UN Mission in Sierra Leone (UNAMSIL): Expanded peacekeeping mission.
UN Observer Mission in Sierra Leone (UNOMSIL).

Other actors

Executive Outcomes: South African private military company hired by the NPRC to
    defend against the RUF.

Widespread AFRC and RUF atrocities

The RUF was, nonetheless, not defeated, and committed mass human rights abuses as it fled. The atrocities continued as the RUF turned to guerrilla tactics and carried out attacks on villages in the northern part of the country. Several waves of attacks were carried out by AFRC/RUF forces targeting civilians at random in order to induce absolute terror in the provinces. A systematic campaign of abuse and attack named Operation No Living Thing was initiated by the RUF in April 1998 and continued through the rest of the year. Despite the presence of ECOMOG forces in Freetown, enabling a level of security in the capital and the south of the country, atrocities continued in the Northern province and the Eastern province.

A factor in the continuing attacks was the trial of Foday Sankoh, following his return from house arrest in Nigeria. Although he appeared on television and called upon the RUF to stop hostilities against the civilian population, the RUF did not follow his orders and questioned whether Sankoh's statement had been coerced. Following a short trial in October 1998, Sankoh was sentenced to death after convictions on seven of nine counts of treason. However, this sentence was never carried out, as Sankoh was of greater use to the government alive during the peace process.

ECOMOG and the CDF (primarily the Kamajors) were unable to defeat the AFRC/RUF forces and prevent the violence from reaching Freetown. In January 1999 an AFRC/RUF offensive was able to break through ECOMOG defenses and capture some areas of the city, with particularly heavy attacks occurring in eastern Freetown. Civilians were specifically targeted, with killings, random amputations, and rapes widespread. Thousands of people were made homeless in Freetown and thousands more fled Sierra Leone to become refugees in neighboring countries. Although the AFRC/RUF forces were finally pushed back, the retreat was marked by the now-familiar pattern of human rights abuses and abduction of thousands of civilians as fighting continued for control of towns in the northern province and the eastern province.

Peace agreements and human rights

In the context of this military standoff, under international pressure, Kabbah and the RUF signed a peace agreement in Lomé in July 1999 following a cease-fire in May. Sankoh had been permitted to travel to Lomé in March to negotiate the terms of the agreement. Under Article 3 of the Lomé Agreement, the RUF would be allowed to organize itself as a political party. In addition, Article 9 (see Box 7.3) granted Sankoh and all combatants and collaborators "absolute and free pardon," and guaranteed them immunity from prosecution.

In addition to the pardon, the agreement also, in Article 7, made Sankoh vice president of the country and board chairman of the Commission for the Management of Strategic Resources, National Reconstruction, and Development. The agreement further outlined establishment of the Commission for the Consolidation of Peace, to which Koroma was appointed chairman, and provided for creation of the Truth and Reconciliation Commission. However, the international community found the amnesty clause of article 9 (Box 7.3) unacceptable. The United Nations made a reservation to the agreement stating that amnesty could not cover international crimes.

The Lomé Agreement also called on the **UN Security Council** to expand the mandate of the UN Observer Mission in Sierra Leone (UNOMSIL) beyond its limited monitoring role. This provision came in part from the desire of ECOWAS, and particularly Nigeria as

---

Box 7.3 The Lomé Agreement, Article 9

Pardon and Amnesty

1. In order to bring lasting peace to Sierra Leone, the Government of Sierra Leone shall take appropriate legal steps to grant Corporal Foday Sankoh absolute and free pardon.
2. After the signing of the present Agreement, the Government of Sierra Leone shall also grant absolute and free pardon and reprieve to all combatants and collaborators in respect of anything done by them in pursuit of their objectives, up to the time of the signing of the present Agreement.
3. To consolidate the peace and promote the cause of national reconciliation, the Government of Sierra Leone shall ensure that no official or judicial action is taken against any member of the RUF/SL, ex-AFRC, ex-SLA or CDF in respect of anything done by them in pursuit of their objectives as members of those organizations, since March 1991, up to the time of the signing of the present Agreement. In addition, legislative and other measures necessary to guarantee immunity to former combatants, exiles and other persons, currently outside the country for reasons related to the armed conflict shall be adopted ensuring the full exercise of their civil and political rights, with a view to their reintegration within a framework of full legality.

---

the primary troop contributor, to withdraw. The UN Mission in Sierra Leone (UNAMSIL) was established on October 22, 1999, by UN Security Council Resolution 1270 under Chapter VI of the **UN Charter**. UNAMSIL was a much larger **peacekeeping** mission and its responsibilities for supporting the peace process included assisting in the disarmament, demobilization, and reintegration (DDR) of ex-combatants, monitoring the cease-fire, facilitating humanitarian assistance, and providing support to the elections.

However, despite the detailed provisions and optimism created by the Lomé Agreement, there were successive problems in implementation. RUF and AFRC forces consistently violated the cease-fire and continued to inflict human rights abuses, including sexual violence, in the north and eastern areas of the country under their control. It was clear that the RUF would negotiate only when under military pressure, and did not truly intend to cooperate. The appointment of Sankoh to the Strategic Mineral Resources Commission did not provide the RUF with any incentive to maintain peace, because he already had significant control over diamond-mining regions.

Although the Security Council resolution initially provided for 6,000 UNAMSIL personnel, a second resolution provided for an increase of this number to 11,000 in February 2000 and finally to 13,000 in May 2000. However, provision for troops in a Security Council resolution does not mean that they are immediately deployed to the field. By May 2000, only 8,700 troops had arrived. Collapse of the peace process occurred in the same month when the RUF took 500 members of UNAMSIL hostage, leading to a renewal of the conflict and intensification of human rights abuses.

UNAMSIL numbers were increased following this incident, and British troops were dispatched to calm the situation and secure the capital. In a strange turn of events, Foday Sankoh was captured in May 2000 after being recognized by a civilian and placed in British custody. This presented the government of Sierra Leone with the challenge of deciding what to do with him. It ultimately requested the creation of a **war crimes** tribunal, which was approved by the UN Security Council in Resolution 1315. As discussed in Chapter 12, the Special Court for Sierra Leone, a **hybrid tribunal**, was created by bilateral agreement between the government and the United Nations.

A cease-fire was negotiated between the government and the RUF in November 2000 in Abuja (Abuja Agreement I; see Box 7.4), with both parties agreeing to recommence the DDR program immediately. The cease-fire was initially successful, but the RUF continued to engage in human rights abuses. Fighting spread to Guinea, threatening regional stability. A second agreement was signed in May 2001 (Abuja Agreement II), urging simultaneous disarmament of CDF and RUF forces, and withdrawal of RUF combatants from the area that cross-border attacks were coming from. Notably, the agreement did not address the issue of the Lomé amnesty or future juridical accountability. However, although the DDR process was initiated immediately and did succeed in demobilizing child soldiers, fighting and human rights abuses continued through August 2001. Following completion of the disarmament and demobilization, the conflict was declared ended and the state of emergency was lifted.

Box 7.4 Abuja Agreement I, selected articles

THE GOVERNMENT OF SIERRA LEONE AND RUF,

Reaffirming their determination to establish sustainable peace, stability and security in Sierra Leone;

Also reaffirming their commitment to the Lome Peace Agreement of 7 July 1999 as the framework for the restoration of genuine and lasting peace to the country …

HEREBY AGREE AS FOLLOWS:

1. To declare and observe a cease-fire and to halt hostilities with effect from Friday 10th November 2000 starting at 23:59 hours.
2. The parties agree to refrain from committing any acts or carrying out any activities that might constitute or facilitate a violation of the cease-fire.
3. They agree that the United Nations Mission in Sierra Leone shall supervise and monitor the cease-fire. The United Nations Mission in Sierra Leone shall also investigate and report on any acts of cease-fire violation.
4. Both parties agree that UNAMSIL shall have full liberty to deploy its troops and other personnel throughout Sierra Leone including the diamond producing areas in the discharge of its responsibilities.
5. The parties undertake, with a view to restoring the authority of the Government throughout the entire territory of Sierra Leone, to ensure free movement of persons and goods, unimpeded movement of humanitarian agencies, and of refugees and displaced persons.
6. The RUF commits itself to the immediate return of all weapons, ammunitions and other equipment seized by the RUF.
7. The two parties agree to recommence immediately the Disarmament, Demobilization and Reintegration Programme.

Done at Abuja this 10th Day of November, 2000

Sankoh and other RUF members who had been in custody were charged with a variety of crimes by the Special Court for Sierra Leone in 2003. CDF combatants were considered heroes due to their role alongside the British troops and UNAMSIL in the defeat in of the AFRC/RUF forces, and due to their overall role during the entire conflict. The leader of the CDF, Samuel Hinga Norman, retained a significant following amongst the population.

A refugee resettlement program began, and the RUF transformed itself into a political party to prepare for elections in May 2002, during which Kabbah was re-elected president with 70 percent of the vote. The DDR program was finally completed in February 2004; six years after the government of Sierra Leone had established the National Committee for Disarmament, Demobilization, and Reintegration. The Truth and Reconciliation Commission, authorized in the 1999 Lomé Agreement, began operating in July 2002, and the Special Court for Sierra Leone was established a month later. The Special Court and the relationship between it and the Truth and Reconciliation Commission are discussed in Chapter 12.

Human rights violations in Sierra Leone

Human rights violations as underlying causes of conflict

Although human rights violations such as social and economic deprivation often act as triggers to conflict, in Sierra Leone there were two further dimensions of human rights abuses that fueled the civil war. Human rights abuses were used to strengthen the RUF, which engaged in forced recruitment and abduction, particularly of child soldiers, and which terrorized the civilian population into joining the hostilities. This method perpetuated the conflict and ensured that even though the RUF lacked popular support, it had a sizable membership. Further, combatants fleeing accountability for human rights violations in neighboring countries joined the RUF.

Forced recruitment of children and other forms of coercion

Beginning 1999 there was much international reporting on the plight of child soldiers in Sierra Leone's civil war. The RUF recruited a great number of children at the beginning of the war in order to increase its numbers, and this pattern continued as it gained control over further territories, even after the signing of the Lomé Agreement, which did not provide for the demobilization of children. According to UN statistics, a total of 6,845 child soldiers were demobilized following the end of the war in 2002. However, it is unlikely that this figure represents the true number of child soldiers involved in the conflict. Further, due to the length of the conflict, many who were younger than age 16 at the time of recruitment were demobilized as adults at the end of the war. The recruitment itself was a traumatic process, with children as young as eight years old being abducted. Human rights groups have documented that the RUF forced the abductees to commit atrocities, often in their home villages, so they could not return. The RUF also forced them to take drugs. These child recruits then underwent military training, and both perpetrated and witnessed many atrocities against civilians.

The RUF used terror tactics to coerce many, both children and adults, into joining the front, through threats that mutilation and other abuses would be committed against family members. The overwhelming success of the RUF's terror tactics is demonstrated by the fact that only 10 percent of fighters indicated that they joined the front for political reasons. This was clearly not a situation in which human rights abuses by other actors generated rebel support. Rather, rebels themselves perpetuated a climate of fear to aid recruitment.

Regional fighters and accountability

Although many regional fighters joined the RUF due to bribery or coercion by fear, there were also fighters who had committed gross human rights abuses in their own countries and joined the conflict to flee accountability. These fighters traveled across West Africa as mercenaries, fueling conflict in Liberia, Sierra Leone, and Côte d'Ivoire. Even after peace was established in Sierra Leone, the existence of these mercenaries led to fears that many fighters would not disarm. Rather, there was speculation that they had simply gone to other countries and would return to fight if offered proper inducements.

Abuses causing resentment

Although the Temne and Limba were dominant in government and security forces under Stevens's rule, ethnic divisions were not the basis for conflict. Ethnic relations were strained, and ethnic balance in the government and army was an important consideration after the favoring of northerners. However, the RUF did not seek support on the grounds of ethnic discrimination. Rather, it cited corruption and poor governance by Sierra Leone's leaders since independence to initially justify its actions. The country's low ranking on the UN Human Development Index, despite its mineral wealth, indicates the level of control that a narrow elite had established over power, governance, and material wealth since 1961. The social and economic deprivation caused resentment, allowing the RUF to initially gain support in its claim that the government was corrupt and needed to be brought down. The lack of free elections, coupled with deprivation and discrimination, also enabled the RUF to claim that it was fighting on behalf of the general population. However, although these abuses of rights did take place by successive governments, support for the RUF on these issues quickly disappeared once it began to target civilians. The majority of fighters were recruited through fear or greed.

Human rights violations during the conflict

While the majority of human rights violations during the civil war in Sierra Leone can be attributed to the RUF, all parties to the conflict perpetrated abuses, and systematic, indiscriminate attacks on civilians were frequent.

Sierra Leone's Truth and Reconciliation Commission classified violations into the following categories (ordered from highest to lowest frequency of violation): forced displacement, abduction, arbitrary detention, killing, destruction of property, assault / beating, looting of goods, physical torture, forced labour, extortion, rape, sexual abuse, amputation, forced recruitment, sexual slavery, drugging and forced cannibalism. Although all parties did commit human rights violations, not all groups necessarily committed all categories of abuses. RUF and AFRC forces, however, committed all of these types of abuses at various points, and at varying levels of intensity, during the ten-year conflict.

Until 1997, the RUF was responsible for most of the violations through tactics developed specifically to provoke fear in civilians. As discussed, the RUF undertook forced recruitment and abduction, followed by a cruel and violent training and initiation process. Its campaign of terror throughout the countryside included deliberate mutilation and sexual violence, as well as indiscriminate brutal killings, and burning and looting. The viciousness of mutilations, including against children and the elderly, was used deliberately to punish those who were unwilling to cooperate with the RUF. In addition, rape and sexual violence directed at women and girls were frequent in RUF operations, and many girls were abducted as "wives" for the rebels.

However, the SLA also carried out serious abuses. In fact, significant numbers of Sierra Leonean Army soldiers colluded with the RUF rebels and were financed by "blood diamond" trade. This blurring of lines between the RUF rebels and the supposed government soldiers engendered the phenomenon known as "sobels"—soldiers by day, rebels by night. The CDF, mobilized by Kabbah against the RUF, also inducted child soldiers and executed rebels.

The scale of human rights violations increased following the AFRC coup in May 1997. Once the AFRC invited the RUF into the government, arrests, torture, and killings increased as well as repression of the press and use of the death penalty. After the AFRC/RUF military junta was finally ousted, it rampaged through the countryside carrying out widespread rape, mutilation, and amputation under Operation No Living Thing and Operation Pay Yourself. Although these violations had been occurring for over eight years, the abuses increased and became more systematic under the AFRC/RUF junta. In January 1999, this campaign of terror finally reached Freetown when AFRC/RUF forces broke through ECOMOG defenses.

The AFRC/RUF junta committed atrocities targeting both civilians and military forces. Reports from nongovernmental organizations detail mutilations of children and adults, with junta forces even cutting off their limbs; only a few victims managed to reach medical assistance, and no mercy was shown to children or the elderly. A large number of abductions were carried out, and rape and other forms of sexual violence were widespread. There was rampant destruction of property during the fighting, with many victims fleeing abroad. The TRC attributes about two-thirds of the abuses carried out from 1997 until the end of the conflict to AFRC/RUF forces.

ECOMOG forces and government troops also committed abuses throughout the conflict, and some civilians engaged in extrajudicial killings as well. Some Nigerian troops in ECOMOG have been accused of rape, looting, and heavy involvement in the diamond trade. During the attack on Freetown in January 1999, rebels and rebel collaborators were summarily executed by ECOMOG forces, members of the CDF, and the Sierra Leonean police. Reports document that the majority of executions, including of women and children, were carried out by ECOMOG. Through the duration of the conflict, government, CDF, and ECOMOG forces were known to beat noncombatants. Government and ECOMOG forces occasionally arrested and detained persons arbitrarily; prison conditions were harsh, sometimes resulting in the death of detainees. In addition, the dysfunctional judicial system caused long delays in trials and consequently prolonged detention. Other abusive actions by the government included restrictions on freedom of speech and the press, and harassment and detention of journalists.

After the Lomé Agreement, abuses continued in areas under RUF control, particularly sexual violence against women and girls, who were abducted and enslaved. These abuses increased when fighting broke out again in May 2000. In September, the RUF attacked refugee camps in Guinea, in collaboration with Liberian forces, which resulted in Guinean security forces retaliating against the Sierra Leonean refugees. The refugees had fled the conflict only to suffer further abuses in Guinea. Despite the signing of the Abuja Agreements, abuses such as rape, murder, and abduction persisted as fighting continued between the RUF and the CDF in the east of the country from June until August 2001. The RUF was reluctant during this period to release female child combatants as required under the second Abuja agreement.

The human rights situation improved steadily throughout 2001 until January 2002, when the conflict was declared ended after successful disarmament and demobilization. On January 18, a symbolic burning of weapons took place during an official ceremony to mark the conclusion of the disarmament process, and President Kabbah declared a formal end to the war.

Applicable law and possible subjects of legal accountability

International humanitarian law

Sierra Leone ratified the **Geneva Conventions** in 1965. It is clear that abuses committed during the civil war are in violation of at least two of the conventions. The RUF's targeting of civilians contravenes the Fourth Geneva Convention (Convention Relative to the Protection of Civilian Persons in Time of War), and its torture and killing of combatants violates the Third Geneva Convention (Convention Relative to the Treatment of Prisoners of War). The case could easily be made for violation of specific articles, such as Articles 33–34, which prohibit pillage, destruction of property, and the taking of hostages, and Articles 32 and 13, which protect civilians from murder, torture, or brutality. However, as outlined in Chapter 4, merely violating conventions does not create individual criminal accountability, which only comes from **grave breaches** of the conventions. There is a challenge in terming clear violations of the Geneva Conventions in Sierra Leone "war crimes," because formally the civil war is defined as a noninternational armed conflict.

Nonetheless, **Common Article 3** of the Geneva Conventions does apply to noninternational conflicts, and acts that it prohibits were clearly committed. Violations of this article include violence, murder, cruel treatment and torture, taking of hostages, humiliating and degrading treatment, and sentencing and execution without judgment by a regularly constituted court. While acts by all sides in the Sierra Leonean conflict may have contravened Common Article 3 of the Geneva Conventions, these violations are not grave breaches within it and thus do not constitute war crimes subject to individual criminal responsibility, and any prosecutions would require further legislation or conventional obligations. The violations committed by both the government and nonstate armed rebel groups are also prohibited by Additional Protocol II of the Geneva Conventions, to which Sierra Leone acceded in October 1986. Additional Protocol II includes several key provisions. Article 4 provides for fundamental guarantees, ensuring humane treatment of civilians and prohibiting murder, torture, collective punishments, hostage-taking, humiliating and degrading treatment, rape, enforced prostitution, and pillage. Particularly relevant to the conflict in Sierra Leone is the prohibition of recruitment of children younger than age 15. Article 5 provides further protection for persons whose liberty has been restricted. Article 6 articulates procedures and limitations on penal prosecutions for acts relating to armed conflict. However, the provisions of Additional Protocol II do not criminalize violation of the protections they enumerate, nor commission of acts they prohibit. Thus in internal armed conflicts, neither the Geneva Conventions (through Common Article 3) nor the provisions of Additional Protocol II provide for individualized criminal accountability such as would be available were the conflict international and had grave breaches been committed.

Nevertheless, there are two arguments that might be made to justify prosecuting war crimes committed in Sierra Leone under existing law. It could be argued that under customary law, some acts may have constituted war crimes even though the conflict was internal and as such, these would give rise to individual criminal responsibility. Violations that would fall under customary law from the conflict would include intentionally directing attacks against the civilian population and child enlistment. Further, it could be argued that the actions of the president of Liberia, Charles Taylor, internationalized the conflict. If his involvement meant the conflict could be classed as international, this would provide a basis for application of the grave breaches provision of the Geneva Conventions.

Box 7.5 **Sierra Leone timeline**

1961   Sierra Leone gains independence from Britain and SLPP forms first postcolonial government.

1967   APC victorious in elections. APC leader Siaka Stevens immediately deposed by military coup.

1968   Stevens able to take his position as head of state after another military coup.

1978   New constitution establishing Sierra Leone as a one-party state.

1985   Stevens hands power to General Joseph Momoh.

1987   Declaration of economic emergency.

1991   RUF, led by Foday Sankoh, starts rebellion against government.

1992   Military coup deposes Momoh. Captain Valentine Strasser elected head of NPRC.

1995   Arrival of Executive Outcomes from South Africa to push back RUF.

1996   *January:* Military coup forces Strasser to step down.

February: SLPP candidate Ahmad Tejan Kabbah wins presidential election.

November: Abidjan peace agreement signed.

1997   *May:* Kabbah overthrown in coup.

May: Paul Koroma declared leader of AFRC.

June: AFRC invites RUF to form coalition government.

October: UN sanctions imposed, ECOMOG forces dispatched.

October: Conakry Accords signed.

1998   *February:* Full offensive by ECOMOG drives out AFRC/RUF; retreating rebels commit massive human rights abuses.

1999   *January:* AFRC/RUF offensive captures parts of Freetown; widespread human rights ensue, with fighting and atrocities on both sides.

May: Cease-fire.

July: Kabbah and RUF sign peace agreement.

October: UNAMSIL established.

2000   *May:* 500 UNAMSIL troops taken hostage.

May: British troops arrive.

May: Foday Sankoh captured.

November: Cease-fire agreement.

2001   *May:* Second Abuja agreement signed; DDR process begins.

August: Presidential and parliamentary elections postponed.

2002   *January:* Declaration of end of war.

May: Kabbah reelected president.

International human rights law

Torture was widespread in Sierra Leone. Even though the country did not ratify the **Torture Convention** until 2001, prohibition against torture is enshrined in international customary law as a *jus cogens* norm. **Genocide** is also clearly prosecutable under international law; however, it is unlikely that the indiscriminate attacks on the civilian population could be defined as genocide, since there is relatively little evidence of ethnic bias, or intent to target a specific group. Although there were some ethnically directed killings, particularly of ethnic groups associated with specific political groups, these appear to have been small-scale, tribal and retaliatory rather than systematic or driven by intent to wipe out an entire ethnic group.

Discussion questions

In examining the possibilities for addressing human rights violations in Sierra Leone as part of the broader process of **peacebuilding**, it is important to understand the complexities of the situation. Any strategy concerning justice and reconciliation must build upon comprehensive analysis of the situation as well as the interests and motivations of all key actors involved.

Determining accountability

There are practical problems in identifying perpetrators, further hindered by the Sierra Leonean population's complex perception of the "good" and "bad" sides of the conflict.

- What strategies would be most suitable for dealing with human rights abuses committed by the CDF (such as recruitment of child soldiers)? What about the abuses committed by ECOMOG?
- Why (or why not) would prosecution of an individual such as Samuel Hinga Norman, leader of the CDF (who died in 2007), have posed any risks to the peace process?
- Should low-level perpetrators be held accountable, or is it more effective to concentrate on the highest in command?

Prospects for addressing violations

Selection of institutions

The selection of appropriate institutions of accountability is challenging. Peace negotiators, and both domestic and international actors, face significant challenges when considering possible modes of accountability.

- What is the capacity of the Sierra Leonean court system to prosecute RUF members?
- What is the potential impact of locating the Special Court for Sierra Leone, as established by Security Council Resolution 1315, within the country rather than in a "neutral" country?
- How should the Truth and Reconciliation Commission (as provided in the Lomé Agreement) and the Special Court for Sierra Leone function together? What challenges might result?

Balancing human rights and security

The concept of defining the "rebels" and "heroes" in a conflict is intertwined with the broader issue of security in the country. In any postconflict situation, the security of the country is paramount and prosecutions could be seen as undermining the peace process.

- Was the inclusion of amnesty essential in ensuring that combatants would actually stop fighting and demobilize, or could it have been more limited than the "absolute and free pardon" offered?
- In light of the failure of the Lomé Agreement, what might be discerned about the motivations of the RUF? What else could have been offered to the rebel forces?
- Who has the authority to represent groups during **peace negotiations**, and how should this be decided?

Dealing with the regional dimension

When considering the conflict in Sierra Leone, it is important to recognize the specific challenges posed by regional implications.

- Should Charles Taylor be immune to prosecution for acts he committed while president of Liberia?
- With the disappearance of lower-level perpetrators across borders, which other countries could the Sierra Leonean peace and accountability processes affect?
- When conflict in a region is as intertwined as it has been in West Africa, can the issues of human rights accountability or peace negotiations be dealt with on a country-by-country basis?

Group exercise

Form two groups. One group should deem international justice as the only way to achieve accountability; the other group should deem domestic justice as more legitimate. Debate the regional implications of the conflict in Sierra Leone, as well as the wishes of the population.

Further reading

Hirsch, John, *Sierra Leone: Diamonds and the Struggle for Democracy* (Boulder, CO: Lynne Rienner, 2001).

International Crisis Group, "Sierra Leone: Time for a New Military and Political Strategy" (April 11, 2001), http://www.crisisgroup.org/en/regions/africa/west-africa/sierra-leone/028-sierra-leone-time-for-a-new-military-and-political-strategy.aspx

Mitton, Kieran, "Irrational Actors and the Process of Brutalization: Understanding Atrocity in the Sierra Leonean Conflict (1991–2002)," *Civil Wars* vol. 14, no. 1 (2012): 104–22.

Pugh, Michael, and Neil Cooper, with Jonathan Goodhand, *War Economies in Regional Context* (Boulder, CO: Lynne Rienner 2004), Chapter 4, "Sierra Leone in West Africa".

Reno, William, *Warlord Politics and African States* (Boulder, CO: Lynne Rienner, 1999).

Sriram, Chandra Lekha, and Zoe Nielsen (eds), *Exploring Subregional Conflict: Opportunities for Conflict Prevention* (Boulder, CO: Lynne Rienner, 2005), Chapter 3.

Official documents and sources

Abuja Ceasefire Accord, November 10, 2000, http://www.sierra-leone.org/ceasefire1100.html

Peace Agreement between the Government of Sierra Leone and the Revolutionary United Front of Sierra Leone (Lomé Agreement), July 7, 1999, http://www.usip.org/files/file/resources/collections/peace_agreements/sierra_leone_07071999.pdf

The Final Report of the Truth Commission of Sierra Leone, http://www.sierraleonetrc.org

United Nations, Report of the Security Council mission to Sierra Leone (October 16, 2000), UN Doc. S/2000/992.

United Nations, Reports of the Secretary General on UNAMSIL, http://www.un.org/en/peacekeeping/missions/past/unamsil/UnamsilR.htm

United Nations, Security Council Resolution 1270 (on the establishment of UNAMSIL), (October 22, 1999), UN Doc. S/RES/1270.

United Nations, Security Council Resolution 1315 (on the establishment of a special court), (August 14, 2000), UN Doc. S/RES/1315.

Online sources

United Nations Mission in Sierra Leone (UNAMSIL), http://www.un.org/en/peacekeeping/missions/past/unamsil/index.html

United Nations Observer Mission in Sierra Leone (UNOMSIL), http://www.un.org/en/peacekeeping/missions/past/unomsil/Unomsil.htm

8   The Democratic Republic of Congo

Key points

- The conflict in the Democratic Republic of Congo (DRC) is particularly complex, as is assignment of responsibility for crimes, given multiple armed groups and support provided to them by a number of neighboring states.
- Exploitation and access to the country's natural resources have partly driven the conflict; multinational corporations may bear some responsibility for human rights abuses.
- Sexual and gender-based violence has been used by all groups systematically, and on a massive scale, and some violations committed during the conflict might be characterized as ethnic cleansing or **genocide**.
- Despite a number of peace agreements and the presence of a **United Nations** (UN) mission, violence and human rights violations continue in the east, maintaining the instability in the region.

Overview

The conflict in the Democratic Republic of Congo, which began in 1996, has been among the bloodiest in recent history. It is also a particularly complex one, comprising several African countries, numerous rebel armed groups, and the pursuit of important economic interests by every party involved. Local and regional conflicts did not end after the peace agreements of 2002, and violence still continues in parts of the country, particularly in the east. This chapter examines the historical background of the conflict, human rights violations as both causes and consequences, the **international humanitarian law** and **international human rights law** applicable to the abuses committed, and prospects for accountability. Chapter 13 analyzes in greater depth the prosecutorial activity by the **International Criminal Court** (ICC) in relation to the crimes committed in the Ituri region.

Background to the conflict

From colonial times to post–Cold War

The recent history of the DRC has been affected by the exploitation, trade, and plundering of its vast resource wealth, and has strong roots in the dynamics established during colonial rule. From 1885 to its independence on June 30, 1960, the DRC was under Belgian rule and

Map 8.1 Democratic Republic of Congo
Source: Adapted from the PCL Map Collection, University of Texas Libraries, the University of Texas at Austin, http://www.lib.utexas.edu/maps/africa/congo_demrep_pol98.jpg.

known as the Congo. During this period the main interest of the administrating authorities lay in the exploitation of natural resources, and the period was characterized by dismantling of the social and political cohesion of indigenous groups and disinterest by colonial rulers in establishing a viable political unit in the country.

Anticolonial, national sentiment in the Congo emerged in the mid-1950s and led to the formation of several political parties that channeled claims for independence. In May 1960, a parliamentary election took place and in June, Belgium was forced to accept the independence of the Congo. Patrice Lumumba became Congo's first prime minister. Shortly after the formation of the government, a secessionist movement broke out in Katanga province, backed by Belgian mining interests. In October 1961, Lumumba, dismissed by his allies in government, was arrested, handed over to his enemies, and killed.

Box 8.1 **Key facts: Democratic Republic of Congo**

Geography

Location: Central Africa, bordered by Republic of Congo to the northwest; Central African Republic and Sudan to the north; Uganda, Rwanda, Burundi, and Tanzania to the east; Zambia and Angola to the south

Area: Total area 2,345,410 km^2, land area 2,267,600 km^2, water area: 77,810 km^2

Natural resources: Cobalt, copper, niobium, tantalum, petroleum, industrial and gem diamonds, gold, silver, zinc, manganese, tin, uranium, coal, hydropower, timber

People

Population: 75.5 million

Ethnic groups: Over 200 African ethnic groups, majority of which are Bantu; four largest tribes (composing 45% of population) are Mongo, Luba, and Kongo (all Bantu), and Mangbtu-Azande (Hamitic)

Religions: Roman Catholic 50%, Protestant 20%, Kimbanguist 10%, Muslim 10%, other (including syncretic sects and indigenous beliefs) 10%

Languages: French (official), Lingala (trade), Kingwana (dialect of Kiswahili or Swahili), Kikongo, Tshiluba; more than 400 Sudanese and Bantu dialects spoken

Literacy: 66.8% (male 76.9%, female 57%) aged 15 and older can read and write French, Lingala, Kingwana, or Tshiluba;

Government

Country name: Democratic Republic of Congo (formerly: Congo Free State, Belgian Congo, Zaire)

Government type: Republic

Capital: Kinshasa

Administrative territorial divisions: One city: Kinshasa, formerly Léopoldville; ten provinces: Bandundu, Bas-Congo, Équateur, Kasaï-Occidental, Kasaï-Oriental, Katanga (capital: Lubumbashi), Maniema, Nord Kivu (capital: Goma), Orientale (capital: Kisangani)—which includes the Ituri region (capital, Bunia) and Haut-Uele, (capital, Isiro)—and Sud-Kivu (capital: Bakavu). According to the 2005 Constitution, the administrative divisions were to be subdivided into twenty-six new provinces by 2009 but this has yet to be implemented.

Independence: June 30, 1960 (from Belgium)

Economy

Gross domestic product: US$27.53 billion, GDP per capita US$400; real growth rate 7.1% (2012)

Unemployment rate: Not available

Source: Central Intelligence Agency, *World Factbook,* Democratic Republic of Congo country profile,
https://www.cia.gov/library/publications/the-world-factbook/geos/cg.html (last accessed April 2013)

Western support allowed Colonel Joseph Mobutu to come to power, following a military coup on November 24, 1965. He changed his name to Mobutu Sese Seko Kuku Ngbendu Wa Banga ("the all-powerful warrior who goes from conquest to conquest leaving fire in his wake"), and that of the country to Zaire. His regime was among the most corrupt and dictatorial in the history of the sub-Saharan region. He drove the country to economic disaster through the so-called Zairenization program, nationalizing foreign-owned commercial and industrial assets and distributing them to those close to the regime, Zaire became a center for corruption and the theft and smuggling of natural resources.

After the end of the Cold War in 1989, Western nations, particularly the United States, Belgium, and France, distanced themselves from Mobutu and terminated most economic aid. In 1996, President Mobutu's regime, weakened within and backed by few external supporters, was confronted by a rebellion by the Alliance of Democratic Forces for the Liberation of Congo-Zaire (Alliance des Forces Démocratiques pour la Libération du Congo-Zaïre—ADFL), under the leadership of Laurent Kabila and backed by neighboring Uganda and Rwanda. The latter backed Kabila as part of its attempt to defeat Hutu rebels who had fled to the DRC after the 1994 genocide in Rwanda. Mobutu was ousted in May 1997 in what is known as the First Congo War. He fled to Rabat, Morocco, where some months later he died. Kabila took power and renamed the country the Democratic Republic of Congo.

However, Rwanda and Uganda were only temporarily allies to the DRC. In August 1998, war broke out again and Rwandan troops invaded eastern Congo, initiating what was termed the Second Congo War. Rwanda justified its activities by invoking its own genocide, claiming it necessary to eliminate bases of Hutu extremists on Congolese territory. Uganda, similarly, claimed that Kabila's regime had failed to stop incursions of Hutu extremists into its territory, and occupied the Ituri region for four years. These countries not only intervened directly, but also backed domestic Congolese rebel forces. Rwanda supported the Congolese Tutsi rebel group Rally for Congolese Democracy (Rassemblement Congolais pour la Démocratie—RCD), while Uganda supported the Movement for the Liberation of the Congo (Mouvement de Libération du Congo—MLC).

Africa's war

Following the invasion of Rwandan and Ugandan troops, Kabila called on Zimbabwe, Angola and Namibia for help. Each country's motives for intervening in the war were different, but all had an interest in securing access to Congolese resources. In this bloody five-year conflict, an estimated 3–3.5 million people died, and gross atrocities were perpetrated against the civilian population. Some organizations estimate that the actual number of deaths was closer to 5 million. Most of the victims died from war-related diseases, lack of medical assistance, and starvation. To a greater or lesser degree, apart from the government of the DRC, the following African countries intervened in the conflict: Rwanda, Uganda, Burundi, Zimbabwe, Angola, Namibia, Chad, and Sudan. This involvement led the conflict to become known as "Africa's war." A multiplicity of rebel forces were also involved (see Box 8.2). Resources proved to be important fuel to the conflict in the DRC, which for this reason is often largely depicted as one of greed. However, the conflict was also driven by grievances, or at least the mobilization of fears and grievances. This is most notable in the justifications offered by Rwanda and Uganda for their interventions in the DRC.

During the conflict the country was split into three areas, each effectively controlled by a distinct group. The government controlled the capital and most of central, southern, and

Box 8.2 **Key players in the Second Congo War**

Individuals

Joseph Kabila: Son of Laurent. Took power after his father was assassinated.
Laurent Kabila: Ousted Mobutu, backed by both Rwanda and Uganda.
Laurent Nkunda: Leader of the CNDP in North Kivu.
Mobutu Sese Seko: Dictator. Ruled the country from 1965 to 1997.

Countries

Angola, Burundi, Chad, Namibia, Rwanda, Sudan, Uganda, Zimbabwe.

Armed groups

AFDL (Alliance des Forces Démocratiques pour la Libération du Congo-Zaïre): rebel
   movement that brought Laurent Kabila to power, backed by Uganda and Rwanda.
APC (Armée du Peuple Congolais, or Armée Populaire Congolaise): armed wing of the
   RCD-K-ML, led by Mbusa Nyamwisi.
CNDP (Congrès National pour la Défense du Peuple): split faction of the RCD, operated
   in North Kivu under Laurent Nkunda first and under Bosco Ntaganda later.
FLC: merger of the MLC, RCD-ML, and RCD-N, formed under Ugandan tutelage
   in November 2000 and headed by the MLC's Jean-Pierre Bemba. Collapsed in
   August 2001.
FNI (Front des Nationalistes et Intégrationnistes): a Lendu group.
Mai-Mai: local militia recruited along tribal lines in eastern Congo, supported Kabila
   during the war.
MLC (Mouvement de Libération du Congo): formed in 1998 with extensive Ugandan
   backing, headquartered in the northern DRC's Equateur province, and led by
   Jean-Pierre Bemba.
NALU (National Army for the Liberation of Uganda): Ugandan rebel group now largely
   wiped out.
RCD (Rassemblement Congolais pour la Démocratie): Rwandan-backed rebel group,
   led by Azarias Ruberwa.
RCD-Goma: Faction of the RCD.
RCD-Kisangani: party formed by Wamba dia Wamba when he was ousted from the
   original RCD in May 1999, became the RCD-ML in September 1999.
RCD-K-ML: Kisangani faction of the RCD-ML, led by Mbusa Nyamwisi, controlled
   areas in North Kivu and Ituri. Allied with Mayi-Mayi and Kinshasa. Also the party
   of Jean-Baptiste Tibasima.
RCD-ML (Rassemblement Congolais pour la Démocratie–Mouvement de Libération):
   formed in September 1999 by Wamba dia Wamba after he and Ugandan forces
   were ousted from Kisangani by Rwanda.
RCD-N (Rassemblement Congolais pour la Démocratie–National): formed during the
   splintering of the RCD-ML in mid-2000, led by Roger Lumbala. Originally based
   in Bafwasende. Now allied with the MLC.

UPC (Union des Patriotes Congolais): Hema-dominated group which came to prominence after taking control of Bunia in August 2002. Sometimes referred to as UPC-FRP (Front for Reconciliation and Peace).

National armies

FAC (Congolese Armed Forces): Created by Laurent Kabila in 1997, led by Joseph Kabila. Integrated into the FARDC in 2004.
FARDC (Armed Forces of the Democratic Republic of Congo): New, integrated Congolese national army established in 2004, comprising the former FAC and the rebel groups that integrated during the peace process.
FAZ (Zairian Armed Forces): Zaire's national army, led by Mobutu.
UPDF (Ugandan People's Defense Forces): Uganda's national army, led by Brigadier James Kazini.

International Missions

Artemis: French-led EU mission in Ituri in 2003.
UN Organization Mission in the Democratic Republic of Congo (MONUC). Peacekeeping mission first deployed in 2000. Renamed Stabilization Mission in the Democratic Republic of Congo (MONUSCO) in 2010.

western Congo; the MLC, the rebel group backed by Uganda, controlled northern areas in Équateur province; and the RCD, reliant on Rwanda, controlled Maniema province, most of the Kivus, and parts of Orientale, Kasaï Oriental, and Katanga provinces.

The United Nations, the Organization of African Unity (OAU) (now the **African Union** [AU]), and the **South African Development Community** (SADC) all sought to support and facilitate negotiations to end the conflict. The key state parties involved, namely Rwanda, Uganda, Zimbabwe, Angola, and Namibia, in addition to the DRC itself, and later joined by **nonstate actors**, signed a cease-fire at Lusaka in July 1999. The accord called for the withdrawal of all foreign forces from the DRC and the deployment of UN **peacekeeping** forces to monitor its implementation.

The **UN Security Council** established the UN Organization Mission in the Democratic Republic of Congo (MONUC) in 2000. The Security Council, recognizing the role of natural resources in the war, established a panel of experts in June 2000 to address the illegal exploitation of the Congo's natural resources. In a landmark report in October 2002, the panel highlighted the role of Uganda, Rwanda, and a host of national and multinational corporations in the looting of the Congo's natural resources and the perpetuation of the war.

Despite the 1999 Lusaka Accord and the deployment of MONUC, violence continued and in January 2001 Laurent Kabila was assassinated. His son, Joseph Kabila, took power, becoming president and commander of the armed forces. Joseph Kabila's government enjoyed a warm welcome from Western and African countries, and was offered economic aid by the European Union (EU) and the International Monetary Fund (IMF). **Peace negotiations** were then revived.

The Inter-Congolese Dialogue and the transitional government

On April 19, 2002, the parties to the conflict met in Sun City, South Africa, to resume the process that had begun in 1999 in Lusaka. The peace process was developed through a series of small agreements, known as the Inter-Congolese Dialogue, that led to the adoption of an inclusive peace agreement on December 17, 2002: the Pretoria Accord, also known as the Global and All-Inclusive Agreement. This accord was signed by the eight parties to the peace talks: the former DRC government, the MLC, the RCD, the political opposition, civil society, the Mai-Mai, the RCD-ML, and the RCD-N. In separate agreements signed in July and September 2002, Rwanda and Uganda respectively agreed to withdraw their forces from the territory of the DRC if Interahamwe members and Hutu extremists in the Congo were apprehended, disarmed, and repatriated. It was also agreed that the withdrawal of Ugandan troops from the Ituri region would be followed by the creation of the Ituri Pacification Committee, comprising a group of local parties, which would assume control over administrative and security arrangements in the region.

The peace agreements included the creation of a transitional government to rule in the run-up to the elections, in which President Joseph Kabila would share power with four vice presidents: one from each of the two main rebel movements, one from the government, and one from the political opposition. On June 30, 2003, Joseph Kabila announced the formation of a government of national unity, with the government controlling the interior and finance ministries, the Rwandan-backed RCD controlling the economy and defense ministries, and the Ugandan-backed MLC controlling the budget and foreign affairs ministries. A civilian assumed control of the mining ministry.

The peace agreements also foresaw the integration of rebel groups into the new national army, the Armed Forces of the Democratic Republic of Congo (Forces Armées du République Démocratique du Congo [FARDC]). Kabila's army, the Congolese Armed Forces (Forces Armées Congolaises [FAC]), integrated into the new FARDC. The RCD was given important roles in the land forces and in the defense ministry, and the MLC was given more marginal roles in the naval forces but important commands in financial matters. However, some RCD units later mutinied in North and South Kivu. Most of the Kivu Mai-Mai militias, allied to Kabila during the war, were also given positions in the army and government. However, they split into several groups once in power, and many of the field commanders have since been marginalized. The Ituri militia and the Mai-Mai of northern Katanga did not sign the peace agreement and have since integrated into the army in smaller numbers following deals between the transitional government and various commanders. Most of the RCD-N troops have spontaneously demobilized and joined the new national army, and parts of the RCD-ML have also integrated or demobilized. The integration of the army has been slow and not fully effective, and there are claims that its position is precarious, posing security risks.

The transitional government held a successful constitutional referendum on December 18, 2005, and elections for the presidency, National Assembly, and provincial assemblies took place in 2006. Kabila's Alliance of the Presidential Majority (Alliance de la Majorité Présidentielle [AMP]) won the majority of seats in the National Assembly and in eight of the eleven provincial assemblies. The National Assembly was installed in September 2006, Kabila was inaugurated as President in December, and the provincial assemblies were constituted in early 2007.

Western countries generally supported President Kabila, and the peace process received significant international support, particularly through the International Committee to Accompany the Transition, based in Kinshasa, which comprised ambassadors from the

United States, France, the United Kingdom, Belgium, South Africa, China, Angola, Canada, Russia, the European Union, and the African Union, and was chaired by the **Special Representative of the Secretary-General** (SRSG) for the DRC. However, this interest was perhaps not completely altruistic. Some of the Western nations that supported the process also sought to secure control over strategic reserves of copper, cobalt, and other minerals. Some were also interested in restricting China's future access to these resources.

While violence did not end in the east of the country after the peace agreement and subsequent elections, and in fact was renewed in some areas, the bulk of the country has remained relatively stable. In November 2011, presidential and parliamentary elections were held and Kabila won another term. However, the results were disputed by opposition parties.

Continuation and renewal of violence

Despite the peace accords of 2002, the violence continued in several parts of the country, including in the east, in Ituri and the Kivus, and in the south, in Katanga. While these conflicts were at times depicted as marginal confrontations between local groups and warlords, they had brutal consequences for civilians, who suffered severe human rights violations as patterns of abuse that emerged during the nationwide conflict.

Ethnic strife between the Lendu and Hema groups in Ituri was exacerbated during Uganda's four-year occupation of the region. As part of the peace accords, Uganda agreed to withdraw its forces in September 2002 and started to do so in late April 2003, leaving a significant security vacuum in the region. The long-simmering conflicts over land and mineral wealth, as well as the ethnic rivalries, led to widespread violence and massacres during 2002 and 2003, which not even UN troops were able to stop. The armed groups who participated in the conflict developed on the basis of ethnic loyalties. The two main ones were: the Union of Congolese Patriots (Union des Patriotes Congolais [UPC]), formed predominantly by northern Hemas and the Nationalist and Integrationist Front (Front des Nationalistes et Intégrationnistes [FNI]), comprising mainly Lendus. Each group was militarily and politically supported by the government of the DRC, and by Uganda and Rwanda, respectively.

On May 5, 2003, firefights broke out between armed Lendu and Hema groups in several areas of Bunia, the capital of the Ituri region, targeting MONUC and other UN offices and provoking panic among residents. Both groups sought control of the town in anticipation of the complete withdrawal of Ugandan forces. Following this outbreak, the French led an emergency mission, Artemis, which under EU authority was deployed to the province in July 2003. Artemis managed to contain the situation, which allowed a more robust UN mission to return. It was not until mid-2004, however, that militia groups in Ituri signed an agreement with the government to disarm and participate in the transitional process. After intense work from MONUC, the militias started demobilizing; in April 2007, the FNI, was the last militia to disarm.

Violence in the Kivus continues today. Some dissident members of the former Rwandan-backed RCD rebel movement, which had not been integrated into new national army, briefly occupied Bukavu (South Kivu) on the Rwandan border in June 2004. Their pretext was to save local Congolese Tutsis. The violence, which targeted civilians, resulted in 20,000 to 30,000 people fleeing to refugee camps in Rwanda and Burundi. Following the summary execution of 160 Congolese Tutsi refugees in one of these camps, the UN-operated camp of Gatumba (near Bujumbura, inside Burundi), Rwanda and Burundi threatened intervention in the DRC, either directly or through proxies. Also, in August 2004, following the Gatumba refugee camp massacre, the RCD leadership withdrew from the transition process. It was reported in May 2005 that Rwandan Hutu rebels based in eastern Congo were responsible for hundreds of summary executions, rapes, beatings, and hostage-taking of Congolese civilians in the territory of Walungu (South Kivu). Fighting continued and, in August 2008, intensified greatly, especially in North Kivu. General Laurent Nkunda, who had been integrated into the national army in 2003, left his position and retreated to North Kivu. Backed by Rwanda, Nkunda led a faction of the RCD-Goma, transformed into the National Congress for the Defense of the People (Congrès National pour la Défense du Peuple [CNDP]), in its fighting with ethnic Hutu Rwandans in the area, the Congolese government, and the government-backed Mai-Mai militias. More than a million people fled North Kivu, and the local population was subjected to horrific human rights abuses, while MONUC was unable to stabilize the area and protect them. The treatment of women and girls was particularly harsh, with all the parties, rebel groups and government forces, perpetrating sexual abuses. In November 2008 President Kabila and President Kagame of Rwanda negotiated a secret agreement, which resulted in Rwanda dropping its support for General Nkunda and both countries launched a joint operation against him in January 2009. This joint operation was an offensive against both the CNDP and the Rwandan Hutu militia group operating in the North and South Kivus known as the FDLR (Forces Démocratiques pour la Liberation du Rwanda), which the government of the DRC had previously backed. Nkunda was soon arrested in Rwandan territory. The rapprochement between Rwanda and the DRC was also made official by the re-establishment of diplomatic relations.

On 23 March 2009 the CNDP, now under the leadership of Bosco Ntaganda, signed a peace agreement (referred to as the M23 peace agreement) with the DRC government which included provision for the integration of CNDP soldiers into the Congolese army and the conversion of the group into a political party. The agreement included the commitment of the government to pass a law of amnesty to cover the period from June 2003 to March 2009; the liberation of CNDP prisoners, which the CNDP itself would identify. Among those suspected of war crimes was Ntaganda himself, for whom the ICC had issued an arrest warrant in 2006 for charges relating to his involvement in crimes committed in Ituri (see Chapter 13). In just a few weeks 18,000 fighters from the CNDP and other armed groups were integrated into the armed forces. At the same time, the FDLR continued to resist forcible disarmament and formed alliances with other Congolese militias that refused integration into the national army.

The Kivus are rich in valuable minerals. The power struggles between the government, the CNDP, the FDLR and Mai-Mai groups have all involved control over lucrative mines. In April 2012, violence returned to the Kivus, when Bosco Ntaganda mutinied and started a new rebellion, leading the new group M23. M23 developed its own administration and finance systems in parts of North Kivu. Observers on the ground accused Rwanda of backing the group, but both the M23 and Rwanda deny this claim. Meanwhile, Mai-Mai groups have continued to expand in rural areas and have exacerbated ethnic tensions by committing atrocities. In an unexpected turn, Ntaganda turned himself in at the US embassy in Kigali, on 17 March 2013 and was sent to the ICC.

Terms of the 2002 peace accords and attempts at accountability

As discussed, the new government was installed before the peace process was completed and before local violence had ended. The 2002 peace accords contained power-sharing provisions, including many of the main parties to the conflict within the government as well as a unified national army, in the hopes of stabilizing the state. Integration of rebel forces with the national army proved a challenge as explained, but power-sharing was maintained in large part due to significant support by the international community.

The Inter-Congolese Dialogue did address the importance of prosecuting human rights abusers, passing resolutions on the creation of both an international criminal tribunal and a **truth commission**. However, its discussion of these mechanisms provoked tension and the formal peace accords do not mention them, or other accountability mechanisms, though they have not tried to prevent accountability through amnesties and pardons.

Following a resolution adopted on December 20, 2002, by the Inter-Congolese Dialogue, the transitional government passed a law on June 30, 2003, establishing a truth and reconciliation commission. Lack of sufficient consultation and an apparent politicization of the process of commissioner appointments have been cause for concern. Equally, a national human rights observatory and an anticorruption commission were tainted by their inclusion of known human rights abusers as members.

Another resolution adopted during the Inter-Congolese Dialogue allowed the transitional government to request the UN Security Council to establish an international criminal court for the DRC, modeled on the **International Criminal Tribunal for Rwanda** (ICTR) and the **International Criminal Tribunal for the Former Yugoslavia** (ICTY). President Kabila also raised the topic of a tribunal in an address to the **UN General Assembly** in 2003, but no further steps were taken. The lack of support by the UN itself toward these options for accountability has now effectively ruled them out.

The DRC's domestic judicial system presents few options for accountability. In the wake of the conflict, the judiciary has been seriously damaged, and suffers from widespread corruption. Crimes committed during the armed conflict fall under the jurisdiction of military tribunals rather than civilian courts. There is some doubt from the international community and domestic observers that such tribunals will impose accountability for human rights violations, particularly considering that the peace process included the integration of rebel groups into the national army.

During the pacification of the Ituri region there were some attempts to address the causes of the conflict and the human rights violations it generated. These included the Ituri Pacification Committee, created by the Luanda Accords of September 2002. These accords also established a human rights committee, but it functioned purely to educate the populace. The violations in the North and South Kivus raised numerous international demands for accountability from international human rights organizations, with special attention given to the severe sexual and gender-based violence suffered by women and girls. In response to international pressure, the government created "mobile courts" to prosecute those accused of sexual violence. These courts have had some success in bringing justice to rural areas and fighting impunity. The Open Society Justice Initiative (a funder of the courts) reported in 2012 that one of the gender courts operating in South Kivu held 20 court sessions in remote areas of the province, concluding 382 cases, with 204 convictions for rape, 82 convictions for other offenses, and 67 acquittals in its first 36 months of operation (from October 2009 through October 2012). Sentences for rape ranged from 1 to 20 years imprisonment, with significant financial penalties added in some cases. Despite the doubts concerning military tribunals, some individuals have been successfully prosecuted. In February 2011 Kibbi Mutware, a commanding officer of the Congolese army, was convicted in a mass rape case and sentenced to 20 years imprisonment. This was the first conviction of a commanding officer for sexual violence in eastern Congo.

Accountability has largely taken place outside of the country. Significant strides have been made in addressing crimes committed in the DRC with the referral of the situation in Ituri to the ICC, as discussed in Chapter 13. Nonetheless, the Court will not be able to consider many of the atrocities committed in the DRC, as the majority predate the 2002 entry into force of the ICC's Rome Statute, with some dating back to 1960.

There have also been several attempts to bring claims for accountability before foreign courts using the principle of universal jurisdiction. A Belgian court issued an arrest warrant for the foreign minister of the DRC, accusing him of incitement to genocide, there is an ongoing case in Spanish courts (see Box 8.5) and in 2011 the Rwandan Hutu rebel Ignace Murwanashyaka, former leader of the FDLR, went on trial in Germany accused of crimes against humanity. The DRC has strongly resisted these attempts at justice. In 2000 it brought a case before the ICJ against Belgium concerning the arrest warrant. In 2002 the ICJ ruled that Belgium failed to recognize the immunity of the DRC foreign minister in the Case Concerning the Arrest Warrant of 11 April 2000 (*Democratic Republic of the Congo v. Belgium*).

Human rights violations and in the DRC

Human rights violations as underlying causes of conflict

It is clear that resources constitute one of the primary causes of conflict in the DRC. Many actors, including foreign countries, nonstate armed groups, and multinational corporations, have sought to exploit the country's vast resources, including gold, oil, timber, and coltan, which have been a source of competition and violence. In Ituri and Haut Uele districts, gold mines have been the site of significant conflict and human rights abuses, driven in part by plunder by forces from neighboring Uganda. In 2005, **Human Rights Watch** claimed that more than 60,000 people had died due to direct violence in the northeastern region of the Congo. Human rights abuses connected with the exploitation of gold, particularly from 1998 to 2003, when Ugandan soldiers controlled the area, included coerced labor, beatings, and arbitrary arrest of resistant gold-miners, and several massacres of civilian populations in the area. Irresponsible mining practices caused the death of over a hundred people following the collapse of the Gorumbwa mine. The Ugandan army is also alleged to have plundered a ton of Congolese gold, valued at over US$9 million. The plundering of the DRC mines continues, especially in the east, with devastating consequences for the population which lives in surrounding areas.

However, the conflict in the DRC has been driven not only by resources, but also by human rights abuses and grievances. Abuses have fomented the conflict in at least two ways, through domestic grievances and through transborder intervention.

Domestic grievances

Though demands for access to resources and political power have driven the conflict in the DRC, the impact of real and perceived slights in a country with some 200 distinct ethnic groups has also been an important factor. The violence in Ituri, for example, has been perpetuated by tensions between the Hema and Lendu populations in the region. These tensions have significant roots in colonial favoritism, in claims over land and fishing rights, and in the perceptions of discrimination held by each group. The 2002–2004 conflict in the region developed out of a local land dispute between the Hema and Lendu ethnic groups in 1999, and was exacerbated by the intervention and occupation of the area by Uganda. The armed groups who participated in the conflict represented the ethic divide and originated as ethnic self-help organizations. The continued violence in North and South Kivu is directly related to ethnic tensions following the Rwandan genocide. The CNDP was originally established to defend the interests of the Tutsi community in the east, including against the Hutu-led FDLR. When the CNDP integrated into the army in 2009 their new influence was resented by leaders of other communities, who feared that they would be disadvantaged in future elections.

Transborder intervention by neighbor countries

Defense of human rights, particularly protection of kin populations across borders and defense against attacks on their own populations, has served as a pretext for both Rwanda and Uganda to intervene and even occupy parts of DRC territory. Rwanda's interventions have been driven by its desire to defeat Rwandan Hutu rebels and protect Tutsis following the genocide in 1994. Its participation in the conflict in the Kivus, first backing the RDC in the Bukavu occupation and later supporting the CNDP in North Kivu (allegedly to contain the FDLR) affected both the conflict and human rights abuses. Rwanda was also accused of supporting the M23 rebellion, which both the Rwandan government and the rebels deny.

When Uganda intervened in and occupied Ituri province in 1999, it argued that it was seeking to protect itself from incursions by the Lord's Resistance Army, a Ugandan rebel group that was operating within the eastern DRC. While Uganda has occasionally cited protection of vulnerable populations as a rationale for its intervention, it has also profited considerably, exporting diamonds and gold from the DRC worth millions of dollars. Rwanda has also hoped to similarly exploit resources, although it has been less successful. While both countries have cited human rights concerns as justifications for their incursions, their armed forces, as well as the armed groups to which they offered support, have committed grave atrocities.

Human rights violations emerging from and transforming the conflict

The scale of human suffering that has resulted from the war in the DRC is vast. As mentioned, casualties could number more than the officially estimated 3–3.5 million deaths, reaching up to 5 million, and the atrocities have been horrendous. Violence in the east continues to rise steeply. In 2012 it was estimated that there were a total of nearly 1.7 million people displaced, and a further 476,000 are refugees in neighboring countries. According to the 2007 report of the independent expert of the UN Human Rights Council, abuses have included summary and extrajudicial killings, forced disappearances, **torture**, and arbitrary detention. Other reports have focused on sexual violence against women and girls, the situation of street children *(shegues),* and use of child soldiers by nearly all parties to the conflict. Some human rights organizations have reported instances of cannibalism. In 2010 the UN High Commissioner for Human Rights released a report mapping violations during the period between 1993–2003, which highlighted the systematic and widespread nature of the acts and contains a special section on sexual violence (see Box 8.3).

Much of the violence has been ethnically targeted, even as it has been justified on the grounds of protecting another ethnicity. Ethnic conflicts have in several instances become intertwined with the struggle over natural resources. This is particularly true in the region of Ituri, where the fight over control of the gold mines has rendered the conflict particularly violent, with grave consequences for the civilian population. For example, the fight over the Mongbwalu gold-mining area between Hema and Lendu armed groups in 2002 and 2003

Box 8.3 **Sexual and gender-based violence in the DRC**

Violence in the DRC has involved the widespread and systematic use of rape and sexual assault by all combatant forces, which has targeted women and girls of all ages, including very young girls, and refugees in Rwandans refugee camps. The 2010 UN Office of the High Commissioner for Human Rights mapping report confirmed hundreds of incidents of sexual violence,, but warned that the incidents recorded in its report were only "the tip of the iceberg." The report concluded that sexual violence was frequently used to terrorize and subjugate the population and was generally ethnically targeted, but was also used against women of opposing political parties or due to their relationship with civil society organizations. The abuses included public rapes, gang rapes, systematic rapes, forced incest, sexual mutilation, disembowelling of pregnant women and genital mutilation.

The DRC government has only begun to address impunity for sexual abuse, which has persisted for decades, following years of international pressure and campaigns by human rights organizations. However, sexual and gender-based crimes continue in the east.

Source: UN High Commissioner for Human Rights, Report of the Mapping Exercise documenting the most serious violations of human rights and international humanitarian law committed within the territory of the Democratic Republic of the Congo between March 1993 and June 2003 (August 2010, unofficial translation from French), http://www.ohchr.org/en/Countries/AfricaRegion/Pages/RDCProjetMapping.aspx

---

led to the slaughter of 2,000 civilians, as well as rape, torture, and arbitrary detentions. It resulted also in the internal displacement of tens of thousands of civilians who were forced to flee their homes after their possessions had been looted or destroyed. An estimated 50,000 to 60,000 civilians have died in Ituri since 1999, with more than half a million civilians forced to flee the region with no possibility to return. The armed groups have also prevented delivery of humanitarian assistance to other groups considered enemies. In North and South Kivu, Tutsi and Hutu rebel groups have fought over control of mining of cassiterite and other valuable minerals.

Applicable law and possible subjects of legal accountability

In analyzing the applicable law to determine who might be held accountable for breaches, the distinction between international and noninternational armed conflict becomes salient, potentially affecting whether certain acts by armed groups can be characterized as **war crimes** even if they are clear violations of international humanitarian law. The attacks against the civilian population, many of them against women and children and against the refugee population, involved multiple acts of large-scale violence, often conducted in an organized fashion. Given their nature and the fact that they were addressed to non-combatant population these acts can be qualified as **crimes against humanity**.

Given their scale and nature of the human rights violations committed during the conflict, it might be argued they have transformed organized chaos into genocide, given the ethnically targeted nature of the violence. Abuses targeting ethnic Hutu, especially in refugee camps, and the clashes between the Hema and Lendu in Ituri have prompted allegations of genocide.

The DRC conflict is particularly complex, as many governments have been militarily involved through use of their own armed forces or support to armed groups, alongside the involvement of many other rebel groups. Where states have been directly involved or used proxies who engaged in abuses, the states themselves may be liable, according to the principles of state responsibility. Further, individuals might be held criminally liable. Chapter 13 addresses the cases that have actually been brought at the ICC in greater detail.

State responsibility: the DRC v. Uganda and Rwanda

On June 23, 1999, the DRC brought a case against Uganda before the **International Court of Justice** (ICJ) for the latter's activities on DRC territory, particularly its acts of armed aggression, use of force, violation of the principles of peaceful settlement of disputes and noninterference, and violation of obligations under international humanitarian and human rights law.

In its decision of December 19, 2005, the Court found that Uganda, by engaging in military activities against the DRC on the latter's territory, by occupying Ituri, and by providing military, logistic, economic, and financial support to irregular forces operating on DRC territory, had violated the principle of nonuse of force in international relations and the principle of nonintervention. It found that Uganda's armed forces had engaged in killing, torture, and other inhumane treatment of the Congolese civilian population, and had destroyed villages and civilian buildings. Further, it found that Uganda had failed to distinguish between civilian and military targets and to protect the civilian population in fighting with other combatants, had trained child soldiers, had incited ethnic conflict, and had failed to take measures to end the conflict. It also found that Uganda, as an occupying power, had failed to take measures to ensure respect for human rights and international humanitarian law in Ituri district, and had therefore violated its obligations under international humanitarian law and international human rights law. Finally, the Court found that Ugandan armed forces had engaged in looting, plundering, and exploitation of Congolese natural resources, and that Uganda, while occupying Ituri, had failed to comply with its obligations as an occupying power to prevent such acts. Therefore, the Court found that Uganda had violated obligations to the DRC under international law and owed it reparations.

In a similar case filed by the DRC against Rwanda on the same date, June 23, 1999, the ICJ found in its of judgment of February 3, 2006, that it had no jurisdiction to hear the case. However, the increase in violence in the eastern DRC since the summer of 2008 drew renewed attention to—and new evidence for—Rwanda's role in perpetrating human rights violations in the DRC, through its backing of the CNDP. In Spain, a case has been brought (see Box 8.5) exercising **universal jurisdiction** to address human rights abuses committed in the region, including the killings of nine Spanish nationals, missionaries, and aid workers. In February 2008, a Spanish judge issued an arrest warrant against 40 members of the Rwandan Patriotic Army accused of committing international crimes in Rwanda that also spilled over into DRC territory. Among those who have been prosecuted by the Spanish courts is General Karake Karenzi, deputy-commander of the UN-AU Hybrid Mission in Darfur (UNAMID) at the time of the indictment. The Spanish courts have also considered the responsibility of Paul Kagame, president of Rwanda, but have found him immune to prosecution as a sitting head of state. The case is ongoing but no arrests have been made.

***Box 8.4* The DRC's case against Uganda, ICJ Hearing of April 27, 2005**

"The Congo requests the Court to adjudge and declare:

1. That the Republic of Uganda, by engaging in military and paramilitary activities against the Democratic Republic of the Congo … has violated the following principles of conventional and customary law:
    - the principle of non-use of force in international relations, including the prohibition of aggression;
    - the obligation to settle international disputes exclusively by peaceful means so as to ensure that international peace and security, as well as justice, are not placed in jeopardy;
    - respect for the sovereignty of States and the rights of peoples to self-determination, and hence to choose their own political and economic system freely and without outside interference;
    - the principle of non-intervention in matters within the domestic jurisdiction of States, including refraining from extending any assistance to the parties to a civil war operating on the territory of another State.
2. That the Republic of Uganda, by committing acts of violence against nationals of the Democratic Republic of the Congo … has violated the following principles of conventional and customary law:
    - the principle of conventional and customary law imposing an obligation to respect, and ensure respect for, fundamental human rights, including in times of armed conflict, in accordance with international humanitarian law;
    - the principle of conventional and customary law imposing an obligation, at all times, to make a distinction in an armed conflict between civilian and military objectives;
    - the right of Congolese nationals to enjoy the most basic rights, both civil and political, as well as economic, social and cultural.
3. That the Republic of Uganda, by engaging in the illegal exploitation of Congolese natural resources … has violated the following principles of conventional and customary law:
    - the applicable rules of international humanitarian law;
    - respect for the sovereignty of States, including over their natural resources;
    - the duty to promote the realization of the principle of equality of peoples and of their right of self-determination, and consequently to refrain from exposing peoples to foreign subjugation, domination or exploitation;
    - the principle of non-interference in matters within the domestic jurisdiction of States, including economic matters."

Source: http://www.icj-cij.org.

Box 8.5　The cases against the FPR in Spain

Juzgado Centrad de Instrucción N.4 Audiencia Nacional

Case Reference Number: "Sumario 3/2008-D". Order of indictment. 6-February-2008. (Official translation)

"III. LEGAL ARGUMENTS

FIRST

The criminal conducts as described above could constitute the following offences established in the current Penal Code:

A) Offence of Genocide …

B) Offences against humanity …

C) Offences against persons and property protected in the case of armed conflict …

D) Common Provisions …

E) Belonging to a Terrorist Organization …

F) Terrorists Acts .

…

THIRD

… there is reasonable evidence that the persons with the most responsibility for the military political organization **FRONT PATRIOTIQUE RWANDAIS (FPR)– ARME PATRIOTIQUE RWANDAISE (APR)**, among whom the persons indicted in this case have unfolded a whole range of criminal methodology in their operations firstly carried out from outside of Rwanda, from Uganda and later from Rwanda and in its territory. They seized power by force by means of strategic terrorist attacks and open war operations, and took absolute control off the structure of the State, generating from then on a real terror regime.

This terror regime was generated not only from the dictatorial structure of the State itself but, above all, from a complex hierarchical parallel structure which was put in charge of perpetrating heinous criminal acts against the population both national and foreign, which were previously selected for ethnical and/or political reasons. Their criminal plan, for alleged security reasons, culminated in the invasion and conquest in two phases of the immense Democratic Republic of Congo, which the support of their political-military groups or allies created for this purpose. An indeterminate number of persons were exterminated through these two phases of hostilities at the hand of a systematic, organized and strongly hierarchical structure.

According to some sources, the number of persons exterminated during the periods to which these case refers to, could be four million people, approximately, a figure that includes Rwandan refugees belonging to the Hutu ethnic group, as well as the civilian population of the Congo, mainly Congolese Hutus.

Furthermore, pillage and large scale looting was carried out centred above all in valuable natural resources such as timber and high valued and strategic minerals. The criminal network created for the exploitation and pillage of these riches enables them to maintain a powerful position and geostrategic domination of the zone, as well as to finance their wars, enriching both individuals and the group, and to continue and extend their criminal plan for extermination and domination."

Box 8.6 DRC timeline

1908	Established as a Belgian colony.
1960	Independence.
1965	Mobutu's military coup.
1996	Laurent Kabila's rebellion (supported by Rwanda and Uganda).
1997	Mobutu deposed and dies in Morocco.
1998	Insurrection backed by Rwanda and Uganda.
1998–9	Uganda occupies Ituri region.
1999	Lusaka Accord signed.
2000	MONUC established.
2001	Laurent Kabila assassinated. Joseph Kabila named head of state.
2002	*April 19:* Peace talks in Sun City.
	July: Peace accord signed.
	September: Luanda Accords signed.
	October: Withdrawal of Rwandan forces occupying eastern Congo negotiated.
	December 17: Pretoria Accord signed by all remaining warring parties, ending fighting and establishing government of national unity.
2003	Uganda begins withdrawing troops from Ituri region and confrontation between the Lendu and Hema intensifies.
	June: EU emergency mission in Ituri.
	July: Government of national unity confirmed.
2004	Militia groups in Ituri sign agreement with government to disarm and participate in transitional process.
	June: Dissidents from RCD occupy Bakavu (Sud-Kivu).
2005	*December*: Constitutional referendum.
2006	Elections for presidency, National Assembly, and provincial legislatures.
	March: Thomas Lubanga is charged by the ICC.
	September: National Assembly installed.
	December: Joseph Kabila inaugurated president.
2007	*January*: Provincial assemblies constituted; governors and national senators elected.
2008	Renewed clashes in Nord-Kivu. Laurent Nkunda consolidates control of the East.
2009	Joint operation DRC–Rwanda to defeat Nkunda.
	March: Peace deal with CNDP, now led by Bosco Ntanganda.
	May: Kabila approves amnesty law for armed groups in the East.
2010	Jean-Pierre Bemba stands trial in the ICC for crimes in Central African Republic (2002–2003).
2011	*July:* Lubanga sentenced to 14 years imprisonment at the ICC.
	November: Presidential and parliamentary elections. Kabila gains another term.
2012	*April:* Ntaganda abandons the army and commands a rebellion as leader of M23
	November: The group M23 enters Goma.
2013	*March:* Ntaganda surrenders and is transferred to the ICC.

International humanitarian and human rights law

The DRC ratified the **Geneva Conventions** in 1961 and its two additional protocols in 1982 and 2002, respectively. The first issue to resolve in trying to identify the international humanitarian law that is applicable to the conflict in the DRC is whether the conflict should be considered internal or international, as it presents characteristics of both. At the beginning of the conflict the UN Special Rapporteur on the Situation of Human Rights in the DRC, Roberto Garretón, considered that, notwithstanding the internationalization of the conflict, it still remained an internal one. However, following the ICJ's judgment that Uganda bore responsibility for many breaches of international humanitarian law, it is arguable that the conflict should be categorized as international. Thus the Pre-Trial Chamber in the Lubanga case at the ICC found that the conflict was international until Uganda withdrew from Ituri on June 2, 2003, in contrast to the position of the prosecutor but consistent with the position of the defense. The Office of the Prosecutor argued that the conflict was noninternational, and that Uganda's involvement (even if it was found to have constituted occupation), would not automatically mean the armed conflict was international in character, or alternatively that even if Ugandan involvement did create an international armed conflict, the UPC was involved in a distinct, simultaneous noninternational armed conflict. The verdict of March 14, 2012 was that the conflict in Ituri was of a noninternational character.

Beyond the ICC, the impact of the international–noninternational armed conflict distinction could significantly affect what crimes can be prosecuted. If the conflict is deemed noninternational, only one provision of the Geneva Conventions is applicable. **Common Article 3** prohibits a host of activities by all parties to a conflict, and the rapes, massacres, mutilations, and cannibalism perpetrated during the DRC conflict clearly violate this article. This means that the various rebel groups and the government of the DRC violated Common Article 3. Such violations are not automatically war crimes, as they cannot be termed "**grave breaches**" under the Geneva Conventions, which can only be committed in the context of an international armed conflict. While Additional Protocol II further regulates the conduct of internal armed conflict, and the DRC is a state party, as discussed in Chapter 4, traditional international humanitarian law does not define violations in such internal conflicts as grave breaches or war crimes.

As highlighted previously, the devolvement of the conflict in the eastern DRC into ethnic violence and deliberate targeting of civilian populations according to their membership in specific ethnic groups could arguably be considered genocide. As we have seen (Box 8.5), the Spanish courts have considered the claim that some of the acts perpetrated in the eastern DRC amounted to genocide, crimes against humanity, war crimes, and terrorist offenses.

Discussion questions

Determining accountability

The conflict in the DRC is complex, involving many actors, including foreign governments, national and multinational corporations, which might have had a role in aggravating and perpetuating the conflict.

* Why did the International Court of Justice take a different stand in the case against Uganda compared to the case against Rwanda?
* Can the abuses carried out in the DRC be considered to fall within the definition of genocide? If so, what criminal responses do these abuses merit? Consider the conflicts in Ituri and the Kivus separately.

- To what extend are multinational corporations responsible for some of the human rights abuses perpetrated in the DRC? To answer this question study the reports of the UN Expert Panel on the Illegal Exploitation of Natural Resources and Other Forms of Wealth in the Democratic Republic of Congo and the UN Group of Experts on the DRC (see "Official Documents and Sources" at the end of this chapter).

Prospects for addressing violations

The fragile state of peace implementation and the continuing violence in the east has imposed limitations on accountability. The ICC only has the capacity to prosecute those with responsibility for the most serious violations. Thousands of crimes will not be addressed by the court.

- Given the state of the national judiciary, is it realistic to expect domestic criminal accountability in the DRC?
- Are mobile courts a solution to the limited presence of courts in rural communities?
- Given that the ICC cannot address all crimes committed, are there other venues such as foreign courts that might be utilized?
- Would a **hybrid tribunal** be a viable solution in this case? Why? Would the resources needed to establish a hybrid tribunal be better used for other purposes, such as rebuilding the judicial system?
- How beneficial would it be to establish a truth and reconciliation commission for the DRC? Can a politicized truth commission function as a viable instrument for domestic accountability?

Achieving stability

As we have seen, violence has not stopped in several areas of the DRC. Mistrust and fear engendered by the ethnically targeted abuses and attacks in the Ituri region and in the eastern DRC have made conflict resolution much more difficult. Even if there is low risk of renewed war involving the whole country, which external powers would likely prevent, it is important to consider that increased corruption, continuation of local violence, **impunity**, and economic stagnation may lead to increased instability.

- How could the continued violence in Ituri and the Kivus impact the stability of the country as a whole?
- Could externally imposed accountability processes, such as those before the ICC and the Spanish courts, impact in the stability of the country?

Group exercise

The DRC's transitional government, in discussions in May 2004 designed to engage the armed groups in Ituri, made the following statement: "There will not be a peace without justice, but the government will firstly privilege the restoration of peace and security before justice starts." Form two groups. One group should argue the advantages of this strategy, and the other group should argue its disadvantages.

Further reading

Autesserre, Séverine, *The Trouble with the Congo: Local Violence and the Failure of International Peacebuilding* (Cambridge: Cambridge University Press, 2010).

Human Rights Watch, "The Curse of Gold: Democratic Republic of Congo" (2005), http://www.hrw.org/doc/?t=africa_pub&c=congo.

International Centre for Transitional Justice (Federico Borello), "A First Few Steps: The Long Road to a Just and Democratic Peace in the Democratic Republic of Congo" (October 2004), http://www.ictj.org/downloads/ictj.drc.eng.pdf

International Crisis Group, "Congo: Consolidating the Peace," *Africa Report* no. 128 (July 5, 2007), http://www.crisisgroup.org/en/regions/africa/central-africa/dr-congo/128-congo-consolidating-the-peace.aspx

International Crisis Group, "Maintaining Momentum in the Congo: The Ituri Problem" (August 2005), http://www.crisisgroup.org/en/regions/africa/central-africa/dr-congo/084-maintaining-momentum-in-the-congo-the-ituri-problem.aspx

Juma, Laurence, "The War in Congo: Transnational Conflict Networks and the Failure of Internationalism," *Gonzaga Journal of International Law* vol. 10 (2006): 97–163.

Nest, Michael, with François Grignon and Eminzet F. Kinsangani, *The Democratic Republic of Congo: Economic Dimensions of War and Peace* (Boulder, CO: Lynne Rienner, 2006).

Open Society Justice Initiative, *Justice in DRC, Mobile Courts Combat Rape and Impunity in Eastern Congo* (2012), http://www.opensocietyfoundations.org/publications/justice-drc-mobile-courts-combat-rape-and-impunity-eastern-congo

Turner, Thomas, *The Congo Wars: Conflict, Myth, and Reality* (New York: Zed Books, 2007).

Official documents and sources

International Court of Justice, Case of Armed Activities in the Territory of the Congo (*Democratic Republic of Congo v. Uganda*) (December 19, 2005).

International Court of Justice, Case Concerning the Arrest Warrant of 11 April 2000 (*Democratic Republic of the Congo v. Belgium*) (February 12, 2002).

United Nations, *Report of the Panel of Experts on the Illegal Exploitation of Natural Resources and Other Forms of Wealth of the Democratic Republic of the Congo* (April 12, 2001), UN Doc. A/2001/357.

United Nations, *Report of the Independent Expert on the Situation of Human Rights in the Democratic Republic of the Congo, Titinga Frédéric Pacéré* (February 21, 2007), UN Doc. A/HRC/4/7.

United Nations High Commissioner for Human Rights, *Report of the Mapping Exercise Documenting the Most Serious Violations of Human Rights and International Humanitarian Law Committed within the Territory of the Democratic Republic of the Congo between March 1993 and June 2003* (August 2010, unofficial translation from French), http://www.ohchr.org/en/Countries/AfricaRegion/Pages/RDCProjetMapping.aspx

United Nations Group of Experts on the Democratic Republic of Congo, Reports submitted pursuant to UN Security Council Resolution 1533 (2004), all reports available http://www.un.org/sc/committees/1533/egroup.shtml

9 Sudan

Key points

- There are two main conflicts in Sudan: the north–south conflict between the government of Sudan and the Sudanese People's Liberation Movement/Army (SPLM/A), and the conflict in the Darfur region between the government of Sudan and the Sudan Liberation Movement/Army (SLM/A) and the Justice and Equality Movement (JEM), also involving the Janjaweed militia.
- Widespread atrocities have been carried out in both conflicts by all parties, with systematic targeting of civilians by the Janjaweed in Darfur.
- There is no consensus in the international community as to whether the events in Darfur can be considered **genocide**.
- The north–south conflict did not result in accountability mechanisms, while the Darfur situation is under consideration by the **International Criminal Court** (ICC).

Overview

After decades of conflict, the war between the Sudanese government and the Sudanese People's Liberation Movement/Army came to an end in 2005 with the signing of the Comprehensive Peace Agreement, which included provision for a referendum on the independence of the south, as well as for SPLM/A inclusion in both governance and security structures, but does not provide for accountability mechanisms. However, the situation remains fragile. Further, conflict has continued to rage in Western Darfur, where genocide may have been committed. The **UN Security Council** referred the situation to the International Criminal Court (ICC), as discussed in Chapter 13. The Sudan case is an example of peace without justice in the south, and justice without peace in Darfur.

This chapter examines the background to the conflict between the north and the south as well as in the Darfur region, the human rights violations committed by all parties, and the applicable **international humanitarian law** and **international human rights law**. It considers the violations both before and after the independence of South Sudan.

Background to the conflict

The conflict in the south

The north–south conflict in Sudan occurred in two phases: from independence until 1972, and again from 1983 until 2005. We focus here on the more recent conflict, although the underlying causes of both conflicts were substantially the same.

Map 9.1 Sudan and South Sudan
Source: *The World Factbook* 2013–14. Washington, DC: Central Intelligence Agency, 2013.

Box 9.1 Key facts: Sudan

Geography

Location: Northern Africa, bordering the Red Sea, between Egypt and Eritrea.
Area: Total area 1,861,484 km².
Natural resources: Petroleum; small reserves of iron ore, copper, chromium ore, zinc, tungsten, mica, silver, gold; hydropower.

People

Population: 35 million.
Ethnic groups: Sudanese Arab (approximately 70%), Fur, Beja, Nuba, Fallata.
Religions: Sunni Muslim, small Christian minority.
Languages: Arabic (official), English (official), Nubian, Ta Bedawie, Fur.
Literacy (est. 2003)*:* 61.1% (male 71.8%, female 50.5%) age 15 and older can read and write.

Government

Country name: Republic of the Sudan (local name: Jumhuriyat as-Sudan).
Government type: Federal republic.
Capital: Khartoum.
Administrative territorial divisions: 17 states (wilayat, singular – wilayah); Al Bahr al Ahmar (Red Sea), Al Jazira (Gezira), Al Khartoum (Khartoum), Al Qadarif (Gedaref), An Nil al Abyad (White Nile), An Nil al Azraq (Blue Nile), Ash Shimaliyya (Northern), Gharb Darfur (Western Darfur), Janub Darfur (Southern Darfur), Janub Kurdufan (Southern Kordofan), Kassala, Nahr an Nil (River Nile), Sharq Darfur (Eastern Darfur), Shimal Darfur (Northern Darfur), Shimal Kurdufan (Northern Kordofan), Sinnar, Wasat Darfur (Central Darfur).
Independence: January 2, 1956 (from Egypt and the United Kingdom).

Economy

Gross domestic product: US$80.43 billion (2012 est.).
Unemployment rate: 20% (2012 est.).

Source: Central Intelligence Agency, *World Factbook,* Sudan country profile, https://www.cia.gov/library/publications/the-world-factbook/geos/su.html (last accessed June 2013).

Many of the contemporary grievances in the conflict are directly related to the colonial administration of the territory that is now Sudan. Beginning in 1821, Sudan was under Ottoman-Egyptian rule, and later was subject to the Anglo-Egyptian condominium administration. The colonial powers helped to reinforce the distinctions between the cultural and religious identities from the peoples of the north and the south. During the Anglo-Egyptian rule, the population in the northern two-thirds of the country, who had intermarried with Arab migrants, were under Arabic and Islamic influence, and those in the southern portion of the country, populated by animists and Christians, were regarded as African. This administration also promoted a disparate economic and social development, in which the

---

***Box 9.2.* Key facts: South Sudan.**

Geography

Location: East-Central Africa; bordering Sudan, Uganda and Ethiopia.
Area: Total area 644,329 km².
Natural resources: Hydropower, fertile agricultural land, gold, diamonds, petroleum, hardwoods, limestone, iron ore, copper, chromium ore, zinc, tungsten, mica, silver.

People

Population: 11 million.
Ethnic groups: Dinka, Kakwa, Bari, Azande, Shilluk, Kuku, Murle, Mandari, Didinga, Ndogo, Bviri, Lndi, Anuak, Bongo, Lango, Dungotona, Acholi.
Religions: Animist, Christian.
Languages: English (official), Arabic (includes Juba and Sudanese variants) (official), regional languages include Dinka, Nuer, Bari, Zande, Shilluk.
Literacy: 27% (male 40%, female 16%) age 15 and older can read and write.

Government

Country name: Republic of South Sudan.
Government type: Republic.
Capital: Juba.
Administrative territorial divisions: 10 states; Central Equatoria, Eastern Equatoria, Jonglei, Lakes, Northern Bahr el Ghazal, Unity, Upper Nile, Warrap, Western Bahr el Ghazal, Western Equatoria.
Independence: January 9, 2011 (from Sudan).

Economy

Gross domestic product: US$9.664 billion (2012 est.).
Population below the poverty line: 50.6% (2009 est.).

Source: Central Intelligence Agency, *World Factbook,* South Sudan country profile, https://www.cia.gov/library/publications/the-world-factbook/geos/od.html (last accessed June 2013).

---

north was considerably more advanced and gave rise to an elite who controlled government following decolonization. The government sought to force the Islamization of the country, including in the south. Discriminatory treatment, which continued into independence, fostered insecurity and resentment in the south. A mutiny in 1955 led to a 17-year war between the government and the Southern Sudanese Liberation Movement (SSLM), also known as Anya Nya. The conflict ended with the 1972 Addis Ababa Agreement, which granted political and economic autonomy to the south and established the conditions for resource and power-sharing between the regions.

It would be simplistic to understand this conflict exclusively as a religious and racial conflict between the Arab Muslims of the north and the Christian blacks of the south. The conflict was complicated with the development of oil exploitation in the south, following discoveries at the beginning of the 1970s. The concession for exploitation was granted to the Chevron Corporation in 1975. In 1980, President Jaafar Nimeiri began to change the administrative provincial borders so that the north could control oil resources. In 1983, he recentralized political and economic power, rescinded the autonomy of the south, and transferred its financial powers to the central government, abrogating the Addis Ababa Agreement. He also officially transformed Sudan into an Islamic state, declaring Arabic the official language (it had been English in the south), and imposed *sharia* law throughout the whole country, even though one-third of the population was non-Muslim. Southern resistance was mobilized through the SPLM/A, led by Colonel John Garang, and the war resumed.

From 1989 onward, several attempts to achieve peace were unsuccessful, with the revocation of *sharia* law as one of the main points of disagreement. By 1989 the SPLA controlled most of the south and was exercising a considerably military pressure on the government. In that year, Brigadier-General Omar Hassan Ahmad al-Bashir, supported by the National Islamic Front (NIF), seized power in a coup d'état and established an authoritarian government, which intensified the war. Also, the SPLA split when some among its military command questioned Garang's leadership, resulting in the creation of the SPLA-United— later the Southern Sudan Independence Movement—under the command of Riek Machar. Internal fighting within the south had devastating repercussions for both the Bor Dinka and Nuer ethnic groups.

Peace negotiations and agreements

Several **peace negotiation** attempts between the government, the SPLA, and the Southern Sudan Independence Movement failed. In 1993, the Inter-Governmental Authority on Development (IGAD), an African subregional organization, began facilitating the peace process, under the leadership of Kenya's president. International pressure escalated, promoted by the United States in part because of its global "war on terror" and including the imposition of UN sanctions, until the first peace agreement, the Machakos Protocol, was signed in July 2002.

The Machakos Protocol provided the basic framework for peace, including the right of the south to hold a referendum on independence after an interim period of six years, freedom of religion, and guarantees that *sharia* law would not be imposed in the south. The protocol also established the Assessment and Evaluation Commission to monitor implementation of accords during the interim period. The commission comprised equal membership from the SPLA and the government, as well as representation from the IGAD subcommittee on Sudan and from four observer states: Italy, Norway, the United Kingdom, and the United States.

Subsequent agreements, including a framework agreement in 2003 and several others in 2004, established an internationally monitored cease-fire, deployment of the UN Mission in Sudan (UNMIS), and security arrangements for the interim period, which included the formation of integrated as well as separate armed units, wealth- and power-sharing provisions, and provisions for the resolution of related regional conflicts, including those in Southern Kordofan/Nuba Mountains and Blue Nile States, and the Abyei conflict. The power-sharing provisions allowed the national government to protect the sovereignty and people of the whole country, while the government of South Sudan would exercise authority in relation to people in the south. The executive was to comprise a president and two vice-presidents, with John Garang to be first vice-president as well as president of the autonomous government of South Sudan, with Juba as the capital.

On January 10, 2005, in Nairobi, the government of Sudan and the SPLA signed the Comprehensive Peace Agreement. This agreement, like its predecessors, established no mechanisms for accountability for the human rights violations committed during the conflict.

Six months after signature of the Comprehensive Peace Agreement and shortly after his inauguration, Garang was killed in a helicopter accident, sparking riots in the capital of Sudan, Khartoum; many southerners suspected that the crash was no accident. The riots caused over a hundred deaths as well as fears that the growing civil unrest would derail the peace process. Salva Kiir Mayardit took over the presidency in the south. The peace process was fragile and significant clashes repeatedly threatened it, and in October 2007 the SPLA temporarily suspended participation in the government of national unity. Much of the tension was located in the oil-rich border region between the north and the south, particularly in the disputed area of Abyei, claimed by both the government and the autonomous government of South Sudan. In 2008, both parties agreed to international arbitration over the status of Abyei. In July 2009 the parties announced acceptance of an arbitral ruling which redrew the borders, decreased the size of the region and placed one of the major oil fields, the Heglig, in the north. A referendum on Abyei's future status was supposed to follow, but it has not taken place amidst increased tension. By the end of 2009 the government and the autonomous government of South Sudan agreed on the terms of the referendum on independence for the south. In January 2011 the south overwhelmingly voted for independence, resulting in the creation of the state of South Sudan. Salva Kiir was appointed president. A new UN mission was established on the ground to help maintain stability in the new country, the UN Mission in the Republic of South Sudan (UNMISS). This, however, did not conclude the fighting in the border region, and in May 2011, northern troops invaded the town of Abyei, causing thousands to flee and escalating the conflict between north and south. The violence around Abyei has provoked a renewed conflict between the government of Sudan and the SPLM-North (SPLM-N), a northern affiliate of the SPLM, based in the Nuba Mountains. The SPLM-N and the Justice and Equality Movement (JEM) operating in Darfur announced in July 2011 that they had joined forces in the area of South Kordofan, linking the north–south and the Darfur conflicts. Other Darfurian rebels joined their alliance and the Sudan Revolutionary Front (SRF) was created. The clashes between the SPLM-N and the government of Khartoum continued in South Kordofan and the Blue Nile states. In June 2012, under the mediation of African Union's envoy Thabo Mbeki, Sudanese President Omar al-Bashir and South Sudanese President Salva Kiir recommended negotiations. On September 27 they signed eight agreements in Addis Ababa, Ethiopia, which included establishing the parameters in regards to demarcating their border, an economic-cooperation agreement, an agreement to protect each other's citizens and the creation of a six-mile demilitarized zone along their border. The agreements allowed the resumption of oil exports and in March 2013, both countries began to withdraw their forces from the border area.

Regional dimensions

The conflict in Sudan has significant regional dimensions. Some neighbors, such as Kenya, Uganda, Ethiopia, and Eritrea, have been positively engaged in supporting negotiations in Sudan through the IGAD process.

However, regional dynamics have also fomented conflict. Until 1991, Ethiopia provided support to the SPLA because, among other things, it suspected that the Sudanese government was fostering Islamist movements in Ethiopia and Eritrea. Uganda has also provided support to the SPLA, as part of its strategy to fight the Lord's Resistance Army, which operates in Uganda along the border with Sudan, as well as in South Sudan.

In 2005, Chad declared war on Sudan, after the Chadian rebel group Rally for Democracy and Liberty launched an attack on the Chadian town of Adre, located near the Sudanese border and within the Darfur region, killing about a hundred people. Chad accused the Sudanese government of supporting the rebel group and its attacks, and claimed that Sudanese militias were responsible for their daily incursions into Chad to steal cattle, killing civilians and burning villages along the way. In turn, Chad supported the JEM in their fight against the government. Both countries signed several peace agreements between 2006 and 2008, but fighting continued. It was only after the two states agreed to normalize relationships and cooperate in January 2010 that Chad renounced its support of the JEM, and both countries committed to joint border patrols. Sudanese refugees have fled to neighboring countries, particularly Eritrea, Chad, Ethiopia, Uganda, and the Central African Republic.

Despite the issuance of an arrest warrant by the International Criminal Court for Sudanese President Omar al-Bashir, neighboring states have refused to arrest him when present for regional conferences, in line with wider African Union condemnation of the court for its exclusively African caseload.

The conflict in Darfur

Even as the north–south conflict drew to a close, violence raged elsewhere in the country. Reports of massacres and potentially genocidal attacks in Western Darfur began to emerge in early 2003. According to human rights advocates, the government of Sudan is responsible for ethnic cleansing and **crimes against humanity** in Darfur, one of the world's poorest and most inaccessible regions, on Sudan's western border with Chad. This region comprises 250,000 square kilometers, has an estimated population of six million persons, and is home to several sedentary and nomadic tribal groups, some predominantly agricultural, some mainly cattle herders. All of the tribes practice Islam, and Arabic is widely spoken. This conflict has historical roots but escalated in February 2003 when two rebel groups, the Sudan Liberation Army/Movement and the Justice and Equality Movement, drawn from members of the Fur, Masalit, and Zaghawa ethnic groups, initiated attacks against the government, demanding an end to economic marginalization and seeking a power-sharing deal. They also demanded government action against abuses they had suffered from rival groups, mainly Arab pastoralists driven onto African farmlands by drought and desertification—and who had a nomadic tradition of armed militias.

The government responded to this armed and political threat by targeting the civilian populations from which the rebels were drawn, with the fighting reaching its peak in 2002–3. The government called on local tribes to assist fighting against the rebels in order to supplement its lack of military presence in the region, much of which was devoted to the conflict in the South. This ethnic manipulation by the government sought to exploit existing tensions between different tribes. It was mostly Arab nomadic tribes without a traditional homeland who responded to the call, forming the "Janjaweed" militias with the support, arms, training, and organization provided by the government. The term was traditionally used in the region to refer to armed bandits or outlaws on horses or camels. The government has effectively shielded these militias from any accountability process.

The Sudanese government and the Arab Janjaweed militias have committed numerous attacks on civilians of the African Fur, Masalit, and Zaghawa ethnic groups. Together, they are responsible for killing thousands of civilians, raping women, and destroying villages, food stocks, and other supplies essential for survival. The abuses have virtually emptied rural areas that were previously populated by Masalit and Fur farmers. By 2009, more than two million people had been displaced and nearly two million others were in need of humanitarian aid, according to UN reports. The population has been driven into camps and settlements in Darfur, where they live at the very edge of survival, subject to Janjaweed abuses, or has fled to neighboring countries, often Chad.

In August 2003 the first meeting between representatives of the rebel groups and the government was convened to seek a solution to the conflict. The host was President Idriss Deby of Chad. In November, the government, the SLA, and the JEM signed two protocols, one on improvement of the humanitarian situation and the second on enhancement of the security situation in Darfur. In October 2004 an African Union mission, the AU Mission in Sudan (AMIS), was authorized to monitor the cease-fire between the parties and to help establish a secure route for refugees and **internally displaced persons**. The cease-fire was ineffective; AMIS was unable to protect civilians and stop the violence, and the humanitarian situation continued to worsen.

The Darfur Peace Agreement, between the government and the main faction of the SLA, led by Minni Minnawi, was signed in May 2006 in Abuja. Another faction of the SLA and the JEM refused to participate, undermining the process. The Janjaweed militias were not party to the negotiations, nor did they sign the agreement; instead, the government promised to control and disarm them. The agreement established the so-called Darfur–Darfur Dialogue and Consultation, to address the challenges of restoring peace and overcoming the divisions between communities. The agreement also contained provisions on wealth and power sharing. It established the Transitional Darfur Regional Authority to oversee the implementation of the agreement and to help administer the region until a referendum to decide on the level of autonomy of the region within the country could be held. However, the agreement did not address some of the core issues at the heart of the conflict, among them land tenure and the powers and structure of local government, which were left to the Darfur–Darfur Dialogue and Consultation process. Nor was accountability addressed in the agreement, although the UN Security Council, on March 31, 2005, almost contemporaneous with the negotiations, passed Resolution 1593 to refer the situation in Darfur to the ICC (see Chapter 13).

The humanitarian situation in Darfur did not improve after the signature of the Darfur Peace Agreement and attacks on civilians continued. Camps for internally displaced persons became increasingly violent, with residents being co-opted by all sides to join the fighting while the government sought to force them to return to unsafe areas. The conditions for humanitarian organizations became much more difficult, with attacks on their personnel and assets by all sides, and some withdrew for security reasons. After much pressure, the Sudanese government agreed to the establishment of a joint United Nations–African Union force, the UN-AU Hybrid Mission in Darfur (UNAMID), which was authorized in July 2007 by Security Council Resolution 1769 and began deploying troops in December. The first months of the mission proved difficult; there were staff shortages, and seven peacekeepers were killed in an attack on July 9, 2008. The mission continues to be operational.

At the end of 2007 and beginning of 2008, the humanitarian crisis worsened and violence increased as some groups splintered and confrontations multiplied. The government launched major aerial bombardments and ground attacks in Western Darfur in February 2008. In turn, JEM rebels assaulted Khartoum in May, leaving at least 200 dead. This was a milestone in the Darfur conflict, the first military strike on the capital in 30 years.

Fighting continued until 2011 when the Liberation and Justice Movement (a new group composed of several rebel groups formed in 2010) and the JEM resumed talks with the government of Sudan in Doha. After very difficult negotiations, the 2011 Doha Peace Agreement was signed in July between the government of Sudan and the Liberation and Justice Movement. The agreement established a power-sharing arrangement which allows for the rebel movement signing the accord to nominate government ministers and have

---

Box 9.3 Key players in Sudan

Individuals

Omar Hassan Ahmad al-Bashir: President of Sudan.
John Garang: Late leader of the SPLA.
Salva Kiir Mayardit: President of South Sudan.
Minni Minnawi: Leader of the main faction of the SLA and later president of the Darfur Regional Authority.

Government of Sudan

NIF (National Islamic Front): Dominates the National Congress Party, the party in government.
NCP (National Congress Party): The party in government, comprising a coalition of parties including the Southern National Congress, an important representative of South Sudan.

Armed groups

Janjaweed: Government-supported militia (based in Darfur).
JEM (Justice and Equality Movement) (based in Darfur).
LJM (Liberation and Justice Movement): Umbrella organization composed of different rebel groups in Darfur (formed in February 2010).
SPLM/A (Sudanese People's Liberation Movement/Army).
SPLM-N (Sudanese People's Liberation Movement–North): Northern affiliate of the SPLM (based in the Nuba Mountains).
SLM/A (Sudanese Liberation Movement/Army) (based in Darfur).
SRF (Sudanese Revolutionary Front): Coalition of rebel groups fighting the government of Sudan, including the SPLM-N, JEM and SLM.

Regional organizations

African Union (AU).
Inter-Governmental Authority on Development (IGAD).

International missions

AU Mission in Sudan (AMIS) (deployed in Darfur).
UN-AU Hybrid Mission in Darfur (UNAMID).
UN Mission in Sudan (UNMIS).
UN Mission in the Republic of South Sudan (UMMISS).

representation in the national legislature. The agreement established a new Darfur Regional Authority to oversee the region until a referendum to determine its permanent status, and allowed the president of Sudan to appoint a vice-president from Darfur. Finally, the Doha Agreement established a compensation fund for victims of the conflict in Darfur, which would receive contributions from the government of Sudan, charitable organizations; Islamic, Arab and African countries and their funds; the EU and other donors; and UN agencies.

Human rights violations in Sudan

Certain human rights abuses have been important factors in both the conflict in the South and the conflict in Darfur. In particular, exclusion and marginalization in language policy, access to resources, and violations of freedom of religion significantly motivated the attempts by the SPLA to either secede from the country or defeat the Khartoum government. Similar concerns also prompted the rebel movements in Darfur. The conflicts themselves, however, sparked far greater violations of human rights, by all sides, although the government does appear to bear particular responsibility.

Human rights violations as underlying causes of conflict

As we have seen, several causes underpin the conflict in Sudan, including religion, access to resources, race, and geographic distinctions. Each is contentious, and their impact on the conflict and motivation have changed over time. Further, they are interrelated, as geographic distinctions are clearly linked to racial and religious divides, whether perceived or real.

Among the apparent human rights causes of the conflict are real and perceived discrimination, and attempts to impose religion and constrain freedom of religion. So too are demands for self-rule, enshrined in part for the first time in the 1972 Addis Ababa Agreement. This autonomy worked relatively well, at least until the discovery of oil and the northern government's attempt to control it spurred old resentments. Demands over governance, self-determination claims, and access to resources also underpinned the conflict.

Elitism and discrimination based on race and ethnicity

Southern resentment and at least some of the impetus for armed conflict have been rooted in historical and contemporary inequities, with the south largely excluded from access to power and wealth.

Colonial rules exploited the racial distinction between north and south. Even if racial distinctions between Arabs in the north and black Africans in the south may have been artificial and constructed, they were embedded and reinforced through colonialism and had long-term effects on the perceptions of both groups. The Anglo-Egyptian administration encouraged separate development of the two groups, favoring the economic and political development of the Arab elites of the north and generally denying education, especially Arabic language skills, and development to black Africans of the south. Under colonial rule, slave trade of southerners by northern Sudanese was encouraged. Slavery has continued to the modern day, disproportionately targeting members from the non-Muslim Dinka ethnic group, and has also been common during the conflict, particularly as part of the government's strategy to depopulate parts of South Sudan.

After independence, discriminatory policies continued. The race issue should not be overemphasized, but understood as part of a dynamic interaction between race, religion, and geography, and within the context of elite dominance of a few tribes in the north, who also dominated other northerners. Not only has the north been traditionally disproportionately represented in state institutions of the country as a whole, but also even within the north, three Arab tribes, the Shaigiyya, the Jaalyee and the Dongollawis, have dominated key institutions. For example, the head of state security forces has always been a member of one of these three tribes, and the National Council for the Distribution of Resources, formed for oil exploration and exploitation, was dominated by Arab elites of the north, while most of the oil is located in the south.

In Darfur, the conflict is mainly related to ethnicity rather than religion, as all involved are generally Muslim. Fighting is linked to control over land and livestock.

In both conflicts, the government has sought to stoke pre-existing ethnic tensions, such as those between the Nuer and the Dinka in the area around the Upper Nile oilfield, and those between the Zaghawa, Fur, and Masalit tribes and Arab nomads.

Restrictions on freedom of religion and Islamization

Islamists of the National Islamic Front have dominated the current government since it came to power, while the SPLA has remained mainly secular and pushed for a clear division between religion and state. The attempts by the north to impose *sharia* law in the south are often signaled as the cause of the second civil war. It was clearly and explicitly an aim of the government of Khartoum to Islamicize parts of the country that were home to non-Muslims, and to promote its own version of Islam to those who were already Muslim. International organizations and religious groups have accused the government of persecuting Christian churches and believers, and of punishing apostasy or conversion by Muslims to other religions with death. However, while freedom of religion has been a demand in the conflict, the war actually began before the imposition of *sharia* law, with disbandment of the provincial Juba assembly and alteration of provincial borders to allow for northern control of oil resources.

Human rights violations emerging from and transforming the conflict

The consequences of the conflict in the south have been catastrophic. An estimated two million people lost their lives, and the conflict has generated an estimated four million internally displaced persons out of a total national population of 38 million. In addition to the many civilian deaths resulting from the conflict, severe human rights abuses have been committed. The government's forces and their associates have conducted the great majority of these abuses, but the SPLA has also been responsible for killing and injuring civilians.

In Darfur the death toll is strongly disputed, with the UN estimating a minimum of 300,000 killed, a number contested as being both too low, according to nongovernmental organizations (NGOs) and too high, according to the government, which estimates 10,000 have died. Over two million people have been displaced in a worsening humanitarian situation in the region. All parties to the conflict have committed human rights violations, but the tactics of the government and the Janjaweed militias it sponsors have been particularly cruel.

The serious violations of human rights and humanitarian law have themselves further fuelled resentment and conflict. Security forces and associated militias have carried out extrajudicial killings and disappearances, and regularly beat, harass, arbitrarily arrest, and detain incommunicado, opponents and suspected opponents of the government; there have been reports of **torture** as well. Both security forces and associated militias have beaten refugees, raped women abducted during raids, and harassed and detained internally displaced persons, acting with complete **impunity**. The government has also manipulated humanitarian aid in some areas and prevented the delivery of food, using famine as a weapon in the war. Antigovernment insurgent groups, too, have committed numerous, serious abuses. The particularly cruel and bloody tactics used in attacking civilians in Darfur have attracted international outrage, with many arguing that they amount to genocide.

Violations in the south and access to resources

As discussed, the discovery of oil in the south of Sudan in the 1970s helped reignite the conflict. Sudan's oilfields are mainly located in the boundary between north and south, with the largest deposits located in the southern region of the Upper Nile, which the government has aggressively exploited since the 1989 coup. The government has continued its operations even in areas that were abandoned by the major oil companies due to security concerns when the civil war erupted. For example, Chevron abandoned oil exploitation in 1984 after a number of its expatriate employees were kidnapped and killed. However, other companies were prepared to build the infrastructure for oil development, including Chinese and Malaysian companies, and the Canadian company Talisman Energy. Talisman Energy withdrew in 2003 following allegations of its complicity in serious human rights abuses. It faced a lawsuit in the United States for such alleged violations, as discussed in greater detail later in this chapter and in Chapter 11.

Government tactics have included coordinated attacks on civilian settlements involving aerial bombardment and raids by helicopter gunships, followed by ground attacks in which government forces and militias burn villages and crops, loot livestock, and kill and abduct civilians. Oil companies such as Talisman Energy have been accused of providing launching areas for these attacks.

Clashes over agricultural lands and livestock led to further abuses during the north–south conflict. Since the mid-1980s, successive governments have supported armed groups that raid villages and abducted people to be sold as slaves to commercial farms and children to act as "domestic helpers." The SPLA has also been accused of abducting people for the slave trade. The government denies that slavery is practiced, and there are serious disagreements about the extent of it. Nongovernmental organizations estimate that 5,000 to 200,000 people have been abducted as slaves since the mid-1980s. Those enslaved often live in appalling conditions. They are denied access to their families and cultural background and identity, and are even forced to adopt Islam. Some are sexually abused as well. Attempts to escape are harshly punished, including by death.

Abuses in Darfur as transformer of the conflict

Despite the peace process, the conflict, abuses, and humanitarian crisis have continued in Darfur, with wide-scale destruction of villages throughout the three states of Darfur resulting in deaths of civilians and massive displacement of the population.

In 2004 the Security Council asked the **UN Secretary-General** to commission a report on the situation of Darfur. The International Commission of Inquiry, instituted by the UN Secretary-General, issued its report on January 15, 2005. The commission established that Janjaweed attacks, with government support and with direct government involvement in some cases, include massacres, summary executions of civilians (including women and children), burning of towns and villages, and the forcible depopulation of wide swathes of land long inhabited by the Fur, Masalit, and Zaghawa. The Janjaweed militias, although Muslim like the African groups they attack, have destroyed mosques, killed Muslim religious leaders, and desecrated Qurans belonging to their enemies.

The atrocities in Darfur have transformed the internal conflict into ethnic cleansing and perhaps even genocide. The International Commission of Inquiry established that persecution and "ethnic cleansing" have taken place, but did not term the abuses "genocide." It is clear from the facts of the situation that African tribes have been targeted. The rebel groups allege that the government and the Janjaweed have committed genocide by specifically targeting people from African tribes and specifically the Fur, Masaalit, Zaghaba, Birgit, Aranga, Jebel, and Tama. Rebel groups allege that extensive rapes have been committed by the government and the Janjaweed forces, targeting only women from African tribes. They accuse the government and the Janjaweed of abducting women and children and systematically looting property, including livestock, cash, and utensils. Conversely, the government insists that the conflict has no ethnic dimension, but instead that it is related to historical intertribal conflict. The government maintains that it is protecting civilians in the area. It justifies attacks as counterinsurgency responses, accusing the SLA and JEM of most of the atrocities committed in Darfur and of the displacement and destruction. The government admits that its forces follow rebels into villages, where the latter hide, but claims that destruction of villages is caused by the subsequent fighting and that casualties are the consequence of civilians being caught in the crossfire.

Rebel groups in Darfur, the SLA (particularly the SLA faction led by Minni Minawi) and the JEM are also responsible for abuses, including killings, beatings, rape, robbery, destruction of property, forced conscription, restricting freedom of movement of populations under their control, kidnapping, restricting access of relief workers and supplies, killing NGO workers, as well as targeting AU peacekeeping personnel. The ICC has indicted members of the JEM, including Saleh Mohammed Jerbo Jamus and Abdallah Banda Abakaer Nourain.

Applicable law and possible subjects of legal accountability

The north–south conflict

The widespread abuses that took place in the conflict in the south—disappearances, rapes, and massacres—are clearly violations of human rights law and humanitarian law. Sudan is party to the four **Geneva Conventions**, which it ratified in 1957, and to their two additional protocols, ratified in 2006. This conflict, despite its regional repercussions, is an internal one. Therefore, **Common Article 3** of the Geneva Conventions applies, as does Additional Protocol II. This would mean that the violations committed during the conflict do not amount to **grave breaches** of the Geneva Conventions, excepting, perhaps, the violations committed in the context of the Sudan–Chad confrontation between 2005 and 2007. However, they can be considered crimes against humanity, as the violations have involved systematic and widespread attacks against civilians.

Government-related militias have allegedly engaged in slave raiding and trading. The Slavery Convention, which entered into force on March 9, 1927, established that state parties are obligated to prevent and suppress the slave trade, and to bring about the complete abolition of slavery in all its forms, in the territories under their jurisdiction. Sudan ratified this convention in 1957; regardless, the prohibition on slavery has achieved the status of a *jus cogens* norm.

During the north–south conflict, there were also numerous violations for which the state might be responsible, such as its failure to protect human rights under its jurisdiction.

Militias and rebel groups have also been responsible for violations of human rights and violations of international humanitarian law. Companies involved in the exploitation of natural resources in Sudan may also be liable, if they participated in the abuses. As discussed, the Chevron Corporation withdrew in 1984, but Talisman Energy, one of the companies that took over the concession, currently faces civil suit in the United States under the **Alien Tort Claims Act** (see Chapter 11) brought forward by the Presbyterian Church of Sudan (see Box 9.4).

Once South Sudan became independent, the conflict became an international one. Thousands of civilians have been displaced or killed in confrontations in the border regions.

Box 9.4 *Presbyterian Church of Sudan v. Talisman Energy*

In 2001 in the United States, a number of Sudanese individuals and the Presbyterian Church of Sudan brought a claim against the Canadian company Talisman Energy under the Alien Tort Claims Act. The plaintiffs alleged that the company had been complicit in the Sudanese government's human rights abuses against non-Muslim Sudanese living in the area of Talisman's oil concession in southern Sudan. From 1998 to 2002, Talisman owned a 25 percent share of an oil pipeline project in the area. The plaintiffs argued that the acts committed by the government, to which the company was complicit, amounted to genocide. They claimed that these acts were part of an armed campaign of ethnic cleansing against the non-Muslim Sudanese that included massive civilian displacement, extrajudicial killing of civilians, torture, rape, and the burning of villages, churches, and crops. The primary allegation involved the use of Talisman's facilities as a base for government bombing missions. On September 12, 2006, the District Court of the Southern District of New York granted Talisman's motion to dismiss the case. In February 2007, the plaintiffs appealed this dismissal to the US Court of Appeals for the Second Circuit.

The lawsuit attracted international attention, and the Canadian government even intervened, urging the Second Circuit not to hear the case on the basis of lack of jurisdiction, and warning that such a move would create friction in Canada–U.S. relations.

The Second Circuit dismissed the complaint, finding that plaintiffs failed to establish that defendant "purposefully" aided and abetted the alleged including war crimes and crimes against humanity. The plaintiffs asked the Supreme Court to review this ruling in 2010, but it was denied later that year.

Even if the case never reached a verdict, the repercussions have been important. Partly due to the security situation in the area but also due to adverse public relations, Talisman withdrew from Sudan in 2006. Talisman strongly denies any participation in human rights abuses, maintaining that it did not know that government troops were using its facilities for bombing missions, and that it successfully demanded a halt to these operations as soon as it learned of them in the fall of 1999. The company insists it conducts business with integrity and respect for human dignity and the rights of the individual.

Abuses in Darfur: Genocide?

Most of the types of human rights violations committed during the north–south conflict have also been committed in Darfur. The attacks that have taken place appear to target civilians, not rebels, offering a clear case for crimes against humanity. However, it is less clear whether the attacks in Darfur also meet the definition of genocide—that is, whether attacks by the government and the Janjaweed militias demonstrate an intent to destroy a group in whole or in part. Many advocacy groups have characterized the abuses as genocide.

The International Commission of Inquiry concluded that both the government of Sudan and the Janjaweed militias were responsible for serious violations of international human rights law and international humanitarian law, amounting to crimes against humanity. However, it asserted there was no evidence of intent to destroy a group, in whole or in part. Therefore, the acts committed in Darfur could not be considered genocide (see Box 9.5).

Box 9.5   Genocide in Darfur? Conclusions of the International Commission of Inquiry

Extract from *Report of the International Commission of Inquiry on Darfur to the United Nations Secretary-General,* January 25, 2005, paras. 507–518:

507. *General.* There is no doubt that some of the objective elements of genocide materialized in Darfur. … The Commission has collected substantial and reliable material which tends to show the occurrence of systematic killing of civilians belonging to particular tribes, of large-scale causing of serious bodily or mental harm to members of the population belonging to certain tribes, and of massive and deliberate infliction on those tribes of conditions of life bringing about their physical destruction in whole or in part (for example by systematically destroying their villages and crops, by expelling them from their homes, and by looting their cattle). However, two other constitutive elements of genocide require a more in depth analysis, namely whether (a) the target groups amount to one of the group protected by international law, and if so (b) whether the crimes were committed with a genocidal intent. …

    518. *Conclusions.* … the Commission concludes that the Government of Sudan has not pursued a policy of genocide. Arguably, two elements of genocide might be deduced from the gross violations of human rights perpetrated by Government forces and the militias under their control. These two elements are: first, the *actus reus* consisting of killing, or causing serious bodily or mental harm, or deliberately inflicting conditions of life likely to bring about physical destruction; and, second, on the basis of a subjective standard, the existence of a protected group being targeted by the authors of criminal conduct. Recent developments have led to the perception and self-perception of members of African tribes and members of Arab tribes as making up two distinct ethnic groups. However, one crucial element appears to be missing, at least as far as the central Government authorities are concerned: genocidal intent. Generally speaking the policy of attacking, killing and forcibly displacing members of some tribes does not evince a specific intent to annihilate, in whole or in part, a group distinguished on racial, ethnic, national or religious grounds. Rather, it would seem that those who planned and organized attacks on villages pursued the intent to drive the victims from their homes, primarily for purposes of counter-insurgency warfare.

According to the Sudanese government, the attacks are carried out by the Janjaweed militias and are therefore not attributable to it (or that its involvement, where acknowledged, is for counterinsurgency purposes). The government claims that it is actually trying to restrain these militias, and that what is taking place is "tribal warfare." In June 2005, the Sudanese government established a tribunal, the Special Criminal Court on Events in Darfur, purportedly to try individuals guilty of abuses. However, this appears to have been an attempt to prevent international trials. None of the first cases tried by the new tribunal concerned major crimes associated with the conflict. No mid- or high-level government officials or militia leaders were suspended from duty, investigated, or prosecuted for serious crimes in Darfur. The government also tried to prevent international trials by establishing "tribal" or "traditional" justice courts for Darfur, which also have not conducted significant proceedings.

The government's denial of cooperation with the Janjaweed is not convincing, as documented in a 2003 report authored by **Human Rights Watch** . This report documents joint attacks, often with air support from the Sudanese military. According to the report, although the Janjaweed always outnumber regular soldiers, during attacks the government forces usually arrive first and leave last. Following the Security Council's referral of the Darfur situation to the ICC, the court is now in a position to determine whether the campaign of violence undertaken by the Sudanese government and the Janjaweed militias constitutes genocide. During its investigation, the Office of the Prosecutor of the ICC collected evidence that suggests the violations may have constituted genocide. In 2009 the ICC issued an arrest warrant for al-Bashir on charges of war crimes and crimes against humanity, and in 2010 the warrant was amended to include three counts of genocide: genocide by killing; genocide by causing serious bodily or mental harm, and genocide by deliberately inflicting on each target group conditions of life calculated to bring about the group's physical destruction. Al-Bashir is the only suspect indicted in genocide charges. The rest of the members of his government under investigation by the ICC, include Ahmad Muhammad Harun, former Minister of State for the Interior and current Minister of State for Humanitarian Affairs of Sudan, Abdel Raheem Muhammad Hussein, former Minister of the Interior and Sudanese President's Special Representative in Darfur and current Minister of National Defense, as well as the alleged leader of the Janjaweed, Ali Muhammad Ali Abd-Al-Rahman ("Ali Kushayb"). They all face charges of war crimes and crimes against humanities. The cases before the ICC are discussed further in Chapter 13.

Box 9.6 The Prosecutor v. Omar Hassan Ahmad al-Bashir. Second Warrant of Arrest, 12 July 2010

PRE-TRIAL CHAMBER I of the International Criminal Court ("Chamber" and "Court" respectively);

HAVING EXAMINED the "Prosecution's Application under Article 58" ("Prosecution's Application"), filed by the Prosecution on 14 July 2008 in the record of the situation in Darfur, Sudan ("Darfur situation") requesting the issuance of a warrant for the arrest of Omar Hassan Ahmad Al Bashir (hereinafter referred to as "Omar Al Bashir") for genocide, crimes against humanity and war crimes; …

…

CONSIDERING that that there are also reasonable grounds to believe that in furtherance of the genocidal policy, as part of the GoS's unlawful attack on the above-mentioned part of the civilian population of Darfur and with knowledge of such attack, GoS forces throughout the Darfur region (i) at times, contaminated the wells and water pumps of the towns and villages primarily inhabited by members of the Fur, Masalit and Zaghawa groups that they attacked; (ii) subjected hundreds of thousands of civilians belonging primarily to the Fur, Masalit and Zaghawa groups to acts of forcible transfer; and (iii) encouraged members of other tribes, which were allied with the GoS, to resettle in the villages and lands previously mainly inhabited by members of the Fur, Masalit and Zaghawa groups;

CONSIDERING therefore that there are reasonable grounds to believe that, from soon after the April 2003 attack on El Fasher airport at least until the date of the Prosecution's Application, GoS forces, including the Sudanese Armed Forces and their allied Janjaweed Militia, the Sudanese Police Force, the NISS and the HAC, committed the crimes of genocide by killing, genocide by causing serious bodily or mental harm and genocide by deliberately inflicting conditions of life calculated to bring about physical destruction, within the meaning of article 6 (a), (b) and (c) respectively of the Statute, against part of the Fur, Masalit and Zaghawa ethnic groups;

CONSIDERING that there are reasonable grounds to believe that Omar Al Bashir has been the de jure and de facto President of the Republic of the Sudan and Commander-in-Chief of the Sudanese Armed Forces from March 2003 until at least the date of the Prosecution's Application 14 July 2008, and that, in that position, he played an essential role in coordinating, with other high-ranking Sudanese political and military leaders, the design and implementation of the above-mentioned GoS counter-insurgency campaign;

CONSIDERING, further, that the Chamber finds, in the alternative, that there are reasonable grounds to believe: (i) that the role of Omar Al Bashir went beyond coordinating the design and implementation of the common plan; (ii) that he was in full control of all branches of the "apparatus" of the Republic of the Sudan, including the Sudanese Armed Forces and their allied Janjaweed Militia, the Sudanese Police Force, the NISS and the HAC; and (iii) that he used such control to secure the implementation of the common plan;

CONSIDERING that, on the basis of the standard of proof as identified by the Appeals Chamber, there are reasonable grounds to believe that Omar Al Bashir acted with dolus specialis I speciiic [sic] intent to destroy in part the Fur, Masalit and Zaghawa ethnic groups;

CONSIDERING that, for the above reasons, there are reasonable grounds to believe that Omar Al Bashir is criminally responsible as an indirect perpetrator, or as an indirect co-perpetrator, under article 25(3)(a) of the Statute, for:

i. Genocide by killing, within the meaning of article 6(a) of the Statute;
ii. Genocide by causing serious bodily or mental harm, within the meaning of article 6(b) of the Statute; and
iii. Genocide by deliberately inflicting conditions of life calculated to bring about physical destruction, within the meaning of article 6(c) of the Statute.

Source: International Criminal Court, Office of the Prosecutor, http://www.icc-cpi.int/en_ menus/icc/situations%20and%20cases/situations/situation%20icc%200205/related%20cases/ icc02050109/court%20records/chambers/ptci/Pages/95.aspx

Box 9.7 Sudan timeline

1899–1955	Sudan under joint British-Egyptian rule.
1956	Independence.
1958	Military coup against the civilian government elected earlier in the year.
1962	Civil war begins in the south, led by the Anya Nya movement (SSLM).
1964	"October Revolution" overthrows the government; new national government established.
1969	New military coup, the "May Revolution," led by Jafar Numeiri.
1972	Addis Ababa Agreement between the government and the Anya Nya movement; the south becomes a self-governing region.
1978	Oil discovered in Bentiu in the south.
1983	Civil war breaks out again in the south, involving government forces and the SPLM, led by John Garang. President Numeiri declares introduction of *sharia* law.
1985	Numeiri deposed by a group of officers; Transitional Military Council established to rule the country.
1986	Coalition government formed after general elections, led by Sadiq al-Mahdi as prime minister.
1989	National Salvation Revolution takes over in military coup.
1993	Omar al-Bashir appointed president; Revolution Command Council dissolved.
1999	President Bashir dissolves National Assembly and declares state of emergency. Sudan begins to export oil.
2000	al-Bashir re-elected president for further five years.
2001	Islamist leader Hassan al-Turabi's party, the Popular National Congress (PNC), signs memorandum of understanding with the SPLA; al-Turabi arrested the next day, with more arrests of PNC members in following months. Government accepts Libyan-Egyptian initiative to end the civil war after failure of peace talks between President Bashir and SPLM leader John Garang in Nairobi.
2002	*July:* Government and SPLA sign the first peace agreement: the Machakos Protocol.
2003	*February:* Rebels in Western Darfur rise up against government.
	January: Army moves to quell rebel uprising in Western Darfur; hundreds of thousands of refugees flee to neighboring Chad.
	May: Government and southern rebels agree on power-sharing protocols as part of peace deal to end the north–south conflict.
2005	*January:* Government and southern rebels sign peace agreement that includes permanent cease-fire and accords on wealth and power sharing.
	March: UN Security Council votes to refer those accused of war crimes in Darfur to International Criminal Court.

June: Government and exiled opposition group National Democratic Alliance (NDA) sign reconciliation deal allowing NDA into power-sharing administration. President Bashir frees Islamist leader Hassan al-Turabi, detained since March 2004 over alleged coup plot.

July 9: Former SPLM leader John Garang sworn in as first vice president; constitution giving significant autonomy to the south is signed.

August 1: Vice president and former rebel leader John Garang killed in plane crash and succeeded by Salva Kiir; Garang's death sparks deadly clashes in the capital between southern Sudanese and northern Arabs.

September: Power-sharing government formed in Khartoum.

October: Autonomous government formed in the south, in line with January 2005 peace deal; administration dominated by former rebels.

2006   *May:* Khartoum government and main rebel faction in Darfur, the SLM, sign peace accord, but fighting continues.

November: African Union extends mandate of its peacekeeping force in Darfur for six months.

2007   *April:* Sudan says it will accept partial UN troop deployment to reinforce AU peacekeepers in Darfur, but not a full 20,000-strong force.

May: International Criminal Court issues arrest warrants for both a minister and a Janjaweed militia leader suspected of committing war crimes in Darfur.

July: UN Security Council approves resolution authorizing UNAMID.

October: SPLM temporarily suspends participation in national unity government, accusing Khartoum of failing to honor 2005 peace deal.

December: SPLM resumes participation in national unity government.

2008   *January:* UN takes over Darfur peace force; Sudanese government bombs rebel positions in Western Darfur, preventing access by aid workers.

March: Presidents of Sudan and Chad sign accord aimed at halting five years of hostilities between their countries.

May: Southern defense minister Dominic Dim Deng killed in plane crash in the south; tension increases between Sudan and Chad, resulting in severed diplomatic relations; intense fighting breaks out between northern and southern Sudanese forces in disputed oil-rich town of Abyei.

June: President Bashir and southern leader Salva Kiir agree to seek international arbitration to resolve dispute over Abyei.

July: International Criminal Court's top prosecutor calls for arrest of President Bashir for genocide, crimes against humanity, and war crimes committed in Darfur, representing first ever request to the ICC for arrest of a sitting head of state; Sudan rejects the indictment.

November: President Bashir announces an immediate cease-fire in Darfur, but the region's two main rebel groups reject the move, saying they will fight until the government agrees to share power and wealth in the region.

2009	*March*: The ICC issues its first arrest warrant for President Bashir on charges of war crimes and crimes against humanity in Darfur.
	July: North and south Sudan accept ruling on the status of Abyei by the arbitral tribunal in The Hague.
	December: Leaders of north and south reach deal on terms of 2011 referendum on independence.
2010	*February–March*: The Justice and Equality Movement and the government sign a peace accord, prompting President al-Bashir to declare the Darfur war over.
	April: al-Bashir is re-elected as president
	July: The ICC issues second arrest warrant for al-Bashir on charges of genocide.
	August: The Kenyan government refuses to enforce the ICC warrant when al-Bashir visits the country.
2011	*January*: Referendum of independence in South Sudan overwhelmingly approved.
	May: The town of Abyei is invaded by northern troops.
	July: South Sudan is declared independent.
	September: State of emergency declared in Blue Nile state, and thousands flee.
	October: South Sudan and Sudan agree to set up several committees to resolve their outstanding disputes.
	November: Sudan accused of bombing refugee camp in Yida, Unity State, South Sudan.
	December: The OTP of the ICC requests arrest warrant for Sudan's defense minister, Abdelrahim Mohamed Hussein, for alleged war crimes in Darfur.
2012	*January*: South Sudan halts oil production after talks on fees for the export of oil via Sudan break down.
	February–April: Sudan and South Sudan sign non-aggression pact at talks on outstanding secession issues, but border fighting breaks out.
	May: Bilateral peace talks resume between Sudan and South Sudan.
	August: Sudan and South Sudan agree on resumption of South Sudan's oil exports via Sudan's pipelines.
	September: Agreement between Sudan and South Sudan on trade, oil and security, including setting up a demilitarized zone on the border. They fail to resolve border issues including the disputed Abyei territory. Clashes with rebels in Darfur and South Kordofan region.
2013	*March*: Sudan and South Sudan agree to resume pumping oil following a yearlong shutdown over disputes over fees. They also agreed to withdraw troops from their border area to create a demilitarized zone.

Discussion questions

Determining accountability

As we have seen, all parties to the conflict in Sudan—the government, the militias, and the rebel groups—have taken part in atrocities. We now consider the extent to which the actions of the Janjaweed militias may be attributed to the government, and the potential role of foreign corporations in aggravating the conflict.

- According to the International Commission of Inquiry, the actions in Darfur do not constitute genocide. What does this mean in terms of individual responsibility for those involved?
- Could the actions of the Janjaweed militias be attributed to the state? If so, what difference would this make in identifying specific acts as international crimes?
- Could managers and employees of Talisman Energy be prosecuted for violations of international law?

Prospects for addressing violations

The government of Sudan has no evident interest in pursuing extensive accountability, which could implicate its high-level officials. To date, no proceedings, either outside or inside Sudan, have been initiated to address abuses committed during the north–south civil war, excepting the case concerning Talisman Energy. However, a great deal more attention has been paid to the violence and abuses being committed in Darfur, including the case before the ICC, which has triggered vigorous opposition from the government. But as we have seen, there have been few Darfur-related domestic trials.

- How does the absence of accountability provisions in the Comprehensive Peace Agreement affect the possibility of prosecutions for violations committed during the north–south conflict?
- Given the nature and behavior of the Sudanese government to date, do you think that domestic trials could provide accountability for the human rights violations?

Achieving stability

Despite the peace agreement between the government of Sudan and the SPLA, and the referendum granting southern independence, tensions, especially in the border region are high and the stability of the situation remains fragile. Despite the signing of the Darfur Peace Agreement in 2005, the conflict and human rights violations have continued.

What are the main risks of a return to conflict between Sudan and South Sudan?

- Now that South Sudan is an independent country, would the crimes committed in the border region be treated differently under the Geneva Conventions and their Additional Protocols?
- Would investigations and prosecutions by the ICC help, or jeopardize, the chances for achieving peace in the region and ending human rights abuses?

> **Group exercise**
>
> Form two groups. Gather evidence from reports by international and state bodies on the human rights abuses committed in Darfur. One group should argue for treating the acts in Darfur as genocide, and the other group should argue against. Both groups should discuss the legal repercussions that such a designation would have.

Further reading

Abass, Ademola, "Proving State Responsibility for Genocide: The ICJ in *Bosnia v. Serbia* and the International Commission of Inquiry for Darfur," *Fordham International Law Journal* vol. 31, no. 4 (2008): 871–910.

Abass, Ademola, "The United Nations, the African Union, and the Darfur Crisis: Of Apology and Utopia," *Netherlands International Law Review* vol. 54, no. 3 (2007): 415–440.

Human Rights Watch, "Sudan, Oil, and Human Rights" (2003), http://www.hrw.org/reports/2003/sudan1103/sudanprint.pdf

Idris, Amir, *Conflict and Politics of Identity in Sudan* (London: Palgrave Macmillan, 2005).

International Crisis Group, "God, Oil, and Country: Changing the Logic of War in Sudan" (2002), http://www.crisisgroup.org/en/regions/africa/horn-of-africa/sudan/039-god-oil-and-country-changing-the-logic-of-war-in-sudan.aspx

International Crisis Group, "Sudan's Spreading Conflict (I): War in South Kordofan" (14 February 2003), http://www.crisisgroup.org/en/regions/africa/horn-of-africa/sudan/198-sudans-spreading-conflict-i-war-in-south-kordofan.aspx

Iyob, Ruth, and Gilbert M. Khadiagala, *Sudan: The Elusive Quest for Peace* (Boulder, CO: Lynne Rienner, 2006).

Johnson, Douglas, *The Root Causes of Sudan's Civil Wars* (Oxford: James Currey, 2003).

Lathrop, Coalter G. "Government of Sudan v. Sudan's People's Liberation Movement/Army (Abyei Arbitration)", *American Journal of International Law* vol. 104 (2010): 66–73.

Nouwen, Sarah and Wouter G. Werner, "Doing Justice to the Political: The International Criminal Court in Uganda and Sudan," *European Journal of International Law* vol. 21, no. 4 (2011): 941–965.

Sriram, Chandra Lekha, *Peace as Governance* (London: Palgrave, 2008), Chapter 4.

Official documents and sources

United Nations, *Report of the International Commission of Inquiry on Darfur to the United Nations Secretary-General* (January 25, 2005), http://www.un.org/news/dh/sudan/com_inq_darfur.pdf

United Nations, Office of the UN Deputy Special Representative of the UN Secretary-General for Sudan, *Darfur Humanitarian Profile* no. 29 (October 1, 2007), http://www.unsudanig.org/docs/hnp%2029_narrative_1%20october%202007.pdf

Online source

International Criminal Court, http://www.icc-cpi.int/

Part III
Building peace and seeking accountability

Recent mechanisms and institutions

10 Ad hoc tribunals

Key points

- The **International Criminal Tribunal for the Former Yugoslavia** (ICTY) and the **International Criminal Tribunal for Rwanda** (ICTR) are international tribunals established by the **UN Security Council.**
- The ICTY and ICTR prosecute violations of international law during the conflict in the former Yugoslavia and the Rwandan genocide respectively.
- Both tribunals have carried out a number of landmark cases leading to important advances in **international humanitarian law**, particularly regarding gender related crimes.
- Criticisms of the tribunals include the relatively low numbers of indictments when compared to the enormous costs involved, as well as the slow progression of cases.
- The **Mechanism for International Criminal Tribunals** (MICT) has been created to carry out a number of functions for both tribunals after the completion of their mandates.

The International Criminal Tribunal for the Former Yugoslavia

History and legal basis

The International Criminal Tribunal for the Former Yugoslavia was established in order to bring to trial those responsible for the atrocities committed during the conflict in the region. See Chapter 6 for a detailed analysis of the conflict in the former Republic of Yugoslavia (FRY).

A number of **United Nations** (UN) and **UN Security Council** actions laid the groundwork for the development of the ICTY. The first comment of the Security Council on the situation in Yugoslavia came in Resolution 713 of September 1991. This was followed by another 10 resolutions through 1992 reaffirming concern about the fighting and stating that continuation of the conflict constituted a threat to international peace and security. In addition to this concern, the Security Council noted in Resolution 764 that all parties to the conflict were bound to comply with international humanitarian law and that those who committed **grave breaches** of the **Geneva Conventions** were individually responsible. This led to the establishment of a UN commission of experts, under Resolution 780, tasked with examining grave breaches of the Geneva Conventions and other violations of international humanitarian law committed in the FRY. The commission of experts confirmed that grave breaches and other violations of international humanitarian law, including ethnic cleansing, mass killings, **torture**, and rape had been committed, and recommended the establishment of an ad hoc international tribunal. This led to the Security Council decision of February 1993, under Resolution 808, to establish a tribunal to address the widespread violations of international humanitarian law in the FRY.

Resolution 808 asked the **UN Secretary-General** to make recommendations on the establishment of such a tribunal. His subsequent report considered the legal basis and suggested that the tribunal be established through a **UN Security Council resolution**. Although the normal procedure would be to establish an international tribunal by treaty, drafting such a treaty and getting enough countries to ratify it would take significant time. In addition, the treaty process would also be unable to guarantee ratification from the states involved. Establishing the tribunal by decision of the Security Council under Chapter VII of the **UN Charter** was quicker and would ensure that all states were under a binding obligation to carry out the decision. The Secretary-General also noted that the Council had previously established subsidiary organs for the maintenance of peace and security, so the only difference here was that this would be a judicial organ. Although established by Security Council resolution, the tribunal would be independent of any political considerations in its operations and instead apply existing international humanitarian law.

Resolution 827 established the ICTY in May 1993 and adopted the statute of the tribunal (see Box 10.1). The ICTY website stated four objectives in carrying out the purposes of this resolution:

- to bring to justice persons responsible for violations of international humanitarian law;
- to contribute to the restoration of peace by holding these persons to account;
- to bring justice to the victims;
- to deter further crimes.

ICTY organs

Chambers

The Chambers consist of 16 permanent judges divided between three trial chambers and one appeals chamber. At any one time, there are a maximum of 16 *ad litem* (ad hoc) judges, who join particular trials as necessary. All judges are appointed by the **UN General Assembly** for four-year terms; the 16 permanent judges can be reelected, but the *ad litem* judges cannot. The *ad litem* judges were appointed in November 2000 in order to maximize the efficiency of the court following criticism of the time taken for trials.

Office of the Prosecutor

The Office of the Prosecutor conducts investigations and is independent of any country or organ of the ICTY. It prepares indictments and initiates prosecutions. The office is staffed by police officers, crime experts, analysts, lawyers, and trial attorneys as necessary to carry out its activities. There have been four prosecutors: Richard Goldstone (1994–96), Louise Arbour (1996–99), Carla Del Ponte (1999–2007), and Serge Brammertz (2008–).

Registry

The Registry carries out the administration and judicial support services of the tribunal, including record-keeping, translation, and has responsibility for custody of defendants and protection for witnesses.

***Box 10.1* Key articles from the statute of the ICTY**

Statute of the International Criminal Tribunal for the Former Yugoslavia

Article 1: Competence of the International Tribunal

The International Tribunal shall have the power to prosecute persons responsible for serious violations of international humanitarian law committed in the territory of the former Yugoslavia since 1991....

Article 2: Grave breaches of the Geneva Conventions of 1949

... shall have the power to prosecute persons committing or ordering to be committed grave breaches of the Geneva Conventions....

Article 3: Violations of the laws or customs of war

... shall have the power to prosecute persons violating the laws or customs of war. ...

Article 4: Genocide

... shall have the power to prosecute persons committing genocide....
... the following acts shall be punishable:
a. genocide
b. conspiracy to commit genocide
c. direct and public incitement to commit genocide
d. attempt to commit genocide
e. complicity in genocide

Article 5: Crimes against humanity

... shall have the power to prosecute persons responsible for the following crimes when committed in armed conflict, whether international or internal in character and directed against any civilian population. ...

Article 7: Individual Criminal Responsibility

A person who planned, instigated, ordered, committed or otherwise aided and abetted ... shall be individually responsible for the crime.

Detention Unit

The Detention Unit holds the accused until the completion of proceedings. If the accused are found guilty, the Detention Unit transfers the prisoners to appropriate states, as previously agreed with the UN, to serve their sentences.

Functioning of the ICTY

The ICTY's first session was from November 17–30, 1993; its first indictment was issued a year later. This delay was due to political challenges in establishing the tribunal, such as funding, appointing the chief prosecutor, and staffing the court. It took time to build the logistical and procedural infrastructure needed for the court to function, as well as to establish agreements with governments to provide assistance. As a result, the ICTY was not really a fully functioning international court until 1999. Beyond the initial organizational problems in establishing the tribunal, there has been an ongoing lack of cooperation by key governments, hindering the gathering of evidence and enforcing of arrest warrants. When states do cooperate, they have tended to want evidence kept confidential; and even if evidence is shared during early stages, it might still be blocked at trial. In the FRY, there was no cooperation with the ICTY, with the Yugoslav authorities failing to arrest two key accused—Radovan Karadžić and Ratko Mladić. With the 1999 Kosovo conflict and indictment of Slobodan Milošević, the situation worsened. The Croatian government publicly stated that it would cooperate with the ICTY, but in reality used legal arguments to obstruct the court's work. Still, in November 2000, the ICTY prosecutor acknowledged that cooperation by Croatia had improved compared to the past. The situation was better in Bosnia, where there had been some ad hoc interaction with the UN Protection Force (UNPROFOR). The difficulties in apprehension are shown by the fact that between 1994 and 1996 there were 44 indictments but only eight arrests. These arrests steadily grew over the following 17 years, with a large proportion captured by the NATO led Stabilization Force (SFOR) for Bosnia and the others by Austria, Germany, Bosnia, Croatia and Serbia. By mid-2011, and in contrast to the ICTR, all indicted suspects had been successfully arrested. Of 161 indicted persons, 131 were captured, 20 had their indictments withdrawn and the rest died before apprehension. Karadžić was captured in July 2008 and Mladić in 2011, with Goran Hadžić—the last of the ICTY indictees—apprehended in July 2011. These particular arrests were made following pressure by the European Union on Serbia to arrest the war criminals as a pre-condition of membership.

The ICTY has experienced ongoing organizational and logistical difficulties. Dealing with such complex cases means that a great deal of evidence needs to be collected, as well as translated. And with public indictments, some suspects went into hiding to avoid prosecution. In response, the ICTY shifted to using sealed indictments in order to better enable the arrest of suspects.

ICTY jurisprudence

Competence

The ICTY recognizes the principle of **nullum crimen sine lege**, meaning that a person cannot be accused of a crime unless it was a crime under law at the time it was committed. In order to avoid accusations of applying the law retroactively, the tribunal applies principles of international humanitarian law that are customary law. This avoids the question of ratification of specific conventions. The tribunal thus goes to great lengths to justify the customary bases that it uses as its source of law, and this elaboration of customary law through its jurisprudence provides an important basis for future decisions beyond the ICTY (and ICTR). The tribunal can prosecute the following offenses that have been committed on the territory of the former Yugoslavia since 1991:

- grave breaches of the 1949 Geneva Conventions;
- violations of the laws or customs of war;
- genocide;
- crimes against humanity.

The court has the authority to try natural persons only, and as such cannot indict organizations, political parties, administrative entities, or other legal subjects. Bosnian courts are unable to prosecute cases where the ICTY has jurisdiction.

Focus

The ICTY has focused on cases of human rights abuse against civilians, with its first trials indicting lower-level perpetrators. This enabled the tribunal to operate during the ongoing conflict, and to be seen as proceeding with its mandate. The reasoning behind this strategy was that trying lower-level perpetrators would eventually lead to enough evidence to indict the higher-level perpetrators. As the work of the ICTY continued and its legitimacy grew, outside pressure increased, there was more cooperation, and higher-level perpetrators began to be indicted. This approach was consolidated in the completion strategy for the ICTY as elaborated in Security Council Resolutions 1503 and 1534. These resolutions stated that the ICTY should finish its work by 2010 and that, in order to achieve this, the tribunal should concentrate on the prosecution of those who bear the most responsibility and refer lower-ranking individuals to the national courts. The most famous of these high-level indictments came in May 1999, when the ICTY charged President Slobodan Milošević Milošević with **crimes against humanity** and **war crimes** against Kosovar Albanians. He was arrested in April 2001, following his fall from power, and the trial started in February 2002. The prosecution took two years, finishing in February 2004, and the defense phase started several months later, in August, due to Milošević's ill health. Milošević represented himself, would not speak to the court-appointed defense lawyers, refused to enter a plea, and questioned the legitimacy of the court. Milošević died in March 2006, toward the end of the trial, before a verdict could be rendered. The prosecutor, Carla del Ponte, stated at the time that Milošević's death deprived his victims of the justice they needed and deserved.

The final arrests of Karadžić, Mladić and Hadžić put to rest earlier criticism of the ICTY that it had failed to put key fugitives on trial. Karadžić was captured on July 21, 2008, 13 years after his first indictment. He was the president of the self-proclaimed Serbian Republic of Bosnia (Republika Srpska). He was accused of orchestrating the Srebrenica massacre, the shelling of Sarajevo, and the use of peacekeepers as human shields. He went into hiding in 1996 and assumed the life of an alternative health therapist, changing his appearance and fooling all those around him. His trial is expected to finish in 2014. Mladić was a prominent figure in the conflict, as he was the commander of Republika Srpska's army. He is also accused of a wide range of crimes during the war, including a major role in the Srebenica massacre and the shelling of Sarajevo. The ICTY estimates that the Hadžić and Mladić trials will finish by 31 December 2015 and 31 July 2016, respectively.

As of June 2013, the ICTY has 12 ongoing trials and 13 before the appeals chamber.

ICTY landmark cases

Tadić

The first determination of individual guilt or innocence by the ICTY was the trial of Duško Tadić in May 1995. Tadić was a leading member of the Serbian Democratic Party and of a Serb paramilitary group. He was accused of taking part in ethnic cleansing against the non-Serbian population in the town of Kozarac in Bosnia–Herzegovina, where 800 civilians out of a population of 4,000 were killed, and the rest were forced to leave the town. After the

---

Box 10.2   The UN Charter, Article 41

Charter of the United Nations
CHAPTER VII
ACTION WITH RESPECT TO THREATS TO THE PEACE, BREACHES OF THE
PEACE, AND ACTS OF AGGRESSION
Article 41

The Security Council may decide what measures not involving the use of armed force
are to be employed to give effect to its decisions, and it may call upon the Members
of the United Nations to apply such measures. These may include complete or partial
interruption of economic relations and of rail, sea, air, postal, telegraphic, radio, and
other means of communication, and the severance of diplomatic relations.

---

takeover of the area, thousands of Muslims and Croats were put into camps and severely
mistreated. Tadić was indicted for crimes against humanity, grave breaches of the Geneva
Conventions, and violations of the laws or customs of war, under Articles 5, 2, and 3 of the
ICTY statute, respectively. This case resulted in several key developments.

JURISDICTION OF THE ICTY

The Tadić defense objected to the ICTY's assertion of jurisdiction, challenging the legality of
the establishment of the tribunal, and its subject-matter jurisdiction. The tribunal determined
that, as a subsidiary organ of the United Nations, it could review Security Council resolutions.
Tadić had objected that the Security Council had acted outside its mandate under Article 41
of the UN Charter by creating a court, which is not one of the measures envisioned in that
article. The tribunal had to consider whether the Council is limited to the measures listed in
Articles 41 and 42 of the UN Charter. However, the tribunal found that the measures listed
in Article 41 (see Box 10.2) are illustrative rather than comprehensive and therefore did not
rule out the establishment of an international tribunal.

INTERNATIONAL V. INTERNAL ARMED CONFLICT

The defense team claimed that under Articles 2 and 3 of the ICTY statute, the alleged acts
needed to have taken place in an international armed conflict. The Tadić defense claimed
that the alleged crimes had been committed in the context of an internal armed conflict and
therefore were outside of the jurisdiction of the ICTY. The tribunal agreed and determined
that Article 2 of the statute, invoking grave breaches of the Geneva Conventions, did require
the presence of an international armed conflict. The court found that after May 19, 1992,
when the Yugoslav People's Army withdrew from Bosnia-Herzegovina, the FRY did not
have effective control over the Bosnian Serb forces. This meant that the conflict could not be
defined as international, and that the victims were not protected persons under the Geneva
Conventions—and Tadić was acquitted on this count (although he was found guilty on the
other counts). The appeals chamber reversed this decision by finding that the conflict was in
fact international. It determined that the trial chamber had used too stringent a test, and that
instead of proving effective control, the prosecution only had to prove overall control of the

Bosnian Serbs by Serbia. This overall control consists of a state organizing, coordinating, or planning military actions of the military group as well as financing, training, equipping, or providing operational support, and does not need to include specific orders or planning of operations. The appeals chamber found Tadić guilty of grave breaches of the Geneva Conventions.

DEFINITION OF ARMED CONFLICT

The ICTY determined that the crimes listed under Articles 5 and 3 of its statute required the presence of conflict, but not one of a specifically international type (see Box 10.1), and so had to consider under what circumstances armed conflict could occur, for the purposes of **Common Article 3** of the Geneva Conventions, in order to try Tadić. The court determined that conflict between states or protracted armed violence between governmental authorities and organized armed groups was required. It found that international humanitarian law applies from the start of such conflict and ends at the peace settlement. It is noteworthy that the decision did not require the armed group to exercise territorial control. This alone did not solve the problem of prosecuting Tadić, since Common Article 3, unlike the grave breaches provisions of the Geneva conventions, does not specifically criminalize specific acts, it just prohibits them. So the ICTY further determined that while Common Article 3 does not explicitly refer to individual criminal liability, as the Nuremberg Tribunal had determined, the absence of specific treaty provisions does not rule out such liability.

Krstić

Radislav Krstić was the deputy commander and chief of staff of the Drina Corps within the Bosnian Serb Army, which was tasked with planning and carrying out "Krivaja 95"—the operation to attack Srebenica. The ICTY trial chamber found that Krstić had participated in plans to ethnically cleanse Srebenica of all Muslims and to kill the men of military age there. He was found guilty of murder, persecutions, and **genocide**. The latter represented an important elaboration of the definition of genocide, with the court finding that intent to destroy a part of a group within a limited geographical area can still be held as genocide. There is therefore no need to show the intent of the accused to destroy the entire group, but only a part that is a distinct entity, in this case Bosnian Muslims in Srebenica. Even though the focus of the killing was on men of fighting age, the perpetrators knew this would have an impact on the group and that, coupled with the forcible transfer of women, children, and elderly, this would result in the Bosnian Muslim population disappearing from that area.

Čelebiči

In this case the ICTY made important advances in attributing command responsibility. The court confirmed that superior commanders have an obligation to ensure that their subordinates do not carry out war crimes and crimes against humanity. The case concerned four individuals who worked in the Čelebiči prison camp: Zdravko Mucić, the camp commander; Hazim Delić, the camp deputy commander; Esad Landzo, a camp guard; and Zejnil Delalić, coordinator of the Bosnian Muslim and Bosnian Croat forces. It was alleged that Bosnian Muslim and Bosnian Croat forces took control of Bosnian Serb villages around the Konjic municipality in central Bosnia. Persons detained during these operations were held at the Čelebiči camp, where it was alleged that detainees were killed, tortured, sexually assaulted, and beaten. In this case, the first concerning command responsibility since the Nuremberg trials, the ICTY found that a superior can be held criminally responsible for failing to prevent crimes committed by subordinates, whether this position was held *de jure* or *de facto*, and whether the superior was a civilian holding a position of authority or a military commander. Mucić was found guilty of command responsibility for murder, torture, and ill-treatment, Delić and Landzo were not found to have had command responsibility for the offenses of others, but were still found guilty for murder, wilful killings, and rape. Delalić was found not to have had command responsibility over the Celibici prison camp and so was acquitted of all charges.

Aleksovksi

The ICTY appeals chamber in this case widened the definition of protected persons under Article 4 of Fourth Geneva Convention. This article states: "Persons protected by the Convention are those who, at a given moment and in any manner whatsoever, find themselves, in case of a conflict or occupation, in the hands of a Party to the conflict or Occupying Power of which they are not nationals." Zlatko Aleksovski, a Bosnian Croat and commander of a prison facility at Kaonik, near Busovača in Bosnia-Herzegovina, was accused of committing abuses against Bosnian Muslim prisoners. It was alleged that detainees under his control were subjected to inhumane treatment such as excessive and cruel interrogation, physical and psychological harm, and forced labor, and that some detainees were used as human shields and killed. He was indicted on charges under Articles 2 and 3 of the ICTY statute. The trial chamber in 1999 first acquitted Aleksovski of inhumane treatment and willfully causing great suffering or serious injury to body or health, because the chamber did not consider the Bosnian Muslim victims to be protected persons as defined by the Fourth Geneva Convention and because the offenses did not take place during an international armed conflict. The appeals chamber overturned this verdict and considered the conflict to be international in character, as shown by the overall control test in the *Tadić* case. The appeals chamber found that the provision of protection to civilians can be widened so that a person can have protected status even if they have the same nationality as their captors. The appeals chamber stated that this understanding of Article 4 is in keeping with the spirit of the Geneva Conventions and is especially important for interethnic conflict, in which the question of nationality is not so clear-cut.

Furundžija

Anto Furundžija was the local commander of a special unit—known as the "Jokers"—of the Croatian Defense Council's military police force. He was accused of being present while a female Muslim civilian was raped and a Croatian solder was beaten during an interrogation at the Jokers' headquarters. The ICTY trial chamber found that the ban on torture has reached the level of *jus cogens* under international law, which means that no derogation is permitted under any circumstance. The definition of torture used by the court was based on that in the **Genocide Convention**:

> the intentional infliction, by act or omission, of severe pain or suffering, whether physical or mental, for the purpose of obtaining information or a confession or of punishing, intimidating, humiliating or coercing the victim or a third person, or of discriminating on any ground against the victim or a third person. For such an act

to constitute torture, one of the parties thereto must be a public official or must, at any rate, act in a non-private capacity, e.g. as a de facto organ of a State or any other authority wielding entity.

Gotovina

Ante Gotovina was Operations Commander of the Croatian Forces and directed "Operation Storm", which was launched to recover Southern Krajina in 1995. The objective of the operation was to recapture the area from the Serbs and expel them. He was accused of expelling 150,000 individuals and responsibility for the death of 150 Serb civilians resulting from the operation. He was indicted in 2001, arrested in 2005 and charged with individual criminal responsibility and also as a hierarchical superior on five counts of crimes against humanity (persecution, deportation, forcible transfer, inhumane acts, murder) and four counts of war crimes (plunder, wanton destruction, murder, cruel treatment). After a number of delays, his trial began in March 2008, together with two other Croatian generals, Ivan Čermak and Mladen Markač. In April 2011, the Trial Chamber acquitted Čermak and convicted Gotovina and Markač of eight counts of crimes against humanity and war crimes (finding them not guilty of forcible transfer as a crime against humanity). Gotovina was sentenced to 24 years and Markač to 18 years. However, they both appealed and the hearing was held in May 2012. In November of that year the Appeals Chamber acquitted Gotovina and Markač of crimes against humanity and war crimes and ordered their release. The Appeals Chamber stated that the Trial Chamber had erred in finding there was a joint criminal enterprise to permanently and forcibly remove the Serb population from Krajina. The Appeals Chamber also found that the Trial Chamber had erred in finding that the artillery attacks ordered by Gotovina and Markač were unlawful.

Definition of rape and sexual violence

The ICTY (and the ICTR) made great advances in the recognition of rape and sexual violence as crimes of genocide, torture, war crimes, or crimes against humanity. In the Čelibiči case, the court determined that "there can be no question that acts of rape may constitute torture under customary law." The court found that because Delić was a public official, any rapes committed by him would constitute torture, since in this circumstance rape would always involve "punishment, coercion, discrimination, or intimidation." The court also found that rape was also a crime against humanity. In the *Kunarac* (or *Foča*) case, sexual slavery too was defined as a crime against humanity. Foča and its surrounding villages were occupied by Serb military forces, and Muslim and Croatian inhabitants were detained under deplorable conditions in facilities in the area. Dragoljub Kunarac was the head of a special unit of the Serb military forces, and Radomir Kovač and Zoran Vuković were paramilitary commanders. Among other indictments, the three were charged with rape as a crime against humanity, and Kunarac and Kovač were charged with enslavement as a crime against humanity. It was alleged that they had taken women and girls from the detention centers and held them in sexual slavery. The ICTY judgment defined enslavement, including control of sexuality, exploitation, sex, prostitution, and trafficking, as a crime against humanity. This is important because it broadened the definition of enslavement beyond an economic crime. In the *Furundžija* case, the accused was convicted of torture even though he did not personally commit the rapes, and the ICTY expanded the definition of rape to mean:

the sexual penetration, however slight, either of the vagina or anus of the victim by the penis of the perpetrator, or any other object used by the perpetrator, or of the mouth of the victim by the penis of the perpetrator, where such penetration is effected by coercion or force or threat of force against the victim or a third person.

The trial chamber noted in the *Kvocka* case that sexual violence included sexual mutilation, forced marriage, and forced abortion, as well as the crimes listed in the Rome Statute (see Chapter 13, on the **International Criminal Court** [ICC]): rape, sexual slavery, forced prostitution, forced pregnancy, and forced sterilization.

ICTY sentencing

In determining sentencing under the ICTY statute, the trial chamber can look to the practice of the courts of the FRY, but is not obligated to follow their precedent. When the trial chamber is sentencing, it must look to the gravity of the offense and circumstances of the convicted person as well as to other mitigating and aggravating circumstances. There is no minimum sentence required and life is the maximum penalty. In practice, sentencing is at the discretion of the court, and its practices have differed with those of the ICTR. Early release can be granted depending on the law of the state where the sentence is being served, such as after two-thirds of sentence has been served.

ICTY completion strategy and case transfer

The ICTY completion strategy was endorsed by the Security Council in Resolutions 1503 and 1534. The three-phase plan envisioned completion of investigations by the end of 2004, completion of all first instance trials by the end of 2008, and completion of all work in 2010. In order to ensure effective closure of the ICTY, the completion strategy narrowed prosecutions to the senior leaders most responsible for war crimes. This meant that cases for lower ranked accused needed to be transferred to national courts, and is detailed in Article 11*bis* of the ICTY Rules of Procedure and Evidence (see Box 10.3). Although investigations were completed on time, the arrests of Karadžić, Mladić and Hadžić mean that the projected completion date of the tribunal's work is 2016.

Eight cases involving 13 lower-level perpetrators were transferred to Bosnia, Croatia and Serbia between September 2005 and June 2007. Six of these cases went to the War Crimes Chamber (WCC) in Bosnia. The WCC is part of the Criminal Division of the State Court of Bosnia and aims to provide the justice system with the capacity to prosecute and carry out war crimes trials to international justice standards.

The International Criminal Tribunal for Rwanda

History and legal basis

The ICTY paved the way for the International Criminal Tribunal for Rwanda. With the events following the death of Rwandan president Juvenal Habyarimana, ethnic tensions in the country escalated, leading to a genocide in April 1994 during which 800,000 Tutsis and moderate Hutus were killed. Outraged over the slaughter, the international community demanded prosecutions. As with the establishment of the ICTY, many allege that the establishment of the ICTR was to assuage the international community of its guilt from failing to act to stop the atrocities.

Box 10.3 **Rule 11*bis* of the ICTY**

Referral of the Indictment to Another Court

(A) … the President may appoint a bench of three Permanent Judges selected from the Trial Chambers (hereinafter referred to as the "Referral Bench"), which … shall determine whether the case should be referred to the authorities of a State:

i. in whose territory the crime was committed; or
ii. in which the accused was arrested; or
iii. having jurisdiction and being willing and adequately prepared to accept such a case,

so that those authorities should forthwith refer the case to the appropriate court for trial within that State.

(B) The Referral Bench may order such referral … after being satisfied that the accused will receive a fair trial and that the death penalty will not be imposed or carried out.

(C) In determining whether to refer the case in accordance with paragraph (A), the Referral Bench shall, in accordance with Security Council resolution 1534 (2004)1, consider the gravity of the crimes charged and the level of responsibility of the accused.

The establishment of the ICTR followed a pattern similar to that of the ICTY. Following the genocide, on April 30, 1994, the president of the Security Council stated that those who had participated in breaches of international humanitarian law in Rwanda were individually responsible, and requested the Secretary-General to investigate these violations. The Secretary-General's report on the situation led to Security Council Resolution 935, which established a commission of experts to examine the evidence for grave violations and possible acts of genocide. Their commission found that individuals from both sides of the Rwandan conflict had perpetrated serious breaches of international humanitarian law, that both sides had perpetrated crimes against humanity, and that Hutus had perpetrated acts of genocide. The commission recommended that those responsible for the human rights violations be brought to justice before an independent and international criminal tribunal.

The Security Council established the International Criminal Tribunal for Rwanda, under Chapter VII of the UN Charter, through Resolution 955 in November 1994. Following the experience of the ICTY, it was decided that a single resolution was sufficient. The statute of the ICTR (see Box 10.4) was adapted from that of the ICTY, and certain institutional links were made between the two international courts, such as sharing a prosecutor and the appeals chamber. There was a great deal of discussion about where to situate the court; although the Rwandan government wanted the court to be situated in its own country, suitable premises were lacking in Kigali due to damage caused by the war. Citing that it would be too expensive to build appropriate infrastructure in Rwanda in sufficient time, as well as concerns of fairness and impartiality, the Secretary-General recommended that the tribunal be located in a neutral country. Nairobi, Kenya, and Arusha, Tanzania were both considered, although Kenya was ultimately unable to offer a seat for the tribunal; Tanzania, on the other hand, could provide an international conference center. In Resolution 977 of February 1995, the Security Council decided that the ICTR would be located in Arusha.

Box 10.4 **Key articles from the Statute of the ICTR**

Statute for the International Criminal Tribunal for Rwanda

Article 1: Competence of the International Tribunal for Rwanda
The International Tribunal for Rwanda shall have the power to prosecute persons responsible for serious violations of the international humanitarian law committed in the territory of Rwanda and Rwandan citizens responsible for such violations committed in the territory of neighbouring States between 1 January 1994 and 31 December 1994, in accordance with the provisions of the present Statute.

Article 2: Genocide
… shall have the power to prosecute persons committing genocide …

Article 3: Crimes Against Humanity
… shall have the power to prosecute persons responsible for the following crimes when committed as part of a widespread or systematic attack against any civilian population on national, political, ethnic, racial or religious grounds …

Article 4: Violations of Article 3 Common to the Geneva Conventions and of Additional Protocol II
… shall have the power to prosecute persons committing or ordering to be committed serious violations of Article 3 common to the Geneva Conventions … and of Additional Protocol II …

Article 6: Individual Criminal Responsibility
1. A person who planned, instigated, ordered, committed or otherwise aided and abetted in the planning, preparation or execution of a crime … shall be individually responsible for the crime.
2. The official position of any accused person, whether as Head of State or Government … shall not relieve such person of criminal responsibility …
3. The fact that any of the acts … was referred to by a subordinate does not relieve his or her superior of criminal responsibility if he or she knew or had reason to know that the subordinate was about to commit such acts or had done so and he superior failed to take the necessary and reasonable measures to prevent such acts.

ICTR organs

The Tribunal completed all trial activities at the end of 2012. Some of the functions undertaken by ICTR Organs have been taken over by the Mechanism for International Tribunals (see the section on the Mechanism below).

Chambers

The chambers consisted of nine judges divided between three trial chambers. The appeals chamber, shared with the ICTY, is based at The Hague and comprises seven judges. Security Council Resolution 1431 of 2002 established a pool of 18 *ad litem* judges, with four *ad litem* judges attached to the trial chambers. Security Council Resolution 1512 of 2003 increased the latter number of *ad litem* judges to nine. As with the ICTY, judges for the ICTR were elected by the UN General Assembly for four-year terms.

Office of the Prosecutor

The Office of the Prosecutor was initially shared with the ICTY, until September 2003. This was to ensure that both tribunals were operating under the same prosecutorial strategy. Hassan Bubaca Jallow was eventually appointed as the ICTR's prosecutor. The office had two divisions: the Prosecution Division, which collected evidence and assembled trial teams to handle cases (and has completed its work), and the Appeals and Legal Advisory Division, which is responsible for appeals and providing advice to trial teams.

Registry

The Registry is responsible for administration and management of the tribunal, judicial and legal support services for the work of the trial chambers, and prosecution.

Witnesses and victim support

Support and protection was provided for the witnesses for both the prosecution and the defense, including physical and psychological rehabilitation. These tasks are now the responsibility of the MICT.

Defense counsel and detention management

The detention facility had 56 cells within the Arusha complex. There were 200 lawyers available for defense counsel to ensure the accused their right to a fair trial.

Functioning of the ICTR

The first accused arrived in Arusha in May 1996, and the first trial started in January 1997. The delay between Resolution 955 and the first trial was due to a number of logistical and operational problems. Arusha is less well-equipped and considered less prestigious than The Hague, which made it harder to staff the court, and the conference center in Arusha was not intended to house court facilities. Two courtrooms were operating in 1997, and a third was added in 1998. The ICTR faced the same challenges as the ICTY: for example, the cases were complex, testimony in Kinyarwanda, the most widely spoken language in Rwanda, had to be translated into English and French (the two official languages of the tribunal) and witnesses were difficult to transport and often unavailable.

ICTR jurisprudence

Competence

The statute of the ICTR covers:

- genocide;
- crimes against humanity;
- violations of Common Article 3 and Additional Protocol II of the Geneva Conventions.

Although the statute of the ICTR draws heavily on the statute of the ICTY, there is a key difference: the conflict in Rwanda was clearly noninternational. Therefore the ICTR statute considers only violations of humanitarian law that can be committed in both internal and armed conflict as well as genocide and crimes against humanity. The ICTR statute is more expansive than the ICTY statute in that the former includes international instruments, whether or not they are part of customary law, and so includes violations of Common Article 3 as well as breaches of Additional Protocol II of the Geneva Conventions. The ICTR also has a much more limited temporal jurisdiction, covering events only from January 1 to December 31, 1994.

Focus

In contrast to the ICTY, the ICTR has targeted those bearing the greatest responsibility for the genocide from the beginning. Lower-level perpetrators have been dealt with through national courts and the *gacaca* process, which uses a modified traditional mechanism of conflict resolution. The completion strategy imposed by Security Council Resolution 1503 of 2003 is the same as that for the ICTY and confirms the emphasis on leaders of the genocide. There has been a great deal of criticism that only Hutus and no Tutsis have been indicted.

In contrast to the lack of cooperation experienced in the former Yugoslavia, in Rwanda the government requested a tribunal. Rwanda was a member of the Security Council and participated in all discussions concerning the ICTR's establishment. However, Rwanda voted against the resolution that established the tribunal due to several concerns, including its location outside Rwanda and limited temporal jurisdiction. There was also a difficult relationship between the Rwandan government and the joint ICTY and ICTR prosecutor, Carla del Ponte, who, contrary to the wishes of the government, insisted on carrying out investigations into the Rwandan Patriotic Front (RPF). The RPF, a Tutsi-led rebel group, committed atrocities during the genocide but afterward became the ruling political party, leading to a conflict of interest between the government and the ICTR. It was partly due to these ongoing problems that a separate prosecutor for the ICTR was appointed to the tribunal. Despite these problems with the Rwandan government, West African countries have been more cooperative with the ICTR, with successes such as Operations NAKI and Kiwest, which resulted in the arrest of key former ministers who had sought refuge abroad.

As of June 2013, the ICTR has completed its work at the trial level with respect to all 93 accused. There have been 55 first-instance judgments for 75 accused, ten referrals to national jurisdictions (four apprehended and six fugitives), three referrals of top-level fugitives to MICT, two withdrawn indictments and three indictees who died prior to or during the course of trial. Seventeen cases are on appeal and nine accused are still at large.

ICTR landmark cases

Akayesu

This case provided the first definition of rape in international law. Jean Paul Akayesu was a prefecture head (*bourgmestre*) who was accused of failing to prevent acts of sexual violence and ordering and instigating acts of sexual violence against Tutsi women. The ICTR observed that rape is included in its statute as an element of several crimes. It also offered a definition, for purposes of international law, of both rape and sexual violence. Article 3(g) of the ICTR statute states that rape constitutes a crime against humanity if it was committed as part of a widespread or systematic attack against a civilian population on national, political, ethnic, racial, or religious grounds. In *Akayesu,* the ICTR found that the targeting of Tutsi women constituted a widespread attack due to ethnicity and so could be punishable as a crime against humanity. Another important aspect of the case was the inclusion of rape as a possible element of the *actus reus* of genocide—that is, one of the acts that constitute genocide. According to Article 2 of the ICTR statute, genocide means any of the following acts committed with intent to destroy a group: (a) killing members of the group, (b) causing serious bodily or mental harm to members of the group, (c) deliberately inflicting on the group conditions calculated to bring about its physical destruction in whole or in part, (d) imposing measures intended to prevent births within the group, and (e) forcibly transferring children of the group to another group. The ICTR found that rape and sexual violence were among the worst ways to inflict bodily and mental harm and that the rapes were carried out as part of the process of specifically targeting Tutsi women for destruction. This systematic campaign of sexual violence resulted in physical and psychological destruction of Tutsi women and as such constituted genocide.

The ICTR also interpreted the definition of genocide from the Genocide Convention, specifically in considering how to define a "protected group." The ICTR gave a fairly broad interpretation, stating that whether someone belongs to a protected national, ethic, racial, or religious group depends on whether that person is treated as belonging to a group, and whether that person considers him- or herself as belonging to a group. This concept of self-identification (subjective) or identification of others (objective) is elaborated in the *Kayishema* case.

Although the ICTR could not find that Akayesu had personally raped women, it concluded that he had aided and abetted the offenses, and as such was subject to individual criminal responsibility. Akayesu was found guilty of genocide and incitement to genocide, and of crimes against humanity, including rape. The court determined that the Rwandan conflict was of sufficiently noninternational character that Article 4 of its statute applied.

Nahimana et al.

Also known as the *Media* case, this was the first international trial involving the media since Julius Streicher, the publisher of a Nazi propaganda newspaper, had been convicted at Nuremberg in 1946. In December 2003, the ICTR trial chamber found Ferdinand Nahimana, Hassan Ngeze, and Jean-Bosco Barayagwiza guilty of genocide, direct and public incitement to commit genocide, and persecution and crimes against humanity, due to their broadcasts on Radio Television Libre des Mille Collines (RTLM) and articles in the *Kangura* newspaper throughout 1994. The appeal chamber reversed this decision and found that only the RTLM broadcasts after April 6, 1994, which specifically encouraged extermination of Tutsis, constituted incitement to commit genocide; there was lack of proof that broadcasts before that date had any causal connection. The appeals chamber also found that hate speech can be as serious as other crimes against humanity where it is accompanied by other acts of persecution, such as violence and destruction of property. It therefore found that the broadcasts after April could be considered persecution as a crime against humanity. The appeals chamber did not rule on whether hate speech that is not accompanied by violence constitutes persecution as a crime against humanity.

Kambanda

This case, the first concerning a former head of state to be brought by either the ICTY or the ICTR, which was significant in demonstrating the nonimmunity of the accused from prosecution. Jean Kambanda became prime minister of the interim government of Rwanda on April 9, 1994, after President Juvenal Habyarimana was killed in a plane crash on April 6. It was also the first case in which the accused entered a guilty plea to all counts. No agreement was made between the prosecution and defense concerning Kambanda's sentencing to life in prison. The trial chamber found that although Kambanda had cooperated, that his guilty plea could encourage others to recognize their responsibilities, and a guilty plea is usually considered a mitigating circumstance, this did not mean that the sentence could be reduced. The ICTR found that Kambanda's crimes were extremely grave and shocking to the human conscience, that he had committed the crimes knowingly and with premeditation, and that he had abused the trust of the Rwandan population. The court deemed that the aggravating circumstances thus negated the mitigating circumstances. The life sentence was upheld by the appeals chamber in 2000.

Bagosora

The Bagosora verdict was significant in holding those most responsible for the genocide accountable for their crimes. Théoneste Bagosora held a powerful position in the Ministry of Defense and was accused of being one of the masterminds behind the genocide. He was indicted with three other high-level military officials in what was known as the "Military I case". In its judgment, the Trial Chamber found that Bagosora was the highest authority in the Ministry of Defense and exercised effective control over the Rwandan army and gendarmerie from 6 until 9 April. He was therefore responsible for the murder of the prime minister, four opposition politicians, ten Belgian peacekeepers and the extensive military involvement in the killing of civilians in Kigali during this period. He was found guilty of genocide, crimes against humanity and war crimes and sentenced to life imprisonment. One of the other military officials was acquitted while the other two were also found guilty and sentenced to life in prison. However, in 2011 Bagosora's sentence was reduced on appeal to 35 years. The other two military officials also had their sentences reduced to 15 years and 35 years respectively. The Appeal Chamber upheld Bagosora's convictions for genocide, crimes against humanity, and war crimes. However, it reversed his convictions for two specific killings (Augustin Maharangari and Alphonse Kabiligi), the Belgian peacekeepers, and the killings at Gisenyi town, at Mudende University, and at Nyundo Parish. There was some disappointment and confusion expressed by victims at this reduced sentence.

ICTR sentencing

The ICTR statute is similar to that of the ICTY in that it can look to general sentencing practices in Rwanda and provides no minimum sentence. The ICTR has handed down harsher sentences than the ICTY, including a number of life sentences (the ICTY has only issued term imprisonments) and much higher average sentence lengths.

ICTR completion strategy and case transfer

The Security Council resolutions 1503 and 1534 also endorsed the ICTR completion strategies as well as the ICTY. The ICTR was originally expected to complete investigations by 2004, trial activities by 2008 and all of its work in 2010. At the time of writing, the ICTR had completed all of its work at the trial level, and the remaining appeals were projected to finish by the end of 2014. Rule 11*bis* of the ICTR Rules and Procedures is similar to that of the ICTY.

Due to a number of concerns about the standard of justice, the first case was transferred to Rwanda only in June 2011. Even after the abolition of capital punishment by Rwanda in 2007, there were concerns about the possibility of life imprisonment in isolation and insufficient witness protection. The case of Jean Uwinkindi was the first time that the Referral Chamber was convinced based on the evidence that Rwanda possessed the ability to accept and prosecute Uwinkindi's case. In its decision the Referral Chamber expressed its hope that the Republic of Rwanda:

> in accepting its first referral from this Tribunal, will actualize in practice the commitments it has made in its filings about its good faith, capacity and willingness to enforce the highest standards of international justice in the referred cases.

Subsequently, the case of Bernard Munyagishari was transferred to the national jurisdiction of Rwanda in 2012 as well as the cases of six fugitives still at large. Two cases were transferred to France in 2007 but had not yet gone to trial by 2013. In 2007, the ICTR revoked an earlier decision to transfer the case of Michel Bagaragaza to the Netherlands, after the Dutch courts failed to find a jurisdictional ground in Dutch law to try him.

Box 10.5 **Rule 11*bis* of the ICTR**

Rule 11*bis*: Referral of the Indictment to another Court

(A) If an indictment has been confirmed, whether or not the accused is in the custody of the Tribunal, the President may designate a Trial Chamber which shall determine whether the case should be referred to the authorities of a State:

i.   in whose territory the crime was committed; or
ii. in which the accused was arrested; or
iii. having jurisdiction and being willing and adequately prepared to accept such a case,

so that those authorities should forthwith refer the case to the appropriate court for trial within that State.

(B) The Trial Chamber may order such referral *proprio motu* or at the request of the Prosecutor, after having given to the Prosecutor and, where the accused is in the custody of the Tribunal, the accused, the opportunity to be heard.

(C) In determining whether to refer the case in accordance with paragraph (A), the Trial Chamber shall satisfy itself that the accused will receive a fair trial in the courts of the State concerned and that the death penalty will not be imposed or carried out.

Mechanism for International Criminal Tribunals (MICT)

The MICT was established by Security Council Resolution 1966 to continue the "jurisdiction, rights and obligations and essential functions" of the ICTR and ICTY. One branch inherited functions from the ICTR on July 1, 2012 and is based in Arusha. The other branch is located in The Hague and took over functions from the ICTY on July 1, 2013.

The ad hoc functions of the MICT include:

- Tracking and prosecution of remaining fugitives: nine fugitives are still wanted for trial by the ICTR. The MICT retains jurisdiction over three accused and the remaining six have been referred to Rwanda.
- Appeals proceedings: the MICT will conduct any appeals that may arise from the cases of the outstanding fugitives and from the cases of Karadžić, Mladić and Hadžić.
- Retrials: the MICT will conduct retrials ordered by the Appeals Chamber of the ICTR after July 1, 2012 and retrials ordered by the Appeals Chamber of the ICTY after July 1, 2013.
- Trials for contempt of the Tribunal and false testimony
- Proceedings for review of final judgment

Continuing functions of the MICT include:

- Protection of victims and witnesses: continuity in this function is particularly important. The MICT will assume tasks related to protection for ongoing cases and completed cases from both tribunals and the MICT. On July 1, 2012 MICT became responsible for 3,000 protected witnesses who testified at the ICTR.
- Supervision of enforcement of sentences: persons convicted by the ICTR and ICTY serve their sentences in one of the countries that has signed an agreement on enforcement of sentences. The MICT has jurisdiction to designate states of imprisonment for those convicted after July 1, 2012 for ICTR cases and July 1, 2013 for ICTY cases. The President of the MICT will have jurisdiction to supervise the enforcement of sentences and decide on requests for pardon or commutation of sentences.
- Assistance to national jurisdictions: the MICT will respond to requests for assistance from national authorities in relation to national investigations, prosecutions and trials. The MICT will assist national courts conducting related proceedings, including transferring dossiers, responding to requests for evidence and protective measures for witnesses.
- Preservation and management of MICT, ICTR and ICTY archives: the MICT will be responsible for the ICTY and ICTR archives, which is important to preserve the legacy of the tribunals. The archives include documents, maps, photographs, audiovisual recordings and objects. These document the investigations, indictments and court proceedings, the work relating to the detention of accused persons, protection of witnesses and enforcement of sentences. The MICT will preserve the archives as well as ensuring wide access to them.

Criticism of the tribunals

A major criticism of the ICTY and ICTR has been the enormous costs incurred by both courts and the lengthy time taken for trials. The ICTY began with a budget of US$276,000 in 1993, which progressively increased over the next decade to US$223,169,800 for 2002–3 (two-year budget) reaching US$310,952,100 in 2008–9. The budget for 2012–13 was US$250,814,000. Similar amounts were also allocated to the ICTR. Although the trials are complex and involve high-profile cases, some have doubted that they were worth the cost compared to relatively low numbers of indictments and sentences. The Security Council resolution that allowed the addition of *ad litem* judges to increase the overall number of judges did try to address the criticism of slowness. Extra trial chambers were added to both tribunals, and standby witnesses were also allowed when witnesses were unable to testify. When sentences have resulted, many of the ICTY's have been particularly short, although the ICTR has imposed longer sentences. At the ICTR, seven individuals have completed their sentences. At the ICTY, many of those shorter sentences have been completed, while some convicted were granted early release having served only two-thirds of their time. Some victims and members of wider society in the former Yugoslavia have expressed disappointment at the release of these individuals.

Although many have welcomed the ICTY and ICTR for bringing perpetrators of human rights abuses to account, some have criticized the locations of the trials, in The Hague and Arusha. This argument centers around the distance between the courts and those to whom they were meant to bring justice. As well, both tribunals have been criticized for their lack of engagement with the local populations and the late establishment of their outreach programs. Another criticism has been that the tribunals have not built the capacity of the Yugoslav and Rwandan domestic systems, which were left shattered following the conflicts. Although both courts were mandated to assist domestically, capacity building has been neglected. It was hoped that international legal norms would penetrate into the national legal systems and that the proceedings of the tribunals would have a pedagogic effect, but demonstrable results have yet to be achieved. However, the ICTR's outreach program, initiated in November 2007, has helped to train Rwanda's judicial sector in international criminal law, indictment and prosecution, advocacy, information management, and legal research. This training has been aimed at judges, the Rwandan Bar Association, court staff, and judicial and academic institutions. The role of the ICTY in the establishment of the WCC has sought to assist Bosnian capacity to prosecute war crimes.

Beyond criticisms based on distance and lack of capacity building, serious concerns have been raised about the jurisdictional relationship between the ICTR, based in Arusha, Tanzania, and domestic prosecutions in Rwanda, with the ICTR trying organizers and leaders while the Rwandan courts handle more ordinary cases. The ICTR and Rwanda's domestic courts have concurrent jurisdiction over crimes relating to genocide. However, the Rwandan courts use a specialized plea-agreement system in cases of genocide, which helps to expedite cases and elicit more information, though there is potential for miscarriage of justice. The ICTR had far greater resources, and far fewer defendants to process, but was slow to render sentences and was not capable of handling the vast number of cases that the Rwandan courts have sought to address.

One argument made by advocates for the establishment of the tribunals was that they would act as deterrents to future abuses. It was hoped that, by showing that war crimes and crimes against humanity would be prosecuted, combatants and leaders would be dissuaded from carrying out such acts. However, history shows that the situation in the former Yugoslavia worsened with the 1999 Kosovo conflict, and that the ICTY did not have such a deterrent effect in this instance. Both tribunals did have an effect, though, in that those indicted were arrested and kept in detention while others were forced into hiding or had their assets frozen. It was perhaps unrealistic to believe that courts would prove a deterrent on their own, outside their role in a broader strategy.

The local reaction to the Gotovina acquittal also demonstrates the divisive nature of tribunal verdicts and its potential effects on reconciliation efforts. Gotovina and Markač were welcomed home to Croatia as heroes, while the Appeals Chamber decision was heavily criticized in Serbia, with the president and prime minister claiming that it was a political decision that harmed the credibility and public opinion of the tribunal.

Contributions of the tribunals

Despite the criticisms leveled at the tribunals, they have achieved much. It is a success that both tribunals gained custody of those indicted persons who held high-level positions and bore the greatest responsibility for serious crimes. The focus of both the ICTY and ICTR on abuses against civilians has demonstrated a stance against conflict that specifically targets noncombatants and allowed the Yugoslav and Rwandan peoples to see that justice is being done on their behalf, although the extent of their engagement with tribunals that are located outside their countries is debatable. Despite the criticism over lengthy trials, the ICTY and ICTR are comparable to domestic courts in terms of the time and resources needed to try complicated cases such as murder. As an innovative response of the international community, the tribunals were bound to experience problems, but crucial lessons have been learned that can provide a basis for the work of **hybrid tribunals** and the International Criminal Court, discussed in Chapters 12 and 13, respectively.

Advances in international humanitarian law will be the long-term legacy of the tribunals. The ICTY and ICTR have enabled international humanitarian law to be applied to domestic as well as international conflicts. The ICTY has applied its provisions creatively, and the ICTR has been able to treat violations of Common Article 3 of the Geneva Conventions as criminal. These advances have helped to address the potential datedness of international humanitarian law and its inability to cope with contemporary, largely internal, armed conflicts, and serve as precedents for future cases. As stated in the statute of the ICTR and in the jurisprudence of ICTY, violating Common Article 3 leads to individual criminal responsibility in both internal and international conflict. It is also highly significant that the ICTR, soon followed by the ICTY, indicted a head of government, setting the precedent that leaders are not immune from prosecution.

The ICTY and ICTR have been widely acknowledged for their advances in terms of gender crimes. It is now clear in international humanitarian law that rape is a crime against humanity and can also be part of genocide, torture, and war crimes—a development long overdue despite substantial advocacy within the human rights community. It is the jurisprudence of the ICTY and ICTR that provides the basis for future cases of gender crimes, whose pioneering judgments has led to the broad definitions of sexual violence in the ICC's Rome Statute.

Discussion questions

- What do the experiences of the ICTR and ICTY demonstrate about the reliance of ad hoc tribunals on political goodwill?
- What difficulties did the Office of the Prosecutor face in assembling cases for the ICTY and ICTR?
- Were the Rwandan government's reasons for wanting the ICTR to be situated in Kigali valid?
- How do the international courts affect perceptions of justice, domestically and internationally?

- What do you think has been the most important development in international humanitarian law to result from the ICTY and ICTR?
- What are the most important ad hoc and continuing functions of the MICT?

Group exercise

Form two groups to debate the value of the ICTY and ICTR.

Group 1: Argue in support of the tribunals. Think about how to justify the enormous resources (time, money, personnel) they required. You may wish to consider the scale of the atrocities, the role of the international community, and important jurisprudence.

Group 2: Argue that the tribunals were not worth the time or resources required. Think about the number of people that have been indicted and sentenced, the length of trials, organizational and operational difficulties, and alternative prosecution options.

Further reading

Cassese, Antonio and Paola Gaeta, *International Criminal Law* (Oxford: Oxford University Press, 2013).

Drumbl, Mark A., *Atrocity, Punishment, and International Law* (New York: Cambridge University Press, 2007).

Gow, James, Rachel Kerr and Zoran Pajić, eds, *Prosecuting War Crimes: Lessons and Legacies of the International Criminal Tribunal for the Former Yugoslavia* (London: Routledge, 2013).

Kerr, Rachel, and Eirin Mobekk, *Peace and Justice: Seeking Accountability After War* (Cambridge: Polity, 2007), Chapter 2, "Ad Hoc International Criminal Tribunals: The ICTY and ICTR."

Meron, Theodor, "Reflections on the Prosecution of War Crimes by International Tribunals," *American Journal of International Law* vol. 100, no. 3 (July 2006): 551–579.

Meron, Theodor, *The Making of International Criminal Justice. A View from the Bench* (Oxford: Oxford University Press, 2011).

Møse, Erik, "Main Achievements of the ICTR," *Journal of International Criminal Justice* vol. 3, no. 4 (September 2005): 920–943.

Ratner, Steven R., and Jason S. Abrams, *Accountability for Human Rights Atrocities in International Law: Beyond the Nuremberg Legacy* (Oxford: Oxford University Press, 2001), Chapter 9, "The Progeny of Nuremberg: International Criminal Tribunals".

Riznik, Donald, "Completing the ICTY-Project Without Sacrificing Its Main Goals Security Council Resolution 1966 – A Good Decision?" *Göttingen Journal of International Law* vol. 3 (2011): 907–922.

Sloane, Robert D., "The International Criminal Tribunal for Rwanda" in Chiara Giorgetti (ed.), *The Rules, Practice and Jurisprudence of International Courts and Tribunals* (Leiden: Martinus Nijhoff Publishers, 2012).

Steinberg, Richard. H. (ed.), *Assessing the Legacy of the ICTY* (Leiden: Brill, 2011).

Official documents and sources

United Nations, *Assessment and Report of Judge Theodor Meron, President of the International Tribunal for the Former Yugoslavia, provided to the Security Council pursuant to paragraph 6 of Security Council resolution 1534 (2004), and covering the period from 23 May 2012 to 16 November 2012*, (19 November 2012), UN Doc. S/2012/847.

United Nations, *Interim report of the Commission of Experts Established Pursuant to Security Council resolution 780 (1992)*, (10 February 1993), UN Doc. S/25274.

United Nations, *Preliminary Report of the Independent Commission of Experts Established in Accordance with Security Council resolution 935 (1994)*, (4 October 1994), UN Doc. S/1994/1125.
United Nations, *Report on the Completion Strategy of the International Criminal Tribunal for Rwanda (as at 5 November 2012)*, (14 November 2012), UN Doc. S/2012/836.

Online sources

International Criminal Tribunal for Rwanda, http://www.ictr.org
International Criminal Tribunal for the Former Yugoslavia, http://www.un.org/icty
Mechanism for International Criminal Tribunals, http://www.unmict.org

11 Enforcing human rights transnationally

Key points

- Accountability for past abuses may be sought not only in the country where crimes occurred or in international courts, but also in national courts of other states.
- Such accountability may involve criminal charges or civil claims.
- Criminal accountability through **universal jurisdiction** is controversial, but actively practiced in a number of European jurisdictions, and may be utilized in developing countries as well.
- Civil claims are widespread in the United States under the **Alien Tort Claims Act** (ACTA), and may include claims against multinational corporations.
- Transnational options for accountability may be gap-fillers where domestic or international courts are not available, but have been increasingly limited in recent years.

Overview

Elsewhere in this book, we consider accountability mechanisms in international courts, whether ad hoc, such as those for the former Yugoslavia and Rwanda (Chapter 10); hybrid, such as the Special Court for Sierra Leone (Chapter 12); or permanent, such as the **International Criminal Court** (ICC) (Chapter 13). In such situations, international law, both **international human rights law** and **international humanitarian law**, are applied by international or internationalized courts, not wholly domestic courts. However, there are also processes by which accountability is imposed transnationally. What is unusual about such processes is that they involve the application of international law in domestic courts, but not in the domestic courts of the country where the abuses or crimes actually took place. Instead, accountability may be found extraterritorially through the exercise of universal jurisdiction, imposing criminal accountability, or civil accountability processes in a number of states. In such situations, accountability is ultimately imposed quite far from the locus of the crime. The phenomenon of universal jurisdiction is widely known, thanks to cases brought against former Chilean dictator Augusto Pinochet Ugarte in Spain and elsewhere. You may be less familiar with another tool, that of civil accountability. It is particularly available in the United States through the use of the Alien Tort Claims Act. However, the United States and Europe are not the only locations where accountability might be exercised for past abuses: as discussed below, Argentina is seeking to exercise universal jurisdiction, and Senegal has come under some pressure to do so as well.

This chapter discusses universal jurisdiction and civil accountability in turn, considering critical cases and debates. The debates include both legal—about the scope of and limits to extraterritorial jurisdiction—but also political—about the appropriateness of the courts of one nation sitting in judgment over the actions of citizens and officials of another nation.

Criminal accountability through universal jurisdiction

It is important to understand that universal jurisdiction is a principle of international law, but one that has emerged in customary law over time, with little mention in international treaties or conventions, even by implication. It permits and perhaps requires prosecution of certain serious crimes in the domestic courts of any state in the world, regardless of where the crimes occurred.

Universal jurisdiction can be exercised only in response to a very limited number of crimes. These include **war crimes**, **crimes against humanity**, **genocide**, and **torture**; slavery is sometimes included, as is piracy, for largely historical reasons. The cases brought against Pinochet in Spain, and complaints filed against Ariel Sharon in Belgium, and Donald Rumsfeld in Germany, are but a few of the most famous examples of the exercise of universal jurisdiction to prosecute a defendant accused of crimes committed far from the nation and from the court seeking to try him or her. The exercise of universal jurisdiction may potentially fill gaps in accountability globally, where domestic courts are unable or unwilling to try alleged perpetrators, and where no international venue is available or where those that are lack jurisdiction. However, universal jurisdiction is controversial, precisely because it does involve the exercise of jurisdiction by one state over the citizens of another, and often over high-profile officials or former officials, and its scope has been limited by legislation in two key states: Belgium and Spain.

Under the principle of universal jurisdiction, a state is competent to judge someone alleged to have committed certain international crimes and found in its territory, or to seek the extradition of that person from the territory of another state. Unlike other bases for jurisdiction, specific contacts with the state that is seeking to assert jurisdiction are not required. The nationality of the victims and the location of any alleged crimes are not relevant. The ability to exercise such jurisdiction over international crimes enables states to fulfill treaty commitments (such as the ***aut dedere aut judicare*** principles in treaties such as the **Genocide Convention**) to try or extradite individuals suspected of certain crimes.

Universal jurisdiction and national sovereignty

It is important to recognize that the exercise of universal jurisdiction may constitute a significant infringement upon national sovereignty, and may even violate the principle of noninterference in the internal affairs of states, as enshrined in Article 2(7) of the **UN Charter**. Historically, juridical jurisdiction has been closely tied to territorial sovereignty, with states generally exercising exclusive jurisdiction over acts committed on their own territories or by their own nationals. The instances in which a state could exercise jurisdiction extraterritorially have been very limited. The exercise of extraterritorial application of jurisdiction has tended to require a nexus—some kind of connection—between the alleged act and the state that is seeking to hear a case. Universal jurisdiction is the only form of extraterritorial jurisdiction that requires no such nexus. The other generally recognized bases for extraterritorial jurisdiction, apart from universal jurisdiction, are:

- *territorial,* in that jurisdiction is based upon the location where the offense had its effects, but is in fact extraterritorial in that it is exerted over a nonnational acting outside the territory;
- *national,* based upon the nationality of the offender;
- *protective,* based upon injury to the national interest; and
- *passive personal,* based upon the nationality of the victim.

The reason why extraterritorial jurisdiction is limited is perhaps obvious—respect for sovereignty. There is a concern not to have the courts of one country sitting in judgment upon the internal activities of others, but also a concern to avoid jurisdictional conflicts—with courts of several countries considering what is essentially the same case. Infringement upon sovereign powers is not taken lightly in international law, and states emerging from conflict often defend their sovereignty as strongly as do stable states.

While universal jurisdiction is a general principle in international law, it is not one that most domestic judges are prepared to exercise. Even those who do exercise universal jurisdiction often do so cautiously, relying upon other bases such as passive personality or the nationality of the victims of crimes. Judges may also rely upon a range of domestic legislation enacted by states to incorporate international treaty obligations, and to fulfill their obligations under such treaties to enact effective domestic legislation. Such may explicitly refer to universal jurisdiction, or spell out the power of state courts to hear cases involving specific crimes, in the absence of any nexus. Some scholars have referred to the use by judges of universal jurisdiction and other bases of jurisdiction simultaneously as *universal jurisdiction plus.*

As we have seen, this exceptional jurisdiction can only be exercised in the event of exceptional crimes: war crimes, crimes against humanity, genocide, and torture, as well as slavery and piracy. It is justified on the grounds that such crimes are of concern to all humankind and all nations. It is claimed that such jurisdiction signals that certain crimes are so heinous that they both threaten the international community and are forcefully condemned by it, and that it is in the interests of justice everywhere that perpetrators be brought to account. However, such cases are politically charged, and states and individuals may vigorously resist extradition and trial, particularly where the accused are current or former state officials. As discussed later in this chapter, official immunity is often raised as a defense against such charges, although prosecutors may argue, and judges may concur, that official immunity cannot apply where the crimes alleged are international crimes such as genocide. The question of official immunity is hotly contested by potential defendants who are state officials or sitting or even former heads of state, such as Pinochet. Similarly, states may object to the exercise of universal jurisdiction by other states to prosecute their citizens, and in two cases, discussed later, they have brought cases before the **International Court of Justice** (ICJ) to prevent its exercise over their sitting or former officials.

The *Pinochet* cases

The cases against Augusto Pinochet Ugarte arise from events that took place between the coup that carried Pinochet and his junta to power in Chile on September 11, 1973, and the return of the country to democratic rule in April 1990. During that time, thousands of individuals who supported the democratically elected leader, Salvador Allende, and the return to democracy in the country, were kidnapped, detained, tortured, killed, or "disappeared," allegedly at the direction of Pinochet and his regime. The regime passed self-amnesty legislation in 1978, and Pinochet sought to insulate himself further with "senator for life" status when he stepped down from power.

Cases seeking to bring General Pinochet to justice for killings, torture, disappearances, and genocide during his rule have been filed in several countries in recent years. These include cases brought in Spain, Belgium, and the Netherlands. We focus here upon proceedings against him that were initiated in Spain, and that were consequently triggered in the United Kingdom by a Spanish request for his extradition. We also highlight a related civil case in Spain dealing with assets looted by Pinochet during his rule (see Box 11.2) Finally, we briefly consider proceedings within Chile not based upon universal jurisdiction, but that appear to have been inspired by the proceedings against Pinochet abroad.

Proceedings in Spain

Proceedings in Spain began with the submission of a complaint in July 1996 by the Progressive Prosecutors Union (Union Progresista de Fiscales [UPF]), a group of Spanish prosecutors, against Pinochet and others for crimes against humanity and genocide committed during his rule. The complaint was submitted in a penal chamber of the Spanish Audiencia Nacional— the court having competence over particularly serious crimes such as offenses to the crown, fraud, drug trafficking, and crimes committed outside Spanish territory, among others—and articulated the legal basis and factual allegations that formed the foundation of subsequent actions against Pinochet.

The complaint alleged, and Spanish judges claimed, that Spain had jurisdiction, through a combination of domestic and international law, to address crimes of genocide, torture, and terrorism. Under the Law on Judicial Power (see Box 11.1), Spanish courts are competent to hear cases that address these crimes even if they occur outside Spanish territory and whether they are committed by a Spaniard or a foreigner. The legislation thus empowers courts to exercise universal jurisdiction. The complaint thus claimed that under domestic law, Spain could address these crimes even if no Spanish citizen had been killed in Chile, although there were in fact Spanish victims. In addition to articulating domestic legislation as grounds for the exercise of jurisdiction to pursue these crimes, Spain also emphasized its obligations under international law.

The complaint had to further establish not only that there was potential jurisdiction, but also that acts committed under Pinochet's rule constituted crimes for which that jurisdiction could be exercised, under Spanish or international law. The complaint sought to undermine any potential immunity defenses to genocide and torture in several ways. First, it argued that Spanish national interests in the crimes, due to the presence of Spanish victims, would override the 1978 self-amnesty, which in any event would not have extraterritorial application. Similarly, the complaint argued that defenses of official status or superior orders are excluded under the **Torture Convention**, and that the International Covenant on Civil and Political Rights (ICCPR) indicates no immunity for persons acting in an official capacity.

The complaint thus requested judicial assistance, including provision of information, and the extradition of those responsible to Spain, under the treaty of judicial assistance and extradition between Spain and Chile. It was this aspect of the request that brought about the most notorious aspect of the case—efforts to extradite Pinochet from the United Kingdom, where he was seeking medical treatment.

Late in 1998, Judge Baltasar Garzón of Investigating Court no. 5 of the Audiencia Nacional, acting on the complaint, agreed with the complainants that Spain had jurisdiction to hear allegations of genocide and torture that took place under Pinochet's leadership. This provoked a diplomatic outcry, with the Chilean government objecting vehemently to the assertion of jurisdiction, and to the principle of universal jurisdiction

---

Box 11.1 **The Spanish law that established universal jurisdiction**

Law on Judicial Power (1 July 1985) Spain

Article 23.4 creates Spanish judicial competence over acts committed by Spaniards or foreigners outside Spanish national territory, for the following crimes:

a. Genocide;
b. Terrorism;
c. piracy and airplane hijacking;
d. counterfeiting foreign currency;
e. acts relating to prostitution;
f. traffic in illegal drugs;
g. and any other acts that Spain ought to pursue under its international treaty and convention obligations.

The law was reformed in 2005 and 2007 to include female genital mutilation and human trafficking among the crimes, respectively. In 2009 it was reformed again to limit the scope of extraterritorial jurisdiction, as discussed below.

Source:http://www.derecho.com/xml/disposiciones/trini/disposicion.xml?id_
disposicion=33022; informal translation.

---

generally. Chile argued that Spanish courts were not competent to judge allegations of crimes against humanity committed in any third countries, and that in any event, Pinochet would have immunity, either as a former head of state or as a "senator for life." Despite these objections from Chile, in October 1998 Judge Garzón ordered that Pinochet be subjected to "provisional imprisonment," issued an international arrest warrant, and issued an extradition request to the UK. He also ordered that Pinochet's assets, and those of his accused associates, be frozen.

These orders were issued on the grounds that the alleged acts could constitute genocide, terrorism, and torture subject to universal jurisdiction. Having found that extraterritorial jurisdiction was granted by the Law on Judicial Power, the judge further reasoned that, beyond domestic law, Spain had the power to address the crime of genocide under the Genocide Convention, which was incorporated into domestic law in 1971. The proscription of genocide was further found to be a *jus cogens* norm—a customary norm of international law that cannot be derogated from, and for which the exercise of universal jurisdiction is permitted. Finally, Spain was not a party to the Torture Convention at the time that torture allegedly occurred in Chile, and thus would in principle have been barred from seeking extradition of individuals accused of acts that were not at the time criminalized in Spain. However, the decision rejected this objection, reasoning that if Spain had jurisdiction over crimes of genocide and terrorism, of which torture forms a part, then it would also have jurisdiction over crimes of torture as defined by the Torture Convention.

Critical judicial action then moved to the United Kingdom, where courts deliberated upon whether to honor the Spanish extradition request. As we shall see, Pinochet would ultimately be returned to Chile, but other proceedings against him, civil rather than criminal, continued in Spain (see Box 11.2).

Box 11.2 **Civil actions in Spain**

In addition to committing serious violent crimes, Pinochet and his cohorts were also alleged to have looted the Chilean state, smuggling out millions of dollars to overseas accounts. In September of 2004, private individuals and the Fundación Salvador Allende filed civil and criminal claims for concealment of assets and money laundering by Pinochet. The claims were filed using the tool of *actio popularis,* which allows individuals to act, in essence, as "private prosecutors." The civil claim asked the Spanish courts to seek action by the courts of the United States and Chile to address those responsible for economic the crimes by freezing their foreign assets. The complaint specifically requested that the United States be asked to embargo funds in Riggs Bank identified as belonging to Pinochet, in the amount of €10,300,000, which the Investigative Court no. 5 of the Audiencia Nacional so ordered. While these cases were not explicitly based upon universal jurisdiction, and indeed involved civil penalties, they were related directly to the earlier criminal charges against Pinochet. Further, as with use of the Alien Tort Claims Act in the United States, discussed later in this chapter, these cases brought attention to the use of freezing and confiscating assets as an alternative form of punishment.

Extradition proceedings in the United Kingdom

On October 16, 1998, Pinochet was arrested in the United Kingdom, where he was seeking medical treatment, based on Judge Garzón's international arrest warrant. Pinochet's attorneys promptly claimed privilege and immunity from arrest on grounds that he was a former head of state and that he had parliamentary immunity based on his status of "senator for life." His attorneys further argued that he had never been a subject of Spain and thus that there was no crime in Spain for which he could be extradited. Chile then intervened in the proceedings in the United Kingdom, arguing that Spain's request and any UK extradition involved an exercise of jurisdiction over Chilean subjects contrary to international law, and directly affected Chile's "rights," including its transition to democracy and its relations with the UK and Spain. Arguing that the appropriate place to judge Pinochet was in Chile, the Chilean government asserted national "sovereignty" and, like Pinochet's attorneys, immunity for Pinochet as a former head of state. The Chilean government further invoked international policy and practice supporting noninterference in the "sovereign" acts of nations.

The law lords in the UK—part of the House of Lords, which exercises judicial functions and acted as the highest court of appeal for most domestic issues—examined the issue. They first rejected the claim that immunity as a head or former head of state could be a bar to prosecution, finding that such immunity does not apply where certain grave international crimes such as torture and hostage-taking have been alleged, in line with the reasoning laid out by the complaint in Spain, discussed above. However, the decision was set aside on appeal because one of the law lords had undisclosed links with human rights advocacy group **Amnesty International**, which had been active in condemning Pinochet and advocating his accountability.

Thus the case was reheard before a new panel. It held that while former heads of state did enjoy immunity in the UK for acts engaged in as part of their official functions, torture could not be viewed as an official function. There were other limits, though—specifically temporal ones, as the lords indicated that the UK could only extradite Pinochet for crimes that would have been crimes not just in Chile or Spain, but also in the UK when they were committed;

as the UK had not ratified the Torture Convention until 1988, only events in Chile after 1988 could then be extraditable crimes. This was due to the application of the principle of double criminality—the crime had to be one under both UK and Spanish law at the time it was committed. Conspiracy in Spain to murder someone in Spain was also found to be an extraditable crime. Because of the application of the principle, then, only a few of the many crimes for which Pinochet was alleged to have been responsible constituted crimes for which he could be extradited. On the basis of the decision, Pinochet was to have been extradited to Spain. However, in light of concerns about Pinochet's health and his mental fitness to stand trial, the British home secretary ultimately ordered him returned to Chile in March 2000.

Proceedings in Chile

When Pinochet returned to Chile, he was not able to escape attempts to prosecute him for past abuses. Charges were filed for a number of killings of political prisoners in 1973. However, the issue of Pinochet's parliamentary immunity based on his "senator for life" status was an obstacle to his prosecution, removed ultimately by the Chilean courts. A judge charged Pinochet with kidnapping and ordered his arrest, but this decision was overruled by the Supreme Court in 2000 on procedural grounds—that his house arrest had been improperly ordered. Several further proceedings followed, but never reached fruition. Pinochet died in Chile in December 2006 while under house arrest.

Beyond *Pinochet*: other critical cases

We have focused on the *Pinochet* cases because they are familiar and raise important issues such as official immunities, but advances in universal jurisdiction have been more dramatic in other cases. We discuss here a number of other cases that have been brought in Spain and Belgium (see "Further reading" and "Official documents and sources" at the end of this chapter for more detail).

As discussed, Pinochet was not ultimately extradited to Spain but was returned home for reasons of health. By contrast, Spain has been able to pursue cases against former members of Argentina's junta such as Adolfo Scilingo and Miguel Cavallo, who were responsible for disappearances, torture, and killing during military rule in that country from 1977 to 1983. Scilingo was already present in Spain voluntarily when his arrest was ordered; he was subsequently sentenced to 640 years in prison. While his convictions for genocide, torture, and terrorism were overturned, those for his role in murder and illegal detention were upheld in 2007. This was because torture was not yet defined as a crime in Spanish law when Scilingo allegedly committed those acts; however, those acts did fall within the definition of crimes against humanity in customary law. In the case of Cavallo, Spain issued an extradition request to Mexico, and Mexico duly complied, assisting in the extradition of an Argentine not back to Argentina, but to Spain. In March 2008, Spain transferred Cavallo to Argentina, and he was convicted and sentenced to life imprisonment in October 2011.

Also, as we saw in Chapter 8, in February 2008 a Spanish judge indicted 40 high-ranking Rwandan Tutsi military officials for crimes committed during the 1994 conflict and genocide in Rwanda, sparking an outcry from the government (see Box 8.5 on p. 131). The government, controlled by the Rwandan Patriotic Front (RPF), a Tutsi former rebel group, rejects any claims that its troops committed crimes during the conflict, and presents RPF members rather as heroes who brought a halt to the genocide. Political pressure is alleged to have prevented the International Criminal Tribunal for Rwanda (ICTR), discussed in

Chapter 10, from pursuing any such cases, although it has investigated allegations of crimes by the RPF. Philip Reyntjens, a former employee of the ICTR, calls its failure to prosecute any Tutsis perverse victors' justice. He suggests that the only chance of a trial for members of the RPF is in other countries.

Spain is of course not the only state that has actively pursued cases through the exercise of universal jurisdiction. Belgium has as well, although it has radically limited its legislation in response to political pressure following high-profile attempts to bring cases against Ariel Sharon and US officials. In 2006, Belgium issued a request to Senegal for the extradition of ex-Chadian dictator Hissène Habré, who had been in exile in Senegal since 1990. Habré had been in fact indicted in Senegal in 2001 for crimes, such as torture, allegedly committed while he was dictator of Chad, but the Senegalese courts declined to try him. In response to the Belgian request, the Senegalese president indicated he would never extradite Habré to Belgium. The political controversy was taken up by the **African Union** (AU), which tasked a group of African jurists to examine the issue. The expert panel determined that Habré must be tried, and that Senegal would be the most appropriate location. The experts found not only that the Senegalese courts had jurisdiction over the case, but also that Senegal had an obligation to act in response to allegations of torture in accord with its duties under the Torture Convention. In addition, the expert panel found that several other locations would also be feasible, including Chad and any other African nations that had ratified the Torture Convention.

Legal limits to universal jurisdiction

However, at the same time, some restrictions have been imposed on the exercise of universal jurisdiction by the ICJ and legislatively by two countries which have actively exercised it in Europe. In two instances where courts of European countries (Belgium and France) have sought to exercise jurisdiction over criminal charges against sitting officials of African states engaged in or emerging from conflict (the Democratic Republic of Congo [DRC] and its neighbor the Republic of Congo), those states challenged that jurisdiction before the ICJ. The ICJ issued a ruling in one of the cases that restricts the exercise of universal jurisdiction, and provides some clarity as to the status of official immunities. Further, both Spain and Belgium have revised their universal jurisdiction legislation such that it remains extraterritorial but not universal.

DRC v. Belgium

In April 2000, a Belgian magistrate issued an international arrest warrant for the Democratic Republic of Congo's minister of foreign affairs, Abdoulaye Yerodia Ndombasi, for crimes alleged to constitute "serious violations of international law." The DRC filed a case before the ICJ challenging Belgium's jurisdiction and seeking provisional measures to discharge the warrant immediately on the grounds that Belgium's attempt to arrest Yerodia constituted a violation of its international legal obligations. The DRC argued that there was no evidence of jurisdiction based on any of the normal tools of extraterritorial jurisdiction: territory, *in personam* jurisdiction, or harm to the security or dignity of Belgium. The DRC contended that while several treaties created universal jurisdiction, they did so *only* where the alleged perpetrator was on the territory of the state seeking jurisdiction. It further argued that Belgium had violated the principle of sovereign legal equality, and asserted that Yerodia was protected by diplomatic immunity.

Box 11.3 Universal jurisdiction and immunity

Case concerning the arrest warrant of 11 April 2000
(*Democratic Republic of the Congo v. Belgium*)
International Court of Justice Judgment of 14 February 2002

54. The Court accordingly concludes that the functions of a Minister for Foreign Affairs are such that, throughout the duration of his or her office, he or she when abroad enjoys full immunity from criminal jurisdiction and inviolability. That immunity and that inviolability protect the individual concerned against any act of authority of another State which would hinder him or her in the performance of his or her duties.
55. In this respect, no distinction can be drawn between acts performed by a Minister for Foreign Affairs in an "official" capacity, and those claimed to have been performed in a "private capacity," or, for that matter, between acts performed before the person concerned assumed office as Minister for Foreign Affairs and acts committed during the period of office. Thus, if a Minister for Foreign Affairs is arrested in another State on a criminal charge, he or she is clearly thereby prevented from exercising the functions of his or her office.

In February 2002, the ICJ issued its decision in the case, finding that Belgium had indeed violated its own legal obligations toward the DRC in its failure to respect the immunity from criminal jurisdiction enjoyed by an *incumbent* minister under international law. However, it did not reject the principle *per se*, but only its exercise in this instance. Instead, the ICJ indicated that the warrant would have undermined the conduct of foreign relations by the minister (see Box 11.3). The court thus issued an order that Belgium cancel the international arrest warrant. However, one line in the judgment did indicate that this immunity was only in relation to national courts, not international courts.

The reasoning of the ICJ meant that efforts to pursue a case against Israeli leader Ariel Sharon while he was in office were dropped. The judgment clarifies limits upon the exercise of universal jurisdiction imposed by diplomatic immunity so long as the accused remains in an office of diplomatic importance (although the parameters of what offices are significant has not been articulated), but gray areas remain. In particular, whether immunities attach to *former* diplomats or heads of state for acts undertaken in office has not been addressed, although the logic in the *Pinochet* cases, which has precedent only in the UK, would dictate that only legitimate acts are covered by any official immunity.

Republic of Congo v. France

Similar issues arose in a case brought against France, which has not been decided but could eventually result in a more direct pronouncement on the legality and extent of universal jurisdiction by the ICJ. Judicial proceedings were initiated in France against the sitting president, Denis Sassou Nguesso, of the Republic of Congo, and against the sitting interior minister, for torture and crimes against humanity under Articles 689-1 and 689-2 of the French Code of Criminal Procedure. The Republic of Congo brought a case against France at the ICJ, challenging its attempts to initiate investigations, and sought provisional measures to compel France to suspend judicial proceedings. The Republic of Congo argued that a sitting head of state, or cabinet minister, is immune from any "act of authority" by another state that would hinder them in the exercise of their duties, and further that the "unilateral" exercise by a state of universal jurisdiction is a violation of the sovereign equality enshrined in Article 2(1) of the UN Charter. This constituted a more direct challenge to the principle of universal jurisdiction than that raised by the DRC in the *Yerodia* case. The ICJ rejected the Republic of Congo's request for provisional measures in 2003, on the grounds that France recognized official immunities and thus had made it clear there was no risk that the case would go forward while the officials were in office.

Limits to universal jurisdiction in Belgium and Spain

Universal jurisdiction has been politically controversial, and two countries with a significant number of politically contentious cases—Belgium and Spain—came under international and domestic pressure to limit their legislation and activities. In 2009, the Spanish legislature revised the legislation enabling universal jurisdiction to require that Spanish courts would only have jurisdiction where the accused is present in Spain, victims are of Spanish nationality, or there is some other demonstrated link to Spain and that there is no competent country or international tribunal where proceedings have been initiated. Belgian legislation was similarly revised even earlier, in 2003, to limit jurisdiction over international crimes to situations in which the accused is Belgian or has primary residence in Belgium; where the victim is Belgian or has lived in Belgium for at least three years at the time the crimes were committed; or if Belgium is required by treaty to exercise jurisdiction over the case. Nonetheless, both countries continue to exercise extraterritorial jurisdiction over abuses committed abroad, with Belgium notably seeking to prosecute former Chadian dictator Hissène Habré, and seeking assistance from the ICJ when Senegal failed to prosecute him or extradite him. At the same time, Argentina has become the first "developing" country to invoke the principle (see Box 11.4).

Civil accountability

The Alien Tort Claims Act

The Alien Tort Claims Act, passed in 1789, established US federal district court jurisdiction over "any civil action by an alien for a tort only committed in violation of the law of nations or a treaty of the United States." Because there is virtually no legislative history, it is unclear what the original purpose of the ATCA was, although some argue that it was meant only to address piracy, slave-trading, and attacks on foreign diplomats, while others offer a wider interpretation. Today, cases interpreting the act have enabled *civil* claims to be brought for acts beyond this limited list; however, *criminal* charges cannot be brought. Courts have interpreted "the law of nations" to be customary international law—a norm is so considered for the purposes of ATCA cases when it is "specific, universal, and obligatory." Like universal jurisdiction, civil accountability under the ATCA has proven controversial, particularly as judgments have been rendered against corporate actors.

The landmark Filartiga case

While the ATCA is over 200 years old, it was rarely invoked until 1980, when a federal court issued a historic decision. In a case brought against a Paraguayan police inspector-

---

Box 11.4 A new wave of universal jurisdiction venues?

Even as universal jurisdiction has faced political challenge and legal limitations in Europe, it may be gaining favor in a few developing countries. Former Chadian dictator Hissène Habré, who went into exile in Senegal in 1990, has been the subject of a range of efforts to prosecute him, including by Belgium under its universal jurisdiction legislation. When Senegal refused to extradite him, it came under pressure to prosecute him domestically, and a range of proposals ensued, including the exercise of universal jurisdiction. In a suit before the ICJ, Belgium sought to assert that Senegal's failure to prosecute or extradite Habré was in violation of its obligations under the Torture Convention, which the court confirmed. *Questions related to the obligation to prosecute or extradite (Belgium v Senegal)* (20 July 2012). Facing international pressure and with the promise of foreign funding, Senegal agreed to create a special tribunal to try the case in Senegal, with trials to begin in 2014. The agreed tribunal will be a hybrid one, using Senegalese magistrates working with a president from elsewhere in Africa.

An Argentinean court has explicitly invoked universal jurisdiction to consider claims of violations committed in Spain under the dictatorship of General Francisco Franco. In January 2012, investigations began into military officers involved in the Franco regime in relation to disappearances and summary executions, as well as into companies which are alleged to have benefited from forced labor.

Source: Marcela Vicente, "Argentina Investigates Human Rights Crimes of Spain's Franco Era," *IPS* (1 January 2012).

---

general that arose from the torture and murder of Paraguayan citizen Joelito Filartiga, a New York appellate court determined that human rights violations such as torture could constitute violations of the law of nations for the purposes of the ACTA. *Filartiga v. Peña-Irala* was a landmark case in establishing a reading of the ATCA never previously discussed, but falling within the language of the statute. Subsequent jurisprudence has established that extrajudicial execution, disappearances, war crimes and crimes against humanity, and genocide are also acts contrary to the law of nations for the purposes of interpreting the statute.

Kadić v. Karadžić

As we saw in Chapter 4, nonstate armed groups, and their leaders, may fall through the cracks of international humanitarian law and international human rights law. Internal armed conflicts could not traditionally be the sites of **grave breaches**, even though the same acts could have constituted grave breaches in international armed conflict. Also, human rights obligations are undertaken exclusively by states—by signing treaties or once they become customary law—and in some instances appear on their face to require official action, implying action by state actors rather than **nonstate actors**.

Radovan Karadžić, the leader of Bosnian Serbs during the conflicts in the former Yugoslavia (discussed in Chapter 6), has been accused of bearing direct and indirect responsibility for a wide range of abuses during that time. He was indicted by the International Criminal Tribunal for the Former Yugoslavia (ICTY) (discussed in Chapter 10) and after years in hiding, was arrested in mid-2008. However, over a decade earlier in the United States, he was the subject of a civil suit for a range of abuses. In the *Kadić v. Karadžić* case, attorneys acting on Karadžić's behalf objected that US courts lacked subject-matter jurisdiction, because Karadžić, as a nonstate actor, could not have committed the crimes alleged, which were not attributable to a state. While a lower court held that acts committed by nonstate actors do not violate the law of nations, a US appellate court found that Karadžić could be found liable for genocide, war crimes, and crimes against humanity in his private capacity, and for other violations in his capacity as a state actor. Because he exercised effective control of a territory as the head of Republika Srpska, his regime could satisfy the criteria of a state, and, in the alternative, he might be found to have acted in collaboration with a recognized state, then Yugoslavia. The case was thus an important step forward in treating an individual—head of a nonstate armed group but not of an internationally recognized state—as an official actor for the purposes of international criminal accountability. A similar issue was confronted by the ICTY in the *Tadić* jurisdiction case, discussed in Chapter 10.

Corporations as targets of litigation

More recently, corporations have also been held liable under the ATCA, either for direct commission of abuses or, more frequently, for complicity in abuses. Transnational corporations have been the subject of increasing attention by human rights advocates precisely because of the difficulty of regulating them internationally, and because many of them engage in, or are complicit in the perpetration of, significant human rights violations, particularly when they operate in conflict-affected countries. However, finding the appropriate links and legal personality to establish jurisdiction over corporations has proven difficult. During the negotiations for the Rome Statute for the International Criminal Court, it was proposed that jurisdiction be extended to both legal and natural persons. However, legal persons (such as corporations) were ultimately excluded from the court's jurisdiction. This means that subjecting corporations to criminal sanctions in international law remains impossible, subject to any revisions in the Rome Treaty. Given the difficulty of prosecuting corporations directly before the ICC, the use of the ATCA has proven attractive for filing cases against corporations in the United States.

Numerous cases have extended the *Filartiga* line of reasoning to pursue corporate accountability for crimes committed directly or when they act in complicity with state actors in violation of human rights. For corporate complicity or aiding and abetting a government to be found, in civil cases, it is not sufficient to have simply operated in a country where widespread abuses occurred, but rather that specific projects were connected with specific violations, and that the corporation knew or should have known that such violations would occur.

A crucial corporate case was *Doe v. Unocal,* brought against Unocal, a California-based petroleum company, on behalf of 15 Burmese villagers, for abuses such as forced labor, rape, torture, and murder perpetrated by the Burmese military, which had been hired by Unocal to protect and assist its construction of a pipeline. The case was also brought against the Burmese government and the French company Total. While cases against the state authorities and subsidiaries were dismissed, those against Unocal were not. The court found that corporations could be liable not only for their own actions, but also for actions of their partners or joint venturers, including governments. Unocal was found to be complicit in these acts because it hired the military for security and other support with full knowledge of its history of serious human rights abuses. Unocal appealed and then, just before the appellate court was to begin its review of the case, settled with a group of villagers for an undisclosed sum.

As discussed in Chapter 9, the Canadian oil company Talisman Energy has faced similar allegations and a lawsuit for its alleged complicity with abuses in southern Sudan. In 2001 the Presbyterian Church of Sudan filed a case under the ATCA against Talisman. The case alleges that the company assisted the government's military assaults on minority villages in order to help the government clear the way for Talisman's oil exploration. Talisman attempted several times to have the case dismissed; in its last attempt, in 2003, the judge held that because the alleged acts of genocide, war crimes, torture, and enslavement constituted violations of international law, plaintiffs had actionable ATCA claims. The judge further found that under international law, Talisman could be alleged to have aided and abetted these acts. However, an appeals court dismissed the case for lack of jurisdiction, on the grounds that the plaintiffs failed to establish that the defendants purposefully aided and abetted the abuses. The US Supreme Court denied plaintiffs' writ of certiorari, effectively terminating the proceedings (see Box 9.4 on p. 149). The US Supreme Court has progressively limited the scope of the ATCA, both in terms of the violations covered and in terms of the range of potential accused.

Limits to the ATCA: the Sosa *and* Kiobel *cases*

However, while civil liability through the ATCA has resulted in landmark judgments against individuals and, to a lesser degree, against corporations, there are limits which have been shaped by the strong political and legal opposition both from the US government of the administration of George W. Bush and corporations. The Bush administration argued that ATCA cases potentially undermine the "war on terror." It also argued that ATCA is nothing more than a jurisdictional grant. The US Supreme Court concurred with the latter point in considering the scope of the ATCA in 2004. Its decision in *Sosa v. Alvarez-Machain* found that the ATCA does not create a new cause of action and is merely a jurisdictional grant. The Court also suggested that there are limits to what the law can construe as violating the "law of nations" for the purposes of the act. While the exact scope is unclear, the court indicated that extrajudicial kidnapping would not fall within the law, and suggested that the law might be restricted to its supposed original intent—protection of diplomats and responding to piracy. This judgment does not repeal the earlier decisions, but leaves open the possibility that courts could restrict application of the ATCA.

In 2012, the application of the ATCA to corporations faced a fresh challenge, in a case involving activities by the oil company Royal Dutch Shell in Nigeria, *Kiobel et al v. Royal Dutch Petroleum et al* (April 17, 2013). Plaintiffs alleged that the company aided and abetted atrocities committed by Nigerian police and military forces against the Ogoni people. Two challenges were raised by the case: whether corporations had legal personality and could be sued under this law, and the extraterritorial scope of US law. The majority determined that litigation over abuses abroad could only take place where there was a sufficient connection to the United States, which was deemed not to be present in this case. Some human rights groups have viewed this as a significant defeat, while the opinion and several concurring opinions purport to leave the door open to cases, so long as they involve sufficient connection to the United States, and involve violations of settled international legal norms.

Civil liability in the United Kingdom

The United States is not the only country in which civil accountability may be imposed for abuses. The United Kingdom does not have a statute like the ATCA, though this has

---

Box 11.5 **Landmark ATCA cases: extension and limitation**

Filartiga v. Peña-Irala (1980)
Venue: US Federal Court of Appeals
Issue: Torture by noncitizen of noncitizen
Development: Law of nations includes human rights law; torture now banned as part of customary international law

Kadić v. Karadžić (1995)
Venue: US Federal Court of Appeals
Issue: Extent of state actor requirement; color of law requirement
Development: Liability of nonstate actors established; appears limited to actors that have effective control

Doe v. Unocal (1997–2004)
Venue: US Federal District Court / Court of Appeals
Issue: Complicity for acts of others
Development: Corporations can be complicit for acts of joint venturers; case appealed, then settled out of court

Sosa v. Alvarez-Machain (2004)
Venue: US Supreme Court
Issue: Extent of law of nations for ATCA
Development: ACTA contracted to include only *clearly established* violations of law of nations; implications still unclear

Kiobel et al v. Royal Dutch Petroleum et al (2013)
Venue: US Supreme Court
Issue: Extent of extraterritorial application of US law under ATCA
Development: Claims must not only touch and concern the United States territory, but must do so with sufficient force to displace a presumption against extraterritoriality

---

not prevented its courts from deciding civil cases against foreign state officials for torture, in situations similar to those that are addressed by many ATCA cases. In October 2004, the Supreme Court of Judicature issued a decision regarding immunity in two civil cases involving alleged torture by foreign officials. In both cases, *Jones v. The Ministry of the Interior* and *Mitchell v. Al-Dali,* British and/or Canadian citizens claimed that they had been tortured by Saudi officials, and brought civil claims for damages arising from the alleged torture, including "aggravated and exemplary damages for assault and battery, trespass to the person, torture, and unlawful imprisonment." The government of Saudi Arabia sought to challenge the suits on the grounds of immunity under the UK's State Immunity Act of 1978. The court distinguished between official acts and acts that could not be viewed as in pursuit of official functions, and the distinction between official and private acts, before turning to the crime of torture, which is by definition an act that occurs in an "official" capacity. The court reviewed a range of recent cases, including the *Pinochet* cases and US ATCA

Box 11.6 **Domestic accountability abroad**

Universal Jurisdiction

Type of justice: Criminal
Countries: Canada; multiple European countries including Spain and Senegal
Key cases: Pinochet and many more

US ATCA

Type of justice: Civil
Countries: United States
Key cases: Filartiga v. Peña-Irala and many more

UK Civil Cases

Type of justice: Civil
Countries: United Kingdom
Key cases: Jones v. The Ministry of the Interior

---

cases, and determined official immunity for official acts could not preclude prosecution for systematic torture. The court also considered the extent of civil immunity and held, building upon reasoning in relevant criminal cases, as well as in *Sosa v. Alvarez-Machain,* and other US practice, that even if the Saudi government was immune from civil suits, Saudi officials were not.

Transnational accountability after (or during) conflict

This chapter has examined two tools for transnational accountability after, or indeed during, conflict, where victims may seek redress through criminal or civil processes in the courts of another country. In many instances, after conflict, or while conflict still rages, it may be difficult for domestic courts to act, and where the ICC or other international or internationalized courts do not have jurisdiction, such transnational processes may provide the only feasible venue. It is therefore worthwhile, when considering options for accountability for gross violations of human rights and international humanitarian law during conflict, where other venues such as domestic courts or ad hoc or permanent international courts are not available, to also consider transnational accountability processes.

Discussion questions

*   What limitations did the ICJ impose upon universal jurisdiction in the *DRC v. Belgium* case?
*   What was the original purpose of ATCA and do you think its use to address human rights abuses is consistent with it?
*   What limitations have been placed by courts on the use of ATCA for civil trials for alleged international crimes?
*   How can corporations be held responsible for crimes committed by other actors?

- What are some specific potential problems with the use of either civil or criminal accountability in the courts of other nations?
- Considering the four country studies presented in Part 2 of this book—the former Yugoslavia, Sierra Leone, the Democratic Republic of Congo, and Sudan—can you think of specific cases that might be brought through universal jurisdiction or civil accountability?

Further reading

Aceves, William J., "*Doe v. Unocal* 963 F. Supp. 880," *American Journal of International Law* vol. 92, no. 2 (April 1998): 979–987.

Ballentine, Karen, and Heiko Nitzschke (eds), *Profiting from Peace: Managing the Resource Dimensions of Civil War* (Boulder, CO: Lynne Rienner, 2005).

Burley, Anne-Marie, "The Alien Tort Claims Statute and Judiciary Act of 1789: A Badge of Honor," *American Journal of International Law* vol. 83 (1989): 461–493.

De la Rasilla del Moral, Ignacio, "The Swan Song of Universal Jurisdiction in Spain," *International Criminal Law Review* vol. 9 (2009): 777–808.

Macedo, Stephen, ed., *Universal Jurisdiction: National Courts and the Prosecution of Serious Crimes Under International Law* (Philadelphia, PA: University of Pennsylvania Press, 2004).

Martin-Ortega, Olga, "Business and Human Rights in Conflict," *Ethics & International Affairs* vol. 22, no. 3 (2008): 273–83.

Reydams, Luc, *Universal Jurisdiction: International and Municipal Legal Perspectives* (Oxford: Oxford University Press, 2003).

Sriram, Chandra Lekha, *Globalizing Justice for Mass Atrocities: A Revolution in Accountability* (London: Routledge, 2005).

Vicente, Marcela "Argentina Investigates Human Rights Crimes of Spain's Franco Era," *Inter-Press Serice* (1 January 2012).

Official documents and sources

Alien Tort Claims Act, Title 28, Pt. IV, Chap. 85, Sec. 1350, http://www4.law.cornell.edu/uscode/28/1350.html

Doe v. Unocal, http://www.escr-net.org/docs/i/1054008

Filartiga v. Pena Irala, http://homepage.ntlworld.com/jksonc/docs/filartiga-630F2d876.html

International Court of Justice, *Arrest Warrant of 11 April 2000 (DRC v. Belgium)* (14 February 2002), http://www.icj-cij.org/docket/index.php?p1=3&p2=3&k=36&case=121&code=cobe&p3=4

International Court of Justice, *Questions related to the obligation to prosecute or extradite (Belgium v Senegal)* (20 July 2012) http://www.icj-cij.org/docket/index.php?p1=3&p2=3&case=144&code=bs&p3=4

Kadić v. Karadžić, 70 F.3rd 232 (2nd Cir. *1995*), Rehearing Denied, 74 F.3rd 377 (2nd Cir. 1996), Cert. Denied 518 U.S. 1005 (1996).

Kiobel et al v Royal Dutch Petroleum et al US Supreme Court No. 10-1491 (April 17, 2013).

Sosa v. Alvarez-Machain, 542 US 692 (June 29, 2004).

Regina v. Bartle and the Commissioner of Police for the Metropolis and Others Ex Parte Pinochet, 38 I.L.M. 581 (H.L. 1999).

Wiwa v. Royal Dutch Petroleum 226 F.3d 88 (2d Cir., September 14, 2000).

12 Hybrid tribunals

Key points

- **Hybrid tribunals** combine both domestic and international systems of justice to provide a mixed court system.
- The organization of a hybrid tribunal depends on the context, and can range from insertion of international judges into a domestic system, such as in Kosovo, to the creation of a special court, such as in Sierra Leone.
- Supporters of hybrid tribunals maintain that they combine the benefits of international tribunals, such as impartiality and legitimacy, with the strengths of the domestic courts, including ownership by the local populace and efficiency.
- In practice, experience in Kosovo, Timor-Leste, and Sierra Leone has been mixed, and it remains to be seen how the second trial in Cambodia will proceed and whether there will be any additional prosecutions.
- Despite difficulties, hybrid tribunals will probably continue to be used in the future to provide a measure of justice and potentially assist with rehabilitation of the domestic system.

The development of hybrid tribunals

Given the expense and scale of the **International Criminal Tribunal for Rwanda** (ICTR) and the **International Criminal Tribunal for the Former Yugoslavia** (ICTY), it is unlikely that further international tribunals will be created, especially in light of the establishment of the **International Criminal Court** (ICC). However, the ICC will not be able to address all possible cases, both because it will not have sufficient resources and because it may not have temporal or territorial jurisdiction over all cases of interest. Hybrid tribunals, a recent development in international attempts to seek accountability for serious crimes, are an alternative. These are known as "hybrid", "mixed" or "internationalized" tribunals because they involve both domestic and external judges, as well as a mixture of domestic and international law, and are most often located in the country where the conflict took place.

Hybrid tribunals have been established for Kosovo, Timor-Leste, Bosnia, Sierra Leone, Cambodia, and Lebanon. The Democratic Republic of Congo is in the process of passing legislation for specialized chambers within the domestic court system. The United States suggested that such a mechanism would be appropriate to address the situation in Darfur, preferring it to the **UN Security Council** referral to the ICC, but ultimately engaged in negotiation over a compromise resolution that limited jurisdiction over nationals of nonstate parties. Although hybrid tribunals have also been suggested as a possibility for Afghanistan and Iraq, the Supreme Iraqi Criminal Tribunal was fully domestic.

Defining a hybrid tribunal

Unlike the international ad hoc criminal tribunals or the ICC, a hybrid tribunal is not purely a creation of the international community, employing solely international law and international prosecutors and judges. It is also distinct from domestic processes such as prosecutions, in that it does not solely use domestic judges and law. Instead, it is an attempt to address the limitations of domestic and of international models. There is no particular model that hybrid tribunals follow, but rather each institution deploys a different mix of domestic and international law, and domestic and international judges and staff.

Combining national and international justice

Supporters of hybrid tribunals argue that such mechanisms combine the best of both national and international justice. They expect that the combination of domestic and international judges can avoid the risks of political manipulation and potential bias that domestic courts face. They also suggest that the combination of domestic and international law can avoid the use of domestic laws that do not meet international standards, ensuring that hybrid tribunals are better suited to the needs of countries emerging from conflict. By locating hybrid tribunals in the countries where the conflicts occurred, trials take place relatively close to where the crimes were committed, which should in principle make it easier to obtain information and witnesses. Presence in the country of conflict, advocates argue, should also in principle serve to inform and educate the populace at large, enable a sense of participation in the process, and ideally promote reconciliation. Several hybrid tribunals also have specific mandates to help to build the capacity of collapsed domestic legal institutions. Although each hybrid tribunal is unique, they can be described generally as either domestic courts with international elements, or international courts with domestic elements.

This chapter examines the hybrid tribunals created for Kosovo, Timor-Leste, and Cambodia, as well as the Special Court for Sierra Leone in greater depth, building on the discussion in Chapter 7.

Kosovo

Background

As examined in greater detail in Chapter 6, escalating tension and violence between ethnic Albanians and Serbians in the mid-1990s culminated in the Kosovo Liberation Army (KLA) targeting Serbs. In 1998, Slobodan Milošević retaliated through an ethnic-cleansing campaign against Kosovar Albanians, and in March 1999 rejected a peace deal. This led to a three-month airstrike by the **North Atlantic Treaty Organization** (NATO), and Serbia was forced to withdraw in June 1999. Creation of the UN Interim Administration Mission in Kosovo (UNMIK) was authorized through a **UN Security Council resolution**, Resolution 1244, in 1999. This resolution provided UNMIK with a broad mandate to provide:

> an interim administration for Kosovo under which the people of Kosovo can enjoy substantial autonomy within the Federal Republic of Yugoslavia, and which will

***Box 12.1* Hybrid tribunals to date**

Tribunal	*Type*
"Regulation 64" Panels, Kosovo, established in 2000.	Domestic courts, special courts within, with significant international elements.
Special Panels for Serious Crimes, Timor-Leste, established in 2000.	Domestic court, special court within, with significant international elements.
War Crimes Chamber, Bosnia, established in 2005.	Domestic court, special court within, with significant international elements during its first years of operation.
Special Court for Sierra Leone, established in 2002.	International court with domestic elements.
Extraordinary Chambers in the Courts of Cambodia, agreement reached between UN and Cambodian government in 2003 and became operational in 2006.	Domestic courts with international judges.
Special Tribunal for Lebanon, established in 2007.	International court with domestic elements.

provide transitional administration while establishing and overseeing the development of provisional democratic self-governing institutions to ensure conditions for a peaceful and normal life for all inhabitants of Kosovo.

Mandate and structure

Although the ICTY did have jurisdiction over crimes during the Kosovo conflict, it had a limited capacity to try cases. However, the **United Nations** (UN), the Organization for Security and Cooperation in Europe (OSCE), and international nongovernmental organizations realized that there were significant problems with the Kosovar courts. There were few Serb judges left, and there was risk of ethnic bias as well as intimidation of Albanian judges. As a result, Serbs were often detained for the same crimes for which Albanians would be released. UNMIK Regulation no. 2000/6, passed in February 2000, gave the **Special Representative of the Secretary-General** (SRSG) the power to appoint an international judge and an international prosecutor to assist in the administration of justice. It was hoped that this would improve the situation and secure a foundation for due process. The first international judge and prosecutor were appointed in Mitrovica district in February 2000. UNMIK Regulation no. 2000/64, passed in December 2000 (see Box 12.2), then gave the SRSG the right to appoint enough judges to form the majority in any decisions. These were known as Regulation 64 panels.

The Regulation 64 panels differed from other hybrid models because the international judges and prosecutors worked on a broad range of cases, not only serious crimes. Since their role was to support domestic trials and ensure prevention of ethnic bias, they worked exclusively with domestic law, using international law only where it was a part of the

---

***Box 12.2* UNMIK Regulation no. 2000/64**

UNMIK Regulation no. 2000/64
December 15, 2000

On Assignment of International Judges/Prosecutors and/or Change of Venue

The Special Representative of the Secretary-General …
Hereby promulgates the following:

Section 1
Recommendation for Assignment of International Judges/Prosecutors and/or Change of Venue
1.1. At any stage in the criminal proceedings, the competent prosecutor, the accused or the defence counsel may submit to the Department of Judicial Affairs a petition for an assignment of international judges/prosecutors and/or a change of venue where this is considered necessary to ensure the independence and impartiality of the judiciary or the proper administration of justice
1.2. At any stage in the criminal proceedings, the Department of Judicial Affairs, on the basis of the petition referred to in section 1.1 above or on its own motion, may submit a recommendation to the Special Representative of the Secretary-General. …
1.3. The Special Representative of the Secretary-General shall review a recommendation submitted by the Department of Judicial Affairs and signify his approval or rejection thereof. …

Section 2
Designation of International Judges/Prosecutors and/or New Venue
2.1. Upon approval of the Special Representative of the Secretary-General … the Department of Judicial Affairs shall expeditiously designate:
   a. An international prosecutor
   b. An international investigating judge; and/or
   c. A panel composed only of three (3) judges, including at least two international judges, of which one shall be the presiding judge,
   as required by the particular stage at which the criminal proceeding has reached in a case.

---

applicable domestic law. They were able to try **genocide** and **war crimes** due to the fact that these crimes were incorporated within the domestic code.

There were no clear criteria to determine which cases should have international judges and prosecutors, in order to ensure that they could be appointed to a broad range of cases to guarantee impartiality. In contrast to normal panels, which consisted of two professional and three lay judges, Regulation 64 panels had three professional judges and at least two international judges.

Evaluation

The Regulation 64 panels were first assigned to pending cases concerning war crimes. There were a number of Serbs already in detention when Regulation 64 came into effect. Also in this backlog of cases was a high-profile case against former KLA leaders. Subsequent proceedings dealt increasingly with cases that were considered particularly difficult for security or political reasons such as organized crime and corruption, which were also tied to terrorism and interethnic violence.

Selection of cases

The appointment of international judges and prosecutors was completely at the discretion of the SRSG, as detailed in Article 1.3 of UNMIK Regulation no. 2000/64 (see Box 12.2). This discretion, combined with a lack of guiding criteria, meant that these appointment decisions could potentially be political, rather than decided on the merits of the cases. There has been criticism that UNMIK was in a position to influence the justice process, with **Amnesty International** claiming that international judges and prosecutors were subject to executive interference. International judges and prosecutors were not accountable to an independent body, unlike local judges, who were regulated by the Kosovo Judicial and Prosecutorial Council. Whether true or not, there was a perception of political interference on behalf of Serbs, which was potentially damaging to the work of the Regulation 64 panels.

Lack of cooperation

Most Serb perpetrators fled to Serbia following the conflict. There were problems regarding the extradition of indicted individuals from Serbia, due to both Kosovo's status as a UN protectorate and internal Serbian politics. This added to the perception that only Albanians were being prosecuted.

Problems with recruitment of international judges and prosecutors

There were also difficulties in attracting qualified staff. Because Regulation 64 panels worked only on domestic cases, international judges were sometimes unaware of applicable law, lacked substantive knowledge of **international humanitarian law** and **international human rights law**, or lacked experience with criminal prosecutions.

Due process

While international judges and prosecutors were relatively well resourced, there was concern that local defense lawyers did not have sufficient resources, potentially undermining the possibility of ensuring a fair trial. There were also difficulties with language: proceedings of trials conducted in English were often available only in summary translation; judgments too were not easily accessible.

Lack of focus on war crimes

There was an increasing focus on cases dealing with organized crime, and between 2002 and 2007 only six new cases concerning war crimes were opened. This shift in focus meant that many atrocities committed during the conflict were not prosecuted. This shift was criticized as reflecting international interest in combating terrorism and corruption, rather than reflecting local demands for justice.

Legacy

The Regulation 64 panels were an innovative way of dealing with a justice system incapable of investigation and prosecution of serious crimes after conflict. Although it was hoped that the inclusion of international judges and prosecutors would help the domestic system, through capacity building of prosecutors, defense lawyers, and judges, there was concern that, in practice, the domestic justice system was still no better equipped. The lack of progress is demonstrated by the fact that after the withdrawal of UNMIK after seven years, the international component continues under the European Union Rule of Law Mission to Kosovo (EULEX). The EULEX Executive Division investigates, prosecutes and adjudicates cases related to: war crimes, terrorism, organized crime and high-level corruption, property and privatization cases and other serious crimes. The Executive Division is staffed by judges, prosecutors, police officers and customs officers. It is envisaged that the executive role of EULEX will gradually reduce as Kosovo's rule of law institutions assume greater responsibilities in these areas.

Timor-Leste

Background

Timor-Leste was a Portuguese colony from the beginning of the seventeenth century until 1974. During the process of self-determination, with political parties divided over whether Timor-Leste should become fully independent, integrate with Indonesia, or maintain relations with Portugal, civil war broke out. In December 1975, Portugal withdrew completely as Indonesia invaded and annexed Timor-Leste; in 1976, Indonesia declared Timor-Leste its 27th province. Until 1999, the Armed Forces of Indonesia (Tentara Nasional Indonesia [TNI]) carried out military campaigns against nationalist guerrilla fighters from the Revolutionary Front for an Independent East Timor (Revolucionária de Timor-Leste Independente [FRETILIN]). The TNI targeted not only combatants, but also huge numbers of civilians, killing many and displacing even more. The TNI carried out widespread human rights abuses, including **torture** of FRETILIN supporters, rape, disappearances, and massacres. Following the resignation of Indonesia's President Suharto in 1998, his replacement, Jusef Habibie, suggested that Timor-Leste could be given a special status of limited autonomy. This approach was unacceptable to the TNI, which encouraged widespread intimidation and violence toward the general population through support of pro-integration militias.

In May 1999, Indonesia and Timor-Leste agreed that a referendum would be held to decide whether Timor-Leste would have special autonomy or be completely independent. The referendum took place on August 30, 1999, with 78 percent of voters supporting independence and rejected the proposed autonomy. This was followed by a campaign of "scorched earth" tactics by the pro-integration militias and the TNI, resulting in the deaths of many civilians and the displacement of thousands. In response, the Security Council authorized a multinational force, the International Force for East Timor (INTERFET) to restore peace and security. The TNI and the Indonesian police withdrew, and on September 28, 1999, Portugal and Indonesia agreed to transfer authority in Timor-Leste to the

United Nations. In October 1999 the Security Council established the UN Transitional Administration in East Timor (UNTAET), authorized by Resolution 1272, to administer the country through the transition to independence. Having legislative and executive powers, including the administration of justice, UNTAET effectively acted as the government of the country. Timor-Leste became independent in 2002.

Mandate and structure

Once UNTAET was established, there were calls for an international ad hoc tribunal like the ICTY or ICTR, but this was not seriously considered by the UN, in part because of emergent criticisms of those institutions (see Chapter 10). UNTAET created the Serious Crimes Unit (SCU) to investigate and lead prosecutions, and created the Special Panels for Serious Crimes to try the suspects. UNTAET established the special panels through its own Regulation no. 2000/15 (see Box 12.3), but they were placed within the domestic legal framework—within the Dili district court.

The special panels had exclusive jurisdiction for serious crimes, war crimes, genocide, and **crimes against humanity** committed from January 1 to October 15, 1999. They also had exclusive jurisdiction, and therefore primacy over domestic courts, for the national crimes of murder and sexual offenses committed within this time period.

Box 12.3 **UNTAET Regulation no. 2000/15**

UNTAET Regulation no. 2000/15
June 6, 2000

On the establishment of panels with exclusive jurisdiction over serious criminal offences

Section 1
Panels with jurisdiction over serious criminal offences

1.1. … there shall be established panels of judges (hereinafter: "panels") within the District Court in Dili with exclusive jurisdiction to deal with serious criminal offences
1.3. The panels … shall exercise jurisdiction … with respect to the following serious criminal offences:
   a. Genocide
   b. War Crimes
   c. Crimes against Humanity
   d. Murder
   e. Sexual Offences; and
   f. Torture
1.4. At any stage of the proceedings, in relation to cases of serious criminal offences … a panel may have deferred to itself a case which is pending before another panel or court in East Timor.

Each special panel had one domestic and two international judges. The same type of judicial mechanism was added to the Court of Appeal in Dili, although in some cases three international judges and two domestic judges could be appointed. There was only one special Panel until mid-2003, and then a second and third panel were subsequently established.

Evaluation

The special panels and SCU did achieve some success. The SCU indicted over 400 people, with all charges involving crimes against humanity or violations of domestic law. Between 2002 and 2005, the special panels carried out 55 trials, which resulted in the convictions of 83 people. However, there were challenges to the process.

Gaps between domestic and international law

The special panels had exclusive jurisdiction for certain crimes under domestic law (murder and sexual crimes) between January and October 1999. However, outside this time period, there was inconsistency in determining how crimes would be prosecuted, because the Timorese courts had jurisdiction only from October 25, 1999, the date that UNTAET was established. Crimes that occurred before January 1, 1999, would be under the jurisdiction of Indonesian courts. Further, because the special panels were prosecuting murder and sexual crimes under domestic law, they had jurisdiction only for the territory of Timor-Leste. This meant that rapes and murders committed in camps in West Timor between January and October 1999 were outside the jurisdiction of the special panels. Again, domestic courts could not prosecute these crimes, because their jurisdiction began only on October 25, 1999. Finally, domestic legislation concerning these crimes did not necessarily meet international standards; for example, the definition of rape meant that it was only a crime when the victim was female.

Lack of cooperation

Despite the signing of a memorandum of understanding between the Indonesian government and UNTAET, there was never any cooperation by the Indonesian government with the special panels. This created a difficult obstacle to the work of the special panels. Most of the accused were in Indonesia, and the Timorese government was not able to arrest them. As a result, the special panels were not able to target those who were most responsible for the atrocities; only people from Timor-Leste were convicted, and most perpetrators remain free and have even been promoted to higher military and political appointments in Indonesia.

The work of a hybrid tribunal is drastically limited if it cannot reach indicted suspects in a country that won't cooperate. An international tribunal such as the ICTY or ICTR, authorized under Chapter VII of the **UN Charter**, has greater capacity to access suspects, as all countries are obliged to cooperate. If the special panels had been established in this way, greater international pressure could have been brought to bear on Indonesia.

Organizational problems

In the absence of a Chapter VII commitment, funding for the special panels was provided only on a voluntary basis, and thus the budget of the panel was limited. There were difficulties with staffing and recruitment. The judges, in particular, were not well paid, and it was difficult to appoint them according to the language criteria established by the government. Thus many judges had little experience in international criminal law. Similarly, defense counsel lacked skills in representation, potentially undermining the right of the accused to a fair trial.

Lack of an integrated reconciliation strategy

The Commission for Reception, Truth, and Reconciliation (CAVR) not only acted as a **truth commission**, working to create a narrative of the events and human rights abuses between 1974 and 1999, but also involved community reconciliation procedures. The community reconciliation mechanism was nonjudicial, with people taking part in local hearings to confess their crimes. However, only lesser crimes could be included within the reconciliation process, and serious crimes were not addressed. All those who wished to take part in the reconciliation process were required to submit a statement to the SCU, which decided whether the individual could take part or whether it, the SCU, had jurisdiction and should prosecute the crime. However, with limited resources, it was evident that the SCU would never be able to prosecute all perpetrators of serious crimes. This led to a confusing situation, with individuals excluded from both processes if the SCU could not prosecute. Those who participated in the reconciliation process felt that those who had committed worse crimes had effectively been allowed to act with **impunity**, because the special panels and SCU lacked the capacity to try them all.

Legacy

In 2006, the UN Integration Mission in Timor-Leste (UNMIT) created the Serious Crimes Investigation Team (SCIT) to carry on the investigative functions of the Serious Crimes Unit. However, the SCIT has a more limited mandate—to investigate, not to prosecute; the latter responsibility lies with the domestic Office of the Prosecutor-General (OPG). The SCIT is part of the UN, but SCIT officers work under the direction and supervision of the OPG. Once SCIT has concluded its investigation in a case, it sends all the collected evidence and its recommendations to the OPG. The OPG then decides whether there is enough evidence to file an indictment or close the case. The SCIT began work in February 2008, and has prioritized cases from those still pending before the SCU. Once it has concluded all investigations into serious crimes of 1999, SCIT will be closed. Apart from this investigative function, the SCIT provides legal and forensic training for national agencies, such as the police.

Cambodia

Background

The Khmer Rouge, led by Pol Pot, invaded and gained control of Cambodia in April 1975 and for four years the country suffered repressive rule. The Khmer Rouge forced millions of people into rural areas to start a communist agrarian society. Human rights abuses were widespread, with hundreds of thousands of people tortured and executed, including individuals belonging to religious and ethnic minorities, intellectuals, and members of other political parties. One of the most notorious prisons was a former high school in Phnom Penh named Security Prison 21 (S-21), or Tuol Sleng, where thousands of people were imprisoned, tortured, and killed.

The number of people killed through starvation, forced labor, as well as execution is estimated at around two million. The Vietnamese managed to invade and capture Phnom

Penh in January 1979, forcing the Khmer Rouge to retreat to an area bordering Thailand. The Khmer Rouge engaged in guerrilla warfare for another 20 years, resulting in the displacement of hundreds of thousands. In 1981 the Kampuchean People's Revolutionary Party won National Assembly elections, but the international community did not recognize the government. The Vietnamese withdrew in 1989, and a peace agreement was signed in 1991 in Paris. The UN Transitional Authority in Cambodia (UNTAC) was established by Security Council Resolution 745. UNTAC ensured that a free and fair general election was held in 1993, which was won by the National United Front for an Independent, Neutral, Peaceful, and Cooperative Cambodia (Front Uni National pour un Cambodge Indépendant, Neutre, Pacifique, et Coopératif [FUNCINPEC]). Following the election, the monarchy was restored and the country was renamed the Kingdom of Cambodia. In 1994 thousands of guerrillas surrendered to a government **amnesty**, and in 1996 the deputy of the Khmer Rouge, Ieng Sary, was granted amnesty by the country's king. Pol Pot died in 1998.

Mandate and structure

In 1997, the Cambodian government asked the UN for assistance in establishing a tribunal to prosecute the Khmer Rouge. A long period of negotiation over the structure and mandate of the tribunal followed. In 1998 a UN group of experts was appointed, which recommended that a UN tribunal be established under Chapter VI or VII of the UN Charter, similar to the ICTY and ICTR. The United Nations and many states supported this approach because of fears that the Cambodian justice system was susceptible to corruption and manipulation, and that it was not fully independent of the government. However, the Cambodian government insisted that the tribunal be located within Cambodia. A Cambodian task force put forward the suggestion of a domestic process with international involvement and a supermajority system requiring the support of one international judge. Several UN member states—the United States, France, Japan, Australia, and India—supported this proposal. The UN and the Cambodian government began lengthy negotiations concerning the establishment and operation of the tribunal. The Cambodian National Assembly approved a law in 2001 to create the Extraordinary Chambers in the Courts of Cambodia (ECCC) in order to bring genocide charges against Khmer Rouge leaders for crimes committed between 1975 and 1979. However, the UN had many concerns with the law, fearing that the ECCC process would be too weak to succeed, and withdrew when negotiations with the Cambodian government broke down. The negotiations started again in 2003 and an agreement was finally reached on May 13 of that year. After waiting for funding from voluntary contributions from UN member states, the United Nations announced on April 19, 2005, that the ECCC was ready to proceed.

The ECCC is constituted within the Cambodian legal system, but includes domestic and international judges. While Cambodian judges outnumber international judges in both the trial chamber and supreme court (which generated concerns about bias during the establishment of the ECCC) voting is conducted on the basis of supermajority, so that domestic judges are not able to simply outvote the international judges (see Box 12.4). Therefore the Cambodian judges are not able to make a majority decision on their own, but rather require the support of one international judge. It was hoped that this model would prevent political interference. Nevertheless, as discussed below, it is alleged that the Cambodian government has managed to influence decisions regarding further prosecutions.

The ECCC is part of the Cambodian court system and uses both Cambodian and international law. The court has jurisdiction over crimes committed between April 17, 1975,

Box 12.4 The Law on the Establishment of the Extraordinary Chambers

Law on the Establishment of Extraordinary Chambers in the courts of Cambodia for the prosecution of crimes committed during the period of Democratic Kampuchea (with inclusion of amendments as promulgated on 27 October 2004)

Chapter I
General Provisions
Article 1
The purpose of this law is to bring to trial senior leaders of Democratic Kampuchea and those who were most responsible for the crimes and serious violations of Cambodian penal law, international humanitarian law and custom, and international conventions recognized by Cambodia, that were committed during the period from 17 April 1975 to 6 January 1979.

Chapter II
Competence
Article 2
Extraordinary Chambers shall be established in the existing court structure, namely the trial court and the supreme court to bring to trial senior leaders of Democratic Kampuchea and those who were most responsible for the crimes and serious violations of Cambodian laws related to crimes, international humanitarian law and custom, and international conventions recognized by Cambodia, that were committed during the period from 17 April 1975 to 6 January 1979.
Senior leaders of Democratic Kampuchea and those who were most responsible for the above acts are hereinafter designated as "Suspects."

Chapter III
Composition of the Extraordinary Chambers
Article 9
The Trial Chamber shall be … composed of five professional judges, of whom three are Cambodian judges with one as president, and two foreign judges; and before which the Co-Prosecutors shall present their cases. …
The Supreme Court Chamber, which shall serve as both appellate chamber and final instance, shall be … composed of seven judges, of whom four are Cambodian judges with one as president, and three foreign judges. …

Chapter V
Decisions of the Extraordinary Chambers
Article 14
1. The judges shall attempt to achieve unanimity in their decisions. If this is not possible, the following shall apply:
   a. a decision by the Extraordinary Chamber of the trial court shall require the affirmative vote of at least four judges;
   b. a decision by the Extraordinary Chamber of the Supreme Court shall require the affirmative vote of at least five judges.
2. When there is no unanimity, the decision of the Extraordinary Chambers shall contain the opinions of the majority and minority.

Source: Council of Jurists and the Secretariat of the Task Force, unofficial translation, revised August 26, 2007.

and January 6, 1979, specifically genocide as defined in the **Genocide Convention**, crimes against humanity as defined in the Rome Statute, **grave breaches** of the **Geneva Conventions**, torture, homicide, religious persecution, and destruction of cultural property.

Evaluation

The first individual to stand trial before the ECCC was Kaing Guek Eav (Duch), the head of the S-21 prison. His trial was known as Case 001 and it started in early 2009. Duch was charged with crimes against humanity (murder, extermination, enslavement, imprisonment, torture, rape, persecution on political grounds, and other inhumane acts) and grave breaches of the Geneva Conventions (willful killing, torture or inhumane treatment, willfully causing great suffering or serious injury to body or health, willfully depriving a prisoner of war or civilian of the rights of fair and regular trial, and unlawful confinement of a civilian). In the 2010 judgment, Duch was found guilty of crimes against humanity and grave breaches of the Geneva Conventions. He was sentenced to 35 years in jail. The Trial Chamber ruled that the Cambodian Military Court illegally held Duch in pre-trial detention and so took five years off his sentence, as well as 11 years for time already served. The alteration of the length of his sentence confused some, and disappointed victims and the general population. Both the defense and prosecution appealed in March 2011, with the defense appealing the judgment and looking for an acquittal and the prosecution appealing the verdict and requesting a maximum sentence of life in prison. In February 2012 Duch's sentence was increased to life imprisonment by the Supreme Court Chamber. The completion of his trial was considered a success for the ECCC, which had encountered difficulties and criticism in its first years of operation, including charges of corruption, budgetary constraints as well as political interference. The trial received widespread media coverage in the country, and the ECCC carried out outreach programs to inform the public of proceedings. This was also the first time that victims had taken part as civil parties in such a trial (see Box 12.6) and 22 victims were able to testify against and face Duch themselves.

Initially, Case 002 at the ECCC concerned four individuals. They were: Ieng Sary, former deputy prime minister and former foreign minister, charged with crimes against humanity and war crimes; Khieu Samphan, president during the Khmer Rouge occupation and charged with crimes against humanity and war crimes; Nuon Chea, second in command to Pol Pot and charged with crimes against humanity and war crimes; and Ieng Thirith, minister of social affairs and charged with crimes against humanity. At the end of 2011, Ieng Sary was declared mentally unfit to stand trial due to symptoms of Alzheimer's disease and was released. In March 2013, her husband Ieng Thirith passed away during the ongoing trial. During the protracted negotiations for the ECCC, there had been concerns about the age of the accused and worries about the expediency of the trial. There are only two senior leaders left in case 002, both over 80 years old with ongoing health problems.

Cambodia has a civil law system, and the ECCC uses the same inquisitorial model. Therefore in addition to the two co-prosecutors, (one Cambodian and one international) there are also two co-investigating judges (one Cambodian and one international). Disputes between the co-prosecutors and co-investigating judges regarding prosecutions beyond the five accused in Cases 001 and 002 generated allegations that the Cambodian government is interfering politically. In December 2008, the Cambodian co-prosecutor opposed the submission of five additional suspects by the international co-prosecutor (known as Cases 003 and 004). When a dispute such as this occurs, the Pre-Trial Chamber decides on the matter. In September 2009, the Pre-Trial Chamber announced that it had failed to reach

Box 12.5 The civil party system

The Cambodian judicial system allows victims of the accused to participate as civil parties in criminal proceedings. Since the ECCC uses a mix of domestic and international law, this practice was included in its Internal Rules. The ECCC was the first hybrid or international court to allow victims to participate in courtroom proceedings beyond acting as witnesses (the ICC and Special Tribunal for Lebanon also now have limited mandates for victim participation). Anyone who has suffered physical, psychological or material harm as a direct consequence of the Khmer Rouge regime can apply to become a civil party. They have the same rights as other parties to the proceedings and also have the right to seek reparations. However, the participation of civil parties for the first time in a mass atrocity trial posed some challenges, and a number of changes were made during Case 001 to make things easier for the subsequent proceedings. For example, in Case 001, 90 civil parties participated, divided amongst four groups. Each group had one Cambodian and one international lawyer, so eight lawyers could be questioning witnesses on behalf of civil parties, after judges, the prosecution and the defense. There were nearly 4,000 civil party applicants for Case 002, and it was apparent that this system would be completely unworkable for such large numbers, so changes were made to victim participation in February 2010. One international and one Cambodian lead co-lawyer were appointed to represent all of the civil parties as one consolidated group. Although some victims' groups were concerned that this would limit their input into the trial, there was no other evident solution.

In Case 001, the four groups of civil parties made requests concerning reparations, including: the publication of the judgment, individual monetary awards, a national commemoration day, construction of pagodas, preservation of archives, access to medical care and education. Nonetheless, the ECCC took a narrow view of reparations, declaring all of the suggestions outside of its competence. The only reparations awarded were the inclusion of the names of admitted civil parties and their deceased family members in the judgment and the compilation and publication of all statements of apology and acknowledgment of responsibility made by Duch. The rule concerning reparations was revised, and now there can only be one collective claim for reparations from the civil parties. It remains to be seen how this will be interpreted and work in practice in Case 002.

a supermajority on the matter. The three Cambodian judges agreed with the Cambodian co-prosecutor, whilst the international judges agreed with the international co-prosecutor. Without a supermajority in the Pre-Trial Chamber, the Cambodian co-prosecutor was unable to block the submission of suspects and the judicial investigation stage was able to begin. However, the work by the co-investigating judges during this stage has been just as complicated and resulted in widespread criticism of the ECCC. In 2011, many international staff from the Office of Co-Investigating Judges (OCIJ) resigned in protest at the failure to properly investigate Case 003. Two international co-investigating judges have resigned amidst claims of interference by the Cambodian government. One of them also described a dysfunctional situation within the OCIJ resulting from confrontation with the Cambodian co-investigating judge. In addition, Prime Minister Hun Sen and other politicians have indicated on several occasions that there will be no additional prosecutions, despite the fact, as observed by UN Secretary-General Ban Ki-Moon that decisions regarding additional prosecutions are made by the ECCC, not the government. There has been widespread condemnation from international observers regarding the lack of progress in Cases 003 and 004 and Ban Ki-Moon stated that he had serious concerns about the judicial process in relation to these cases. Nevertheless, a fourth international co-investigating judge has been appointed and has announced that the OCIJ is actively investigating Cases 003 and 004.

Although it is difficult to prosecute crimes committed three decades ago, particularly in terms of gathering evidence and the age of the accused and witnesses, no other **transitional justice** processes have taken place in Cambodia. The ECCC may represent the only opportunity to address the country's abusive past. The verdict in Case 001 is thus important as the first measure of justice for victims of atrocities committed during the Khmer Rouge regime. If the new international co-investigator faces the same obstacles as his predecessors, the cases may stall, limiting accountability at the ECCC, and indicating the degree to which some hybrid tribunals may be limited by political will.

Sierra Leone

Background

As discussed in Chapter 6, conflict between the government of Sierra Leone and the Revolutionary United Front (RUF) broke out in 1991 and endured for over a decade, leading to some 50,000–75,000 deaths and widespread atrocities, including mutilation and sexual violence. The conflict also involved widespread use of child combatants—often abducted and drugged—who were in many instances both victims and perpetrators of abuses. The first real possibility of peace came when negotiations in 1999 resulted in the Lomé Agreement between the government and the RUF, as well as a Security Council–mandated **peacekeeping** force, the UN Assistance Mission in Sierra Leone (UNAMSIL), authorized by Resolution 1270. The United Nations, which acted as a "moral guarantor" of the peace agreement, issued a reservation objecting to an amnesty provision that it did not consider to cover international crimes. Notwithstanding the agreement, fighting and atrocities resumed, and the RUF staged attacks on UNAMSIL. In May 2000, notorious RUF leader Foday Sankoh was captured, provoking discussions about the appropriate venue to try him and other perpetrators. In June, the government asked the UN to establish an international court to try such cases.

Mandate and structure

The Special Court for Sierra Leone (SCSL) was an entirely new court, distinct from the judicial system of the country. The United Nations created the SCSL through Security Council Resolution 1315 in August 2000, following an agreement with the government of Sierra Leone.

The SCSL statute (see Box 12.6), completed on January 16, 2002, gives the court the power to prosecute persons who bear the greatest responsibility for serious violations of national and international humanitarian law since November 30, 1996. The crimes under the jurisdiction of the SCSL include crimes against humanity, violations of **Common Article 3** and Additional Protocol II of the Geneva Conventions, other serious violations of international humanitarian law, and crimes under national law.

The SCSL's first trial chamber, in Freetown, consists of two international judges appointed by the **UN Secretary-General**, based on nominations from UN member states, and one

Box 12.6 The Statute of the Special Court for Sierra Leone

Statute of the Special Court for Sierra Leone

… established by an Agreement between the United Nations and the Government of Sierra Leone pursuant to Security Council resolution 1315 (2000) of 14 August 2000. …

Article 1
Competence of the Special Court
1. The Special Court shall …. have the power to prosecute persons who bear the greatest responsibility for serious violations of international humanitarian law and Sierra Leonean law committed in the territory of Sierra Leone since 30 November 1996. …

Article 2
Crimes against humanity

Article 3
Violations of Article 3 common to the Geneva Conventions and of Additional Protocol II

Article 4
Other serious violations of international humanitarian law
…
c. Conscripting or enlisting children under the age of 15 years into armed forces or groups or using them to participate actively in hostilities.

Article 5
Crimes under Sierra Leonean law
Offences relating to the abuse of girls under the Prevention of Cruelty to Children Act
i. Abusing a girl under 13 years of age … .
ii. Abusing a girl between 13 and 14 years of age … .
iii. Abduction of a girl for immoral purposes … .

Offences relating to the wanton destruction of property under the Malicious Damage Act
i. Setting fire to dwelling, houses, any person being therein
ii. Setting fire to public buildings
iii. Setting fire to other buildings.

Article 7
Jurisdiction over person of 15 years of age
1. The Special Court shall have no jurisdiction over any person who was under the age of 15 at the time of the alleged commission of the crime…

Article 8
Concurrent jurisdiction
1. The Special Court and the national courts of Sierra Leone shall have concurrent jurisdiction.
2. The Special Court shall have primacy over the national courts of Sierra Leone … .

Article 10
Amnesty
An amnesty granted to any person falling within the jurisdiction of the Special Court in respect of the crimes referred to in articles 2 to 4 of the present Statute shall not be a bar to prosecution.

appointed by the government of Sierra Leone. The second trial chamber, in The Hague (established solely to try Charles Taylor) has two international judges appointed by the UN Secretary-General and one appointed by the government of Sierra Leone. The SCSL's appeals chamber consists of two international judges appointed by the UN Secretary-General and two judges appointed by the government of Sierra Leone.

Evaluation

The question of immunity of Charles Taylor

As discussed in Chapter 7, the conflict in Sierra Leone was not confined to that country, but was also affected by conflicts and political leaders elsewhere. In particular, Charles Taylor, president of Liberia at that time, was heavily involved, through support to the RUF. In 2003, the prosecutor of the SCSL unsealed an indictment against him while Taylor was attending **peace negotiations** in Ghana for his own country. Rather than arrest Taylor, Ghana allowed him to leave the country. This was in part out of concern that arresting him would be a diplomatic affront, but also out of fear that it might undermine the Liberian peace process. Taylor went into hiding in Nigeria, which granted him asylum and refused to surrender him to the SCSL. The Nigerian high court, however, said that it would honor a request for extradition from any permanent Liberian government once it was installed, rather than from the interim government in power at the time.

Taylor claimed he was immune from prosecution because at the time of the indictment he was president of Liberia and enjoyed immunity as head of state. The SCSL rejected this challenge to jurisdiction on immunity grounds, invoking the decision of the **International Court of Justice** (ICJ) in the *Yerodia* case (discussed in Chapter 11), in which the ICJ stated that while national courts must respect official immunity, international courts need not. The special court considered itself to be an international court created by agreement between the government of Sierra Leone and the UN rather than a domestic court, and thus that it had jurisdiction.

After President Ellen Johnson Sirleaf was elected in the 2005 Liberian national elections, she requested Taylor's extradition from Nigeria. He attempted to escape but was captured at the Cameroon border. The UN Mission in Liberia (UNMIL) had been mandated under Security Council Resolution 1638 to take responsibility for his "apprehension, detention and transfer to the Special Court for Sierra Leone, in the event of his return to Liberia." Taylor was taken into custody by the SCSL on March 29, 2006, and transferred to The Hague on June 20.

Taylor's trial was moved to the ICC in The Hague because it was feared that holding the trial in Sierra Leone might threaten peace and stability in the country. However, the SCSL retains exclusive jurisdiction over the case. Taylor was originally indicted on 11 charges, for acts alleged to constitute crimes against humanity, violations of Common Article 3 and Additional Protocol II of the Geneva Conventions, and other violations of international humanitarian law, including murder, physical violence, rape and sexual slavery, use of child soldiers, abductions and forced labor, and looting. His trial began on June 4, 2007, and the verdict was delivered in May 2012. The prosecution alleged that Taylor had links with both RUF leaders and the AFRC and provided military training and support. The prosecution's argument rested on the fact that as a superior to the perpetrators, Taylor failed to take measures to prevent the abuses. Taylor pleaded not guilty to all charges and the defense claimed that the only contact he had with rebel groups was in negotiating a peace settlement.

The defense argued that it was impossible for Taylor to have contact with the RUF since the Liberia/Sierra Leone border was controlled by rebel groups. It also argued that it he should not be held responsible for any unauthorized behavior of Liberian security forces, such as trading weapons or arms with RUF. Taylor was found guilty on all 11 counts and sentenced to 50 years in prison. This was the first time a former head of state was found guilty by an internationalized court since the Nuremberg judgments. Taylor appealed the verdict in 2013, while the prosecution appealed to increase the sentence to 80 years. His conviction and sentence was upheld by the appeals chamber in September 2013.

The problem of the blanket amnesty

There was a potential technical legal problem with the blanket amnesty included in the Lomé Agreement. This amnesty was raised by defendants seeking to challenge the jurisdiction of the SCSL, claiming that the amnesty was still in force and reduced the court's temporal jurisdiction to crimes committed only after the signing of the peace accord in 1999. However, Article 10 of the court's statute (see Box 12.6) provides that any amnesty for the crimes covered in the statute would not be a bar to prosecution. Furthermore, the amnesty's validity can be challenged on several grounds. First, the UN reservation at the time stated that the amnesty could not cover international crimes such as genocide, crimes against humanity, war crimes, or other serious violations of international humanitarian law. Thus, even if the amnesty were valid, it would be valid only in respect of domestic crimes. Further, the UN was not party to the 1999 agreement, but rather (along with a number of other institutions and governments) agreed to act as guarantor of the agreement. The government of Sierra Leone was in a different position. It was a party to the Lomé Agreement, and also entered into a contract with the UN for the creation of the SCSL. Nonetheless, the government argued, as have others, that the amnesty provision, along with the rest of the peace accord, was nullified by the continued violation of the accord by the RUF. In March of 2004, the Special Court found that the Lomé Agreement could not be considered a treaty, and that the amnesty contained in the peace accord would therefore only have domestic effect and could have no effect upon an international court.

Perceptions of the court as driven by the government

As discussed in Chapter 6, Sam Hinga Norman was seen by many in Sierra Leone as a hero and defender of a democratically elected government. Many objected to his indictment in March 2003 for war crimes, crimes against humanity, and recruitment of child soldiers. Cadres of the Civil Defense Forces (CDF), and some domestic human rights advocates, saw the indictment as proof that the SCSL was biased in favor of the government. Although many Sierra Leoneans approved the creation of the SCSL, some wanted the court to address only the actions of the Armed Forces Revolutionary Council (AFRC) and the RUF, and resented the fact that former CDF fighters were being called to account. There were even concerns that CDF fighters might seek to destabilize the country. Others argued that Hinga Norman was made a scapegoat and that if he was responsible for the excesses of his forces, then President Kabbah, to whom he had reported, should also be tried. Hinga Norman died in February 2007 during his trial. The SCSL tried two other CDF leaders and found them guilty of war crimes, in a controversial trial that even the prosecutor admitted had been challenging. The prosecutor stated, however, that even though the CDF had sought to restore a democratically elected government, its crimes could not be justified.

Limitations on the court's ability to extradite suspects

The SCSL was dependent on other countries to agree to extradite the accused. This meant that indictees who sought asylum elsewhere could evade prosecution if the sheltering states chose not to extradite them. The lack of power to compel extradition was a problem precisely because the Sierra Leonean conflict had regional dimensions. However, the jurisdiction of the Special Court was limited to the territory of Sierra Leone, meaning that even if it had the power to compel extradition, it could not consider cases arising from events taking place outside the country, even if they involved atrocities related to the conflict. Although Charles Taylor was finally arrested and brought to trial after three years at large, another important accused, Johnny Paul Koroma, continued to elude the court. Another key accused, Foday Sankoh, died in detention.

Funding problems

The SCSL has had difficulty securing funding, which may have affected the court's operation. Its budget was to be US$30.2 million for its first year of operation, and US$84.4 million for the next two years, but has averaged only about $25 million annually. For the last three years of the SCSL, the budget was around $26 million total.

The SCSL's relationship with the Truth and Reconciliation Commission

The special court was established at about the same time as the Truth and Reconciliation Commission (TRC). In principle, their responsibilities did not overlap, as the role of the TRC was not to prosecute crimes, but rather to investigate the causes, nature, and extent of the violence, and also to make recommendations regarding reparations and legal, political, and administrative reform. There was a risk that evidence disclosed to the commission, which had different remit and evidentiary requirements, might be used by the court, but the SCSL prosecutor made clear that this was not an option. Some may not have believed him, and may have refused to testify before the commission. There was also tension between the two institutions when, in an attempt to avoid disrupting stability and undermining its own proceedings, the SCSL did not allow Hinga Norman to testify publicly before the TRC.

Legacy

Despite the many limits to the SCSL, including to its capacity and mandate, and the danger that key trials such as those of CDF members and Taylor would destabilize the country or even the region, the court has successfully prosecuted key perpetrators. The SCSL's strategy has been to prosecute only those most responsible for the crimes, focusing on all parties involved in the conflict: Taylor and members of the CDF, AFRC, and RUF. It has indicted 13 people, and arrested 12, with Johnny Koroma still at large. Three accused have died: RUF leader Foday Sankoh, former RUF battlefield commander Sam Bockarie, and Hinga Norman. In sum, once the Taylor appeal proceedings are completed, nine of those most responsible for war crimes will have been prosecuted by the SCSL, a significant achievement in imposing accountability for atrocities committed during the conflict. After the Taylor appeal is completed, the SCSL will be the first of the ad hoc or hybrid tribunals to finish its work and close.

The SCSL has reached landmark convictions on the use of child soldiers. In June 2007 in the trial of three members of the AFRC, the court found them guilty of the recruitment and use of child soldiers as a war crime. The court also convicted the three accused of war crimes based on charges of sexual violence, particularly taking young girls as forced "wives." This was the first time that an international tribunal ruled on the use of both child soldiers and sexual violence, resulting in an expansion of international criminal jurisprudence to include these violations.

Also important is the SCSL's indictment of Taylor as a sitting head of state. However, holding his trial in The Hague made it more difficult to ensure that the people of Sierra Leone were connected to the outcome.

The future of hybrid tribunals

While it was hoped that hybrid tribunals would combine the best of international and domestic justice, they have serious limitations. Hybrid tribunals have been limited precisely because they are partially domestic courts, in contrast to ad hoc tribunals. Because hybrid tribunals are not created by Security Council resolutions under Chapter VII of the UN Charter, they do not have the authority of ad hoc tribunals to demand extradition of suspects from other countries, nor are they entitled to compulsory UN contributions by member states. As a consequence of the latter, the budgets of hybrid tribunals are much more limited, in some instances totaling less for their entire mandates than the biennial budgets of the ICTY and ICTR. Conversely, hybrid tribunals also suffer from being partially international, since they are viewed by some as foreign courts. In particular, the limited allocation of funds for translation appears to have exacerbated this perception. Although trials undertaken by hybrid tribunals are inherently logistically complex, it seems that many of the lessons from the experiences of the ICTR and ICTY concerning staffing and organization have not been adequately learned.

Nevertheless, these trials offer another venue for seeking accountability in a postconflict context, where the domestic judicial system is likely to be severely underfunded, corrupt, biased, or incapable of processing cases. Where it seems unlikely that legitimate cases could be pursued by the domestic system, or if the ICC is unable to do so because of jurisdictional limitations, hybrid courts can still provide a measure of justice. Some, although not all, of the difficulties identified here could potentially be addressed with more money, commitment, and support from the international community.

Discussion questions

- What are the potential benefits and limitations of hybrid tribunals?
- What should the relationship of hybrid tribunals be to other domestic processes, such as truth commissions?
- What is the difference between tribunals that are largely national, with international elements grafted onto them, such as in Kosovo, and tribunals that are international with a domestic element such as Sierra Leone?
- What are the specific legal objections that have been raised to hybrid tribunals?
- Consider the experience of the ECCC in holding trials for aged accused. What are the challenges in carrying out prosecutions many years after abuses have taken place?
- Compare the experiences of two hybrid tribunals, including their capacity to enhance **peacebuilding** in their respective countries.
- Should victims participate in mass atrocity trials, or is it logistically too difficult?

Group exercise

Evaluate the different permutations of hybrid tribunals and determine which arrangement would be appropriate for Afghanistan. Consider the actors involved during the period from the Soviet invasion of the country in 1979 to the fall of the Taliban in 2001, keeping in mind that many of them still hold positions of power today.

Further reading

Amnesty International, *Kosovo (Serbia): The Challenge to Fix a Failed UN Justice Mission* (London: Amnesty International, January 2008).

Carey, Henry F., and Stacey Mitchell (ed), *Trials and Tribulations of International Prosecution* (Plymouth, MA: Lexington Books, 2013).

Hartmann, Michael E., *International Judges and Prosecutors in Kosovo: A New Model for Post-Conflict Peacekeeping* (Washington, DC: US Institute for Peace, 2003).

Kerr, Rachel, and Eirin Mobekk, *Peace and Justice: Seeking Accountability After War* (Cambridge: Polity, 2007), Chapter 4, "Internationalized Courts".

Open Society Justice Initiative, "The Future of Cases 003/004 at the Extraordinary Chambers in the Courts of Cambodia", October 2012 http://www.opensocietyfoundations.org/publications/future-cases-003-and-004-extraordinary-chambers-courts-cambodia.

Open Society Justice Initiative, "Recent Developments at the Extraordinary Chambers in the Courts of Cambodia" (regular updates), http://www.opensocietyfoundations.org/topics/southeast-asia.

Perriello, Tom, and Marieke Wierda, *Lessons from the Deployment of International Judges and Prosecutors in Kosovo* (New York: International Center for Transitional Justice, 2006).

Reiger, Caitlin, and Marieke Wierda, *The Serious Crimes Process in Timor-Leste: In Retrospect* (New York: International Center for Transitional Justice, 2006).

Sriram, Chandra Lekha, *Globalizing Justice for Mass Atrocity: A Revolution in Accountability* (London: Routledge, 2005).

Worden, Scott, and Emily Wann, *Special Court of Sierra Leone Briefing: The Taylor Trial and Lessons from Capacity-Building and Outreach* (Washington, DC: US Institute of Peace, 2007).

Official sources

Cambodia Tribunal Monitor, http://www.cambodiatribunal.org/

Extraordinary Chambers in the Courts of Cambodia, http://www.eccc.gov.kh

Open Society Justice Initiative, Charles Taylor Trial monitoring website, http://www.charlestaylortrial.org/

Special Court for Sierra Leone, http://www.sc-sl.org

Track Impunity Always (TRIAL), http://www.trial-ch.org

United Nations assistance to the Khmer Rouge trials, http://www.unakrt-online.org/01_home.htm

United Nations Transitional Administration in East Timor (UNTAET), http://www.un.org/peace/etimor/etimor.htm

13 The International Criminal Court

Key points

- The **International Criminal Court** (ICC) provides the first permanent forum for international justice since the Nuremberg process following World War II.
- The jurisdiction of the court is based on the principle of **complementarity**; it can only act when states are unwilling or unable to prosecute international crimes.
- The crimes under the jurisdiction of the court are aggression, **genocide**, **war crimes**, and **crimes against humanity**.
- The first cases before the court are all related to conflicts in Africa.
- The work of the court is necessarily embedded in the delicate balance between peace and justice when dealing with ongoing conflicts.

Background and rationale

Attempts to address serious crimes after war date from the end of World War I, when the Versailles Treaty provided for criminal responsibility of German state officials. Since the end of World War II, the establishment of a permanent international criminal court was part of the agenda of the **United Nations** (UN) and some international lawyers. Since 1948, the International Law Commission (ILC), the UN body devoted to the progressive development and codification of international law, worked to develop two aspects of international criminal law: the drafting of a code of crimes against humanity, and the drafting of a statute for the establishment of an international criminal court. In 1954, the ILC produced the Draft Code of Offences Against the Peace and Security of Mankind, which was updated several times until its final draft was completed in 1996.

Work on an international criminal court was deferred pending the adoption of the draft code and an agreed definition of the crime of aggression. The UN appointed a special rapporteur to draft the statute for the future court, for submission to the ILC. Even though the ILC produced a draft statute in 1951, which was revised in 1953, the political climate was not yet right for such an agreement and the initiative was shelved. The process started again in 1989, and five years later, in 1994, the ILC prepared a draft statute that served as the starting point for the Preparatory Committee for the Establishment of an International Criminal Court, which began its work in 1996. In 1998, the preparatory committee submitted a final draft statute to the United Nations Conference of Plenipotentiaries on the Establishment of an International Criminal Court, which in July of that year adopted the draft as the final statute of the International Criminal Court, known as the Rome Statute.

The rationale for the establishment of the ICC comes from a conviction that the most heinous human rights should not go unpunished, which emerged during the Nuremberg and Tokyo Tribunals. Prior to the establishment of the ICC, the international community had undertaken only ad hoc attempts in its pursuit of criminal accountability: through the Nuremberg and Tokyo Tribunals, and through the tribunals for the former Yugoslavia and Rwanda. Such ad hoc approaches were obviously limited, and subject to a variety of criticisms. The Nuremberg and Tokyo Tribunals were criticized for violating the principles of ***nullem crimen sine lege*** and ***nulla poena sine lege***. The ad hoc tribunals created in 1993 and 1994 for the former Yugoslavia and Rwanda, respectively, were limited in their territorial and temporal jurisdiction, and raised questions about why similar institutions were not created in response to other situations involving serious violations of **international humanitarian law** and **international human rights law**. In the interim period, the international community had been immersed in the Cold War, which prevented any consensus for creating more comprehensive accountability measures. The end of the tension between East and West, together with the new balance in the **UN Security Council**, provided the context for establishment of the ad hoc tribunals. These tribunals helped to create political momentum for the idea of a permanent court. The international community recognized the necessity of such a court after the proliferation of bloody internal armed conflicts in Eastern and Central Europe following the fall of the Berlin Wall, and elsewhere in the world, which demonstrated that cruelty and human rights abuses had not ended with World War II.

There was broad support for an international forum in which to try the most serious crimes against humanity, with 160 states and, perhaps equally noteworthy, some 250 nongovernmental organizations participating in the negotiations. These organizations arguably had a significant influence in shaping the Rome Statute, and in encouraging its rapid ratification. The statute entered into force relatively quickly, on July 1, 2002, following its sixtieth ratification.

As of May 2013, 122 states have signed and ratified the Rome Statute. However, several highly influential countries, such as the United States, Russia, and China, have not. The United States played an important role during the Rome negotiations and originally did sign the statute, but then, on May 6, 2002, famously "unsigned" the law and has since fiercely opposed the ICC. The arguments put forth by the United States for such opposition are discussed later in the chapter.

The Rome Statute requires, in Article 123, that a review conference be held seven years after its entry into force. This conference took place in June 2010, one year late, in Kampala, Uganda. More than 4,600 state, intergovernmental and non-governmental representatives met at the Review Conference. At the conference, the Assembly of State Parties amended the Rome Statute to include a definition of the crime of aggression, which had not been included in 1998, and the conditions under which the court could exercise jurisdiction with respect to the crime. The states parties also amended article 8, as explained below. They also retained article 124, which allows new state parties to exclude from the court's jurisdiction war crimes allegedly committed by its nationals or on its territory for a period of seven years after the entry into force for the state concerned, but left this provision open to future review. The Review Conference also undertook an important stock-taking exercise, reflecting on the impact to date of the ICC. Discussions considered the interaction between peace and justice, discussed below; the impact of the court's work on victims and affected communities, and the capacity of the court to assist and strengthen domestic systems addressing international crimes at the national level. At the closure of the conference, UN Secretary General Ban Ki-moon declared that the era of impunity was now over and participants were witnessing the birth of a new age of accountability.

Structure of the court

The ICC sits in The Hague in the Netherlands. It comprises four organs: the Presidency, the Chambers, the Office of the Prosecutor, and the Registry. The chambers are organized into three divisions: Pre-Trial, Trial, and Appeals. The First Vice President and six other judges sit in the Pre-Trial Chamber. The Second Vice President and five other judges sit in the Trial Chamber. The President and four other judges sit in the Appeals Chamber. All judges must be nationals of state parties to the Rome Statute. They can be appointed for terms of three, six, and nine years. Three- and six-year terms can be renewed for up to a total maximum of nine years,.

The Office of the Prosecutor (OTP) is in charge of examining information received on crimes committed within the jurisdiction of the court, and examining referrals to the court. The OTP also conducts the investigations that may lead to prosecutions before the court. The first head of the OTP was the Argentinian Luis Moreno Ocampo, who was replaced by Fatou Bensouda, from Ghana, in June 2012.

Jurisdiction of the court

The ICC has jurisdiction over a limited set of crimes committed after the Rome Statute entered into force (July 1, 2002). This temporal limitation leaves countless crimes committed in the framework of contemporary conflicts outside the jurisdiction of the court. In practice, this limitation has proved frustrating for human rights victims and advocates alike. This frustration is based on a lack of understanding of the ICC's mandate and its limited role in responding to human rights abuses.

The four crimes over which the ICC has jurisdiction, as listed in the Rome Statute, are genocide, crimes against humanity, war crimes, and aggression. The statute basically adopts the definitions of genocide, crimes against humanity, and war crimes that are already present in customary and conventional law, as discussed in Chapter 4. These definitions (Articles 6–8) should be read in conjunction with the "Elements of Crimes" (Article 9), adopted by the Assembly of State Parties on September 9, 2002. Some commentators and nongovernmental organizations have argued that the statute defines the jurisdiction of the court in rather conservative terms, which was a missed opportunity to develop international humanitarian law more progressively, through widening the definition of some international crimes or overcoming the distinction between international and internal conflicts.

Crimes under ICC jurisdiction

Genocide

The International Criminal Court follows the same definition of genocide established in the **Genocide Convention**, identical to the concept established by customary international law: a set of acts committed with the *intent* to destroy, in whole or in part, a national, ethnic, racial, or religious group. These acts, listed in Article 6 of the Rome Statute, are killing members of a group; causing serious bodily or mental harm to members of a group; deliberately inflicting on a group conditions of life calculated to bring about its physical destruction in whole or in part; imposing measures intended to prevent births within a group; and forcibly transferring children of one group to another group.

The Genocide Convention includes among punishable acts not only genocide itself but also conspiracy to commit genocide, direct and public incitement to commit genocide, attempt to commit genocide, and complicity in genocide. However, Article 6 of the Rome

Statute does not refer to any of these crimes. During drafting negotiations there was a lack of agreement on the treatment of complicity, and other aspects of genocide crimes, such as attempt and incitement, are already dealt with in Article 25, where the grounds for individual criminal responsibility for all the crimes are laid out.

As in the Genocide Convention, Article 6 of the Rome Statute does not specify the actual harm that needs to be done to a group in order to give rise to responsibility. The definition only refers to the *intent* to destroy a group *in whole or in part*. In theory, the customary international rule, as codified in Article 6, does not require that the victims of genocide be numerous; in principle, genocide can be found even if only a small number of persons have been killed. However, in practice, genocide has been found only when victims are numerous.

Crimes against humanity

The definition of crimes against humanity in the Rome Statute builds upon customary international law. Observers have praised the statute's definition for clarifying and broadening the scope of the customary definition in some aspects; but it is also limiting in other aspects.

Crimes against humanity comprise a number of acts, as part of a widespread or systematic attack, directed against any civilian population. They thus cover a host of atrocities that might not be covered by war crimes, because official armed conflict may not be present. The specific acts are listed in Article 7(1): murder; extermination; enslavement; deportation or forcible transfer of a population; imprisonment or other severe deprivation of physical liberty in violation of fundamental rules of international law; **torture**; rape, sexual slavery, enforced prostitution, forced pregnancy, enforced sterilization, or any other form of sexual violence of comparable gravity; persecution against any identifiable group on political, racial, national, ethnic, cultural, religious, gender, or other grounds that are universally recognized as impermissible under international law in connection with any of the acts that constitute crimes under the jurisdiction of the court; enforced disappearance of persons; the crime of apartheid; and any other inhumane acts of similar character undertaken to intentionally cause great suffering or injury to the body or mental or physical health of a person. As we can see, these acts include "ordinary" crimes such as murder, but it is the context—the widespread or systematic attack directed against any civilian population—that qualifies them as crimes against humanity. The Rome Statute defines "attack directed against any civilian population" as a course of conduct involving multiple commissions of the mentioned acts against any such population pursuant to or in furtherance of a state or organizational policy to commit such attack (Article 7.2[a]).

War crimes

War crimes are defined in the Rome Statute in great detail. The statute advances the definition of war crimes by extending it to offenses committed in internal armed conflicts; however, it still distinguishes between the two contexts.

The statute establishes jurisdiction over war crimes, in particular, when committed as part of a plan or policy, or as part of a large-scale operation (Article 8.1). It draws heavily upon the definitions of war crimes arising from within the four **Geneva Conventions**. As discussed in Chapter 4, not all acts outlawed or regulated by the Geneva Conventions constitute war crimes, only those that are enumerated as **grave breaches**. The Rome Statute defines three categories of war crimes: grave breaches of the Geneva Conventions (Article 8.2[a]), other serious violations of the laws and customs applicable in international armed conflicts under international law (Article 8.2[b]), and serious violations of **Common Article 3** of the four Geneva Conventions (Article 8.2[c–e]):

The first category includes the following acts: willful killing; torture or inhuman treatment, including biological experiments; willfully causing great suffering or serious injury to body or health; extensive destruction and appropriation of property not justified by military necessity and carried out unlawfully and wantonly; compelling a prisoner of war or other protected person to serve in the forces of a hostile power; willfully depriving a prisoner of war or other protected person of the right to a fair and regular trial; unlawful deportation, transfer, or confinement; and hostage-taking. As grave breaches of the Geneva Conventions, these crimes can only be committed in the context of international armed conflicts.

The second category, acts that constitute serious violations of the laws and customs applicable in international armed conflicts, includes the following: intentional attacks against civilian populations (and their facilities) who do not take part in the hostilities, such as relief workers and **peacekeeping** personnel; intentionally launching attacks that will cause incidental loss of life or injury to civilians; and improper use of a flag of truce, or the flag of the United Nations.

Finally, the third category of war crimes are related to noninternational armed conflict, those offenses enumerated in Common Article 3 of the Geneva Conventions. The Rome Statute therefore criminalizes acts not only against civilians but also against combatants who have laid down arms or are injured, such as murder, torture, outrages upon personal dignity, hostage-taking, and extrajudicial execution. Other acts that are considered war crimes in the context of a noninternational armed conflict include attacks upon the civilian population, attacks upon designated relief workers and peacekeepers, pillaging, attacks upon religious sites, and conscription of children.

The Rome Statute makes a clear distinction between internal armed conflicts and internal disturbances and tensions. Article 8.2(d–f) includes acts committed in the context of riots, isolated and sporadic acts of violence, and other acts of a military nature. The described acts must occur within the territory of a state where a protracted armed conflict is present between governmental authorities and organized armed groups, or between such groups.

The Review Conference amended article 8 of the Rome Statute to give the court jurisdiction over the war crime of employing specific poisonous and harmful weapons in noninternational armed conflict.

Aggression

The crime of aggression was contained in the original Rome Statute, Article 5(2) but not defined. Jurisdiction of the court over this crime was deferred until a definition had been reached. This was one of the main elements in the agenda of the Review Conference in Kampala, which amended the statute to include a new Article 8*bis*. The new article defines the individual crime of aggression as the planning, preparation, initiation or execution of an act of aggression by a person in a leadership position. An act of aggression is defined as the use of armed force by one state against another state without the justification of self-defense or authorization by the Security Council. The act must constitute a manifest violation of the United Nations Charter.

In order for states to refer a situation and for the OTP to initiate an investigation *proprio motu*, the alleged acts of aggression must have been committed on the territory of or by the nationals of a state party that has not refused to accept the court's jurisdiction over this crime. The UN Security Council however, can refer acts of aggression, irrespective of whether the states involved are parties or not to the Rome Statute.

Parties decided at Kampala that the ICC will only be able to exercise jurisdiction over the crime of aggression once states parties have approved its activation, which cannot be done until after January 1, 2017. So far only five states have ratified the amendments to the Rome Statute with regards to the crime of aggression.

Preconditions for jurisdiction

In order for the court to be able to exercise jurisdiction over an accused individual, there must be a nexus with a state party to the Rome Statute. This nexus may be territorial, or one of nationality. Therefore the court has jurisdiction over an individual when the offense has been committed on the territory of a state party (including aboard vessels or aircraft registered in that state), or when the individual is a national of a state party.

There is a possibility that a national of a nonparty state could be tried if the crimes he or she is accused of were committed on the territory of a state party. This was a primary source of US opposition to the court. The US feared that the ICC would be in a position to bring a case against its personnel deployed in military operations abroad, and that they could potentially be subject to frivolous and politically motivated suits. It also argued that the jurisdiction of the court could jeopardize the willingness of countries to contribute to peacekeeping operations when their personnel could be made criminally responsible, and claimed that prosecutions could upset local compromises and amnesties promulgated in the framework of **peace negotiations**. In reaction to the entry into force of the Rome Statute, the US threatened to veto the renewal of the ongoing peacekeeping operations in the Security Council if protections for personnel of nonstate parties were not promised, and also signed bilateral agreements with all UN member states to avoid jurisdiction over US nationals. These agreements made use of an option under Article 98 of the Rome Statute that establishes that the court may not proceed with a request for surrender or assistance that would require the requested state to act inconsistently with an obligation under international law. Thus if these member states were to surrender US nationals to the ICC, they would be breaching their legal obligation toward the United States as established in these bilateral agreements. Domestically, in 2002, the US Congress passed the American Servicemembers' Protection Act, which established a prohibition on cooperation with the ICC for all US courts, agencies, and entities of any state or local government, as well as a prohibition on any military assistance to parties to the court. The act also placed restrictions on US participation in certain UN peacekeeping operations and granted the US president the power to authorize the use of any means necessary to free members of the US armed forces and other US nationals detained or imprisoned by or on behalf of the ICC. In 2009, after a change of administration, the US Secretary of State, Hillary Clinton, declared that the US was no longer opposed to the ICC and expressed regret that the US was not a signatory to the Rome Statute.

Exercise of jurisdiction and the principle of complementarity

In order for the court to initiate prosecution and exercise jurisdiction, either a case has to be referred to the ICC prosecutor, or the prosecutor can initiate it himself. Only state parties (Articles 13[a] and 14 of the Rome Statute) and the Security Council, acting under Chapter VII of the **UN Charter** (Article 13[b]) can refer a situation to the prosecutor, but the prosecutor can initiate a case *proprio motu* on the basis of any information he has over the crimes (Article 15). In principle, this allows anyone—an individual, a state, a nongovernmental organization—to submit a petition to the prosecutor seeking an investigation. Once the prosecutor has reviewed the information in the preliminary examination phase and concluded that there is a reasonable basis to proceed with an investigation, the situation must be submitted to the Pre-Trial Chamber, the organ that has the power to authorize the official opening of an investigation. If the Pre-Trial Chamber refuses to authorize the investigation, the prosecutor can still request a reconsideration of the situation when new facts or evidence emerge. Of the cases that are now under investigation by the court, two, regarding the situation in Sudan and in Libya, have been referred by the Security Council. Those regarding the situations in the Democratic Republic of Congo (DRC), Uganda, the Central African Republic and Mali, were self-referrals. The OTP initiated investigations *propio motu* into situations in Kenya and Côte d'Ivoire, both confirmed by the Pre-Trial Chamber.

This does not mean that the court has jurisdiction over every possible international crime. A key criteria for jurisdiction is that the state in which the crimes have been committed or whose national has been accused of such crimes is unwilling or unable to prosecute. This is because the jurisdiction of the court is based on the principle of complementarity. Therefore the court will not take up cases where a legitimate legal process is under way in a relevant national jurisdiction, or if the accusation has been seriously investigated and dismissed domestically (art. 17).

The different avenues by which a case reaches the court have an impact on the level of government cooperation with the investigations and proceedings, including the arrest of suspects and their surrender to the court. Experience so far demonstrates this disparity, and it is likely that the court will receive little cooperation from the government of Sudan concerning the situation in that country.

Finally, an investigation or prosecution may be suspended for 12 months by the Security Council, acting under the framework of Chapter VII of the UN Charter (Article 16 of the Rome Statute).

Applicable principles of international criminal law

The functioning of the International Criminal Court is subject to a host of general principles of criminal law (see Chapter 4). These principles, listed in Part 3 of the Rome Statute (Articles 22–33), comprise the following: *nullem crimen sine lege* (no crime without law); *nulla poena sine lege* (no punishment without law); nonretroactivity; no punishment of persons younger than age 18; irrelevance of official capacity (including that heads of state or government shall not enjoy immunity from jurisdiction); command responsibility (a military commander shall be criminally responsible for crimes committed by the forces under his or her effective command and control, or a result of his or her failure to exercise proper control); rejection of the superior orders defense; necessary presence of mental element (intention and knowledge in the commission of the offense), and grounds for excluding criminal responsibility based on lack of capacity to acknowledge the wrongfulness of acts (such as mistakes of fact or mistakes of law that negate the mental element required by the crime, the presence of mental disease or state of intoxication, and acting in self–defense or under threat of imminent death). The Rome Statute also states expressly the principle of presumption of innocence (Article 66).

Further, only natural persons can be prosecuted by the ICC. After much debate in the treaty negotiations, the suggestion that legal persons—such as corporations or other groups—could be prosecuted was rejected. Under the Rome Statute (Article 25), individual criminal responsibility arises when a person materially commits a crime; orders, solicits, or

---

***Box 13.1* The Rome Statute, Article 25**

Article 25: Individual Criminal Responsibility
1. The Court shall have jurisdiction over natural persons pursuant to this Statute.
2. A person who commits a crime within the jurisdiction of the Court shall be individually responsible and liable for punishment in accordance with this Statute.
3. In accordance with this Statute, a person shall be criminally responsible and liable for punishment for a crime within the jurisdiction of the Court if that person:
    a. Commits such a crime, whether as an individual, jointly with another or through another person, regardless of whether that other person is criminally responsible;
    b. Orders, solicits or induces the commission of such a crime which in fact occurs or is attempted;
    c. For the purpose of facilitating the commission of such a crime, aids, abets or otherwise assists in its commission or its attempted commission, including providing the means for its commission;
    d. In any other way contributes to the commission or attempted commission of such a crime by a group of persons acting with a common purpose. Such contribution shall be intentional and shall either:
        i. Be made with the aim of furthering the criminal activity or criminal purpose of the group, where such activity or purpose involves the commission of a crime within the jurisdiction of the Court; or
        ii. Be made in the knowledge of the intention of the group to commit the crime;
    e. In respect of the crime of genocide, directly and publicly incites others to commit genocide;
    f. Attempts to commit such a crime by taking action that commences its execution by means of a substantial step, but the crime does not occur because of circumstances independent of the person's intentions. However, a person who abandons the effort to commit the crime or otherwise prevents the completion of the crime shall not be liable for punishment under this Statute for the attempt to commit that crime if that person completely and voluntarily gave up the criminal purpose.
4. No provision in this Statute relating to individual criminal responsibility shall affect the responsibility of States under international law.

---

induces the commission of such crime; aids and abets or otherwise assists in the commission of the crime; or in some other way contributes to its commission or attempted commission by a group of persons acting with a common purpose (see Box 13.1).

Punishments are also elaborated in the Rome Statute. International criminal tribunals do not now impose the death penalty, so the maximum term to which a person can be imprisoned by the ICC is 30 years. Exceptionally, for particularly grave crimes, life imprisonment is authorized. Imprisonment sentences are served at correctional facilities of the states that indicate their willingness to accept sentenced persons. Once prison sentences are ready to be enforced, the court designates which state will house the prisoner. Those found guilty may also be fined, or be forced to forfeit property. Fines collected may be placed in the trust fund set up to compensate victims and families of victims.

Victim trust fund

Prior to establishment of the ICC, one of the main criticisms of the ad hoc tribunals had been their limited ability to address the needs of the victims of conflict, as discussed in Chapter 10. Aware of the potential obstacle that geographical distance poses to the participation of victims, with the ICC sitting in The Hague, the Rome Statute foresaw the need to function as a redress mechanism for victims and not exclusively as a punishment mechanism for perpetrators. Article 75 of the statute provides that the court shall consider reparations for victims, including restitution, compensation, and rehabilitation, in its decisions. Such reparations are channeled through a victim trust fund, which was established by the Assembly of State Parties in 2002 and it began its operations in early 2007. The main aim of the fund is to provide victims, including child soldiers, victims of rape, sexual assault, and other abuses, and those who have had their property and livelihood destroyed, the necessary help and compensation to enable them to rebuild their lives. The trust is funded by money collected through fines and forfeitures (Article 79), and by contributions from governments, international organizations, and individuals.

Functioning of the court: the first ten years

Once the ICC prosecutor concludes that there is a reasonable basis to proceed with an investigation, he must seek authorization from the Pre-Trial Chamber. If the case appears to fall within the jurisdiction of the court, based on the prosecutor's supporting material, the Pre-Trial Chamber will authorize commencement of the investigation, without prejudice to subsequent consideration by the court of its own jurisdiction and the admissibility of the case (Article 15). Once the formal investigation has been authorized, the prosecutor can ask the Pre-Trial Chamber to issue orders and warrants (Article 57), including warrants of arrest or summons to appear before the Pre-Trial Chamber. The Pre-Trial Chamber can issue a warrant of arrest when there are reasonable grounds to believe that a person has committed a crime within the jurisdiction of the court, in order to ensure his or her appearance at trial, to ensure that he or she does not obstruct or endanger the court's investigation or proceedings, or to prevent him or her from continuing to commit the crime of which he or she is accused, or from committing a related crime within the jurisdiction of the court (Article 58). The state party that receives a request for arrest must immediately take steps to proceed with that arrest and then surrender the accused to the ICC (Article 59).

Once the accused has been surrendered to the court, or appears before it voluntarily or under a summons, the Pre-Trial Chamber confirms the charges established by the prosecutor at a hearing in which the accused and his or her counsel are present. However, the Pre-Trial Chamber can hold such a confirmation hearing in the absence of the accused if he or she has waived the right to be present, or has fled or cannot be found, in which case the Pre-Trial Chamber appoints a defense counsel for the absent accused. At the confirmation hearing, the accused can object to the charges and the evidence and present his or her own evidence. Finally, on the basis of this hearing, the Pre-Trial Chamber determines whether there is sufficient evidence to believe that the person committed each of the crimes charged, and then confirms or declines to confirm those charges (Article 61).

After the charges have been confirmed, the case is initiated before the Trial Chamber. Trials are held in public, excepting for special circumstances requiring that certain proceedings take place in closed sessions (Article 64). The accused must be present during the trial. However, if his or her behavior is disruptive, the Trial Chamber has the power to remove the accused from the courtroom. In this case, the accused can observe the proceedings and instruct counsel from outside the courtroom (Article 63).

The first cases under investigation by the ICC do not begin to encompass the scope of possible referrals, or indeed the myriad communications received by the Office of the Prosecutor suggesting that investigations be launched. By the end of 2012 the OTP had received 9,717 communications.. Most of these communications were found to be manifestly outside the jurisdiction of the court—temporal, subject matter, or territorial—but the OTP undertook intensive analysis (preliminary examination) of at least 18 situations. During this process the OTP has maintained the confidentiality of its inquiries to protect the interests of those involved and the investigations themselves. In general, the OTP explains the reasons not to initiate an investigation only to the originators of the communications. However, in the cases of refusal to initiate investigations on Iraq, Venezuela and Palestine, the prosecutor made his decisions public, in the interests of transparency. The OTP is currently conducting preliminary examinations into the situations in Afghanistan, Georgia, Guinea, Colombia, Honduras, Korea, and Nigeria.

Current situations

The first cases before the court concern the situations in the Democratic Republic of Congo, Sudan, Uganda, the Central African Republic, Kenya, Libya, and Côte d'Ivoire. The situation of Mali was referred to the ICC by the government in July 2012, but no cases had begun at the time of writing. The conflicts in the DRC and Sudan are addressed in greater detail in Chapters 8 and 9, respectively.

Democratic Republic of Congo

The DRC is a party to the Rome Statute, which it signed on September 8, 2000, and ratified on April 11, 2002, when the conflict was still ongoing. This is the first situation for which the Office of the Prosecutor opened an investigation. The OTP began considering the possibility of initiating an investigation into the crimes committed in DRC territory, especially in the Ituri region, shortly after the entry into force of the Rome Statute. In September 2003, after several months of preliminary examination, the prosecutor announced that he was prepared to exercise his *proprio motu* powers and seek authorization from a Pre-Trial Chamber to start an official investigation of the case. He also made it clear that a referral and active support from the government of the DRC would be welcomed. In April 2004, the government of the DRC referred to the court the crimes within its jurisdiction allegedly committed since the entry into force of the Rome Statute, and the investigation was opened in June 2004. This referral, unlike the initial investigation, does not limit itself to the Ituri region, but asks for the consideration of crimes committed "anywhere in the territory of the country." The investigation could also address crimes committed by any DRC faction, including, in theory, the DRC government, or foreign governments acting in the DRC, because this conflict was characterized by the involvement of the government and multiple militias and rebel groups, as well as the direct and indirect participation of several neighboring countries (see Chapter 7). So far, however, cases concerning the situation in the DRC have only involved crimes committed in the Ituri region.

There are several ongoing cases in the DRC situation and one conviction. The case against Thomas Lubanga Dyilo was the first to reach a verdict, and he was also the first person to stand trial. This judgment was a landmark that came on the tenth anniversary of the entry into force of the Rome Statute. Lubanga, the leader of the Patriotic Congolese Union (Union Patriotique Congolais [UPC]), was found guilty of the war crimes—specifically enlisting and conscripting of children under the age of 15 years and using them to participate actively in hostilities. He was sentenced to 14 years imprisonment. Mathieu Ngudjolo Chui, alleged former leader of the Front des Nationalistes et Intégrationnistes (FNI) was acquitted of all charges against him in December 2012 and he was released from custody that same month. The verdict was appealed by the OTP. Other ongoing cases include those against Germain Katanga, alleged commander of the Force de Résistance Patriotique en Ituri (FRPI); Callixte Mbarushimana, alleged Executive Secretary of the Forces Démocratiques pour la Libération du Rwanda—Forces Combattantes Abacunguzi (FDLR-FCA, FDLR); Sylvestre Mudacumura, alleged Supreme Commander of the Forces Démocratiques pour la Libération du Rwanda; and Bosco Ntaganda, alleged former Deputy Chief of the General Staff of the Forces Patriotiques pour la Libération du Congo (Patriotic Forces for the Liberation of Congo [FPLC]) and alleged Chief of Staff of the Congrès National pour la Défense du Peuple (CNDP) armed group, active in North Kivu in the DRC, as discussed in Chapter 8. Katanga was arrested by the Congolese authorities in 2007, whilst Mbarushimana was arrested by the French authorities in 2010. Both their trials are ongoing. Ntaganda surrendered voluntarily in 2013 (see Chapter 8).

Sudan

Just when Sudan reached a comprehensive peace agreement in its long-running civil war between north and south, violence exploded in Western Darfur, where Janjaweed militias, with links to the government, have been carrying out campaigns of intimidation and terror against the civilian population (see Chapter 9). The systematic nature of the attacks has led to their characterization as crimes against humanity, and possibly genocide.

The International Commission of Inquiry on Darfur, in its 2005 report to the **UN Secretary-General**, concluded that both the government of Sudan and the Janjaweed militias were responsible for serious violations of international human rights and international humanitarian law, amounting to international crimes. The commission did not determine that genocide had occurred, as it could not find evidence of an intent to destroy a group, in whole or in part. Rather, it largely accepted the claim by the government that these acts had been undertaken in the context of "counterinsurgency."

The government of Sudan had made clear that it would not refer a case to the ICC itself— it is a signatory to the Rome Statute but has not completed ratification. It even tried to shortcut the risk that a case might be referred by the UN Security Council by setting up "tribal" or "traditional" justice courts for Darfur, which by all accounts have not conducted any genuine proceedings.

In its report, the International Commission of Inquiry considered which venue might be most appropriate to address these crimes. It established that the Sudanese justice system was not fit to do so: specifically, it stated that the system was "unable and unwilling," the requisite language for complementarity. Given this situation, the Commission of Inquiry recommended that the Security Council refer the case to the ICC. The Security Council did so in Resolution 1593 on March 13, 2005 (see Box 13.2).

The resolution was passed by a vote of 11 in favor, with no votes against and four abstentions. Among the abstaining countries was the US, notable given its objections to the ICC in general. Given its permanent seat on the UN Security Council, it could have vetoed the resolution, and there was indeed fear that it would do. However, US politicians

---

Box 13.2 **UN Security Council Resolution 1593 (March 31, 2005)**

The Security Council ... *Acting* under Chapter VII of the Charter of the United Nations,

1. *Decides* to refer the situation in Darfur since 1 July 2002 to the Prosecutor of the International Criminal Court;
2. *Decides* that the Government of Sudan and all other parties to the conflict in Darfur, shall cooperate fully with and provide any necessary assistance to the Court and the Prosecutor pursuant to this resolution and, while recognizing that States not party to the Rome Statute have no obligation under the Statute, urges all States and concerned regional and other international organizations to cooperate fully;
3. *Invites* the Court and the African Union to discuss practical arrangements that will facilitate the work of the Prosecutor and of the Court, including the possibility of conducting proceedings in the region, which would contribute to regional efforts in the fight against impunity;
4. *Also encourages* the Court, as appropriate and in accordance with the Rome Statute, to support international cooperation with domestic efforts to promote the rule of law, protect human rights and combat impunity in Darfur;
5. *Also emphasizes* the need to promote healing and reconciliation and encourages in this respect the creation of institutions, involving all sectors of Sudanese society, such as truth and/or reconciliation commissions, in order to complement judicial processes and thereby reinforce the efforts to restore long-lasting peace, with African Union and international support as necessary;
6. *Decides* that nationals, current or former officials or personnel from a contributing State outside Sudan which is not a party to the Rome Statute of the International Criminal Court shall be subject to the exclusive jurisdiction of that contributing State for all alleged acts or omissions arising out of or related to operations in Sudan established or authorized by the Council or the African Union, unless such exclusive jurisdiction has been expressly waived by that contributing State.

---

had expressed special concern over the situation in Sudan generally and Darfur specifically, so there was a desire to find compromise. The French delegation to the UN played a key role in formulating the compromise. Specifically, paragraph 6 of the resolution contains an exemption for nationals, current officials, and peacekeeping troops of states not party to the Rome Statute. This means that while officials of Sudan may be tried, even though the country has not ratified the Rome Statute, officials and peacekeepers from other nonstate parties cannot be prosecuted by the ICC. With this compromise formulation, the US abstained from voting on the resolution, rather than vetoing it. However, the US did enter into the record of proceedings a statement recognizing the need for action to be taken, but indicating its preference for an ad hoc regional court, perhaps similar to the hybrid court in Sierra Leone.

Following the referral from the UN Security Council, the ICC prosecutor opened the investigation into the situation in Darfur in June 2005 and issued the first arrest warrant against the former minister of interior of Sudan, Ahmad Muhammad Harun, in 2007. In July 2008, in a groundbreaking decision, the prosecutor requested the Pre-Trial Chamber to issue an arrest warrant for Omar Hassan Ahmad al-Bashir, the president of Sudan, on the grounds that he bears criminal responsibility for genocide, crimes against humanity, and war crimes.

The prosecutor alleged that Bashir "masterminded and implemented a plan to destroy in substantial part the Fur, Masalit and Zaghawa groups, on account of their ethnicity."

The government of Sudan has been reluctant to cooperate with the court, and has elicited support for him and promoted opposition to the ICC to other member states of the African Union (AU). He, and they, depict it, as biased as its cases are based exclusively on the African continent. Even with a pending arrest warrant, al-Bashir has been able to travel to numerous countries on the continent, including states parties to the Rome Statute, without fear of arrest. This contravenes the obligations of states parties, as well as UN Security Council Resolution 1593, which explicitly calls for cooperation from governments.

Uganda

The government of Uganda's referral of the situation in its northern territory offers another example of a government voluntarily referring a situation to the ICC. However, the referral is not as virtuous as it may seem, given that it was designed to initiate proceedings against a rebel group while seeking to shield investigation of any misdeeds by Ugandan troops.

The current conflict in Uganda is Africa's longest-running conflict. Tensions arose soon after President Yoweri Museveni took power in 1986. In 1987, a rebel group, the Lord's Resistance Army (LRA), was formed from several splinter groups drawn from the former national army. Fighting has resulted in serious human rights abuses against civilians in the north, including summary executions, torture and mutilation, recruitment of child soldiers, child sexual abuse, rape, forcible displacement, looting, and destruction of civilian property. The LRA's signature tactic is to terrorize the population through mutilation—cutting the hands, ears, or lips of villagers suspected of government sympathies.

LRA fighters are drawn largely from abducted villagers, particularly children, mostly between 11 and 15 years of age, though younger children have been taken. According to human rights organizations, over 85 percent of the LRA's forces are composed of children, who are used as soldiers, porters, laborers, and sexual slaves. As part of their initiation into the rebel movement, abducted children are forced into committing inhuman acts, including ritual killing and mutilation. They are frequently beaten and forced to carry heavy loads over long distances, loot and burn houses, beat and kill civilians and fellow abductees, and abduct other children. In order to evade capture, thousands of children have become "night dwellers," walking great distances to regroup at facilities run by nongovernmental organizations, as well as on the streets, on shop verandas, on church grounds, and at local factories, and then returning to their villages at dawn. It is estimated that over 30,000 children have been abducted by the LRA. However, human rights groups have documented extensive evidence not only of abuses committed by the LRA, but of many abuses by the Ugandan military as well.

Attacks by the LRA in the mid-1990s forced approximately three-quarters of the Acholi population to flee their homes in Gulu and Kitgum/Pader districts in northern Uganda. It is estimated that the conflict has generated over a million **internally displaced persons**.

Uganda was among the first states to sign the Rome Statute, ratifying it in June 2002. The government of Uganda referred the situation to the ICC in December 2003. It explicitly referred only the situation concerning the LRA, effectively shielding any Ugandan officials from prosecution. The ICC prosecutor, however, replied that he would interpret the referral as concerning all crimes under the Rome Statute that had been committed in the region, not just those by the LRA, and that the investigation would be impartial.

The investigation into crimes committed in northern Uganda since July 1, 2002, formally started in July 2004, with the ICC establishing a field office in Kampala to support the proceedings. In October 2005 the court issued arrest warrants for crimes against humanity and war crimes for five senior leaders of the LRA: Joseph Kony, Okot Odhiambo, Dominic Ongwen, Raska Lukwiya, and Vicent Otti. Both Dominic Ongwen and Raska Lukwiya have reportedly been killed. In July 2007 the proceedings against Raska Lukwiya were terminated due to his death. None of the other accused have been arrested and the cases remain open.

Meanwhile, the Ugandan government engaged in peace negotiations with the LRA. In this context it passed an **amnesty** law, but later amended it to exclude LRA leadership. Amnesties are discussed in greater detail in Chapter 1 and later in this chapter.

Central African Republic

The Central African Republic signed the Rome Statute on December 7, 1999, and ratified it on October 3, 2001, among the first states to do so. The conflict in the Central African Republic began in 2001 when François Bozizé, chief of staff of the Central African Armed Forces (Forces Armées Centrafricains [FACA]), took up arms after having been dismissed by presidential decree on accusation of an attempted coup d'état. President Ange-Félix Patassé called on his allies for help, and several groups came to his side in the fighting, including a Libyan military contingent and the Movement for the Liberation of the Congo (Mouvement de Libération du Congo [MLC]), led by Jean-Pierre Bemba Gombo.

Fighting between General Bozizé's rebels and governmental forces began in 2002 and lasted until March 2003, when the rebels took control of the capital, Bangui. Bozizé proclaimed himself president, a position to which he was later elected, in 2005. Patassé went into exile and Bemba Gombo's men returned to the DRC. All combatants perpetrated serious human rights and international humanitarian law violations.

The government of the Central African Republic referred the situation to the ICC in January 2005. The referral included all crimes committed anywhere on the territory of the Central African Republic since July 1, 2002. The decision to refer the case was appealed internally, in view of ongoing national procedures. In April 2006, the highest criminal court of the Central African Republic, the Cour de Cassation, held that its judicial system was unable to carry out effective investigations and prosecutions of the alleged crimes; the national procedures have since been suspended. In order to respect the principle of complementarity, the ICC prosecutor waited for the final decision of the Cour de Cassation before making a determination on the issue of admissibility.

Investigations of the crimes committed in 2002 and 2003 were formally opened in May 2007. The ICC prosecutor announced that the investigations would focus on sexual violence in particular, given that allegations of sexual crimes reportedly far outnumbered alleged killings.

The Pre-Trial Chamber issued an arrest warrant for Jean-Pierre Bemba Gombo, alleged president and commander in chief of the MLC, on May 24, 2008, on two counts of crimes against humanity (rape and torture) and four counts of war crimes (rape; torture; outrages upon personal dignity, in particular humiliating and degrading treatment; and pillage). He was detained by the Belgian authorities and transferred to the court's detention center on July 3, 2008. His trial commenced on November 2010. His is the only case in the Central African Republic situation.

The situation in the Central African Republic deteriorated rapidly in 2012, with the rebel group Séléka Coalition marching into the capital and capturing the presidential palace in March 2013. President Bozizé fled to Cameroon. The ICC Trust Fund for Victims suspended its activities in the country due to the unstable situation and the risk to its personnel.

Kenya

The disputed 2007 Kenyan presidential election sparked a period of both spontaneous and organized violence, killing at least 1,000 and displacing at least 350,000 in the course of two months (see Chapter 2, Box 2.2). Supporters of the Party of National Unity, led by the incumbent Mwai Kibaki, who claimed to have been re-elected, confronted those of the Orange Democratic Movement, led by Kibaki's main opponent, Raila Odinga. The violence brought condemnation from the international community, and the appointment of former United Nations Secretary-General, Kofi Annan as a mediator. He brokered a power-sharing agreement between the two opposing parties, which confirmed Kibaki as president and Odinga as prime minister. As part of the National Dialogue and Reconciliation process, the new coalition government agreed to a Commission of Inquiry into Post-Election Violence. The commission recommended, among other things, the establishment of a special tribunal, similar to the Special Court for Sierra Leone, to try those responsible for the most serious abuses. It also included a failsafe: should such a tribunal not be completed by the appointed deadline, it provided Annan with a sealed envelope containing the names of the top alleged perpetrators of post-election violence and access to boxes of attendant evidence to provide to the ICC OTP. Following the failure of the government to establish a hybrid tribunal or initiate domestic proceedings Annan handed the envelope and evidence to the OTP in July 2009.

In March 2010, Pre-Trial Chamber II of the ICC authorized the prosecutor to open investigations into these events. This was the first use of the prosecutor's *proprio motu* powers. Kenya's reaction was to promise cooperation but to engage in evasion, with parliament passing a nonbinding resolution withdrawing from the Rome Statute and diplomats seeking a 12-month suspension of proceedings by the UN Security Council pursuant to article 16 of the Rome Statute. These and other efforts to halt proceedings were unsuccessful, and six suspects were issued with summons to appear. All six suspects, who were the deputy prime minister, two cabinet ministers, the former head of the police force, the head of the civil service and a leading radio broadcaster, did so voluntarily on April 7–8, 2011. In May 2012 the Pre-Trial Chamber rejected Kenya's objections that the cases were inadmissible, and the charges against four of the accused for crimes against humanity were confirmed. Proceedings against one of the accused were halted in March 2013 following evidentiary challenges and allegations of witness tampering.

In 2013 Kenya held presidential elections, and one of the accused, Uhuru Muigai Kenyatta, was elected president, and another accused, William Samoei Ruto, was elected deputy president. This generated outrage amongst many human rights advocates, and new challenges for the ICC, as Kenya promised cooperation, despite a Kenyan diplomat reportedly requesting that the UN Security Council terminate the proceedings altogether in May 2013.

Libya

In October 2011, a six-month uprising ended the 42-year regime of Colonel Muammar Gaddafi in Libya. The severe repression of the rebellion by Gaddafi and his armed forces prompted the UN Security Council to refer the situation to the ICC just weeks into the uprising. UN Security Council Resolution 1970 (2011) was adopted unanimously by all the members of the Security Council. In June 2011 the OTP brought charges against three individuals: Colonel Gaddafi himself, his son Saif Al-Islam Gaddafi, who acted as *de facto* prime minister during the uprising, and Abdullah Al-Senussi, colonel in the Libyan Armed Forces and head of military intelligence at the time. The case against Muammar Gaddafi was terminated following his capture and execution in October.

The ICC indictments played an important role during the conflict. The rebels, organized around the Libyan National Transitional Council (NTC), demanded that the international community intervene to aid them and stop the violations being committed by the Gaddafi regime. The referral and subsequent charges were by the rebels, and the OTP press releases detailing the abuses of the Gaddafi regime helped increase international pressure on the regime and support for the rebels. However, once the NTC took power, it was reluctant to hand the two remaining accused to the ICC, insisting on a national processes. There have been frequent reports of retaliation by rebels against former members of Gaddafi's regime, armed forces and supporters.

Côte d'Ivoire

Côte d'Ivoire was considered an example of a peaceful state from its independence until a coup d'état in 1999, led by Robert Guéï, who was later himself deposed by a popular uprising. Ethnic confrontations and discrimination against Muslim northerners followed. In 2002, civil war split the country between the north, held by the rebel group New Forces, and the government-controlled south, and resulting in thousands of deaths. Fighting ended in 2004, but the country remained divided and under the threat of violence, which prompted the deployment of the United Nations Operation in Côte d'Ivoire (UNOCI). A power-sharing agreement was brokered in 2007, and in October 2010 presidential elections were held. Alassane Ouattara won the elections, and the international community recognized his victory. However, the incumbent, Laurent Gbagbo, refused to relinquish power and a new wave of violence began. Outtara's forces deposed Gbagbo in April 2011.

Côte d'Ivoire was one of the first states to sign the Rome Statute, in November 1998. However, because of a number of legal and constitutional hurdles, it did not ratify it until 15 February 2013. In the meantime, pursuant to article 12 of the Rome Statute, the country wrote to the ICC in 2003 and again in 2010 expressing its recognition of the competence of the court. The OTP opened a preliminary investigation in Côte d'Ivoire in 2003, and in 2010, using *propio motu* powers, it requested permission from the Pre-Trial Chamber to formally open an investigation in November 2011. The court subsequently issued arrest warrants for Laurent Gbagbo and his wife Simone Gbagbo for crimes against humanity.. The government surrendered Gbagbo to the ICC immediately after and he faces charges of crimes against humanity for murder, rape and other sexual violence, persecution and other inhuman acts, allegedly committed in the context of post-electoral violence in the territory of Côte d'Ivoire between December 16, 2010 and April 12, 2011. The Pre-Trial Chamber rejected Gbagbo's request for provisional release and his claim that poor health would not permit him to stand trial, and charges were confirmed in February 2013. Simone Gbagbo was not surrendered to the ICC and faces domestic proceedings in Côte d'Ivoire for charges which include genocide. The ICC has continued to request her transfer.

The ICC, peace, and justice

There have been numerous concerns voiced by analysts and practitioners during the first ten years of operation of the ICC regarding its work and its legitimacy, with some of the most important debates revolving around the impact of the ICC on conflict resolution, particularly for countries engaged in conflict or in peace processes. Conducting investigations in ongoing conflict situations presents difficulties both from a practical point of view (e.g., protecting investigators, as well as victims and witnesses) and from a wider political point of view. In this regard, one objection to the ICC is that it functions as an external mechanism for providing justice; similar to ad hoc tribunals (Chapter 10) and transnational litigation (Chapter 11), and although it is an alternative for states that are unable or unwilling to prosecute, it is located far from the victims and affected society. This, critics say, could mean that the court will not take sufficient account of local needs in the context of transitions, and in particular could disrupt conflict resolution processes or reconciliation efforts. This complicates the relationship between the international prosecutions of the ICC and national peace processes. The Office of the Prosecutor has tried to address the balance between international justice, national processes, and reconciliation initiatives by firmly rejecting amnesties and demonstrating openness to the complementary role of national processes. But the long-term impact of the ICC remains to be seen.

The tension between the work of the ICC and ongoing peace processes has been raised particularly in the situation in Uganda. The ICC prosecutor has been prepared to proceed with the investigation notwithstanding ongoing peace negotiations. While the impact of the ICC proceedings could be positive in terms of promoting the consideration of national accountability mechanisms in peace agreements, it could also be negative, with those who may have reason to fear prosecution withdrawing from peace negotiations. In April 2008, Joseph Kony, the leader of the LRA, refused to sign a peace accord unless the ICC arrest warrants against the LRA were removed, paralyzing the peace process and resulting in continued fighting, death and abuses. The situation in Sudan has also sparked debate, as concerns have been expressed about the impact of ICC prosecutions on the peacekeeping and humanitarian operations under way in Darfur and elsewhere in the country. As discussed above, UN Security Council referral to the ICC has also been used as part of a conflict management strategy in Libya, although there is disagreement as to its effect.

It is also important to remember that the ICC only has jurisdiction over a small number of serious crimes, and will only focus upon a small number of perpetrators. Thus the majority of perpetrators are unlikely to be pursued by the ICC, which in the absence of appropriate national judicial procedures could contribute to a perception of **impunity**. The first ICC prosecutor tried to address the balance between international justice, national processes, and reconciliation initiatives by firmly rejecting amnesties but also showing openness to the complementary role that national processes can play. Both he and his successor have recognized the role of local initiatives in the use of traditional or customary justice mechanisms as retribution, reparation, and reconciliation tools, as long as they are not used as an excuse for the perpetuation of impunity. When opening his investigation following the UN Security Council's referral of the situation in Darfur, the ICC prosecutor explicitly stated that traditional African mechanisms are complementary to efforts to achieve local reconciliation.

The ICC and Africa

The ICC also faced criticism because all of its situations and cases to date have been in Africa, which has led to accusations by some African leaders and scholars that the court is a neo-colonial instrument. While there are numerous non-African situations under preliminary examination, this fact has not helped dissuade the negative perception.

Discussion questions

- What are some of the novel aspects of the ICC's powers?
- Consider the three different mechanisms by which investigations can reach the Office of the Prosecutor. What might be the impact of each on developing a case for prosecution?
- Consider the two separate situations of your choice from amongst those currently under the scrutiny of the ICC. In each situation, are there any other accountability mechanisms or even nonjudicial mechanisms such as traditional conflict resolution and reconciliation processes that could have a better impact on peacebuilding?
- Would it be possible to use the mechanisms contained in Article 16 of the Rome Statute in any of the ICC's current cases? How do you think such mechanism may work in the future?

Group exercise

Choose an ongoing conflict, or a conflict that has recently reached a peace agreement, as a potential case for the ICC. Form four groups and role play the presentation of an expert report before the Security Council (Group 1), the debate within the Security Council (Groups 2 and 3), and the presentation of a report by the Office of the Prosecutor (Group 4).

- *Group 1:* As a groups of experts, draft a report on the conflict situation, documenting human rights violations that amount to crimes under the jurisdiction of the ICC and recommending a referral from the Security Council to the court.
- *Group 2:* As a group of states in the Security Council who are reluctant to proceed to an ICC referral, prepare a report on your grounds for rejection.
- *Group 3:* As a group of states in the Security Council who are in favor of proceeding to an ICC referral, prepare a report on your grounds for support.
- *Group 4:* As the OTP, prepare a report on the jurisdiction of the court over the alleged crimes.

Further reading

Cryer, Robert, Hakan Friman, Darryl Robinson and Elizabeth Wilmshurst (eds), *An Introduction to International Criminal Law and Procedure* (Cambridge: Cambridge University Press, 2010).

Cassese, Antonio (ed.), *The Oxford Companion to International Criminal Justice* (Oxford: Oxford University Press, 2009).

Cassese, Antonio and Paola Gaeta, *Cassese's International Law* (Oxford: Oxford University Press, 2013).

Human Rights Watch, "Stolen Children: Abduction and Recruitment in Northern Uganda", (March 2003), http://www.hrw.org/reports/2003/uganda0303/uganda0403.pdf

Jessberger, Florian, and Julia Geneuss, "The Many Faces of the International Criminal Court," *Journal of International Criminal Justice,* vol. 10 (2012): 1081–1094.

Schabas, William, *The International Criminal Court: A Commentary on the Rome Statute* (Oxford: Oxford University Press, 2010).

Sriram, Chandra and Stephen Brown, "Kenya in the Shadow of the ICC: Complementarity, Gravity and Impact," *International Criminal Law Review,* vol. 12 (2012): 219–244.

Ssenyonjo, Manisuli, "The Rise of the African Union Opposition to the International Criminal Court's Investigations and Prosecutions of African Leaders," *International Criminal Law Review*, vol. 13 (2013): 385–428.

Official documents and sources

International Criminal Court, *Rome Statute of the International Criminal Court* and related documents, http://untreaty.un.org/cod/icc/index.html

United Nations, *Report of the International Commission of Inquiry on Darfur to the United Nations Secretary-General, Pursuant to Security Council Resolution 1564 of 18 September 2004,* http://www.un.org/news/dh/sudan/com_inq_darfur.pdf

United Nations, *UN Security Council Resolution 1593* (referring the situation in Darfur to the International Criminal Court), hhttp://www.icc-cpi.int/NR/rdonlyres/85FEBD1A-29F8-4EC4-9566-48EDF55CC587/283244/N0529273.pdf

Online sources

Coalition for the International Criminal Court, http://www.iccnow.org
Human Rights Watch, http://www.hrw.org/topic/international-justice/international-criminal-court
International Criminal Court, http://www.icc-cpi.int

14 Enduring and emergent challenges and opportunities

This book has provided an introduction to the intersection of two complex and rapidly developing and compound fields of study and policymaking: human rights and international criminal law; and conflict resolution and **peacebuilding**. It has offered an overview of relevant **international humanitarian law** and **international human rights law**, and presented scholarship and debates about human rights and the causes and consequences of conflict, options for **conflict prevention** and conflict resolution, and options for seeking accountability for past atrocities. There are many tensions between the promotion of human rights and the resolution of conflict, but there may also be opportunities for engaging in each in a more complementary fashion. This book has sought to assist students seeking to work in this hybrid area with these analytic tools, as well as with the study of contemporary situations presenting challenges of protecting human rights while addressing conflict. These situations range from largely internal armed conflicts to those with regional or international dimensions such as those in the former Yugoslavia, Sierra Leone and the Democratic Republic of Congo, and involve a mix of state combatants and nonstate combatants, as well as an increasing range of civilian nonstate actors who may support combat or even engage in it while not being official parties to the conflict, and nonstate actors such as corporations who may operate in conflict zones and even be complicit in serious crimes. Finally, the book has presented a range of critical mechanisms and institutions developed as part of efforts to implement human rights and humanitarian law, generally through criminal accountability, even as conflicts have raged: ad hoc tribunals, transnational mechanisms, **hybrid tribunals**, and the **International Criminal Court** (ICC).

Difficult policy and political decisions must be confronted when seeking to promote justice and resolve conflicts. Though significant challenges remain and will continue to emerge, there are also opportunities for promoting both justice and conflict resolution, rather than choosing one over the other.

Enduring challenges and opportunities

Enduring challenges

Justice v. peace

While great advances in accountability have clearly been made since the early 1990s, beginning with the creation of the ad hoc tribunals for the former Yugoslavia and Rwanda, and continuing through to the negotiation and ratification of the Rome Statute for the ICC, there remain important tensions between the pursuit of accountability and the pursuit of peace agreements. Contemporary peace agreements continue to either set accountability to one side, as in the case of the Comprehensive Peace Agreement concluded in 2005 to resolve the conflict in Sudan between the northern government, based in Khartoum, and the Sudanese People's Liberation Movement/Army, in the south, or explicitly include amnesties for one or more parties, as in the case of the Lomé Agreement in Sierra Leone in 1999. The threat or possibility of accountability also continues to hinder the negotiation of some peace agreements, as in the case of failed negotiations with the Lord's Resistance Army in seeking to end the conflict in northern Uganda during the 2006–2008 Juba Peace Talks, for which many blamed ICC arrest warrants for Joseph Kony and others. . Objections by individuals and groups who may have committed serious human rights violations during the course of conflict, particularly former combatants, whether governmental or nonstate actors, are likely to continue to impede many **peace negotiations**. They may also pose challenges to peace implementation.

Will and capacity to pursue accountability

A related challenge is that while there may be strong demands for accountability from local populations, or from international human rights groups, there may be limited will at the top political levels to pursue it. Alternatively, there may be a desire by the political leadership to pursue accountability, but relatively limited capacity to follow through, as states emerging from violent conflict generally suffer from decimated infrastructure and limited resources. Even when promotion of accountability comes from the national and international levels, some among the most affected populations at the local level may insist that community-based mechanisms are more effective. If national and local will and capacity are lacking, international venues for accountability may be the only option. However, here too there are problems of will, capacity, and sometimes jurisdiction. As discussed in Chapter 13, the ICC's territorial and temporal jurisdiction is limited. While there has been, to date, two referrals to the ICC by the **UN Security Council**, of the situations in Darfur and in Libya, such referrals are likely to be politically contentious and fairly rare. This means that if the ICC is not an option, and if domestic venues in the countries affected by conflict are not available, then accountability for human rights violations would need to be sought in the domestic courts of other nations, or through the creation of ad hoc or hybrid tribunals. However, only in a few countries are courts prepared to hear cases, whether civil or criminal, for abuses committed in other countries, and this is also politically contentious. Similarly, ad hoc and hybrid tribunals can be costly and require significant political will to create. Nonetheless, such avenues for accountability continue to act as complements to the ICC and may help to fill gaps for the foreseeable future.

The Western imposition objection

As discussed in Chapter 3, the scope and content of human rights obligations remain contested, with some groups and some states claiming that these are Western values, or that they are being imposed by Western states. This objection has been vehemently raised by the government of Sudan in the context of the referral to the ICC of the situation in Darfur; by politicians in Kenya following the opening of an investigation in 2010 into post-election violence with some nations branding the ICC as an international court for Africa. Objections have also been raised by a number of African nations in respect to courts exercising **universal jurisdiction** in European countries such as Belgium and Spain over current or former African leaders, with the specter of colonialism often raised. These objections invoke cultural difference or political power, and will likely continue to be raised for the foreseeable future. However, the degree of deference that these objections should be given is certainly debatable, as they are most frequently invoked by the individuals or regimes who most benefit from them.

Enduring opportunities

While it is difficult to identify any significant, long-standing opportunities for pursuing accountability while pursuing **peacemaking** and peacebuilding, there are a number of emergent and increasingly embedded opportunities, discussed below. Certainly, we now have several decades of practice in domestic **transitional justice** to draw upon, as well as the new wave of international criminal accountability efforts that has emerged since the end of the Cold War. Similarly, embedded practices of peacemaking, **peacekeeping**, and peacebuilding are being carried out by the **United Nations** (UN), the European Union (EU), and other **regional organizations**, as well as bilateral donors and international nongovernmental organizations. The professional and technical expertise of networks of human rights activists and practitioners, as well as conflict resolution advocates and practitioners, offer perhaps the most enduring opportunity.

Emergent challenges and opportunities

Pursuit of accountability during conflict

Perhaps one of the most salient emergent challenges involves the growth of efforts to pursue accountability, not after a conflict has reached a negotiated agreement or the victory of one side, but while conflict is still under way. This is not an entirely new phenomenon—the **International Criminal Tribunal for the Former Yugoslavia** (ICTY) was created and began to operate prior to the negotiated end to the conflicts in the former Yugoslavia following the Dayton Accords in 1995—but it is becoming increasingly common. In recent years, the courts of a number of countries in Europe have sought to exercise jurisdiction over accused perpetrators in countries where the conflicts had not yet fully terminated, with attempts by Belgium and Spain to prosecute individuals for crimes in the Democratic Republic of Congo before the conflict had ended. Similarly the ICC has sought to prosecute individuals for crimes in the DRC, Darfur and northern Uganda, and has sought arrest warrants for suspected perpetrators, even though neither conflict has ended, and in the case of Uganda even despite strong concerns that indictments were impeding a peace process.

Venues

Perhaps one of the most significant emergent opportunities for the promotion of human rights during ongoing conflicts or in postconflict situations is the creation or utilization of new venues for accountability. In particular, transnational accountability mechanisms, through the exercise of universal jurisdiction in countries such as Spain, or civil accountability in countries such as the United States and the United Kingdom, have created the possibility of imposing some form of sanction upon human rights abusers who might not otherwise face sanction in their home states. While some of these avenues have been progressively limited, as discussed in Chapter 11, other new ones have been proposed, such as a criminal chamber in the African Court of Human and Peoples' Rights. Similarly, the creation of hybrid mechanisms has offered new opportunities for accountability where previously unavailable. These new venues may be particularly important where purely international accountability is unavailable and domestic accountability is impossible, and can also potentially supplement peacemaking and peacebuilding in countries most affected by conflict and human rights violations.

In situations where the ICC does not have jurisdiction, or the UN Security Council will not refer the situation, or the state affected by the conflict and relevant violations will not initiate a case and the Office of the Prosecutor does not see fit to initiate a case, these mechanisms may help to fill what otherwise might constitute gaps in accountability.

Pursuit of accountability during conflict

Notwithstanding the hurdles it has encountered during its first decade of activity the ICC is now active in eight situations and maintaining a watching brief over numerous other countries. Further, it has now received referrals by the UN Security Council, despite the ongoing US objections to the court. And perhaps most important, the ICC has been able to do something that most previous mechanisms and accountability processes for gross violations of human rights and international humanitarian law have not: initiate investigations and indictments of high-level perpetrators during ongoing conflict. While such investigations may have the potential to disrupt peace negotiations, they may also constitute a positive incentive for negotiations. Optimists argue that ICC investigations may also have the capacity to prevent or deter violations in the midst of ongoing conflict. Even if the ICC does not manage to arrest suspects, experience suggests that indictments may compel suspects to hide, which may prevent them from committing further human rights abuses. Still, it remains to be seen whether such investigations encourage parties to reach peace agreements or prevent them from doing so, and whether such investigations alter the behavior of combatants and prevent abuses that might otherwise have occurred as conflict continues.

The future

It is of course impossible to predict the future of the vast and rapidly intersecting fields of conflict and human rights. Hopefully, however, this textbook has provided the student with the tools and wherewithal to understand the history of the institutions and mechanisms developed for accountability, the dilemmas which confront peacemakers, and hopefully to develop your own recommendations to respond to particular situations. Further, the political and legal analytical skills which students have gained through this study should enable them to think creatively about future, alternative, options: for legal accountability mechanisms, for peace negotiations, and for sustainable political solutions, which enable weak post-conflict states to address accountability while pursuing peace.

Further reading

Davis, Rachel, Benjamin Majekodunmi, and Judy Smith-Höhn, *Prevention of Genocide and Mass Atrocities and the Responsibility to Protect: Challenges for the UN and the International Community in the 21st Century* (New York: UN Office of the Special Adviser on the Prevention of Genocide, International Peace Institute, and Centre for Conflict Resolution, June 2008), http://www.ipinst.org/publication/meeting-notes/detail/25-prevention-of-genocide-and-mass-atrocities-

and-the-responsibility-to-protect-challenges-for-the-un-and-the-international-community-in-the-21st-century.html

Human Rights Watch, *World Report 2004: Human Rights and Armed Conflict,* http://www.hrw.org/legacy/wr2k4/index.htm

Sikkink, Kathryn, *The Justice Cascade: How Human Rights are Changing Global Politics* (New York: Norton, 2011).

Sriram, Chandra Lekha, "Spoilers of Justice," *Nordic Journal of Human Rights* vol. 31, no. 2 (2013): 250–263.

Official documents and sources

United Nations, *Report of the Secretary-General on Peacebuilding in the Immediate Aftermath of Conflict* UN Doc A/63/881-S/2009/304 (June 11, 2009).

United Nations, *A More Secure World: Our Shared Responsibility—Report of the Secretary-General's High-Level Panel on Threats, Challenges, and Change* (2004), http://www.un.org/secureworld.

United Nations, *Nuremberg Declaration on Peace and Justice: Annex to the Letter Dated 13 June 2008 from the Permanent Representatives of Finland, Germany, and Jordan to the United Nations, Addressed to the Secretary-General* (July 19, 2008), UN Doc. A/62/885, http://www.peace-justice-conference.info/download/nuremberg%20declaration%20a-62-885%20eng.pdf

Glossary

African Union (AU). The regional organization that comprises African states. Formerly the Organization of African Unity, it was transformed by a new charter into the AU in 2000.

Alien Tort Claims Act (ATCA). Passed in 1789, this act established the jurisdiction of US federal district courts over "any civil action by an alien for a tort only committed in violation of the law of nations or a treaty of the United States."

amnesty. The blocking of criminal action against alleged perpetrators of crimes.

Amnesty International. An international organization that advocates and campaigns for the protection and promotion of human rights.

aut dedere aut judicare. The legal principle requiring that a nation try an individual accused of certain crimes, such as genocide, or extradite that person to an appropriate jurisdiction on request.

Common Article 3. An article of identical provisions common to all four Geneva Conventions that requires parties in internal armed conflicts not to engage in specific violations, such as violence and denial of due process to persons not taking part in hostilities.

complementarity. The principle that prohibits the International Criminal Court from hearing a case if there is a legitimate legal process under way in a relevant national jurisdiction, or if the accusation has been rigorously investigated and dismissed domestically.

conflict prevention. Activities undertaken to mitigate the risk of imminent conflict, or to address deep-rooted causes of conflict.

crimes against humanity. Specific acts committed as part of a widespread or systematic attack against any civilian population.

Department of Peacekeeping Operations (DPKO). Part of the United Nations, the DPKO assists UN member states and the UN Secretary-General in their efforts to maintain international peace and security.

Department of Political Affairs (DPA). Part of the United Nations, the DPA is the lead UN actor that supports peacemaking, conflict prevention, and peacebuilding.

diplomacy. Efforts by a range of actors, official and unofficial, to promote peaceful settlement of disputes.

Economic Community of West African States (ECOWAS). A regional organization of states in West Africa. Founded in 1975 as an economic body, it now engages in peacemaking and peacekeeping activities through the ECOWAS Cease-Fire Monitoring Group (ECOMOG).

European Convention on Human Rights (ECHR). Drafted in 1950 under the auspices of the Council of Europe, this convention articulates a set of fundamental rights and freedoms that parties are obligated to effect and respect.

European Court of Human Rights. The court that has jurisdiction over claims that rights enshrined in the European Convention on Human Rights have been violated.

Geneva Conventions. A set of four conventions (1949) and two additional protocols (1977):

- *First Geneva Convention.* Addresses treatment of sick and wounded in the armed forces.
- *Second Geneva Convention.* Addresses treatment of sick and wounded at sea.
- *Third Geneva Convention.* Addresses treatment of prisoners of war.
- *Fourth Geneva Convention.* Addresses protection of civilians in armed conflict.
- *Additional Protocol I.* Elaborates obligations and limitations for treatment of victims of international armed conflict.
- *Additional Protocol II.* Elaborates obligations and limitations for treatment of victims of noninternational armed conflict.

genocide. The commission of specific acts with the intent to destroy, in whole or in part, a national, ethnical, racial, or religious group.

Genocide Convention (Convention on the Prevention and Punishment of the Crime of Genocide). Defines and prohibits genocide, and obligates states to prevent and punish genocide.

grave breaches. Specific acts committed during international conflict that are designated in each of the four Geneva Conventions as punishable (war crimes).

hybrid tribunals. Tribunals that utilize a mixture of domestic and international staff, and in some cases domestic and international law, to prosecute crimes of international concern that arise from conflict and gross abuses of human rights. Examples include the Special Court for Sierra Leone and the Cambodia Extraordinary Chambers.

Human Rights Watch. An international organization that advocates for the protection of human rights.

impunity. The failure to bring perpetrators of human rights abuses to account.

internally displaced persons. People who have been forced from their homes, usually by conflict or other humanitarian catastrophe, into another part of their country. Because they have not crossed an international border, they are not protected by the provisions of international agreements regarding refugees.

International Bill of Rights. Comprises the Universal Declaration of Human Rights (UDHR), the International Covenant on Civil and Political Rights (ICCPR), and the International Covenant on Economic, Social, and Cultural Rights (ICESCR).

International Court of Justice (ICJ). The judicial organ of the United Nations, able to adjudicate interstate disputes where it has jurisdiction.

International Criminal Court (ICC). Established by the Rome Statute, which entered into force July 1, 2002, the ICC can try individuals under its jurisdiction for war crimes, crimes against humanity, and genocide, and will be able to prosecute the crime of aggression when and if that crime is defined for the purposes of the Court.

International Criminal Tribunal for Rwanda (ICTR). An ad hoc criminal tribunal created to punish individuals considered most responsible for the 1994 genocide in Rwanda.

International Criminal Tribunal for the Former Yugoslavia (ICTY). An ad hoc criminal tribunal created to punish individuals accused of committing international crimes, such as war crimes and crimes against humanity, during Yugoslavia's armed conflict and breakup.

international human rights law (IHRL). Includes customary and conventional international legal obligations to respect or protect specific rights of natural persons. In addition to the documents included in the International Bill of Rights, key agreements include the

Convention on the Prevention and Punishment of the Crime of Genocide; the Convention Against Torture and Other Cruel, Inhuman, or Degrading Treatment or Punishment; the Convention on the Elimination of Racial Discrimination in All Its Forms; the Convention on the Rights of the Child; and the Convention on the Elimination of Discrimination Against Women.

international humanitarian law (IHL). Includes customary and conventional international legal obligations that regulate activities during internal and international armed conflict. Key documents include the four Geneva Conventions and their two additional protocols.

jus cogens. Obligations that have achieved the status of peremptory norms in international law and from which no derogation is permissible. These include prohibitions on genocide, torture, crimes against humanity, war crimes, piracy, and slavery. Universal jurisdiction may be exercised over those who violate these norms.

Mechanism for International Criminal Tribunals (MICT). Established by the UN to carry out remaining essential functions of the ICTR and ICTY after the completion of their mandates.

nonstate actors. Actors that are not state officials or agents of the state, and may include multinational corporations, private military and security companies, nongovernmental organizations, nonstate armed groups, and terrorist organizations.

North Atlantic Treaty Organization (NATO). Comprises nations of Western Europe and North America that have allied under a treaty of mutual self-defense since the end of World War II. Its membership has grown to involve nations of Central Europe since the end of the Cold War.

nulla poena sine lege. A principle of international criminal law meaning "no punishment without law."

nullem crimen sine lege. A principle of international criminal law meaning "no crime without law."

Nuremberg Charter (Charter of the International Military Tribunal). The charter that established the tribunal to try accused war criminals in Germany following World War II.

peace negotiation. Termination of conflict not through military victory, but through negotiated settlement, whether between states themselves or between states and nonstate armed groups.

peacebuilding. Myriad activities undertaken by individual states and the international community to help states consolidate peace and avoid return to conflict.

peacekeeping. Use of military and civilian contingents by an external third party, most frequently the United Nations, interposed between parties to a conflict, in an effort to halt fighting or to monitor and implement peace agreements.

peacemaking. Reaching a peaceful solution to a conflict through activities such as mediation or negotiation.

private military and security companies. Private companies which provide a range of security, defence and military services.

proprio motu. The power of the prosecutor of the International Criminal Court to initiate a case, if he has jurisdiction.

regional organizations. Organizations formed under multilateral agreements to achieve particular regional purposes, often security or economic coordination. Key examples include the African Union and the European Union.

rule of law. The accountability of all persons, institutions, and entities, public and private, including the state itself, to laws that are publicly promulgated, equally enforced, and independently adjudicated.

South African Development Community (SADC). A regional organization formed in 1980 to coordinate development projects in Southern Africa. The SADC now also engages in peacemaking and other diplomatic activities.

Special Representative of the Secretary-General (SRSG). An eminent person appointed by the UN Secretary-General to engage the situation in a particular country, or with respect to a particular topic. SRSGs often head peacekeeping missions.

torture. Defined by the Torture Convention as "any act by which severe pain or suffering, whether physical or mental, is intentionally inflicted on a person for such purposes as obtaining from him or a third person information or a confession … when such pain or suffering is inflicted by or at the instigation of or with the consent or acquiescence of a public official or other person acting in an official capacity."

Torture Convention (Convention Against Torture and Other Cruel, Inhuman, or Degrading Treatment or Punishment). Defines and universally bans torture.

transitional justice. A range of processes and mechanisms to ensure accountability, justice, and reconciliation after conflict or authoritarian rule.

truth commissions. Nonjudicial fact-finding bodies that investigate patterns of human rights abuses during conflict or authoritarian rule.

UN Charter. The international agreement of 1945 that established the United Nations, setting forth the goals of the organization—to prevent war and to promote human rights—and the obligations of states parties.

UN General Assembly. An intergovernmental organ of the United Nations in which all member states are represented.

UN High Commissioner for Refugees (UNHCR). Office established in1950 by the United Nations General Assembly and is mandated to lead and co-ordinate international action to protect refugees and resolve refugee problems globally.

UN Secretary-General. Described in the UN Charter as the "chief administrative officer" of the United Nations, the Secretary-General engages in a range of diplomatic activities, including through the offer of his good offices to promote conflict resolution.

UN Security Council. One of the principal organs of the UN, established under Article 7 of the UN Charter, comprising fifteen member states, five of which are permanent and have the right of veto. The Security Council's primary responsibility is the maintenance of peace and security.

UN Security Council resolution. A resolution passed by the UN Security Council to effect its primary goal of maintaining of peace and security. Affirmative votes from nine member states are required, with no vetoes by the five permanent member states.

United Nations (UN). Created by the UN Charter in 1945 with the express purpose of saving "succeeding generations from the scourge of war" and reaffirming "fundamental human rights." Key organs include the Security Council, the General Assembly, and the International Court of Justice.

universal jurisdiction. The extraterritorial exercise of criminal jurisdiction over a limited set of international crimes, or violations of *jus cogens* obligations, regardless of the territory in which they were committed.

war crimes. The commission of a range of acts, defined as "grave breaches" in the Geneva Conventions, that are considered violations of the laws and customs of war.

Selected further reading

Abass, Ademola, "The Proposed International Criminal Jurisdiction for the African Court: Some Problematical Aspects," *Netherlands International Law Review* vol. 60, no. 1 (2013): 27–50.

Aceves, William J., "*Doe v. Unocal* 963 F. Supp. 880," *American Journal of International Law* vol. 92, no. 2 (April 1998): 979–987.

Adebajo, Adekeye, and Chandra Lekha Sriram (eds), *Managing Armed Conflicts in the 21st Century* (London: Frank Cass, 2001).

Aksar, Yusuf, *Implementing International Humanitarian Law: From the Ad Hoc Tribunals to a Permanent International Criminal Court* (London: Routledge, 2004).

Almquist, Jessica, "A Human Rights Critique of European Judicial Review: Counter-Terrorism Sanctions," *International and Comparative Law Quarterly* vol. 57 (April 2008): 303–332.

Alston, Phillip, and Ryan Goodman, *International Human Rights* (Oxford: Oxford University Press, 2012).

Andreopoulos, George J., "The International Legal Framework and Armed Groups," *Human Rights Review* vol. 11 (2010): 223–246.

Baetens, Freya and Katrin Kohoutek, "The UN Peacebuilding Commission," in Rüdiger Wolfrum (ed.), *Max Planck Encyclopedia of Public International Law*, (Oxford: Oxford University Press, 2010).

Bakker, Christine and Mirko Sossai (eds), *Multilevel Regulation of Military and Security Contractors: The Interplay between International, European and Domestic Norms* (Oxford: Hart, 2012).

Ballentine, Karen, and Heiko Nitzschke (eds), *Profiting from Peace: Managing the Resource Dimensions of Civil War* (Boulder, CO: Lynne Rienner, 2005).

Bell, Christine, *Peace Agreements and Human Rights* (Oxford: Oxford University Press, 2003).

Call, Charles T., with Vanessa Wyeth, *Building States to Build Peace* (Boulder, CO: Lynne Rienner, 2008).

Carey, Henry F. and Stacey Mitchell (eds), *Trials and Tribulations of International Prosecution* (Plymouth, MA: Lexington Books, 2013).

Cassese, Antonio, "The Multifaceted Criminal Notion of Terrorism in International Law," *Journal of International Criminal Justice* vol. 4 (2006): 933–958.

Cassese, Antonio and Paola Gaeta, *International Criminal Law* (Oxford: Oxford University Press, 2013).

Chesterman, Simon and Chia Lehnardt (eds), *From Mercenaries to Market. The Rise and Regulation of Military Companies* (Oxford: Oxford University Press, 2007).

Clapham, Andrew, "Extending International Criminal Law beyond the Individual to Corporations and Armed Opposition Groups," *Journal of International Criminal Justice* vol. 6 (2008): 899–926.

D'Amato, Anthony, "Peace vs. Accountability in Bosnia," *American Journal of International Law* vol. 88 (1994): 500–506.

Davis, Rachel, Benjamin Majekodunmi, and Judy Smith-Höhn, *Prevention of Genocide and Mass Atrocities and the Responsibility to Protect: Challenges for the UN and the International Community in the 21st Century* (New York: UN Office of the Special Adviser on the Prevention of Genocide, International Peace Institute, and Centre for Conflict Resolution, June 2008), http://www.ipinst.org/publication/meeting-notes/detail/25-prevention-of-genocide-and-mass-atrocities-and-the-responsibility-to-protect-challenges-for-the-un-and-the-international-community-in-the-21st-century.html

Donnelly, Jack, *Universal Human Rights in Theory and Practice* (New York: Cornell University Press, 2003).

Doyle, Michael W., and Nicholas Sambanis, *Making War and Building Peace* (Princeton, NJ: Princeton University Press, 2006).

Duffy, Helen, *The "War on Terror" and the Framework of International Law* (Cambridge: Cambridge University Press, 2005), especially pp. 332–78, 379–442.

Dunne, Tim, and Nicholas J. Wheeler, *Human Rights in Global Politics* (Cambridge: Cambridge University Press, 1999).

Francioni, Francesco and Natalino Ronzitti (eds), *War by Contract. Human Rights, Humanitarian Law and Private Contractors* (Oxford: Oxford University Press, 2011).

Gow, James, Rachel Kerr and Zoran Pajić (eds), *Lessons and Legacies of the International Criminal Tribunal for the Former Yugoslavia* (London: Routledge, 2013).

Hirsch, John, *Sierra Leone: Diamonds and the Struggle for Democracy* (Boulder, CO: Lynne Rienner, 2001).

Ishay, Micheline R., *The History of Human Rights: From Ancient Times to the Globalization Era* (Berkeley, CA: University of California Press, 2004).

Iyob, Ruth, and Gilbert M. Khadiagala, *Sudan: The Elusive Quest for Peace* (Boulder, CO: Lynne Rienner, 2006).

Kaldor, Mary, *New and Old Wars: Organized Violence in a Global Era* (Stanford, CA: Stanford University Press, 2001).

Kerr, Rachel, and Eirin Mobekk, *Peace and Justice: Seeking Accountability After War* (Cambridge: Polity, 2007).

Lauren, Paul Gordon, *The Evolution of International Human Rights: Visions Seen* (Philadelphia, PA: Pennsylvania State University Press, 2011).

Lessa, Francesca and Leigh Payne, *Amnesty in the Age of Human Rights Accountability: Comparative and International Perspectives* (Cambridge: Cambridge University Press, 2012).

Lutz, Ellen, Eileen F. Babbitt, and Hurst Hannum, "Human Rights and Conflict Resolution from the Practitioners' Perspectives," *Fletcher Forum of World Affairs* vol. 27, no. 1 (Winter–Spring 2003), 173–193.

Macedo, Stephen, ed., *Universal Jurisdiction: National Courts and the Prosecution of Serious Crimes Under International Law* (Philadelphia, PA: University of Pennsylvania Press, 2004).

Manikkalingam, Ram, "Promoting Peace and Protecting Rights: How Are Human Rights Good and Bad for Resolving Conflict?" *Essex Human Rights Review* vol. 5, no. 1 (July 2008): 1–11.

Marks, Susan, "Civil Liberties at the Margin: The UK Derogation and the European Court of Human Rights," *Oxford Journal of Legal Studies* vol. 15, no. 1 (Spring 1995): 69–95.

Martin-Ortega, Olga, "Business and Human Rights in Conflict," *Ethics & International Affairs* vol. 22, no. 3 (2008): 273–283.

Martin-Ortega, Olga, "Prosecuting war crimes at home: reflections from the War Crimes Chamber in the State Court of Bosnia and Herzegovina," *International Criminal Law Review,* vol. 12 (2012): 589–628.

Meron, Theodor, "International Criminalization of Internal Atrocities," *American Journal of International Law,* vol. 89 (1995): 554–7.

Mertus, Julie A., and Jeffrey W. Helsing (eds), *Human Rights and Conflict: Exploring the Links Between Rights, Law, and Peacebuilding* (Washington, DC: US Institute of Peace Press, 2006).

Mitton, Kieran, "Irrational Actors and the Process of Brutalization: Understanding Atrocity in the Sierra Leonean Conflict (1991–2002)," *Civil Wars* vol. 14, no. 1 (2012): 104–122.

Nest, Michael, with François Grignon and Eminzet F. Kinsangani, *The Democratic Republic of Congo: Economic Dimensions of War and Peace* (Boulder, CO: Lynne Rienner, 2006).

Nettelfield, Lara, *Courting Democracy in Bosnia and Herzegovina* (Cambridge: Cambridge University Press, 2010).

Nino, Carlos S., "The Duty to Punish Past Human Rights Violations Put into Context: The Case of Argentina," *Yale Law Journal* vol. 100 (1991): 2619–2641.

Orentlicher, Diane, "Settling Accounts: The Duty to Prosecute Human Rights Violations of a Prior Regime," *Yale Law Journal* vol. 100 (1991): 2537–2618.

Paris, Roland, *At War's End: Building Peace after Civil Conflict* (Cambridge: Cambridge University Press, 2004).

Parlevliet, Michelle, "Rethinking conflict transformation from a human rights perspective," (Berlin: Berghof Research Centre, September 2009), http://www.berghof-handbook.net/documents/publications/parlevliet_handbook.pdf,

Paust, Jordan J., M. Cherif Bassiouni, Michael Scharf, Jimmy Gurul, Leila Sadat, Bruce Zagaris, and Sharon A. Williams, *International Criminal Law* (Durham, NC: Carolina Academic Press, 2000).

Pugh, Michael, and Neil Cooper, with Jonathan Goodhand, *War Economies in Regional Context* (Boulder, CO: Lynne Rienner 2004).

Ratner, Steven R., and Jason S. Abrams, *Accountability for Human Rights Atrocities in International Law: Beyond the Nuremberg Legacy* (Oxford: Oxford University Press, 2001).

Reno, William, *Warlord Politics and African States* (Boulder, CO: Lynne Rienner, 1999).

Reydams, Luc, *Universal Jurisdiction: International and Municipal Legal Perspectives* (Oxford: Oxford University Press, 2003).

Schabas, William A., *The Universal Declaration of Human Rights: The Travaux Préparatoires* (Cambridge: Cambridge University Press, 2013).

Schabas, William, *Unimaginable Atrocities: Justice, Politics, and Rights at the War Crimes Tribunals* (Oxford: Oxford University Press, 2012).

Sikkink, Kathryn, *The Justice Cascade: How Human Rights are Changing Global Politics* (New York: Norton, 2011).

Sloane, Robert D., "The International Criminal Tribunal for Rwanda" in Chiara Giorgetti (ed.), *The Rules, Practice and Jurisprudence of International Courts and Tribunals* (Leiden: Martinus Nijhoff Publishers, 2012).

Sriram, Chandra Lekha, *Globalizing Justice for Mass Atrocities: A Revolution in Accountability* (London: Routledge, 2005).

Sriram, Chandra Lekha, *Peace as Governance* (London: Palgrave, 2008).

Sriram, Chandra Lekha, and Suren Pillay (eds), *Peace vs. Justice? Truth and Reconciliation Processes and War Crimes Tribunals in Africa* (Durban: University of KwaZulu-Natal, 2009).

Sriram, Chandra Lekha, and Karin Wermester (eds), *From Promise to Practice: Strengthening UN Capacities for the Prevention of Violent Conflict* (Boulder, CO: Lynne Rienner, 2003).

Sriram, Chandra Lekha, Jemima Garcia-Godos, Johanna Herman and Olga Martin-Ortega (eds), *Transitional Justice And Peacebuilding on the Ground: Victims and Ex-combatants* (London: Routledge, 2012).

Sriram, Chandra Lekha, Olga Martin-Ortega and Johanna Herman (eds), *Peacebuilding and Rule of Law in Africa: Just Peace?* (London: Routledge, 2010).

Turner, Thomas, *The Congo Wars: Conflict, Myth, and Reality* (New York: Zed Books, 2007).

Vandeginste, Stef, and Chandra Lekha Sriram, "Power-sharing and Transitional Justice: A Clash of Paradigms?" *Global Governance* vol. 17, no. 4 (2011): 487–505.

Wippman, David, and Matthew Evangelista (eds), *New Wars, New Laws? Applying the Laws of War in 21st Century Conflicts* (Ardsley, NY: Transnational, 2005).

Worden, Scott, and Emily Wann, *Special Court of Sierra Leone Briefing: The Taylor Trial and Lessons from Capacity-Building and Outreach* (Washington, DC: US Institute of Peace, August 2007).

Zegveld, Liesbeth, *Accountability of Armed Opposition Groups in International Law* (Cambridge: Cambridge University Press, 2002).

Online sources

Crimes of War Project, http://www.crimesofwar.org/
Human Rights Watch reports, http://www.hrw.org
International Center for Transitional Justice reports, www.ictj.org
International Crisis Group reports, http://www.crisisweb.org
Open Society Justice Initiative reports, http://www.osji.org

Index

Abuja Agreement I: Sierra Leone 107
Abyei: Sudan 24, 141, 154–5
accountability 7–9, 61–3, 239, 240, 241; DRC
  124–6, 131; human rights enforcement
  184; individual criminal 46, 53, 54, 66,
  68, 226; institutions 11; international
  community 220; and peacebuilding
  29–30; Sudan 148–51
ad hoc tribunals 161–82; contributions
  of 180–1; criticisms of 179–80; ICTY
  161–70; ITCR 170–8; MICT 178–9
Additional Protocol II 69–70, 75, 111
Africa: and ICC 235; mercenaries 74–5
African Court on Human and People's Rights
  54
African Union (AU) 121, 243
Africa's war 119, 121
aggression: ICC 223–4
Akayesu, Jean Paul 174–5
al-Bashir, Omar Hassan Ahmad 140, 141,
  151–2, 153, 155, 230–1
Aleksovksi, Zlatko 168
Alien Tort Claims Act (ATCA) 11, 192, 243;
  cases 194–5, 196; limits to 195
American Convention on Human Rights 54
The American Declaration of Independence 35
amnesties 8–9
amnesty: definition 243
Amnesty International 41, 243
Anderson, Mary B. 22
Annan, Kofi 19, 233
"Arab spring" 16
arbitration 24
Argentina 8, 41, 187, 191, 193
armed conflict: definition 167; internal 12
Armed Forces Revolutionary Council 103,
  105, 106, 110, 112
armed groups and IHL 67
"Asian values" 43–6
aut dedere aut judicare 243

Bagosora, Théoneste 176
Bangkok Declaration 44–5

Bemba Gombo, Jean-Pierre 234
Bosnia-Herzegovina: Čelebići 167–8,
  169–70; command responsibility 167–8;
  conflict in 86–8; Dayton Accords
  87; genocide 93, 167; international
  v. internal conflict 166–7; *Kadić v.
  Karadžić* 69; Kozarac 165–7; law 94
Bouazizi, Mohamed 16
businesses 77–9, 194–5

Cambodia: background 207–8; civil party
  system 211; Genocide Convention 210;
  tribunal evaluation 210–12; tribunal
  mandate and structure 208–10
Čelebići 167–8, 169–70
Central African Republic: ICC 232
Chad 142
challenges and opportunities 39–48, 238–
  42; accountability 239, 240, 241; the
  future 241; justice versus peace 238–9;
  venues 240–1; Western imposition
  objection 239–40
child soldiers: Sierra Leone 108
Chile: The *Pinochet* cases 185–8
civil accountability 192–7
civil conflict: causes 15–18
civil liability in UK 195–6
civil wars 15
CNDP 124
collective group rights 42
command responsibility 167–8
Common Article 3 60, 180, 223, 243; DRC
  133; nonstate armed groups 66–72;
  Sierra Leone 111; Sudan 148
communist states: human rights 39
communitarians 36
companies 77–9, 194–5; Talisman Energy
  149
complementarity 219, 225, 243
conflict 14–31; causes of 10;
  characteristics and causes 15–18;
  and human rights 5–6, 9, 48–9;
  peacebuilding 27–30; postconflict

reconstruction 27–30; today's conflicts 14–15
conflict analysis 4–5, 9–10
conflict dynamics 6–7
conflict prevention 18–20, 243
conflict resolution 20–7; actors 21–3; mechanisms 23–7; UN 21–2; war and human rights 9–10
Convention on the Elimination of All Forms of Discrimination Against Women (CEDAW) 38, 46, 47
corporate group rights 42
corporations 77–9, 194–5
crimes against humanity 33, 57, 243; Darfur 142–5; DRC 128; ICC 222; Sudan 142; universal jurisdiction 184, 185
crimes: under ICC jurisdiction 221–4
criminal accountability *see* accountability
Croatia 86–8
Côte d'Ivoire: ICC 234
cultural relativism 46
customary international law obligations 55–7

Darfur 141, 146; crimes against humanity 142–5; "ethnic cleansing" 147–8; genocide 150–1; ICC 229–31
Darfur Peace Agreement 143
The Dayton Accords 87
Democratic Republic of Congo (DRC) 116–34; Africa's war 119, 121; background to conflict 116–17, 119, 121–6; case against Uganda 130; FPR case 131; human rights violations 126–8; ICC 228–9; key facts 118; key players 120–1; legal aspects 128–9, 133; map *117*; Second Congo War 120–1; timeline 132; v. Belgium 190–1
Department of Peacekeeping Operations (DPKO) 27, 243
Department of Political Affairs (DPA) 20, 243
diplomacy 18, 23–4, 243
Do no harm 22
Doe v. Unocal: ATCA cases 194–5, 196
domestic accountability abroad 197
domestic grievances 89–90, 126–7
DRC v. Uganda and Rwanda 129–30
drones 61
Dunant, Henri 58

Economic Community of West African States Monitoring Group (ECOMOG) 102, 103, 104, 110
economic rights 39–41
El Salvador 7, 8, 26, 41
"ethnic cleansing": Bosnia-Herzegovina 86; Darfur 142, 147–8, 149; Kosovo 91–2, 93, 214
European Convention on Human Rights (ECHR) 243

European Court of Human Rights 52, 54, 93, 244
Extraordinary Chambers in the Courts of Cambodia (ECCC) 208–12
extraordinary rendition 71

feminist and gender critiques 46
Filartiga v. Peña-Irala 192–3, 196
first generation rights 39
"Five Fables on Human Rights"(Lukes) 36
FPR: case against in Spain 131
Furundžija, Anto 168–9

Gbagbo, Laurent 234
gender and feminist critiques 46
Geneva Call 67
Geneva Conventions 11, 33, 53, 54, 58–9, 244; Additional Protocol II 70; Article 4 of the Third 70; Common Article 3 60; DRC 133; grave breaches. 60; ICTY 161–2; legitimate combatants 69–70; mercenaries 74–5, 76; proscribed violations 68; Sierra Leone 111, 148; war crimes 222–3; Yugoslavia, former 94
genocide: Bosnia-Herzegovina 93, 167; Darfur 150–1; ICC 221–2; ICTR 174–5; ICTY 93; Srebrenica 93; Serbia 93; Sierra Leone 113; state responsibility 93; universal jurisdiction 47–8, 52–3, 184, 185
Genocide Convention 10, 52–3, 54, 244; Article 2 57; Cambodia 210; ICC 221–2; The *Pinochet* cases 187
Global Compact, UN 78
glossary 234–46
gold mining: DRC 126, 127
good offices and mediation 23–4
Gotovina, Ante 169
grave breaches 10–11, 59, 60, 244; Sudan 148, 222–3; Yugoslavia, former 94, 161–2
greed v. grievance: conflict analysis 17–18
group rights 42–3
Guiding Principles on Business and Human Rights 78

Habré, Hissène 192, 193
Hema 123, 126–7
"Homelessness and the Issue of Freedom" (Waldron) 40–1
human rights 32–50; "Asian values" 43–6; communist states 39; and conflict 48–9; conflict resolution 9–10; development 39–41; feminist and gender critiques 46–8; foundations for claims 34–8; homeless 40–1; as idolatry 38; International Human Rights 33–4; and peace negotiation 6–7, 105–8; as politics 37–8; relativism 43–6

human rights abuses: Darfur 147; responses to 11

Human Rights as Politics and Idolatry (Ignatieff) 37

human rights law *see* humanitarian and human rights law; international human rights law

human rights transnational enforcement 183–98; ATCA cases 194–5, 196; civil accountability 192–7; in conflict 197; criminal accountability 184; critical cases 189–90; ICC 190–2; immunity 191; legal limits to 190–2; national sovereignty 184–5; The *Pinochet* cases 185–9

human rights treaties 53

human rights violations: cause of conflict 89–91; as cause of conflict 108–9, 126, 145; during conflict 91–3, 127–8, 146–8; conflict dynamics 6–7; consequence of conflict 6; DRC 126–8; nonstate armed groups 67–8; PMSCs 73–4; Sierra Leone 108–11; and war 5–6; Yugoslavia, former 89–96

Human Rights Watch 126, 151, 244

humanitarian and human rights law 51–64; accountability 61–3; human rights obligations 55–8; humanitarian obligations 58–61; rights and obligations 51–5

hybrid tribunals 29, 180, 199–218, 244; Cambodia 207–12; to date 201; development of 199–200; future of 217; Khmer Rouge 207–12; Kosovo 200–4; Sierra Leone 107, 212–17; Timor-Leste 204–7

ICC: aggression 223–4; crimes against humanity 222; Darfur 229–31; Genocide Convention 221–2; war crimes 222–3

ICJ judgement 92, 93

Ignatieff, Michael 37–8

illegitimate combatants 69–70

immunity 62, 185, 191; Charles Taylor 214–15; *Pinochet* cases 188–9

impunity 147, 244

individual criminal accountability 46, 53, 54, 66, 68, 226

Indonesia: Timor-Leste 205–7

inequality: civil conflict causes 16–17

insecurity: civil conflict causes 16

Inter-Congolese Dialogue 122–3, 125

internal and international conflict 15, 89–90, 94

internal armed conflict 12

internally displaced persons 143, 231–2

international actors 20, 21

International Bill of Rights 10, 55, 244

International Commission of Inquiry on Darfur 147–8, 150–1

International Committee of the Red Cross (ICRC) 58, 60, 75–6, 78–9

international community: criminal accountability 220

International Court of Justice (ICJ) 52, 62–3, 93, 129–30, 244

International Covenant on Civil and Political Rights (ICCPR) 33–4, 52, 54, 55, 56

International Covenant on Economic, Social, and Cultural Rights (ICESCR) 33–4, 41, 52, 54, 55, 56

international criminal accountability: nonstate 61–3

International Criminal Court (ICC) 29, 35, 57, 219–37, 244; and Africa 235; applicable law 225–6; background 219–20; complementarity 225; crimes under 221–4; current situations 228–34; exercise of jurisdiction 225–6; functioning of 227–35; jurisdiction of 221–5; peace and justice 234–5; preconditions 224; Rome Statute, Article 25 226; structure of 221; USA 224; victim trust fund 227

international criminal law 225–6

International Criminal Tribunal for Rwanda (ICTR) 47, 170–7, 244; completion strategy case transfer 177; criticism of 178–80; functioning of 173; history and legal basis 161–2, 170–2; jurisprudence 173–4; landmark cases 174–6; organs of 172–3; sentencing 176; Statute 172

International Criminal Tribunal for the Former Yugoslavia (ICTY) 47, 161–70, 244; completion strategy 170; criticism of 178–80; functioning of 163–4; Geneva Conventions 161–2; genocide 93; jurisprudence 164–5; key articles 163; landmark cases 165–70; organs of 162–3; sentencing 170; United Nations 161–2

international criminal tribunals 11

international human rights law 33–4, 51, 220, 244–5; DRC 133; Sierra Leone 113; Yugoslavia, former 94, 96

international humanitarian law 51, 220, 245; armed groups commitments 67; Bosnia-Herzegovina 94; and business 78–9; companies 77–8; DRC 133; group exercise 114; and human rights law 58; Kosovo 94; and nonstate actors 75–6; obligations 58–61; permissible weaponry 61; PMSCs in 75–6; Sierra Leone 111; Yugoslavia, former 93–4

international humanitarian law obligations 59–62

International Law Commission (ILC) 219
international legal documents 10
international treaties 55–7
international v. internal armed conflict:
   Bosnia-Herzegovina 166–7
intrastate conflicts 15
Iraq, PMSCs in 73–4
Islamization: Sudan 138–40, 145–6

Janaweed militia 142–3, 147–8, 151
jus cogens 57, 245; ICTY 168–9; Sierra
   Leone 113; Sudan 148
justice v. peace 238–9

Kabila, Joseph 121, 122–3
Kadić v. Karadžić 69, 193–4, 196
Kambanda, Jean 176
Karadžić, Radovan 68, 69, 86, 165, 193–4,
   196
Kenya: ICC 233; post-election violence
   19, 24, 57; *proprio motu* 233
Khmer Rouge 207–12
Kiobel et al v. Royal Dutch Petroleum et al
   195, 196
Kosovo: conflict in 88–9; European Court
   of Human Rights 93; human rights
   violations 92–3; hybrid tribunals
   200–4; IHL 94; international human
   rights law 5; NATO 88, 92–3
Kozarac: Bosnia-Herzegovina 165–7
Krstić, Radislav 167

Law on Judicial Power 187
The Law on the Establishment of the
   Extraordinary Chambers 209
law: war and human rights 10–11
Lee Kuan Yew 43–4
legal accountability: DRC 128–31, 133;
   Sierra Leone 111, 113; Yugoslavia,
   former 93–4, 96
legal documents, international 10
legitimate combatants 69–70
Lendu 123, 126–7
Libya: ICC 233–4
Locke, John 35
Lomé Agreement 105, 106, 107, 215
Lukes, Steven 36–7

Mechanism for International Criminal
   Tribunals (MICT) 178–9, 245
mercenaries: Africa 74–5; Geneva
   Conventions 74–5, 76; regulations
   74–5
Milošević, Slobodan 86, 89, 90, 95, 165
Mladić, Ratko 86, 90, 91–2, 94, 95, 164
mobilizing causes of civil conflict 16
Montenegro 63
multinational corporations 77–80

Nahimana et al. case (*Media* case) 175
national sovereignty: universal jurisdiction
   184–5
natural law 34, 35
natural resources 15, 17, 77; Sudan
   139–40, 147
nonstate actors 245; and human rights law
   65–80; human rights violations 67–8;
   multinational corporations 77–80
nonstate armed groups 25, 66–72; human
   rights violations 67–8; legitimate
   combatants 69–70; PMSCs 72–7;
   proscribed violations 68; Sudan 15;
   terrorists and unlawful combatants 70–2
Norman, Sam Hinga 215
North Atlantic Treaty Organization (NATO)
   88, 92–3, 245
Northern Ireland 5
nonstate armed groups 66–7
nuclear weapons 61
nulla poena sine lege 62, 220, 245
nullem crimen sine lege 62, 164–5, 220,
   245
Nuremberg Charter 33, 61–2, 245

oil exploitation: Sudan 139–40, 147
Operation No Living Thing: Sierra Leone
   105, 110
operational v. structural conflict prevention
   18–19

peace agreements and human rights 105–8
peace and justice: ICC 234–5
peace enforcement 26–7
peace negotiation 6–7, 25, 140–1, 245
peacebuilding 5, 27–30, 245
Peacebuilding Commission 29
peacekeeping 25–6, 27, 106, 245
peacemaking: definition 245
permissible weaponry 61
The *Pinochet* cases 185–9; Chile 189; Law
   on Judicial Power 187; Spain 186–8;
   UK 188
piracy 184, 185
political rights 39–41
politics and human rights 37–8
postconflict peacebuilding 6–7
postconflict reconstruction 27–30
*Presbyterian Church of Sudan v. Talisman
   Energy* 149
private incentives: civil conflict causes 17
private military and security companies
   (PMSCs) 72–3, 245; human rights
   violations 73–4; ICRC 75–6; IHL 67,
   75–6; Iraq 73–4; regulation of 74–7;
   Sierra Leone 73
proletarians 37
proprio motu 233, 234, 245

proscribed violations 68
The Prosecutor v. Omar Hassan Ahmad al-Bashir 151–2
proximate causes: civil conflict causes 15–16

rape and sexual violence definitions 47–8, 169–70, 174–5
reconciliation: Yugoslavia 94
regional organizations 22, 245
relativism 43–6
religious freedom: Sudan 146
Republic of Congo v. France 191–2
Revolutionary United Front (RUF) 73, 112, 212; atrocities 105; child soldiers 108; emergence of 102–3; human rights violations 109–10
right of peoples 43
right to development 43
right to environment 43
right to peace 43
Right to Peace, The Draft UN Declaration on 44
rights and obligations 52–4
rights, duties, enforcement and accountability 54
Rome Statute 47–8, 54, 57, 62, 67, 220–6; Article 7 58; Article 25 226
Rousseau, Jean-Jacques 34–5
rule of law 7–8, 15–16, 103, 245
Rwanda 18, 62–3, 123–4; DRC 119, 127

Sankoh, Foday 8, 102, 104, 105, 106–7, 108; hybrid tribunal 212, 216
Sarajevo 91
Saudi Arabia 196
Srebrenica 91–2, 93
Second Congo War 120–1
second generation rights 39–41
security actors 20
Senegal 193
Serbia 63, 93
sexual and gender-based violence 47–8; definitions 169–70, 174–5; DRC 127–8
Sierra Leone 99–114; Abuja Agreement I 107; AFRC 105; background to conflict 99, 101–3, 105–8; Charles Taylor 214–15; Geneva Conventions 5, 8, 73; human rights violations 108–10; hybrid tribunals 212–17; key facts 101; key players 104; legal aspects 111, 113; Lomé Agreement 106; map *100*; PMSCs in 73; timeline 112
slavery: Sudan 145, 147, 148; universal jurisdiction 184, 185
social rights 39–41
solidarist rights 42–3
Sosa v. Alvarez-Machain 195, 196

South Sudan: Abyei 141; key facts 139; map *137*; natural resources 139–40
Soviet bloc 17
Spain: FPR case against 131; The *Pinochet* cases 186–8; Rwandan Patriotic Army 129, 131
Special Court for Sierra Leone (SCSL) 212–14
state responsibility: *DRC v. Uganda and Rwanda* 129–30; genocide 93
states and treaties 52–5
The Statute of the Special Court for Sierra Leone 213
Stevens, Siaka 101–2
structural causes: civil conflict causes 15
structural v. operational conflict prevention 18–19
Sudan 136–57; background to conflict 136, 138–45; causes of conflict 6; conflict in the south 136, 138–40; Darfur 142–5, 150–1; human rights violations 145–8; ICC 227–31, 233, 237; key facts 138; key players 144; legal aspects 148–52; map *136*; South Sudan key facts 139; timeline 153–5
systematic conflict prevention 19

Tadić, Duško 75, 165–7
Talisman Energy 147, 149, 195
Taylor, Charles 214–15
terrorists and unlawful combatants 70–1
terrorism 72
third-generation or group rights 42–3
Timor-Leste: background 204–5; The Commission for Reception, Truth, and Reconciliation (CAVR) 207; hybrid structure: mandate and structure 205–6; hybrid tribunals 204–7; hybrid tribunals: evaluation 206–7; hybrid tribunals: legacy 207; Indonesia 205–7; UN Transitional Administration Administrational Administration in East Timor (UNTAET) 205–6
torture: definition 168–9; Sierra Leone 113; universal jurisdiction 184, 185
Torture Convention 10, 35, 52–3, 54, 55, 68; Article 1 56
transitional justice 29–30
transnational accountability in conflict 197
treaties and conventions 52–5
treaty monitoring bodies 53
Trial Chamber: ICC 227–8
tribunals, hybrid 201
Tunisia 16

Uganda: DRC 119, 123, 126–7; DRC case against 129, 130; ICC 133, 231–2
UN bodies and agencies 21

UN Charter 20, 33, 161–2, 166
UN Draft Declaration on the Right to Peace 44
UN General Assembly Resolution A/
  RES/60/180 (2005) 29
UN Human Rights Council 44; Resolution
  7/21 76
UN mediation and amnesties 8
UN Peacebuilding Commission 28–9
UN peacekeeping operations 27
UN Security Council Resolution 1244 89
UN Security Council Resolution 1593 (March
  31, 2005) 230
UN Transitional Administration in East Timor
  (UNTAET) 205–6
United Nations (UN) 20; ICC 219; ICTY
  161–2; International Human Rights 33;
  peacebuilding 28; peacekeeping 25–6
United States: Alien Tort Claims Act (ATCA)
  192–5; ICC 224; unlawful combatants 71
Universal Declaration of Human Rights 33,
  34, 52, 54
universal jurisdiction 11, 53, 129, 239–40;
  immunity 191; limits to 192; sovereignty
  184–5
universality, problem of 35–8
unlawful combatants 70–1
UNMIK Regulation no. 2000/64 202
Unocal: ATCA cases 194
unofficial actors: conflict resolution 22–3
UNTAET Regulation no. 2000/15 205
utilitarians 36

The Vienna Declaration and Programme of
  Action 47

Waldron, Jeremy 40–1
war and human rights 3–13; accountability
  7–9; conflict analysis 4–5; conflict
  dynamics 6–7; conflict resolution 9–10;
  human rights violations 5–6; internal
  armed conflict 12; law 10–11; response
  to abuses 11; violations as consequences
  6
war crimes 10–11, 47–8, 53; Common
  Article 3 223; Geneva Conventions
  222–3; ICC 222–3; universal jurisdiction
  184, 185
war crimes tribunal 107
weaponry 61
Western imposition objection 239–40
Western view of human rights 35–8
women: human rights history 46–8

Yugoslavia, former 17, 18, 63, 69, 83–98;
  background to conflict 84, 86; Bosnia-
  Herzegovina 86–8, 91–2; Croatia 86–8;
  human rights violations 89–96; IHL
  93–4; key facts 85; key players 90;
  Kosovo 88–9, 92–3; legal aspects 93–4,
  96; map *84*; timeline 95

Zaire 119
Zechenter, Elizabeth M. 46

Taylor & Francis

eBooks
FOR LIBRARIES

ORDER YOUR
FREE 30 DAY
INSTITUTIONAL
TRIAL TODAY!

Over 23,000 eBook titles in the Humanities,
Social Sciences, STM and Law from some of the
world's leading imprints.

Choose from a range of subject packages or create your own!

Benefits for you

▶ Free MARC records
▶ COUNTER-compliant usage statistics
▶ Flexible purchase and pricing options

Benefits for your user

▶ Off-site, anytime access via Athens or referring URL
▶ Print or copy pages or chapters
▶ Full content search
▶ Bookmark, highlight and annotate text
▶ Access to thousands of pages of quality research
at the click of a button

For more information, pricing enquiries or to order
a free trial, contact your local online sales team.

UK and Rest of World: **online.sales@tandf.co.uk**

US, Canada and Latin America:
e-reference@taylorandfrancis.com

www.ebooksubscriptions.com

ALPSP Award for
BEST eBOOK
PUBLISHER
2009 Finalist
sponsored by

Taylor & Francis eBooks
Taylor & Francis Group

A flexible and dynamic resource for teaching, learning and research.